# First Person Plural

# First Person Plural

## Aboriginal Storytelling and the Ethics of Collaborative Authorship

SOPHIE McCALL

UBCPress · Vancouver · Toronto

© UBC Press 2011

All rights reserved. No part of this publication may be reproduced, stored in a retrieval system, or transmitted, in any form or by any means, without prior written permission of the publisher, or, in Canada, in the case of photocopying or other reprographic copying, a licence from Access Copyright, www.accesscopyright.ca.

20 19 18 17 16 15 14 13 12 11     5 4 3 2 1

Printed in Canada on FSC-certified ancient-forest-free paper
(100% post-consumer recycled) that is processed chlorine- and acid-free.

**Library and Archives Canada Cataloguing in Publication**

McCall, Sophie, 1969-
    First person plural : aboriginal storytelling and the ethics of collaborative authorship / Sophie McCall.

Includes bibliographical references and index.
ISBN 978-0-7748-1979-4 (bound)
ISBN 978-0-7748-1980-0 (pbk.)

    1. Native peoples – Canada – Communication. 2. Intercultural communication – Canada. 3. Authorship – Collaboration. 4. Oral tradition – Canada. I. Title.

E78.C2M127 2011          971.004'97          C2010-908005-X

e-book ISBNs: 978-0-7748-1981-7 (pdf); 978-0-7748-5993-6 (epub)

Canadä

UBC Press gratefully acknowledges the financial support for our publishing program of the Government of Canada (through the Canada Book Fund), the Canada Council for the Arts, and the British Columbia Arts Council.

This book has been published with the help of a grant from the Canadian Federation for the Humanities and Social Sciences, through the Aid to Scholarly Publications Program, using funds provided by the Social Sciences and Humanities Research Council of Canada, and with the help of the K.D. Srivastava Fund.

UBC Press
The University of British Columbia
2029 West Mall
Vancouver, BC V6T 1Z2
www.ubcpress.ca

# Contents

Acknowledgments / vii

Introduction: Collaboration and Authorship in Told-to Narratives / 1

1 'Where Is the Voice Coming From?': Appropriations and Subversions of the 'Native Voice' / 17

2 Coming to Voice the North: The Mackenzie Valley Pipeline Inquiry and the Works of Hugh Brody / 43

3 'There Is a Time Bomb in Canada': The Legacy of the Oka Crisis / 76

4 'My Story Is a Gift': The Royal Commission on Aboriginal Peoples and the Politics of Reconciliation / 109

5 'What the Map Cuts Up, the Story Cuts Across': Translating Oral Traditions and Aboriginal Land Title / 137

6 'I Can Only Sing This Song to Someone Who Understands It': Community Filmmaking and the Politics of Partial Translation / 181

Conclusion: Collaborative Authorship and Literary Sovereignty / 205

Notes / 214

Works Cited / 230

Index / 246

# Acknowledgments

*First Person Plural* is dedicated to the memory of Barbara Godard, whose energy, support, and intellectual rigour helped shape this project from its beginnings, and whose words of wisdom and guidance remain with me to this day. I thank her for her generosity in helping me see the bigger picture across a vast range of topics – while at the same time uncannily recalling the smallest details.

This study began in conversation at York University with students, professors, and lifelong friends, and I hope the spirit of exchange and dialogue continues to frequent its pages. While at York University, I was fortunate to work with some outstanding professors, particularly Ken Little, Arun Mukherjee, and Leslie Sanders, as well as Terry Goldie, Rinaldo Walcott, and Ato Sekyi-Otu, the latter who became a special mentor and friend. The legendary community of graduate students at York University helped immeasurably through the long writing process and I would like to mention Gamal Abdel-Shehid, Elena Basile, Gugu Hlongwane, Heather Milne, Lori Moses, Alok Mukherjee, Candida Rifkind, Trish Salah, and Janine Willie.

My graduate and undergraduate students at Simon Fraser University, particularly Dave Gaertner, Keri Petschl, and Christine Lyons, as well as my graduate students enrolled in English 804 in 2005 and my undergraduate students in English 453 over a number of terms, helped immeasurably in leading stimulating discussions of many of the fundamental questions in this study. I am grateful to the community of scholars and friends in various fields who have helped me (sometimes unwittingly) through a challenging political or intellectual entanglement, and my thanks are due to Alessandra Capperdoni, Warren Cariou, Richard Cavell, Julie Cruikshank, Jeff Derksen, Peter Dickinson, Renate Eigenbrod, Kristina Fagan, Margery Fee, Carole Gerson, Susan Gingell, Smaro Kamboureli, Christine Kim, Larissa Lai, Sam McKegney, Roy Miki, Deanna Reder, June Scudeler, and Rita Wong. For indispensable class visits from Aboriginal writers I would like to thank Marie Clements, Sharron Proulx-Turner, Richard Van Camp, Garry Gottfriedson, Gregory Scofield, Michael Nicoll Yahgulanaas, Joanne Arnott, and Steve Sanderson, as well as the SFU English Department, which made these visits possible. I would be remiss if I did not also mention some very special friends and colleagues in Toronto, Vancouver, and elsewhere, who have not only helped me articulate many of the ideas in this book but have supported me as true friends: Joanne Saul, Bronwen Low, Andi Curtis, Joanna Reynolds, Melina Baum Singer, Nick Saul, Nupur and Anju Gogia, Colette Colligan, Roxanne Panchasi, Susan Brook, Tiffany Werth, and Genevieve Fuji-Johnson.

This book underwent extensive revisions over the course of many years, and some dedicated friends, colleagues, and scholars in the field took the time to read over portions of the manuscript. For generously responding to my requests for help and for offering invaluable suggestions that helped me find that missing piece, I would like to thank Hugh Brody, Alan Cairns, David Chariandy, Dave Gaertner, Kathy Mezei, and Roxanne Panchasi. I am especially indebted to Nancy Earle, who went over the entire manuscript with a fine-tooth comb at a particularly critical juncture in the revision process. I would also like to thank the anonymous reviewers for the University of British Columbia Press for their excellent suggestions. Darcy Cullen and Ann Macklem at the Press have been model editors whose kind and thoughtful professionalism I greatly appreciate. I would also like to mention Sigrid Albert, Jillian Shoichet, and Laraine Coates.

This work received generous financial support from Simon Fraser University through the President's Research Grant and the Publications Grant.

Very grateful thanks are due to my parents, Storrs and Ann, who have been unflagging supports in every way, and to my parents-in-law, Rawlins and Claudette, for taking supremely good care of my children during the time I was writing this book. I also wish to acknowledge my extended family, particularly my grandparents, Tony and Kitty, my brothers, Mengo and Kai, and their families. To my best friend and partner, David, I owe my immeasurable gratitude and love. My children, Maya and Skye, you are my inspiration and my joy. Meegwetch to all!

**Permissions**
Permission to quote extensively from the following four texts is gratefully acknowledged:

- Julie Cruikshank, in collaboration with Angela Sidney, Kitty Smith, and Annie Ned, *Life Lived Like a Story: Life Stories of Three Yukon Elders* (UBC Press, 1990), reprinted with the permission of the publisher;
- Harry Robinson, *Write It on Your Heart: The Epic World of an Okanagan Storyteller*, edited by Wendy Wickwire (TalonBooks, 1989), reprinted with the permission of the publisher;
- Hugh Brody, *Maps and Dreams: Indians and the British Columbia Frontier* (Douglas and McIntyre, 1988), reprinted with the permission of the publisher;
- Ila Bussidor and Üstün Bilgen-Reinart, *Night Spirits: The Story of the Relocation of the Sayisi Dene* (University of Manitoba Press, 1997), reprinted with the permission of the publisher.

I also wish to acknowledge that earlier versions of Chapters 5 and 6 were published in *Essays on Canadian Writing* (80 [2003] and 83 [2005], respectively).

# First Person Plural

# Introduction
## Collaboration and Authorship in Told-to Narratives

> Our European concepts of 'voice' are hedged with assumptions and undermined with problems. Voice equals speech. Voice has the floor. Voice is authority. To have voice is to have power. To be dumb or voiceless is synonymous with being ignorant.
>
> – RON MARKEN, FOREWORD TO MARIA CAMPBELL'S *STORIES OF THE ROAD ALLOWANCE PEOPLE*

> The time has passed when privileged authorities could routinely 'give voice' (or history) without fear of contradiction.
>
> – JAMES CLIFFORD, *PREDICAMENT OF CULTURE: TWENTIETH CENTURY ETHNOGRAPHY, LITERATURE AND ART*

> Nowhere is our cultural disorientation better captured, or the ambiguous transitional moment in which we find ourselves more clearly underlined, than in the complex issue of voice appropriation. The issue of who can speak for whom, and who can write for whom, is a major contemporary issue in the social sciences and humanities.
>
> – ALAN CAIRNS, *CITIZENS PLUS: ABORIGINAL PEOPLES AND THE CANADIAN STATE*

> So many of us are a mixed-up lot, a chorus of intermingling voices and
> histories, and I write to tell you of that mixing, of the sounds of that chorus.
>
> – GREG SARRIS, *KEEPING SLUG WOMAN ALIVE*

'Voice' remains a central point of struggle in Aboriginal studies, standing for a range of concepts: from empowerment to appropriation, from individual style to collective identity. *First Person Plural* confronts the complexity of the issue of 'voice' by examining 'told-to narratives,' in which, typically, non-Aboriginal recorders collect, edit, and structure stories by Aboriginal narrators.[1] Historically, collector-editors have submitted the oral performance to numerous changes, omissions, and manipulations, while claiming sole authorship on the title page. At the same time, these editors have effaced their intervention, stating in the preface that the story is in the narrator's 'own voice.' My approach emphasizes the interpenetration of authorship and collaboration. I attend to the degrees of authorship and degrees of collaboration between storytellers, recorders, translators, editors, and authors, and I track the subtle shifts in the balance of power between mediators who are working within a broad range of as-told-to forms, techniques, and arenas.

*First Person Plural* looks at some genre variations of told-to narratives – including ethnography, recorded (auto)biography, testimonial life narrative, documentary, myth, legend, and song – and examines the implications of the choices that editors, translators, narrators, and documentarians make in their textualizations. Collaboratively produced texts, such as Lee Maracle's *Bobbi Lee, Indian Rebel* (1990), Julie Cruikshank, Angela Sidney, Kitty Smith, and Annie Ned's *Life Lived Like a Story* (1990), and Harry Robinson and Wendy Wickwire's *Write It on Your Heart* (1989), are some of the key texts that I analyse in this work; however, I further expand the category of the told-to narrative in order to examine how contemporary Aboriginal voices have been represented in public forums, land claims court cases, commissioners' reports, media representations, and film (both documentary and dramatic). In carrying out this work I have discovered that many of the same issues pertaining to voice and agency that animate discussions of told-to narratives are also at stake in reading the transcripts of public hearings, legal trials, and government reports. My intention is not to demonstrate the limits of the genre of told-to narrative but, rather, its scope. Approaching this hybrid genre in the widest sense of the definition, I explore a variety of contact zones of Aboriginal/non-Aboriginal interactions as overshadowed by colonial legacies in Canada but also as potentially decolonizing. Thus, for example, I read Justice Thomas Berger's report of the Mackenzie Valley Pipeline Inquiry and his approach to the politics of voice in tandem with the ethnographies and films of Hugh Brody, who worked as a writer and consultant for Berger (Chapter 2); I pair an analysis of the media representations of the Oka crisis, which simplified the issues at stake in the standoff and divorced them from their historical context, with readings of the complex chorus of voices in Maracle's recorded (auto)biography and in Alanis Obomsawin's quartet of films relating to Kanehsatake (Chapter 3); and I demonstrate the extent to which Zacharias Kunuk's film *Atanarjuat, the Fast Runner*, which began shooting in the same month and year as the formation of Nunavut in 1999, is shaped by the filmmaker's (at times ambivalent) cultural nationalism (Chapter 6).

The double focus of this study stems from the recognition that literature and criticism are continuously responding to larger public discourses. This double focus also enables me to address more than one audience – an appropriate goal for a book on the politics of voice. While the book is aimed primarily at readers of Aboriginal literary studies in the Canadian context, it also will attract readers interested in Native North American Studies, Canadian literary studies, and postcolonial and cultural theory. In particular, the audience will include scholars investigating the problem of textualizing Aboriginal oral narrative. A primary concern in writing this book has been the search for innovative ways to produce textual readings that meaningfully engage with historical, social, and political contexts. I ask how and why we read texts and histories in conjunction with one another – and why we don't. The wager of this book is that an approach that emphasizes the theoretical elasticity of told-to narratives provides a unique opportunity to bring together texts, histories, and critical approaches whose connections, for disciplinary reasons, have remained understated.

Most of the texts, histories, and case studies addressed in this book are dated from 1990 to 1999. I focus primarily on the 1990s because these years were pivotal in reconceptualizing how we think about voice and representation in Aboriginal cultural politics. In 1990, the 'Oka crisis' (also known as the standoff at Kanehsatake) coincided with an explosion of debates over the 'appropriation of voice' in universities and dominant media outlets. The disputes go to the heart of struggles around the politics of cultural representation: who has the authority to speak, for whom, and under what circumstances? Aboriginal writers have used the issue of the appropriation of voice to highlight struggles over the material conditions of publication and circulation of texts, as well as conflicts over the control of resources, land, and cultural property. The demands for the 'return of voice' have dovetailed into efforts to repatriate cultural treasures held in museums in metropolitan centres in North America and in Europe (Kew 91), as well as legal battles over land and resources. Told-to narratives, historically 'authored' solely by collector-editors, are implicated in these debates over cultural property. The fierce discussions over the appropriation of voice helped to create a shift in the production of told-to narratives: First Nations editors, translators, recorders, and collectors began to take more active roles in recording, translating, editing, and publishing the texts. As a result, new forms of the genre have emerged that emphasize process, debate, and exchange.

Until recently, Canadian literary criticism – which, along with Aboriginal studies, is the core disciplinary space from which this analysis proceeds – has ignored the told-to narrative, labelling this diverse body of texts as anthropological case studies.[2] In the preface to *Contemporary Challenges* (1991), Hartmut Lutz comments that, prior to the 1970s, 'texts stemming from the oral tradition were usually collected, translated, and often heavily edited by non-Native missionaries, anthropologists, and hobbyists.' These editors, Lutz argues, 'tended to represent Native "tales" from the igloo, the smokehouse, or the campfire as "quaint" or "exotic," fit for ethnological inquiry perhaps, but not for serious literary studying' (2). Lutz implicitly concludes that critics should thus dispense with cross-cultural told-to narratives altogether, and turn their attention to First Nations writing produced in the past thirty years. Increasingly, Canadian literary critics have questioned this tendency to leave aside the work of interpreting recorded oral narrative, and have sought new ways to approach these layered texts. In the words of Susan Gingell (2005), 'Canadian literature is ... a rich archive of textualized orature and orality, one whose wealth has only just begun to be recognized by critics' (9). Gingell has played an important role in coordinating scholars working on textualized orality in Canadian contexts.[3]

Despite a recent upsurge in interest, there are several reasons these blurred genres have remained understudied in Canadian literary criticism. Told-to narratives do not fit the criteria that govern European concepts of genre; the collaborative process challenges the author-function and notions of the literary by foregrounding process over product, context over text, and audience over author; and literary critics have assigned the study of oral literature to the departments of anthropology and folklore, contributing to the view that transcribed oral narratives are the domain of linguists or other cultural specialists. Meanwhile, Aboriginal literature in Canada has increasingly come to mean singly authored texts, as if told-to narratives were synonymous with literary colonization. My study, in contrast, argues that told-to narratives play a formative role in both Aboriginal and Canadian literatures. As a meeting ground for multiple voices, told-to narratives offer productive sites for analysing the shifting dynamic of cross-cultural interaction. Exploring the complexity, richness, and depth of the collaborative process provides a way for me to articulate a different kind of cultural politics that avoids reinscribing a sharply oppositional characterization of the relationship between Aboriginal storytellers and non-Aboriginal collectors, writers, and editors in contemporary told-to narratives. By focusing on the processes of mediation and collaboration, I hope to challenge notions of 'voice' that are singular, unmediated, and pure, thereby questioning the discourses of authenticity that continue to perpetuate static notions of Aboriginal identity.

In American (as opposed to Canadian) literary studies, the study of Native North American oral literatures has claimed greater institutional legitimacy. Dell Hymes (1981), Dennis Tedlock (1983), Arnold Krupat (1983, 1992), Brian Swann (1983, 1992, 1996), David Murray (1991), William Clements (1996), and Eric Cheyfitz (1997) are just a few of the critics who have produced extensive critical studies on Aboriginal verbal art. For the most part, these critics focus on translations or re-translations of oral literatures from the nineteenth century or from the first half of the twentieth century. While there are a number of important exceptions,[4] there has developed an historically entrenched split between critics who study historical Native American orature and those who study contemporary Native American writing. Commenting on this phenomenon, Creek-Cherokee scholar Craig Womack (2006) argues that until recently 'all Indian writing was claimed as being based on oral tradition and ceremony, yet there was little actual tribally specific analysis or consideration of how oral tradition itself has a literary history and has changed over time' (154). Similarly, Jace Weaver (1997), also a Cherokee scholar, reacting against the assumptions embedded in these critical studies, persuasively argues that an over-emphasis on 'orature' in Native American literary studies 'is a way of continuing colonialism. It once again keeps American Indians from entering the twentieth century' (23). However, Weaver's conclusion – that

'Native American literature ... is most clearly found in novels written by Native Americans about the Native American experience' (26) – is also problematic. He suggests that only those Native American writers who write novels about the 'Native American experience' are writing Native American literature. He also suggests that an attempt to critically engage with orature will necessarily lead to 'continuing colonialism' (23). In considering the implications of Weaver's statement, the question arises: Are Native American writers who write novels participating more directly in a process of literary decolonization than those who engage in the textualization of oral narratives? In recent decades, as Aboriginal writers, editors, translators, scholars, and community members have become more involved in developing innovative approaches to the task of recording and preserving oral traditions, it has become clear that told-to narratives remain a vibrant form of cultural expression.

Thus, in this book, I do not approach told-to narratives as inherently examples of textual colonization by White recorders of Aboriginal oral narrators. Following the lead of Coast Miwok/Pomo/Jewish writer Greg Sarris, whose book *Keeping Slug Woman Alive* (1993) is a key influence in this study, I argue that there is always a gap between recorder and storyteller, even when the interlocutors belong to the same community or family, and even when they follow a careful collaborative process. I approach the claims made by those collector-editors who state that they have recorded the stories 'exactly as told' with a degree of skepticism. David Brumble in *American Indian Autobiography* (1988) argues that a dominant trend in recorded life narrative is the myth of the 'absent editor,' who 'create[s] the fiction that the narrative is all the Indian's own' (75). The recorder denies his or her role as listener in shaping the story, stressing his or her neutrality or objectivity. There are numerous examples of the absent editor phenomenon. In the preface to the collective testimonial life story *Night Spirits: The Story of the Relocation of the Sayisi Dene* (1997), a searing account of enforced settlement that I discuss in Chapter 4, recorder-editor Üstün Bilgen-Reinart writes that the story 'is told largely by Ila [Bussidor] and the other Sayisi Dene, in their own voices' (xi). Janet Silman, a Métis writer who recorded and edited the stories in *Enough Is Enough: Aboriginal Women Speak Out* (1987), likewise states that the testimonies by the women from the Tobique Reserve in New Brunswick are transcriptions: '[t]he story is not about them but rather *by* them in that it is in their own words'(9, emphasis in original). Rosamond Vanderburgh is one of a minority of recorder-editors who acknowledge that their work – in Vanderburgh's case the biography of Anishinaabe narrator Verna Patronella Johnston, *I am Nokomis, Too* (1977) – is not a direct transcription: 'Much of this story reflects her [Johnston's] manner of speaking and her own phrasing, but inevitably it reflects, as well, the cultural framework and expressions of the interviewer' (15). However, given that Vanderburgh has changed Johnston's first-person account into a third-person biography, and has provided descriptive titles to each 'chapter' of Johnston's life, this admission of editorial intervention seems understated at best.

Avowals of friendship, trust, mutual responsibility, shared agendas, and the relinquishing of authorial control are common in editors' prefaces and introductions to recorded oral narratives. The recorded (auto)biography *During My Time: Florence Edenshaw Davidson* (1992), by anthropologist Margaret Blackman, provides a good example of how the claim to collaboration provides 'an affective or experiential dimension' that 'complements' the norms of the 'standard ethnography' without substantially disrupting the genre (4). Haida elder Florence Edenshaw Davidson might command centre stage in the text, but she does so as exemplary evidence within Blackman's interpretive framework. Blackman downplays her own role in writing the life story, claiming that it was Davidson who initiated the project. Yet Blackman, writing an 'ethnographic life history,' presses Davidson to speak candidly about her experiences 'as a Haida woman': 'Nani was somewhat embarrassed to discuss her puberty seclusion knowing that the account might be published. I, on the other hand, felt the subject significant enough to pursue until she had exhausted her memory' (16). Blackman impels her 'Native informant' to reveal her knowledge about Haida customs to the point of exhaustion, in both senses of the word. The close relationship between the women suggests that Blackman has shared authorial control with her subject, but it should be noted that the claim to sharing increases the text's ethnographic authority.

Nevertheless, storytellers have their own strategies for overturning the authority of the collector-editors. Just as the collector-editor selects, interprets, shapes, and determines the form of the narrative, so too does the narrator choose, arrange, and order her memories. 'I don't tell everything – what's no good,' Davidson insists (19), advising Blackman to 'shut that thing off,' referring to the tape recorder, at certain points in the narrative (xiii). Davidson makes clear that she is addressing more than one audience: one listener may be Blackman, but Davidson often has family and community members present at the recording sessions as well. In addition, she is aware of the interest of outsiders in Haida culture, as numerous anthropologists, including John R. Swanton (1873-1958) and Wilson Duff (1925-76), had worked closely with her family members since the early twentieth century (14). In response to Blackman's detailed questions about Haida cultural practices, Davidson exclaims: 'It wasn't important to me then – how was I supposed to know that white people might be interested years later?' (18). Narrators use a range of strategies, from direct confrontation, to parody, to silence, to avoidance, in order to claim narrative authority in these composite texts. Blackman and Davidson struggle over not only the content, but also the form, genre, and language of the life narrative, and it is a mistake to assume that Davidson relinquishes control in this struggle. Power relationships are volatile and shifting, influencing cross-cultural negotiation in unpredictable ways. The relations of authority in the told-to narrative are open to alteration, recombination, and transformation.

Despite the complexity of the interaction between interlocutors in told-to narratives, critical studies have focused narrowly on the agenda of either the recorder or the narrator. In this book, I depart from those who posit the Aboriginal narrator as a cipher that is vulnerable to the collector-editor's textual manipulations. Poststructuralist literary critic Philippe Lejeune, in his well-known essay 'Autobiography for Those Who Do Not Write' (1989), argues that the recorder overrides the authority of the narrator.[5] The recorder 'is the author in every sense of the term'; 'He [sic] ha[s] the initiative; the collected narrative accomplishes his plan, and not that of the model; he is in control of the work; and he is ultimately its signer and its guarantor' (208). For Lejeune, the collector-editor's frame determines both the form and content of the life narrative. At the same time, my readings also differ from those that merely reverse the unilateral relation and insist that the narrator is the ultimate author-ity. John Beverley (1992), writing about Latin American *testimonios* – collaboratively produced first-person narratives, inspired by Marxism and closely associated with social justice struggles – attributes all agency to the narrator[6]: 'In oral history, it is the intentionality of the recorder – usually a social scientist – that is dominant ... In *testimonio*, by contrast, it is the intentionality of the narrator that is paramount' (96). As a result, '*testimonio* involves a sort of erasure of the function and textual presence of the author' (97). Beverley downplays or even camouflages the role of the collector-editor.

Both Lejeune and Beverley install a sharp opposition between recorder and teller, overlooking the forms of intersubjectivity that the told-to narrative produces. Focusing on the recorder or the narrator in an exclusive way elides the formative impact of other mediating figures, such as translators, editors, and readers. Such an approach also ignores the social contexts in which tellings, re-tellings, or re-readings take place. Social context plays a vital role in shaping told-to narratives, which are based on situated, embodied events of communication. According to Russian philosopher and literary critic Mikhail Bakhtin (1895-1975), it is impossible to consider speakers and listeners in isolation from one another, or disassociated from the world in which they interact. He calls into question the tendency of listeners to deny their own role in shaping the story; indeed, for Bakhtin, 'the listener becomes the speaker' (*Speech* 68). Both listener and speaker participate in the acts of making meaning, while larger political and social contexts impinge upon the intimate setting of a conversation. Interlocutors operate in a contested zone; they cannot overcome or wish away the determinacies of their disparate social locations. He reminds us that these relations of authority exert their force in every act of communication. However, they are especially pertinent to the process of textualizing First Nations' oral texts, a process historically steeped in culturally determined notions of orality and literacy, of ethnicity and difference.[7]

The asymmetric relations between the Native speaker and the (usually) non-Aboriginal recorder bear dramatic consequences in the mediated spaces of public forums, community hearings, media representations, and land claims trials. For example, I track the permutations that transcribed community hearings undergo when they are re-presented in official reports. Reports, which exert a degree of social power that hearings cannot, are important sites of analysis. Their rhetorical features – often downplaying the 'personal' viewpoint of the author(s), who may or may not be named – may tempt a reader to rely upon them as straight, factual accounts, but I emphasize the degree to which they are themselves discursive performances. Similarly, transcribed court documents in land claims trials involve a series of liminal figures (plaintiffs, defendants, cultural translators, expert witnesses, lawyers) who are testifying, performing, recording, translating, debating, editing, and arranging oral utterances. Court transcriptions starkly highlight how the act of recording oral statements is subject to the law's powerful 'ordering imperative' (Boyce Davies 3). This 'ordering imperative' sometimes results in mistranslation or nontranslation of those utterances that do not fit the existing analytical categories. Even when transcriptions demonstrate word-for-word accuracy, the processes of decontextualization and recontextualization potentially transform the range of possible meanings that utterances produce.

The public forums I have selected – the Mackenzie Valley Pipeline Inquiry (1973-77), the Oka crisis (1990), the Royal Commission on Aboriginal Peoples (1991-96), the land claims trial *Delgamuukw v. British Columbia* (1991, 1997), and community debates surrounding the creation of Nunavut (1999) – provide a rich (if contradictory) narrative of the struggle for Aboriginal rights in Canada in the last decades of the twentieth century. Historically, non-Aboriginal governmental representatives have crafted 'Indian policy' in Ottawa behind closed doors. Today, Aboriginal researchers and community activists are actively participating in negotiating self-government agreements, brokering modern-day treaties, and filing land claims. However, there are no guarantees that what is traced here is a narrative of progress towards more equitable relations between the Canadian nation-state and the First Nations. The development of Aboriginal rights in Canada has always been, as Aboriginal studies scholar Peter Kulchyski points out, 'a history of sustained, often vicious struggle, a history of losses and gains, of shifting terrain' (*Unjust* 9-10). If the Oka crisis ignited intense debates over the politics of representation, the formation of Nunavut in 1999 held out the promise that Aboriginal self-government may resolve or at least mitigate the intertwined crises over land, voice, and representation. Yet genuine change in Aboriginal-Canadian relations is still an elusive goal, as ongoing disputes over land, property, and resources make clear. The differential relations of communication in told-to narratives and in public hearings reflect the ongoing colonial nature of the Indigenous-settler relationship in Canada. Profound social, economic, and political inequalities between Aboriginal and non-Aboriginal groups persist today.

Doreen Jensen, Gitksan artist and cultural worker, has said that 'Canada is an image which hasn't emerged yet. Because this country hasn't recognized its First Nations, its whole foundation is shaky' (20). There are yawning gaps and silences between official and alter-Native histories in Canada. Growing up in Montreal, Quebec, in the 1970s and 1980s and living on my parents' farm not far from Oka during the summer of 1990, I learned something about these yawning gaps. My father was involved in the 'No' campaign leading up to the Quebec referendum in 1980 (and, to a lesser extent, again in 1995), and I vividly remember his defence of bilingualism, minority language rights, and multiculturalism. Not surprisingly, as a fourth-generation Anglophone Montrealer, my father opposed René Lévesque's separatist, nationalist vision for Quebec. My father's liberal politics were imbued with a strong sense of fairness and equality, as well as a respect for cultural difference. I have always admired his political engagement, though we have disagreed about the implications of Canadian Liberal politics. In writing this book, I have learned the extent to which well-intentioned liberal ideology has contributed to the deferral of Aboriginal rights. For example, Prime Minister Pierre Trudeau's White Paper (1969) proposed to shred the *Indian Act* and eliminate the special status of Aboriginal peoples from the Canadian constitution. The assimilationist White Paper is classically liberal in its assumption that everyone should be treated 'equally' in a liberal democracy, regardless of race, class, or gender. While liberalism's defense of individual rights can be enabling in certain cases, its de-emphasis of collective rights poses a problem in the struggle for Aboriginal rights. Liberalism may recognize the rights of certain minority groups, but it sometimes ignores how privileges are conferred upon others. Liberal ideology, compounded by the settler mentality – which in this context involves the effacement of differences between Aboriginal and minority groups – often leads to a reluctance to acknowledge the degree to which mainstream society's benefits come at the expense of Indigenous people's rights. Yet Aboriginal communities should not be considered another minority group; they are the First Nations of this continent.[8]

It may come as no surprise to my readers that, as a non-Aboriginal, Canadian critic, I have chosen to write about these genre-bending, hybridized, collaborative texts that model Aboriginal / non-Aboriginal dialogues. To some extent, told-to narratives provide an entry point for me to engage with discussions about Aboriginal literature and criticism. Many Aboriginal critics today (though certainly not all) have adopted sovereigntist perspectives and have articulated tribally specific modes of interpretation. Sovereignty is a key issue not only in political movements but also in literary criticism, as the title of the text *American Indian Literary Nationalism* (2006), by co-authors Weaver, Womack, and Robert Warrior, makes clear. In Cree writer Janice Acoose's words, 'Exercising sovereignty, we must name/define our own literatures and take control of the Indigenous-literary territory' (46-47). She connects her work as a literary critic to current political struggles over land and sovereignty. In this book I both advance sovereigntist arguments and explore cross-cultural, pan-Native, collaborative forms of expression. By working on double-voiced, cross-cultural, composite productions, I am attempting to fashion or at least to imagine new models of shared authority and collaboration that can contribute at the same time to ongoing discussions about land rights and governance. Envisioning models of sovereignty in cross-cultural contexts has implications for my work as a teacher and researcher of Canadian and First Nations literatures at a Canadian, post-secondary institution. I bear a responsibility to do what I can to make more space for Indigenous studies and to help make the university a more welcoming place for Indigenous students. I am inspired by my colleagues in Indigenous studies who have analysed with sharp clarity the imbrications of inequities both at the university and in broader social contexts and have dedicated time, energy, and thought to practising 'an ethics of scholarship' that bridges persistent gaps between academic and community dialogues (Fagan, 'Delicate' 78).[9]

The chapters in this book examine told-to narratives – including ethnography, documentary, life narrative, myth, legend, and song – in conjunction with discussions of political proceedings that dramatize Aboriginal/Canadian (non)exchange – public hearings, media representations of Aboriginal/Canadian conflict, royal commissions, land claims trials, self-government agreements – as a way to talk about how and why social actors engage in collaborative, cross-cultural production. In Chapter 1, I explore some historical roots of told-to narratives: Romantic-nationalist, anti-colonial, and collaborative. In the first half of the twentieth century, Romantic-nationalist collectors sought to salvage what they assumed were the last performances of Aboriginal verbal art as a way to provide the 'ground' for new settler literatures. By deploying an 'art museum' style of exhibition (Clements 186), literary anthologists of Aboriginal verbal art, such as Natalie Curtis (1907), George W. Cronyn (1918), and John Robert Colombo (1981, 1983), presented fragments of song in isolation from larger contexts. Following the rise of Aboriginal political movements in the 1960s, writers such as Lee Maracle (1990) and Craig Womack (1999), who argue for varying forms of literary sovereignty, have disassociated themselves from ethnographic traditions and have drawn attention to multiple forms of appropriation. The emergence of the 'Native voice' as one of anti-colonial resistance has created the necessary conditions for establishing more reciprocal relations of collaboration. In the collaborative approach, critics, writers, and ethnographers such as co-authors Cruikshank, Sidney,

Smith, and Ned (1990), Greg Sarris (1993), and Sharon Venne (2002), attend more carefully to the degrees of collaboration and of authorship that shape these composite texts while at the same time offering new ways to think about Aboriginal sovereignty in relation to ongoing disputes over land, voice, and representation in Canada. Told-to narratives cannot be romanticized as unmediated oral tradition, nor can they be dismissed as corrupted texts. Rather, a collaborative approach acknowledges the volatility of relations of authority between recorders, tellers, interpreters, and editors, and emphasizes the process of making told-to narratives as much as the product itself.

Chapter 2 focuses on the period just following the presentation of the White Paper, introduced by the Liberal government of Pierre Trudeau in 1969, as Native groups struggled to transform Canadian Indian policy from one of assimilation to one of self-government. I examine the Mackenzie Valley Pipeline Inquiry, headed by Justice Thomas Berger, and Hugh Brody's ethnographies and documentary films of the 1970s and 1980s as important precursors in debates over voice and representation that emerged so forcefully in the 1990s in universities and in dominant media coverage. The Berger Inquiry endeavoured to break with the colonial past by actively seeking the opinion of Dene, Inuit, and Métis groups in thirty-five community hearings throughout the Mackenzie Valley regarding a proposed oil and gas pipeline. The hearings, which were televised nationally, introduced a new politics of voice in Canada, in which Native groups sought to speak directly to the Canadian public without mediators such as Indian agents, academics, or legal representatives. While Justice Berger celebrates Northerners speaking 'in their own voices' at the commission, his report reinforces the importance of governmental decision-making. In Hugh Brody's work, in contrast, there is a palpable sense of unease about the problem of speaking for a community, an issue that he explores through a variety of narrative and cinematic strategies. I argue that while both Berger and Brody are motivated by the best of intentions to expose injustice and 'give voice' to marginalized Aboriginal groups, they sometimes overlook their own role as mediators in cross-cultural dialogues and exchanges.

Chapter 3 focuses on the standoff at Kanehsatake as a turning point in First Nations politics and cultural production. This event became the crucible in which debates over the appropriation of voice began to boil over. In this chapter, I examine how two Indigenous artists – Abenaki filmmaker Alanis Obomsawin and Coast Salish writer Lee Maracle – use strategies of the told-to narrative to engage with the Oka crisis, challenging the dominant, starkly oppositional representations of the event. While clearly highlighting asymmetric relations of power so palpable in the televised images of the barricades, Obomsawin and Maracle construct double-voiced, composite productions that are troubling to reified notions of identity, difference, and representation. Both artists, working within the limits of their chosen media, manipulate forms of the told-to narrative – interview, quotation, and collage – to retell and re-frame the events at Oka. Their 'told-to narratives' are 'twice-told narratives,' in which they re-write or re-present the conflict in ways that avoid stereotypical media oppositions.

The Royal Commission on Aboriginal Peoples was struck in 1991 in response to the Oka crisis, and the commissioners released their five-volume report in 1996. In Chapter 4, I discuss the implications of the commission's stated goal to initiate a politics of reconciliation between Aboriginal and non-Aboriginal groups in Canada, and what the turn to reconciliation might signify in light of debates over the appropriation of voice. I argue that the RCAP missed a crucial opportunity for creating the conditions for reconciliation. This is not because, as many critics have argued, its report's vision of self-government was wrong-headed or divisive, its recommendations impractical, or its call for governmental change ineffectual. Rather, I focus on how, in moving from the community hearings to the writing of the report, the RCAP incrementally distanced itself from the testimony, containing and managing it within the language of recommendations. As a result, the commission did not elicit the active participation of Canadians as witnesses in the remaking of a shared history. In contrast, Ila Bussidor and Üstün Bilgen-Reinart, who initially worked with the RCAP and who later became the co-authors of the collective life narrative *Night Spirits* (1997), sought a broader audience to tell the story of the relocation of the Sayisi Dene First Nation in a way that would persuasively convey the urgent need for compensation. The tendency of the RCAP's report to cut out the 'you,' directed for the most part to the non-Aboriginal addressee, is reversed in this publication, thus encouraging the listener to remain accountable to history in a newly crafted politics of reconciliation.

Chapter 5 explores the renewed connection between oral traditions, land, and Aboriginal title in the current era of land claims negotiations, and proposes that the principle of collaborative authorship may provide a model for engaging with land disputes in the courtroom. Though oral traditions have gained legitimacy in the courtroom, problems of translation (cultural and linguistic) remain. In *Delgamuukw v. British Columbia*, the Gitksan-Wet'suwet'en land claims case that took place in the provincial court of British Columbia in 1991, Chief Justice Allan McEachern officially recognized that oral traditions were admissible as evidence of land title, but nevertheless continually questioned their reliability. Because the judge expected the oral traditions to provide stable sets of data, he failed to take into account the dialogic interaction at the heart of the oral traditions. In contrast, Harry Robinson and Wendy Wickwire, in *Write It on Your Heart*, as well as the co-authors of *Life Lived Like a Story*, make clear that storytelling does not occur in a vacuum; storytellers require continuous responses from participating audience members. I suggest that these texts practise oral traditions in ways that rethink the concepts of evidence, ownership, and Aboriginal title to land, and envision the negotiation of a land dispute as an ethical process of 'response and response-ability' (Blaeser, 'Writing' 54).

The film *Atanarjuat, the Fast Runner*, which the filmmakers say is 'part of the continuous stream of oral history' in Inuit traditions, opens with the character Kumaglak declaring: 'I can only sing this song to someone who understands it.' Kumaglak's statement is a kind of manifesto that shapes the politics and poetics of the film: to respond to, contest, and re-imagine the ethnographic traditions of recording, translating, and collecting oral stories in Nunavut (historically referred to as 'the North'). I argue that the subtitled film, as a form of textualized oral narrative, enables the filmmakers to create two parallel texts that interact and speak to each other in imperfect ways. The gap between what is spoken and what appears on the bottom of the screen can be manipulated strategically, for a variety of effects, enabling the filmmakers to address different audiences. *Atanarjuat* is part of a larger body of work by Isuma films that follows an 'Inuit culture of production' ('Filmmaking' par. 2), emerging from the same political movement for Inuit sovereignty as the new territory of Nunavut. The filmmakers take seriously their role of instigating debate and providing social critique of both colonial Canada and Nunavut. Through their work, they continuously remind the country's and the territory's leaders of the vital role that art and culture play in northern communities.

In the conclusion, I discuss the implications for this book, focusing as it does on told-to narratives and other collaborative cultural productions, of the current trend in Aboriginal literary criticism and in Aboriginal studies more generally to draw upon discourses of sovereignty. In recent years, a significant number of Aboriginal literary critics both in the US and in Canada have turned to 'Indigenous literary nationalism' as a way to locate Indigenous writing within specific historical, political, cultural, and aesthetic contexts and traditions, rather than continually responding to, and calibrating ideas to fit, Euro-American critical paradigms. This turn often is accompanied by a turn away from collaborative texts and towards singly authored texts. Following the lead of Temagami scholar Dale Turner, who suggests that 'Aboriginal sovereignty is best understood by listening to the diverse voices of Aboriginal peoples themselves' (Turner, 'Introduction' 4), I argue that attentive listening to Aboriginal voices-in-dialogue, in a wide range of texts and contexts, may generate a productive range of models of sovereignty. I further suggest that reading and writing collaborative, cross-cultural, composite texts such as told-to narratives provides a way to imagine a new politics of voice and of sovereignty, as well as to shift the kinds of questions critics pose in addressing Native cultural production in Canada.

# 'Where Is the Voice Coming From?' Appropriations and Subversions of the 'Native Voice'

1

> And there is a voice. It is an incredible voice that rises from among the young poplars ripped of their spring bark, from among the dead somewhere lying there ... a voice so high and clear, so unbelievably high and strong in its unending wordless cry.
>
> The voice of 'Gitchie-Manitou Wayo' – interpreted as 'voice of the Great Spirit' – that is, The Almighty Voice. His death chant no less incredible in its beauty than in its incomprehensible happiness.
>
> I say 'wordless cry' because that is the way it sounds to me. I could be more accurate if I had a reliable interpreter who would make a reliable interpretation. For I do not, of course, understand the Cree myself.
>
> – RUDY WIEBE, 'WHERE IS THE VOICE COMING FROM?'

The concluding passage of Rudy Wiebe's short story 'Where Is the Voice Coming From?' evokes with great intensity the power of the 'Native voice.' The voice has the force of immediacy; it is 'high,' 'clear,' and 'strong.' It is at once the dying utterance of Almighty Voice, the Cree fugitive shot by the RCMP in 1895, and the voice of the Great Spirit, Gitchie-Manitou, emanating from the land. Yet despite its eruptive energy, the voice is a 'wordless cry,' a pre-discursive unit of sound. The mediating structures of translation are absent, and the Euro-Canadian narrator does not understand the

Cree language. At the same time that he disavows expertise in translation, he conveys the urgent necessity for 'a reliable interpreter' to salvage the elusive voice that would otherwise disappear unheard.

Wiebe's story highlights the central paradox in the transcription and translation of told-to narratives: to simultaneously control and erase the processes of mediation in the making of the 'Native voice.' The voice that speaks for itself, yet cannot be heard without the intervention of a translator, is a recurring construction in the history of recording Aboriginal oral narratives in North America. In this chapter, I explore three competing constructions of the 'Native voice' in told-to narratives in the twentieth century: Romantic-nationalist, anti-colonial, and collaborative. Generally, Romantic-nationalist discourses from the first half of the twentieth century have constructed the 'Native voice' as an isolated fragment or ethnographic object. The 'art museum' style of exhibition in literary anthologies of Native North American verbal art has decontextualized the 'Native voice' and has contributed to myths about the 'vanishing savage' in works dating from the 1910s to more recent decades (Clements 186). In the second construction, critiques of appropriation in salvage anthropology, which began emerging in the 1960s, have produced anti-colonial readings of the 'Native voice,' in which writers have located and problematized the interventions of collector-editors. In this interpretation, told-to narratives are seen to exemplify incommensurable 'parallel voices' (Valaskakis, 'Parallel') vying for authority in conflicts over representation, conflicts that mirror larger political and social struggles. In the third interpretation, told-to narratives are neither simply authentic records of oral performance nor examples of textual colonization. At least two partners, both of whom are involved in complex cross-cultural negotiations that are shaped by relations of power, produce the composite texts. The result of their collaboration is an intersubjective form that emphasizes process over product, exchange over static image. In the process of making told-to narratives, relations of authority are contested, negotiated, and recreated.

## The 'Native Voice' as Ethnographic Fragment: Literary Salvage Projects and Romantic Nationalist Discourses

> Viewing a Pomo basket in a museum is like viewing a movie frame depicting a close-up of water; it could be water anywhere, or nowhere.
>
> – GREG SARRIS, *KEEPING SLUG WOMAN ALIVE*

In the first decades of the twentieth century, the discourse of the 'vanishing Indian' sparked many projects to record, collect, and anthologize Aboriginal oral traditions. While American and Canadian governments were drafting and implementing aggressive policies of assimilation,[1] a number of collector-editors set out to the field to salvage what they assumed were the final dirges of the departing 'child races' (Curtis xxix). Generally, these projects as examples of salvage anthropology – a term used beginning in the 1960s as part of a critique of nineteenth-century ethnography and of early modern anthropology – produced Romantic images of the Native, elegiac in mood. The 'vanishing Indian' became a particularly resonant image for Canadian and American writers who were seeking to define their newly 'indigenous' (read Euro-American invention of 'indigenous') literary traditions. Writers, poets, and critics from the first half of the twentieth century, such as Natalie Curtis, Mary Austin, George W. Cronyn, Lindsay Skinner, and Alice Corbin Henderson, argued that the fresh vitality of spoken Aboriginal art would enrich the new literatures of North America, as if poetic originality would spring from 'Ab-originality.' The confluence of the old and the new, of oral tradition and literary invention, of Aboriginal belonging and American discovery, would provide the ingredients for establishing a genuine American literature. Mary Austin, the American novelist, poet, and critic whose best-known work, *The Land of Little Rain* (1903), was inspired by myths from the Indigenous peoples of the Mojave Desert, expresses the ideology most succinctly when she writes, 'The first free movement of poetic originality in America finds us just about where the last Medicine Man left off,' treating the disappearance of this 'last Medicine Man' as a given (qtd. in Cronyn xvi). This section of the chapter explores how textualized Aboriginal oral narrative, particularly as presented in literary-minded anthologies, has contributed to the production of literary value in American and Canadian nationalist discourses.

The literary anthology of Aboriginal verbal art, whose popularity as a book form has continued to the present day,[2] played a key role in developing and justifying the new settler literatures of the Americas by using and transforming translations of Indigenous oral narrative. William Brandon states that the production of anthologies of Aboriginal verbal art 'became epidemic' during the late nineteenth and early twentieth centuries, 'nearly always with either scientific or Cub Scout overtones, seldom presented as serious literature' (145). Brandon here is critiquing the historical trends in presenting Aboriginal oral narrative either as data for anthropological studies or as simplified tales for children; instead, he argues, presenting examples from the oral tradition as free-standing poems, without encumbering them with further historical or cultural information, confers upon them their proper literary value. Margery Fee has convincingly argued that the development of settler nationhood in North America relied upon the appropriation of Aboriginal oral traditions, collected and displayed in national anthologies, as the 'ground' for the new settler literatures. Since the settlers had 'taken over the soil, they could also take over the myths of Aboriginal peoples, who were believed to be on the verge of extinction' (Fee, 'Writing Orality' 23). In Romantic-nationalist discourses, oral traditions are closely tied to the land and express the spirit of the nation.[3] This one-to-one relation between land, literature, and nation suggests that a people's sense of belonging to a place is dependent upon that people's knowledge of and familiarity with a store of ancient oral traditions. Fee quotes from nineteenth-century German literary critic, Friedrich von Schlegel, who states: 'A nation unendowed with poetic stores that date from some time prior to the period of regular artistic culture ... will never attain to any nationality of character, or vitality of genius' (qtd. in Fee, 'Writing Orality' 23). For the nationalist settler critic, this poses a serious dilemma. How can the new literature attain 'vitality of genius' without drawing upon an oral tradition as its creative source? The answer is to record the myths, epics, and folktales of Indigenous groups, freely translate them, and present them in anthologies that de-emphasize or even efface tribal and language differences. Literary critic Glenn Willmott comments on how 'such backward looking to another's aboriginal past' is at the same time 'so peculiarly pregnant with the contrary, future-premised birth of a nation' (75).

The first anthology of Native American verbal art, Natalie Curtis's *The Indians' Book* (1907), exemplifies the Romantic-nationalist agenda that both Fee and Willmott describe. Curtis was trained as a concert pianist, but soon after hearing Native American music for the first time in Arizona in 1900, she focused exclusively on transcribing Native American songs and stories from many regions and cultural groups.[4] For Curtis, 'We echo Europe, whereas we might develop a decorative art truly American' (qtd. in Clements 171). Truly 'indigenous' American art, she suggests, would rise from the ashes of Aboriginal music and poetry. Curtis was a strong critic of American governmental policies that sought to suppress Native American cultural practices. Yet in a manner commensurate with the racialized discourses of cultural evolution of her time, Curtis wrote of 'the sunset hour of ... native life' whose 'night was soon to come' (Curtis xxii). While in *The Indians' Book* she states that 'the Indians are the authors of this volume' and that the editor's work was secondary – 'the work of the recorder has been but the collecting, editing and arranging of the Indians' contributions' (Epigraph) – she simultaneously asserts the importance of her role. Without writing, Aboriginal oral traditions were doomed to disappear forever. In speaking to one of her informants, Curtis expresses her regret that Aboriginal oral traditions cannot survive without writing:

> As yet your people have no books nor do they read or write. That is why your songs will be forgotten, why even your language may some day pass away. When you sing, your song is heard, then dies like the wind that sweeps the cornfields and is gone, none knows whither. But if you could write you could put your song in a book, and your people, even to the children of their children, could know your song as if you yourself were singing. (475)

For Curtis, writing is purely functional, providing a convenient storage house for Aboriginal songs; she does not acknowledge whether and to what extent writing shaped the narratives that she secured. Struggling with the limited recording technologies of the early twentieth century, Curtis first used a phonograph and wax cylinders to record songs and stories, and later switched to pen and paper. Each method had its disadvantages: on the one hand, the phonograph was bulky and unwieldy, and wax cylinders typically only stored about two minutes of live performance. On the other hand, the accuracy of a written transcript depended upon the storyteller's willingness to pause while an interpreter translated and Curtis wrote. As a result of these technical factors, Curtis collected mostly short performances that were detached from conversation and stripped of their narrative frames. Curtis also showed a strong aesthetic preference for the ethnographic fragment. Though she expressed regret about what she saw as evidence that Native communities were passing out of existence, she also was moved by the elusive quality of cultural remnants: 'A bit of broken pottery, a bone-awl, an arrow-head, a grave-mound, mute testimonies these of the art, the industry, the life, the death of man in the long ago' (xxix). For Curtis, it appears, the more fragmentary the artifacts (including songs), the more powerful their affective influence.

Curtis's presentation of Aboriginal songs as decontextualized poems reminds us that writing, in its role as a technology of recording, is not a neutral conduit. Curtis's work influenced a number of literary anthologies of 'Indian verse' that emerged in the first half of the twentieth century. In 1917, the prestigious journal *Poetry* published a special 'Aboriginal Issue' of recorded oral 'poetry,' including translations by Curtis. Soon after, literary critic and anthologist George W. Cronyn published *The Path on the Rainbow* (1918), which became, in the words of Mary Austin, who wrote the Introduction, 'the first authoritative volume of aboriginal American verse' (in Cronyn xv). Cronyn showcased a vast range of Aboriginal verbal art without even, as William Clements comments, 'the equivalent of a museum exhibit card' (187) – that is, with little or no information on the narratives' cultural contexts, or explanations of the recording process.[5] The fragments reflected the popular literary trend of the day, imagism, which favoured the poetic form of the short, personal lyric. Austin saw affinities between Aboriginal verbal art and new directions in American verse: 'Vers libre and Imagism are in truth primitive forms, and both of them generically American forms, forms instinctively selected by people living in America and freed from outside influence ... The Indian verse form *is* Imagism' (qtd. in Colombo, *Songs I* 104). Thus Aboriginal verbal art becomes a stepping stone in the making of American literature: through the dedicated work of writers and editors who would transform the oral material into written literature, American literature would evolve its way out of these 'primitive forms.' Cronyn included works by Euro-American poets whose contributions reworked Native American songs to fit the pared-down aesthetics of the personal lyric. Because these poets did not know the Aboriginal languages in which the songs were initially recorded, their aim was to create 'versions,' not translations.

Anthropologists and literary critics have long disputed the best way to 'entextualize' oral narrative, which Richard Bauman and Charles L. Briggs describe as the 'process of rendering discourse extractable, of making a stretch of linguistic production into a unit – a text – that can be lifted out of its interactional setting' (73). Disciplinary divisions between anthropology and literature have created two poles in entextualizing styles of told-to narratives: while the former discipline invokes context as a form of authority, the latter seeks to reduce reliance on context in order to emphasize the timeless, artistic value of the fragment.[6] In early literary anthologies of Aboriginal verbal art, the displayed ethnographic fragments are meant to speak for themselves as art by appealing to a universal aesthetic that transcends cultural difference.

The first anthologies of Aboriginal verbal art from what is now Canada drew on material collected over several hundreds of years of Aboriginal-settler contact. *Poems of the Inuit* (1981) and *Songs of the Indians, Volumes I and II* (1983), edited by poet and compiler Robert Colombo, follow the traditions of anthologizing Aboriginal verbal art in the 'minimalist installation style' associated with art museums (Kirshenblatt-Gimblett 391), an approach to entextualization that was popular in the first decades of the twentieth century. Colombo's skills as an anthologist have been well recognized in Canadian letters (he has been called 'the Master Gatherer' for his compilations of diverse forms of Canadiana), but they exert a particular politics in textualizing Aboriginal oral narrative. Colombo drew upon material in the American literary anthologies described above but re-oriented the content to reflect what he claimed was distinctively 'Canadian' Native verbal art, a categorization that ignores how many Native North American cultural groups cut across the forty-ninth parallel. Even though Colombo's anthologies of Aboriginal verbal art are not well known today, their influence persists. One of the most highly respected anthologies of Native literature in Canada – Daniel David Moses and Terry Goldie's *An Anthology of Canadian Native Literature in English* (2005) – uses Colombo's material in the opening sections of the anthology as examples of 'First Nations Orature.' As Moses and Goldie explain, the entries in the orature section provide 'the cultural roots' (1) from which contemporary Native writing springs – but ultimately departs.

As in the American anthologies, Colombo's collections demonstrate how literary value is constructed through the appropriation of Aboriginal oral expression as the basis for new literary innovations. Colombo's two-volume *Songs of the Indians,* a collection of song lyrics that were gathered over a period of four hundred years by a wide range of individuals of diverse backgrounds and trained in different professions (including Henry Rowe Schoolcraft, Frances Densmore, Franz Boas, John R. Swanton, Natalie Curtis, Mary Austin, Marius Barbeau, and others), creates a dehistoricized, transpersonal, and decontextualized 'Native voice.' Colombo makes little or no distinction between the various collecting and translating projects of the original recorders. He rarely names the Native singers or storytellers of the lyrics, usually providing only the name of the cultural group to which the anonymous song or poem belongs. Although the lyrics are expected to 'speak for themselves,' the reader is left with few clues as to the cultural background or meaning of the songs. Furthermore, Colombo re-translates, re-works, and compresses the songs in a number of cases. Each edited fragment is noted as being a 'very free adaptation,' 'an interpretation' (*Songs I* 105), 'reconstructed,' 'reconstituted' (107), or 'reworked because the original is fragmentary' (117). He also runs together disparate songs and rewrites earlier versions of the songs without knowing the languages in which they were performed or the cultural contexts from which they emerged. His anthologies are closely comparable to William Brandon's *The Magic World: American Indian Songs and Poems* (1971), an anthology of eighty 'poems' that Brandon insists 'can speak for themselves' (Brandon n.p.); yet Brandon has radically adapted, fragmented, and conflated different songs to produce his versions (Clements 189-94).

In suggesting that changes to language are mere technical adjustments, Colombo (along with Brandon and other literary anthologists of Aboriginal verbal art) contributes to a further erasure of the original Aboriginal languages. This erasure shows that translation in the Native North American context has come to represent a 'process of domination' (Blaeser, 'Writing' 54). As David Murray writes: 'In a situation of mutual agreement and equality of power, adaptation and translation can be a two-way process. In a situation of dominance, the cultural translation is all one-way. Knowledge of the processes of this translation, though, must be repressed by the dominant side, in favour of a reassuring image of mutual intelligibility which does not register as significant who has had to translate' (6). Effacing language differences has ominous implications, given the policies of assimilation that have severely threatened the survival of some Aboriginal languages. Colombo's one-way process of translation reasserts English as the dominant language over Aboriginal languages.

In a similar vein to Curtis's *The Indians' Book,* Colombo's *Songs of the Indians I* associates 'Indian eloquence' with the elusiveness of its passing. The anthology opens with a three-line song in the Beothuk language, recorded phonetically in 1822. The three lines, printed upon a great expanse of the white paper without translation, paradoxically convey regret at the extinction of the Beothuk people and pleasure in the aesthetic impact of the fragment. In the notes at the back of the anthology, Colombo explains the provenance of the song. According to its recorder, William Cormack, the singer, Nancy Shanawdithit, who died in 1829 at the age of twenty-nine, was at the time 'the sole survivor of her race' (*Songs I* 105). Colombo emphasizes the untranslatability of the song: 'Whatever the nature of the language, the meaning may never be known, the melody may never again be heard. Something special has been lost' (105). He concludes his section on Beothuk song with a final comment that reinforces a rhetoric of disappearance: 'So much for the lyrical legacy of the Beothuk people' (105). In anthologies such as Curtis's, Cronyn's, Brandon's, and Colombo's, the modus operandi is not so much *finding* fragments as *making* them. These anthologies decontextualize the oral texts as museumized fragments frozen in the past, downplaying or erasing the mediation of the transcribers and translators. The editors then re-translate the translations. The project of salvage is represented as necessary to preserve Aboriginal 'oral cultures': 'All the cultures lacked letters ... The Indian spoke a highly structured language, the words of which he had no way of preserving' (Colombo, *Songs I* 11-12). In the name of preserving what orality cannot, the editors justify their interventions on the page.

The collapsing of Aboriginality with orality ignores Aboriginal writing and sign systems such as wampum belts, carvings, pictographs, and paintings,[7] as well as the reams of letters, petitions, sermons, reports, essays, diary entries, and autobiographies that First Nations people wrote throughout the eighteenth and nineteenth centuries.[8] At the turn of the twentieth century, enthusiasm for 'Aboriginal American verse' rarely included an appreciation for Aboriginal writing. In 1918, author and critic Louis Untermeyer, in his review of Walter Cronyn's anthology *The Path on the Rainbow*, made special objection to the inclusion of poems by Mohawk writer Pauline Johnson (1861-1913): 'It is an added disappointment to come across jingles like Pauline Johnson's "The Song My Paddle Sings," which is neither original nor aboriginal'. Johnson's poems, according to Untermeyer, are 'time-dusty', 'rhymed sweet-meats' (qtd. in Colombo, *Songs I* 104). Untermeyer's disparaging comments reflect his interest in fashioning a 'modern' literary aesthetic, a goal shared by Canadian poet and literary critic A.J.M. Smith. While Smith was equally disapproving of Johnson's verse, he nevertheless valued Aboriginality as the ground and source of Canadian modern verse. For example, he admired the poem 'Story, with Song No. 1', attributed to collector Charles G. Leland, a well-respected scholar in his day and editor-collector of the highly influential anthology of verbal art, *Algonkian Legends* (1884), as a 'simple and direct rendering of aboriginal poetry' (A.J.M. Smith 44). While the poem's style appealed to Smith, its content is also of interest here: the speaker is a 'Noble Savage' who declares 'Now I am left on this lonely island to die' six times in a poem of twenty-four lines (44). This poem, which is likely more of a fabrication than a transcription, indicates the extent to which told-to narratives historically have reinscribed the trope of the 'vanishing Indian', as well as the significance of this image for nascent American and Canadian literatures.[9]

The representation of Aboriginal oral narratives as anonymous, such as the one 'attributed to' the collector-editor Leland (above), implies they are unauthored. However, many First Nations view their songs as cultural property that can be exchanged and traded as a form of wealth. For example, Nora Marks and Richard Dauenhauer, collector-editors of oral narrative from the Tlingit First Nation in Alaska, of which Nora Marks Dauenhauer is a member, have produced four anthologies of Tlingit oral performance, including oratory, life histories, songs, and stories. They say that Tlingit tellers invariably begin stories by outlining where and from whom they initially heard the story, and why they have the right to re-tell it (Dauenhauer and Dauenhauer, 'The Paradox' 9). Many of the Tlingit songs are informed by the concept of *at.óow*, which, according to the Dauenhauers, means 'an owned or purchased thing' (*Haa Shuká* 25): 'If a particular story is the *at.óow* of a given clan, it is important to note this somewhere in the telling' (28). In their anthology of Tlingit oral narrative, *Haa Shuká/Our Ancestors* (1987), the songs are integrated into stories; in turn, the stories are embedded in the frame of the storytelling interaction. The stories all begin with the storyteller's notation of the *at.óow* of the narrative, the storyteller's *shagóon* or *shuká* (Tlingit clan or family genealogy), and the story's or song's place of origin. Clan members perform certain songs to begin feasting at a potlatch; no other clan is permitted to use the songs. In some cases, the storytellers may refer to songs without recording them. For example, A.P. Johnson, who tells the story of 'Kaax̱'achgóok',[10] asked the Dauenhauers to delete his performance of the accompanying song (*Haa Shuká* 323n). The song, according to the Tlingit system of oral copyright, is owned by the Kiks.adi clan and cannot be retold without explicit permission (333n). Johnson offered the following lines to replace the song:

> [Kaax̱'achgóok] started singing his song ...
> But this is the only thing
> you won't hear.
> What they did is now ended.
> This is why
> you won't hear it. (107)

For Johnson, each performance of the song acts as a kind of publication, and retellings that do not respect the song's lineage are breaches of oral copyright.

The problem of oral copyright becomes acute with the inclusion of sacred material, procured and then transformed without the permission of the teller. Representing sacred songs or stories without permission has sparked heated controversies over the politics of representation. Laguna Pueblo author Leslie Silko does not mince words when she writes: 'the racist assumption still abound[s] that the prayers, chants and stories weaseled out by the early white ethnographers, which are now collected in ethnological journals, are public property' (qtd. in Swann, Introduction xxix). Anishinaabe author Lenore Keeshig-Tobias similarly insists that debates over voice are symptomatic of 'the case of cultural theft, the theft of voice ... as surely as the missionaries stole our religion, the politicians stole our land, and residential schools stole our language' (72). Here, Keeshig-Tobias makes a clear connection between the appropriation of stories, the expropriation of land, and the loss of language. The history of told-to narratives is tightly bound up in this history of dispossession.

In recent decades, Indigenous writers have disassociated themselves from ethnographic told-to traditions, drawing attention to the fact that the vast majority of told-to narratives recorded over the past five hundred years are closer to appropriations than translations. They have highlighted the incommensurability of agendas between recorders and tellers in order to challenge totalized conceptions of the 'Native voice.' The emergence of the politics of representation that began in earnest in the 1970s with feminist, anti-racist, and civil activist movements has paralleled the efforts of Indigenous writers to highlight concerns about publication and circulation, as well as struggles over land, resources, and repatriation of material property.

## Parallel Voices: A Question of Representation

> There is a time bomb in Canada – a bomb that has developed, in part, because of a lack of voice.
> The lack of aboriginal voice in basic communications, in history, and in politics has created in the dominant society a series of misconceptions that mutate into indifference and racism.
>
> – JORDAN WHEELER, 'VOICE'

The emergence of the 'Aboriginal voice', especially notable in the 1990s in Canada in political, scholarly, and literary debates, cannot be disentangled from the powerful mediating structures that have threatened to contain and manage that voice. For groups that have been historically silenced, cultural critic bell hooks (1989) has argued that 'coming to voice' becomes a 'revolutionary gesture': 'speaking becomes both a way to engage in active self-transformation and a rite of passage where one moves from being object to being subject. Only as subjects can we speak. As objects, we remain voiceless – our beings defined and interpreted by others' (12). However, Cree-Ojibway writer Jordan Wheeler has complicated this notion of 'coming to voice' by drawing attention to the mediating structures that produce the effect of oppositional Aboriginal voices. Systemic discrimination in Canada's 'basic communications' – media, history, politics, education, and publishing – have commodified and homogenized the 'Native voice'. In other words, the 'Native voice' can be heard, but how it is framed or mediated determines the extent of its impact. Wheeler's point is that the movement from silence to speaking is a complex process that does not guarantee a 'hearing'. Pointing to the example of the media representation of the Oka crisis, Wheeler insists that 'there was an aboriginal presence, but it was not voice. The depiction of the Oka crisis relied on the political slant of the various journalists and media outlets that recorded, interpreted, and relayed the events' (37). By drawing attention to the relations of mediation that create an 'aboriginal voice', Wheeler is defying the historical norm of the invisible, silent recorder who produces the effect of 'Indian eloquence' for a (largely) non-Native audience.

Julie Cruikshank, an anthropologist and collector-editor of oral narratives, makes a similar point, observing that since the early 1970s, there has been 'a dramatic shift in popular discourse, and the idea that indigenous peoples should represent themselves rather than be represented by others (such as anthropologists) now meets widespread, commonsense approval.' Cruikshank, however, has questioned the significance of the change, asking whether the incorporation of Indigenous viewpoints amounted to more than strategic acts of accommodation: 'In Arctic and subarctic Canada, one consequence of this shift has been that references to local knowledge or indigenous knowledge are increasingly incorporated in public discussion, suggesting that additional voices are being included in public debates. But are they? And if so, how? And if more voices are included, whose are still left out?' (*Social* 47). She is implying that the 'incorporation' of Indigenous voices in public discussions does not necessarily change the nature of the discussion. This is precisely what Wheeler is suggesting when he says that during the Oka crisis, the apparent inclusion in dominant media representations of the 'aboriginal voice' 'shouting threats of violence' merely provided 'info-tainment' (37).

Cruikshank's questions are crucial to my discussions in the following chapters, in which non-Indigenous collector-editors insist, usually in the preface or introduction of the told-to narrative, that they have recorded exactly what the teller has said. In told-to narratives, collector-editors have adopted textual techniques to create the effect of Indigenous narrators 'speaking for themselves,' but such strategies have not necessarily transformed the asymmetric relations between recorders and tellers. For example, in the introduction to *I, Rigoberta Menchú: An Indian Woman in Guatemala* (1984), anthropologist Elizabeth Burgos-Debray evokes the immediacy of the raw transcription of Menchú's story: 'We have to listen to Rigoberta Menchú's appeal and allow ourselves to be guided by a voice whose inner cadences are so pregnant with meaning that we actually seem to hear her speaking and can almost hear her breathing' (xii). Burgos-Debray downplays her own role in editing, but also presents her mediation as indispensable in retrieving what would otherwise be lost: 'I allowed her to speak and then became her instrument, her double by allowing her to make the transition from the spoken to the written word' (xx). Overcoming the difficulties of collaboration, Burgos-Debray suggests, requires sympathy, patience, and careful listening: 'For the whole of that week, I lived in Rigoberta's world. We practically cut ourselves off from the outside world. We established an excellent rapport immediately' (xv). In creating this immediate, intimate setting, Burgos-Debray attempts to isolate her interaction with Menchú from larger political contexts.

Burgos-Debray and Menchú's 'excellent rapport,' however, later dissolved. Following the allegations of inaccuracy in the *testimonio*,[11] Menchú accused Burgos-Debray of having stolen and misrepresented her story. She claimed that Burgos-Debray denied her authorship (and royalties) of the (auto)biography: 'authorship of the book, in fact, should have been more correctly indicated, shared, no?' (qtd. in Beverley, 'The Real Thing' 268). This breakdown in trust shares some similarities with the eventual rupture between Salish narrator Lee Maracle and Euro-Canadian writer Don Barnett, who collaborated in 1975 to produce a 'history-from-below' testimonial of Maracle's / Bobbi Lee's life story (discussed in Chapter 3).

It is also comparable to the dissolution of the relationship between co-authors Linda Griffiths (a White actress playing the part of Jessica) and Maria Campbell (whose own life provided the basis of Métis character Jessica's story) in *The Book of Jessica* (1989). A common thread between these controversies is the disjuncture between the time of narration, when the collaborators are speaking together in dialogue, and the time of writing and publication, when one of the interlocutors becomes an 'author.' Carole Boyce Davies comments on this moment of transition in her study of recorded oral life narratives:

> The oral narrative contract in life story telling turns on the concept of 'trust.' All of the collectors identified building 'trust' as the critical ingredient in having the stories told at all ... In the written version, however, it seems, this oral life narrating contract is often violated. Rarely is the collector's story a part of the narrative. At the point of writing, then, the dominant-subordinate relationships are enforced and the editor becomes a detached, sometimes clinical, orderer or even exploiter of the life stories for anthropological ends, research data, raw material, or the like. Writing another person's life can become an act of power and control. (12, 13)

The transition from trusted confidant to editor to author often drives a wedge between collaborators. As the author signs the title page and the publisher circulates the text in larger economies, the initial trust between interlocutors dissolves. This is largely due to the function of authorship in print-capitalist economies. As literary critic Philippe Lejeune argues in 'Autobiography for Those Who Do Not Write,' authorship involves not only writing but also disseminating, publishing, and circulating texts (192). Authorship, with its emphasis on individual creative genius, precludes the very existence of collaborative literary production. This is because the singly authored work enables the publisher to use the 'brand name' of the author to maintain control over profit, labour, and property in print-capitalist markets. As a result, challenges to the supremacy of the author are liable to spark explosive and heated controversies. For example, if we study the movement of the spiralling loss of trust in *The Book of Jessica*, the enforcement of 'dominant-subordinate relationships' occurs most conclusively at the moment of the drafting of the copyright contract between Griffiths, Campbell, and Theatre Passe-Muraille. The contract is the cumulative effect of all the authorship activities that engaged Griffiths, Campbell, and Paul Thompson (director) in making *Jessica*, including the public performance of the play. The 'voice' that reaches the page, then, is determined to a significant degree by structures of mediation that frame this voice.

Despite the claims made by many editors of told-to narratives who suggest that their recording projects have been guided by a mutuality of purpose and harmony of perspective, conflicts over the representation of voice highlight the deep divisions between Aboriginal and non-Aboriginal 'collaborators.' To a large extent these divisions reflect the asymmetric social relations between Aboriginal and non-Aboriginal communities in Canada. As Chippewa scholar Gail Guthrie Valaskakis argues, in cultural and political debates between Aboriginal communities and Canadian governments, moments of exchange are few and far between; usually, the so-called exchange consists in a Manicheist staging of 'parallel voices' grounded in a politics of difference. These 'parallel voices' are 'distortions of the communication symbolized in the Two-Row Wampum Treaty of the Iroquois Confederacy, which represents the historical pact between Indians and newcomers' ('Parallel' 284). Writing in the aftermath of the Oka crisis, Valaskakis points to what she sees as an increasing level of distrust between Aboriginal and non-Aboriginal groups: 'Today, we are all caught in a web of conflicting interests and actions, confrontations constructed in dominant cultural and political process and the Native experience of exclusion, or stereotypical inclusion and appropriation' (284). The idea of 'stereotypical inclusion' is a sobering thought with respect to told-to narrative. The Native perspective is either excluded or 'too thoroughly' included in a different space of politics.[12] Valaskakis argues that 'the politicized reality of pluralistic Native experience' is rarely acknowledged in dominant narratives of 'Indian cultural stasis' (294). The legacy of critical thought has positioned First Nations in the past, removed from the cultural and political reality of contemporary life. In situating her analysis in the context of Oka (like Wheeler), Valaskakis argues that 'parallel voices' become especially pronounced when the stakes are high in disputes over property, land, resources, and economic development. In these typically asymmetric exchanges, the possibilities of cross-cultural dialogue are slight.

Disputes over 'voice' that become entangled with the law, an instrument of state power, raise the stakes of collaborative practice considerably, as is evident in Rudy Wiebe and Yvonne Johnson's co-authored (auto)biography, *Stolen Life: The Journey of a Cree Woman* (1998). It is not an incidental detail that during the five years they worked together, Johnson was serving her sentence of life imprisonment without the possibility of parole for twenty-five years following her conviction of first-degree murder. The text, which is more self-conscious about the process of representing another's voice than is evident in, for example, *I, Rigoberta Menchú*, draws attention to its mediated status as well as to the co-authors' widely differing life experiences, levels of education, and socio-economic opportunities. The novel comprises a mix of genres, including (auto)biography, confessional, legal drama, and investigative journalism; Wiebe states that in crafting Johnson's 'voice', he has 'gathered together Yvonne's words ... as she and I agreed from various sources', including Johnson's seventeen prison notebooks, her letters, her comments on official records, her statements to police, Wiebe's notes from their conversations, and numerous audiotapes. The text's techniques of juxtaposition and self-referentiality bring to the fore debates about the appropriation of voice and the politics of representation, acknowledging the constraints underlying the collaborative process between the co-authors.[13]

By jumping from one genre and way of speaking to another, each of which carries varying degrees of legitimacy and authority, *Stolen Life* signals the irrefutable differences between Wiebe and Johnson, who respectively live 'outside' and 'inside' prison. A significant condition of production that underlies this collaborative relationship is the fact that Johnson never testified at her trial for murder. In any case, she questions to what extent she would have been heeded by the jury whose members were White and mostly male. Writing about herself in the third person years after the trial, she recalls her reactions at that time: 'She told her lawyer she did not want to go back into court, it could just go on without her, as her face being there just gave them an Indian face to judge and sneer at, she could say or do nothing anyway' (Wiebe and Johnson 318). Deena Rymhs argues that as much as the book is a story of Johnson coming to terms with her past, as well as finding in Wiebe a witness to her trauma, Correctional Services Canada remains a largely unacknowledged but potent presence, whose power 'extends beyond the jurisdictions of this narrative to suspend the inmate's agency and self-determination at any time' (Rymhs, 'Auto/biographical' 104). Referring to Johnson's transfer from the alternative, minimum-security institution of Okimaw Ohci Healing Lodge to the Edmonton Correctional Institution against her will following the publication of the book, Rymhs suggests that *Stolen Life* cannot be read as a narrative of 'coming to voice' without acknowledging how that voice inextricably is bound up in discourses of criminal law.

Because of the persistence of ongoing colonial state apparatuses such as the law that so palpably shape the interactions between First Nations communities and the Canadian nation-state, strong differences between 'insider' and 'outsider' perspectives continue to haunt Native American and First Nations studies. Some writers, to counteract the predominance of non-Aboriginal writing about Aboriginal communities, have strategically differentiated their work from mainstream discourse 'on' First Nations by insisting upon the importance of doing research 'in' First Nations intellectual traditions, and engaging with the particularities of ethnic, linguistic, national, regional, gender, and sexual differences. Since the early 1990s, Aboriginal literary and cultural critics such as Lee Maracle (1992, 1996), Maria Campbell (1992), Kimberly Blaeser (1993), Jeanette Armstrong (1993), Taiaiake Alfred (1999), Craig Womack (1999), Armand Ruffo (2001), Kristina Fagan (2004), and Daniel Heath Justice (2008), to name only a few, have argued in favour of engaging more profoundly with differences *within* Aboriginal communities, rather than continually re-staging the 'parallel voices' of 'Aboriginal' versus 'non-Aboriginal' (read Euro-Canadian) differences.

Craig Womack's influential and widely cited study, *Red on Red: Native American Literary Separatism* (1999), makes a strong case for 'literary sovereignty' as an antidote to the phenomenon of 'parallel voices' that Valaskakis describes.[14] A Creek-Cherokee author and scholar, Womack 'seek[s] a literary criticism that emphasizes Native resistance movements against colonialism, confronts racism, discusses sovereignty and Native nationalism, seeks connections between literature and liberation struggles, and, finally, roots literature in land and culture' (11). Womack links the struggle against colonialism with the struggle for self-determination and the reconnection to Aboriginal traditions. He imagines an activist, socially engaged criticism whose aim is to build knowledge networks within Aboriginal nations, rather than continually responding to and countering dominant Euro-American epistemologies. For Womack, literary sovereignty becomes a way to assert control in ideological struggles over representation and other political arenas.

The varying articulations of 'literary sovereignty' and cultural autonomy have become the founding narratives of First Nations discourse, connecting to broader social and political struggles to establish 'nation-to-nation' relations between First Nations and the Canadian nation-state, especially since the Oka crisis in 1990. By developing tribally specific research, critics such as Womack are opening up a space in which intra-cultural differences may be explored more fruitfully. Literary or intellectual sovereignty provides release from essentialist stagings of the 'parallel voices' of the Native/White binary. Attending closely to intra-cultural differences enables a more sustained discussion of gender, class, and language differences within Native communities. Furthermore, for Womack, literary sovereignty corrects the historical over-emphasis on Aboriginal oral traditions in Native American literary criticism. Womack argues that during the 1990s, while he was working on his dissertation, Native American criticism was dominated by studies of oral tradition; however, very few of these studies engaged with tribally specific analyses or acknowledged the historical dynamism of oral traditions ('The Integrity' 154). Womack, with his focus on contemporary and historical Creek writing and storytelling, aims to shift the focus away from a pan-Native, transhistorical approach to orality, and towards an analysis of the particular forms of governance and cultural expression of a given Indigenous nation.

The turn to Womack's 'literary sovereignty' as well as to Osage scholar Robert Allen Warrior's 'intellectual sovereignty'[15] has generated significant debate, with some critics claiming that an over-emphasis on sovereignty reinforces the problem of Manicheism. Referring to the two-row wampum belt, which provides an image of Aboriginal and non-Aboriginal communities living side by side harmoniously but never intersecting, political scientist Alan Cairns argues that such a model 'stresses the permanence of difference. [This] parallelism does not address the reality of our interdependence, and of our intermingling' (92). Yet as Valaskakis suggests, such a reading is reflective of the 'distortions' that sometimes accompany interpretations of the vision of cross-cultural coexistence of the Two-Row Wampum Treaty (Valaskakis, 'Parallel Voices' 284). For Valaskakis, the Two-Row Wampum Treaty is more of an acknowledgement of difference than an assertion of a binary opposition.[16] Similarly to Cairns, Arnold Krupat, a well-known critic of Native American literatures, argues that the concept of intellectual sovereignty contributes to a false Aboriginal/non-Aboriginal cleavage: 'To consider these Native thinkers as ... "intellectually sovereign" – as comprehensible apart from Western intellectualism – is simply not possible. Nor, if it were possible, would it be useful for the purposes claimed' (*The Turn* 18). He argues that describing a culture from the 'inside' relies upon essentialist constructions of identity that turn upon a series of colonial oppositions (13). For Krupat, the focus on intellectual sovereignty risks replicating the very terms of racialized difference that colonialism imposes. Yet for critics such as Womack, Warrior, and

Valaskakis, it is only by attending to intra-cultural and intra-national differences that Indigenous scholars can overcome the static opposition of a Native/White binary.

Krupat's critical work on 'bi-cultural composite authorship' attempts to take into account the inter-cultural dynamics of Native American literature. He claims that we cannot view Native American literature as autonomous because what we know as the history of Native American literature begins with collaboratively produced, cross-cultural, told-to narratives:

> We need to be acutely aware of the mode of production of Native American texts, taking into account the varying contributions of Native performers, informants, interpreters, and the like, as well as non-Native editors. Whatever understanding of traditional Native American literature may currently be achieved, it will have to take into account the role Euramericans have played in its textual production. This is only one price of our history of domestic imperialism. (*The Voice* 129n)

I agree with Krupat that we need to attend to the many participants involved in told-to narratives, and he is right to argue that told-to narrative cannot be thought of as purely 'Native American literature.' Ironically, however, his formulation of 'bi-cultural composite authorship' reinforces a strict dividing line between recorder and teller, and goes too far in asserting the control of the recorder over Native oral forms. Figuring the collaborative relation in 'bi-cultural composite authorship' as the 'textual equivalent of the "frontier"' ('Indian Autobiography' 263), Krupat employs a metaphor (the frontier) that underlines the conceptual model of a Native-White impasse. Though he argues that 'bi-cultural composite authorship' is a 'collaborative effort,' he concludes that its production is dependent upon 'some white [who] translates, transcribes, compiles, edits, interprets, polishes and ultimately determines the 'form' of the text in writing' (262). While Krupat is helpful in highlighting the asymmetric relations in 'bi-cultural composite authorship,' his 'bi-culturalism' presents linguistic and cultural relations in binary terms. By assuming that 'bi-cultural' means 'Native/White,' Krupat implies that conversation, dialogue, and exchange can only take place along a Native/White axis. He risks missing the point of the turn to literary sovereignty, which is to attend more carefully to tribal differences and to produce more nuanced representations of Indigenous identity and history.

Kimberly Blaeser, a Chippewa writer of mixed German and Anishinaabe descent, writing in response to Krupat, argues that 'Perhaps the most frequently employed mode for articulating "Native constructions of the category of knowledge" has been oppositional.' However, she adds, 'the emerging critical language expressing this central aesthetic characteristic of Native literature need not or should not have to base its existence or integrity on an oppositional relationship ... Several intriguing experiments in Native critical discourse recognize both the differences between Native and non-Native perspectives and the complexity of the literary voice that arises from the convergence of these different perspectives' ('Native' 58). In tandem with Blaeser, Cruikshank (1990, 1998), Greg Sarris (1993), and Cree community activist and legal scholar Sharon Venne (1997), I attend to degrees of collaboration and degrees of authorship that shape the told-to narrative. In the following chapters, I examine the moments of rupture and cross-cultural misunderstandings that productively disturb the usual staging of 'parallel voices,' while highlighting the volatile and politically charged contexts that shape communication. I discuss a spectrum of techniques of subversion in told-to narrative, including, to name just a few, the politics and poetics of juxtaposition in Hugh Brody's ethnographies, the parody of ethnography in Lee Maracle's 'Rusty,' the complicated layers of tellings in *Night Spirits,* and the multi-directional agendas of the four authors of *Life Lived Like a Story*. In all of these examples, interlocutors develop working intersubjectivities through contact with the other. This approach to told-to narrative offers unique opportunities to think about the dynamics of cultural contact and cultural difference.

## Collaborative Voices: Rethinking Authorship and Ownership

> That slow piling one on top of the other of thin, transparent layers which constitutes the most appropriate picture or way in which the perfect narrative is revealed through the layers of a variety of retellings.
>
> – WALTER BENJAMIN, 'THE STORYTELLER'

A critical focus on collaboration enables us to theorize the interaction between interlocutors in relational and dialogic terms. Attending to the degrees of collaboration and degrees of editorial intervention requires careful attention to the social contexts that affect the process of collaboration, as well as to the role of power in the storytelling / recording relationship. The verb 'collaborate' has two distinct meanings, as *The Concise Oxford English Dictionary* makes clear: '1) work jointly, esp. in a literary or artistic production; 2) cooperate traitorously with an enemy.' Both senses have resonance in the context of cross-cultural interactions with and among Aboriginal communities. Furthermore, while it is evident that power relations shape told-to narratives, power is a volatile relationship that potentially flows in more than one direction.

A groundbreaking collection of told-to narratives that uses collaboration as its methodology is *Life Lived Like a Story* (1990), by Julie Cruikshank and three Athapaskan storytellers, Angela Sidney, Kitty Smith, and Annie Ned (a book I discuss in detail in Chapter 5). One reason that collaboration (in the sense of cooperation) appears to 'work' in this text is that the ownership of the stories – their author-ity – is acknowledged. The text uses as a guiding principle Angela Sidney's claim that 'my stories are my wealth' (Cruikshank et al. 36). The notion that clans own stories forms the basis of the collaborative contract between the four authors. For Sidney, Smith, and Ned, each telling of the 'same' story acts as a kind of publication. For each re-telling, the purpose and audience change. Collaborative authorship acknowledges that stories circulate in different communities, for different reasons, and to different political effect.

*Life Lived Like a Story* brought about something of a sea change in approaches to textualizing oral narratives, with many more recent collections naming Aboriginal storytellers as authors on the title page, listing other community members as translators, editors, and compilers, and developing innovative practices of collaboration.[17] Examples of contemporary recorded oral narrative that, to varying degrees, acknowledge oral forms of authorship and recognize the involvement of Aboriginal co-creators include: Beverly Hungry Wolf's *The Ways of My Grandmothers* (1980); Nora Marks Dauenhauer and Richard Dauenhauer's *Haa Shuká/Our Ancestors: Tlingit Oral Narratives* (1987); Freda Ahenakew and H.C. Wolfart's *Our Grandmothers' Lives, As Told in Their Own Words* (1992); Darwin Hanna and Mamie Henry's *Our Tellings* (1995); Maria Campbell's *Stories of the Road Allowance People* (1995); Ila Bussidor and Üstün Bilgen-Reinart's *Night Spirits* (1997); George Blondin's *Yamoria the Lawmaker: Stories of the Dene* (1997); Nympha Byrne and Camille Fouillard's *It's Like the Legend* (2000); and John Bennett and Susan Rowley's *Uqalurait: An Oral History of Nunavut* (2004). Each of these projects pursues different objectives, including re-telling family histories (Hungry Wolf), (re)learning Indigenous languages (Hanna and Henry; Ahanekew and Wolfart), experimenting with forms of recorded verbal art (Dauenhauer and Dauenhauer; Campbell), constructing narratives of Indigenous nationhood (Bennett and Rowley), healing from historical trauma (Bussidor and Bilgen-Reinart), or gathering evidence for land claims trials (Hanna and Henry; Bussidor and Bilgen-Reinart; Byrne and Fouillard). In many of the texts listed above, the narrators retain the copyright for their stories, and virtually all of these texts have distributed the royalties among the participants or have donated the earnings to an education or land claims fund. As a way of acknowledging the stories as cultural property, many of the recorders describe how they paid for the narratives with tobacco, cloth, food, or money; Maria Campbell, for example, says she gave a 'prize Arab stallion' in exchange for one set of stories (*Stories* 2).

The connection between story and property remains controversial in the field of Native literary criticism. Arnold Krupat opposes the arguments of a number of Native American critics (such as Warrior [1995], Elizabeth Cook-Lynn [1996], and Annette Jaimes [1992]) that assert stories as forms of cultural property. 'To whom does culture "belong"?' he asks. His answer is:

> Contemporary Native American literature is a practice, not a thing, and as a practice, it cannot 'belong' either to American literature or to ... Native American literature ... This is true as well for a good deal of oral literature. Once there is a degree of circulation of stories, that is, once narrators permit 'outside' auditors to record, translate, and publish stories, then ... there is no ground on which they can claim sole rights to possession ... For all these reasons, the cultural property metaphor for most of what is taken as Native American literature obscures far more than it clarifies, and this is the case even for those textualized oral performances of a sacred or traditionally circumscribed kind that probably never should have been transcribed, translated and published in the first place. (*The Turn* 22)

I agree with Krupat's point that Native American literature is a practice, not a thing, and that debates over ownership are problematic in laying claim to a cultural production that might be best thought of in more active terms such as *writing* and *storytelling*. However, Krupat's argument comes close to rationalizing historical practices of appropriation. He suggests that it makes no difference if a recorder has received permission to record stories once the narratives are 'made public.' He continues:

> Rather than say that certain stories and ceremonials, along with certain artifacts, 'belong' to particular lineages of storytellers, clans, or people, acceding to a language of commodity and possession, it seems better to refer to these people or groups as the culturally sanctioned guardians, stewards, or 'friends' of the materials. (22)

Again, Krupat's point about the need to redefine notions of property in opposition to the 'language of commodity' is crucial. However, because he refuses the language of property in a wholesale manner, Krupat does not consider how First Nations cultures and languages create alternative notions of property. The analysis rests on only one possible type of authorship and one possible mode of publication or circulation. It must be kept in mind that oral modes of authorship and publication operate according to a different set of assumptions, as *Life Lived Like a Story* makes clear.

In *Life Lived Like a Story*, 'collaborative authorship' is an active exchange between people from different cultural backgrounds and a collective responsibility shared between four mediators. The author/mediator, who passes the story along from previous storytellers, conveys a sense of the radical polyvocality that collaborative storytelling can potentially create. Opening up the spectrum of possible forms of authorship is key in rethinking the relations of authority in told-to narratives. For Mikhail Bakhtin, using the speech of someone else makes possible 'various types, subcategories and forms of authorship' (*Speech* 104). While Bakhtin 'dispels "authorship" of the old centered-subject private-property type,' he does not reject the notion of authorship altogether (Jameson 185). Instead, he opens up the possibility of conceptualizing collaborative and multiple authorship.

In storytelling performance, there are at least two people and often more involved in the making of the story. Multiple narrators, recorders, translators, and listeners, either present in the room or invoked by the storyteller, push the recorder's role into the background. Sharon Venne, who has worked with Cree elders in collecting oral traditions for the purposes of land claims negotiations, has observed how storytelling can become a collective process that disperses the responsibility of authorship among members of a community. 'When the Elders come together, the stories begin to flow. One Elder alone has many stories, but when a number of Elders are placed in the same room, the stories multiply,' she comments. 'One Elder may know part of a story and another will know the rest of the story ... No one Elder knows the complete story' ('Understanding' 174). Furthermore, the story is dependent upon responses from the audience. The Elders 'tell a piece and wait to see if there is interest in the whole story. The story is then like a puzzle ... There is one piece in this corner, then another piece given at another time. It remains to the listener to put the pieces together and sort out the complete picture' (176). The stories interlock and connect in web-like formations; one story creates the conditions for telling another. In moving from one cluster of stories to another, the storyteller waits for a response from her or his audience. The listener's participation is thus key in shaping the story; different audiences create different inflections, nuances, and references in the narrative. This model of collaborative production is effective in highlighting the limitations of Krupat's characterization of the opposing figures of the White recorder and the Native storyteller and is better able to show that 'listeners' and 'tellers' may include translators, interpreters, editors, and readers of told-to narrative.

As composite texts, told-to narratives dramatize the collision and confluence of at least two voices. Other discourses and other voices, whether the speakers and listeners are aware of these or not, shadow every word and utterance (to paraphrase Bakhtin). As co-productions, told-to narratives conceal and reveal a surplus of contradictory intentions of recorders, tellers, and other intermediaries, all of whom are involved in selecting and shaping the narrative. These collaborative texts produce subjectivities that are multiple, competing, and contradictory. In *Life Lived Like a Story*, there is no absolute opposition between recorder and teller, no clear first/third speaker division. This is not to say that there is no *difference* between recorder and tellers; indeed, at the outset, their agendas are described as divergent.[18] Nevertheless, the stories belong neither to the recorder nor to the teller in an exclusive way.

For Greg Sarris, storytelling creates a gap between teller and listener, but the widely differing cultural and personal worlds between speakers and listeners need not be a hindrance. Indeed, distance between interlocutors can become a creative space of collaboration: 'No one party has access to the whole of the exchange. One party may write a story, but one party's story is no more the whole story than a cup of water is the river' (Sarris 40). As a mixed-blood scholar of Coast Miwok, Pomo, and Jewish descent, Sarris has a complicated relationship to the storytelling traditions he studies. Even the most intimate storytelling moments that he has experienced with his Pomo grandmother do not ensure the same understanding of a story. Sarris attempts to map out some of those creative moments of (mis)understanding in *Keeping Slug Woman Alive,* a book of stories, theory, dialogues, and transcriptions. In telling stories about the telling of stories, Sarris suggests that it is through the static of mediation that one hears best.[19] Cross-cultural, told-to narratives make explicit the social, cultural, and personal dynamics that are at play in exchanges between tellers and listeners.

To return, then, to Wiebe's question, 'Where is the voice coming from?' The narrator of the story implies that he cannot locate the elusive voice because he does not understand the voice speaking in Cree. But if he could re-conceptualize the voice as part of a conversation, rather than straining to hear the isolated utterance, he may begin to piece together the mystery of Almighty Voice. The tendency to isolate the 'Native voice' from context reflects a common strategy employed by some collector-editors to maintain control over the process of making told-to narratives. These collector-editors have justified their control over the representation of told-to narratives by constructing the 'Native voice' as fundamentally oral and unauthored. Especially in anthologies of recorded verbal art from the early twentieth century (as well as in more recent publications), the 'Native voice' as an isolated, oral utterance has reinforced settler ideas about the eventual disappearance of Native cultures. At the same time, literary-minded collector-editors and anthologists have argued that Aboriginal verbal art should provide the ground for 'new' settler literatures. Aboriginal writers and activists have strongly opposed the appropriation of stories, land, and other cultural properties, and have become increasingly outspoken since the 1970s about the wide gaps in socio-economic conditions and opportunities between Aboriginal and non-Aboriginal communities in Canada. These gaps continue to widen and have resulted in the establishment of 'parallel voices' that have, in turn, influenced the production and reception of told-to narratives. Especially when the stakes are high, in legal contests or disputes over property, land, and resources, 'parallel voices' reassert the dividing line between Aboriginal and non-Aboriginal groups in Canada. Nevertheless, there are some intriguing experiments in cross-cultural told-to narrative that place more emphasis on the collaborative process, dialogue, and exchange. It is a mistake to view told-to narratives as either reliable recordings of oral traditions or examples of textual colonization. Two or more mediators produce these composite texts, and their negotiations, shaped by contested relations of power, result in dynamic forms of intersubjectivity that unfold in productively challenging ways.

# Coming to Voice the North
## The Mackenzie Valley Pipeline Inquiry and the Works of Hugh Brody

**2**

The year 1969 was a crucial turning point in First Nations politics. Following Prime Minister Pierre Elliott Trudeau's proposed White Paper of 1969, which sought the rapid assimilation of Aboriginal groups into mainstream Canadian society, a new era of First Nations activism began, shaped by the goals of self-determination and self-government. First Nations groups across Canada formed political organizations, such as the Indian Brotherhood, the Native Women's Association of Canada, and the Inuit Tapirisat of Canada, and launched friendship centres, newspapers, and magazines. In 1973, the Supreme Court of Canada's decision in the Nisga'a land dispute, *Calder v. British Columbia*, which affirmed the continued 'existence of Aboriginal title,' forced Trudeau to concede that Aboriginal groups 'may have more rights than we thought' (qtd. in Culhane 84). Trudeau was further compelled to revise his government's assimilationist agenda after the Mackenzie Valley Pipeline hearings, which took place in the Northwest Territories from 1973 to 1975. These hearings contributed significantly to the revitalization of Native sovereignty movements in Canada, providing Dene activists with a national forum to articulate their demands. In July 1975, at a joint assembly of Dene and Métis people, the Dene Declaration was passed. As a manifesto of Dene rights, the declaration began with the statement, '[W]e the Dene of the Northwest Territories insist on the right to be regarded by ourselves and the world as a nation' (qtd. in Watkins 3). Partly in response to this assertion of Dene nationhood, Indian bands across Canada began calling themselves First Nations (Kulchyksi, *Like the Sound* 86).

Both Thomas Berger, Chief Justice of the Mackenzie Valley Pipeline Inquiry, and Hugh Brody, ethnographer and filmmaker, would play important roles in terms of non-Native participation in the shift from assimilation to self-determination in First Nations politics since 1969. Both men were outspoken opponents of the Canadian Liberal government's policies of assimilation, and both sought to challenge the secretive manner by which the Department of Indian Affairs and Northern Development developed 'Indian policy' in Ottawa. Berger is remembered for conducting extensive public hearings during the pipeline inquiry, undertaking public consultation with Native groups in the North on an unprecedented scale. Brody, who worked as a consultant and researcher for the Berger Inquiry and who wrote portions of *Northern Frontier, Northern Homeland* (1977, 1988),[1] has been widely recognized as uncommonly 'sensitive' and 'empathetic' in his ability to represent a 'variety of points of view' in his texts and films (Huggan 68n).[2]

In this chapter, I examine the politics of voice and representation that animated Berger's *Northern Frontier, Northern Homeland*, the local research projects and community hearings associated with the Mackenzie Valley Pipeline Inquiry, and Brody's ethnographies and documentary films. Significant differences underlie the conditions of production of these diverse manifestations of 'as-told-to' interactions: while Berger was commissioned to produce a particular kind of document and was constrained by the terms of his appointment, the hearings were instrumental in providing an arena for Inuit, Métis, and Dene community members to articulate locally based, socially progressive projects that expanded beyond the immediate aims of the Berger Inquiry. Meanwhile, Brody worked at various points in his career for a range of organizations, including the Department of Indian Affairs and Northern Development, educational institutions, band councils, and land claims research groups.[3] As a result of these shifting job posts, through his reports, films, and books, Brody continually questions whose interests he is representing in his depictions of cross-cultural communication and political negotiation.

Consistent with the momentum of Native activism that challenged Canada's deeply paternalistic history, in their respective work, both Berger and Brody have recognized and valorized the idea of Native people 'coming to voice' and 'speaking for themselves.' Indeed, partly as a result of the politics that sprang from the Berger Inquiry in the North in the 1970s, decolonizing 'voice' and decolonizing First Nations communities became tightly intertwined projects. As we have seen in the previous chapter, however, 'coming to voice' through told-to narratives must be viewed in the context of the power structures that mediate the process. The difficulties of the told-to process – transcription, translation, and interpretation of oral testimony – sharpen in the antagonistic arenas of land claims hearings or governmental consultations with Aboriginal communities over resources. The Berger Inquiry, like all public forums that involve the acts of testifying and witnessing, mobilized a multiplicity of mediated voices that defied a simplistic division between 'speaking for oneself' and 'speaking for others.' Both Aboriginal and non-Aboriginal spokespeople were involved in the hearings, including expert witnesses, advisers, translators, transcribers, writers, and editors, as well as a slew of journalists and camera operators. In analyzing Berger's report, the local presentations at the community hearings, and Brody's texts and films, it becomes evident that each enacts a different politics of voice; yet in assessing these disparate contributions, I argue that each helped forge a renewed sense of Aboriginal nationhood and autonomy through a sense of shared historical accountability. I further argue that while both Berger and Brody are motivated by the best of intentions to expose injustice and 'give voice' to marginalized Aboriginal groups, they sometimes overlook their own role as mediators in cross-cultural dialogues and exchanges.

## Justice Berger's Report: *Northern Frontier, Northern Homeland*

> [R]epeatedly stress[ing] the fact that the text allows the 'voices of the voiceless' to be heard [is] an image that ignores that [Aboriginal people] have always had a voice, that it was the ear that was lacking.
>
> – CARLI COETZEE, 'THEY NEVER WEPT, THE MEN OF MY RACE'

In 1973, Prime Minister Trudeau appointed Thomas Berger to determine the 'social, environmental and economic impact' of a natural gas pipeline stretching over three thousand kilometres from Prudhoe Bay in Alaska, east to Tuktoyayaktuk in the Northwest Territories, south down the Mackenzie River to join up with existing pipelines in British Columbia, Alberta, and finally into the Chicago area. The chief justice, deciding against holding formal hearings in Yellowknife only, as the government had instructed him to do, travelled extensively through the region to conduct public hearings in villages, towns, and reserves. The community hearings opened in Aklavik in the Mackenzie Delta in April 1975 and continued for two summers, closing in Detah, near Yellowknife, in August 1976. In the report, Berger writes: 'All those who had something to say – white or native – were given an opportunity to speak' (Canada, *Northern* vii). He made considerable effort to make the hearings open and democratic; he gathered testimony not only from representatives of political organizations, who 'claim[ed] to speak for all northerners,' but also from non-affiliated community members: 'I decided that I should give northerners an opportunity to speak for themselves' (viii). He was especially concerned that Dene, Inuit, and Métis people had a chance to express their views, and ensured that translators of the six regional languages – Gwi'chin to the northwest, North Slavey in the Sahtu region in the central west, Dogrib in the North Slave region in the central east, Chipewyan in the South Slave region in the southeast, South Slavey in the Dehcho region, and Inuktitut in the Mackenzie Delta in the north (Kulchyski, *Like the Sound* 95) – were present at the community hearings. His approach, of letting community members have their say in their own languages, represented a significant break in the history of government commissions (Hamilton 187). In April 1977, Berger released his report, *Northern Frontier, Northern Homeland*, recommending a ten-year moratorium on resource development. Such time was needed, he argued, to complete environmental and social impact studies and, in particular, for Aboriginal people in the region to consolidate their vision of self-determination and resolve their land claims with the federal government. He challenged the notion of the North as a 'frontier' to be developed for the benefit of the South, insisting it is also a 'homeland' to diverse Northern communities.

Berger emphasized the extent to which the statements voiced at the community hearings directed his findings. He quotes extensively from elders, political leaders, and ordinary citizens who express their sense of commitment to the land. Page after page highlights the voices of Northerners who express their passionate, bodily attachment to Denendeh (the Dene name for their land in the Northwest Territories). 'This land it is just like our blood because we live off the animals that feed off the land,' says Louis Caesar (Canada, *Northern* 94). Georgina Tobac, also of Fort Good Hope, says, 'Every time the white people come to the North or come to our land and start tearing up the land, I feel as if they are cutting our own flesh because that is the way we feel about our land. It is our flesh' (94).

Berger stressed the Native groups' common opposition to the pipeline. In Old Crow, for example, a village with a population almost exclusively of Gwi'chin Dene people, 'the whole village told me they were opposed to the pipeline. I heard 81 people testify; virtually everyone, man and woman young and old, spoke and they spoke with one voice' (Canada, *Northern* 36).

Berger made considerable efforts to ensure that the media covered the inquiry from a local perspective. He saw great potential in the Canadian Broadcasting Corporation's (the CBC's) Northern Service, which had been developing a number of community radio stations since the late 1950s, as well as hiring and training Aboriginal people as broadcasters. In 1975, when the community hearings began, Aboriginal people were receiving extensive radio services in their own languages: the CBC was broadcasting from Yellowknife in Chipewyan, Dogrib, and Slavey; from Inuvik in Gwich'in; and from Montreal to the eastern Arctic in Inuktitut (Hamilton 183). Berger ensured that every community hearing took place before journalists and requested that the CBC broadcast the hearings daily.

There is no doubt that Berger's advocacy was strategically useful in bringing about certain changes in Aboriginal politics within the context of the mid-1970s in the Northwest Territories. My purpose here is not to fault Berger for writing what he was, after all, hired to write; I recognize that Berger was constrained by the conditions of his appointment as commissioner as well as by the genre of the governmental report. Given these limitations, Berger was farsighted in encouraging the Dene, Métis, and Inuit people to use the commission to advance their own interests. Rather, my aim is to assess the report's representation of Aboriginal voices, which, I argue, is symptomatic of larger problems in textualized oral narrative. Indeed, I read *Northern Frontier, Northern Homeland* as a told-to narrative, asking how it incorporates quotations from the public hearings, how it constructs a notion of 'coming to voice', and how it produces a relationship between a collector-editor (Berger) and storytellers (community hearing participants). I interpret *Northern Frontier, Northern Homeland* in this light since its legacy continues to inform commonly held notions about the politics of representation as well as the relationship between Aboriginal peoples and the Canadian nation-state.

The manner in which Berger textualizes the oral statements from the hearings, as well as his facilitation of media coverage, suggest that the inquiry offered a neutral space in which every voice could be heard and recognized equally. 'This Inquiry ... has obtained the views of the native people who live in every settlement and village of the Mackenzie Valley and the Western Arctic,' Berger wrote. 'There the native people, speaking in their own villages, in their own languages and in their own way, expressed their real views. About that I am in no doubt' (Berger 259). Yet what happens in the transmission of these voices from the community hearings to the report? The notion that the Dene, Métis, and Inuit people were 'express[ing] their real views' elides how the report itself produces voices and contains them within an institutionally sanctioned space. It also overlooks the problems involved in translating testimony from an Indigenous language – such as Gwi'chin, North Slavey, or Dogrib – into English, the language of report, interpretation, and archive (Sanders 22). In an interview in the film, *The Inquiry Film: A Report on the Mackenzie Valley Pipeline Inquiry* (1977), Berger urges Native people to 'speak for themselves,' without acknowledging his role in eliciting these acts of speaking:

> We have listened to the anthropologists and the sociologists telling us what the Native peoples think. But we need to hear what the Native peoples think. They need to speak for themselves. The most important opinions of all are those expressed by the Native peoples. This may seem obvious but we need to state it clearly. That is what we are here for – why else are we holding these public hearings?

There is a central paradox in Berger's *Northern Frontier, Northern Homeland*: while he argues it is time for Aboriginal people to 'speak for themselves,' he places considerable importance upon the role of federal leadership to end paternalism and move towards self-government, while leaving unclear the role of Dene, Métis, and Inuit people in bringing about social change.

Reflective of his emphasis on the responsibility (and agency) of those in positions of authority, Berger's report rhetorically emphasizes the crucial role of the narrative 'I.' A preponderance of phrases such as 'I have seen,' 'I have learned' (Canada, *Northern* 2), and 'I decided that' (viii) underlines the influence of the first person and reveals the importance the report places upon Berger's own role in recognizing and listening to Aboriginal voices. In turn, Berger's goal is to persuade Canada's leaders to act in the best interests of Aboriginal peoples. In an anecdote in the introduction to the revised edition of *Northern Frontier, Northern Homeland* (1988), Berger recounts a conversation with Prime Minister Trudeau, soon after he had submitted the report. During this conversation, Berger described the annual journey of the Porcupine herd of caribou that migrate hundreds of miles each year to their calving grounds in the Mackenzie Valley. The sight of this migrating herd, he revealed, was an important factor in his decision to recommend a postponement of the pipeline:

> I ... urg[ed] Trudeau to visit the Northern Yukon in June. I told him that the herd, migrating from the Ogilvie Mountains to the Arctic Coast, reaches the Coastal Plain, like clockwork, at the beginning of June. I had been there and seen the herd on its migration back into the mountains in late summer. I confess the sight of this magnificent aggregation of animals ... had helped me make up my mind to recommend that no pipeline be built along the Coastal Plain. A year later, after my report had been handed in, I read in the newspapers that Trudeau and his sons were camping in the Northern Yukon. I said to my wife, 'That's it.' 'How do you know?' she asked. I replied, 'No one can visit the Porcupine herd, and then decide to build a pipeline that would drive them from their calving grounds. How could you face yourself at the shaving mirror each morning for the rest of your life?' (Berger 3-4)

The story, which ends with the image of Berger/Trudeau shaving at the mirror, underlines the importance of the actions of Canada's leaders. Berger/Trudeau's sense of moral responsibility for the defenseless (in this case, the caribou) will result in morally correct actions. What contribution, then, do the Dene, Métis, and Inuit people make in determining their future? Berger leaves this unclear. The important thing is for people who have power to listen to people who do not. In *Northern Frontier, Northern Homeland,* the struggle for Aboriginal rights relies upon a politics of recognition that locates agency in Canadian leadership.

Berger used his influence to encourage the federal government to take seriously the challenges that the Dene, Métis, and Inuit people were making to Aboriginal/Canadian relations. His main reason to recommend against the pipeline is the unresolved land claims in the region. However, there is a paradox in valorizing the Native voice while at the same time discursively reinforcing the preeminence of Canadian leadership. Though *Northern Frontier, Northern Homeland* supports Aboriginal peoples' demands for local control, it assumes that self-determination is a right that the federal government may choose to grant or not. In the logic of the report, recognition of Aboriginal rights is dependent upon the political will of national leaders, who reserve the authority to 'give [Native peoples] the right to govern their own lives' (Berger 252). Aboriginal rights are dependent upon their recognition by the Crown; it is up to the Crown to do the right thing. While the report puts the responsibility where it belongs – on the government – it simultaneously reaffirms the need for federal control. It also leads to an incremental model for change, in which existing policies and legislation are minimally revised without questioning the colonial institutions that underpin Aboriginal relations with the Canadian nation-state.

Though Berger quotes with approbation from outspoken Dene and Métis community members, such as Georges Erasmus, George Manuel, James Wah-Shee, Robert André, Richard Nerysoo, Phoebe Nahanni, Charlie Snowshoe, and many others, he is ultimately more concerned with Canadian national unity than with Aboriginal self-determination. Indeed, self-determination functions to strengthen the Canadian constitution. Berger points out correctly that for the most part, the Dene, Métis, and Inuit spokespeople at the hearings were supporters of a centralized, federal government: 'It is a disservice to the Dene to suggest that they – or, for that matter, the Inuit or the Métis – are separatists. They see their future as lying with and within Canada, and they look to the Government of Canada, to the Parliament of Canada, and to the Crown itself to safeguard their rights and their future' (Berger 172). It is true that many Dene representatives at the public hearings defined Dene self-determination within the context of Canadian federalism.[4] However, Berger's desire to establish a common ground with all Canadians does not acknowledge how, for Aboriginal people, the granting of Canadian citizenship has been closer to a policy of enforced inclusion. The Dene Declaration puts it bluntly: 'The Dene find themselves as part of a country. That country is Canada. But the Government of Canada ... [and] the Government of the N.W.T. ... were not the choice of the Dene, they were imposed upon the Dene' (qtd. in Watkins 4). The Canadian nation-state has not guaranteed Aboriginal peoples' rights; rather, it has sought to extinguish them by incorporating Aboriginal peoples within the dominant social order through the 'gift' of citizenship. In this light, Berger's inclusion of a broad spectrum of voices may be seen as a strategy of accommodating critique without significantly rethinking or adjusting the main agenda. In what Gail Guthrie Valaskakis in another context calls the 'stereotypical inclusion' of Native voices ('Parallel' 284), Berger's notion of Aboriginal self-determination serves to reinforce Canadian unity and Canadian citizenship.

Historical accounts of the Berger Inquiry have emphasized the importance of Berger, as opposed to the Dene, Métis, and Inuit, in blocking the proposed Mackenzie Valley pipeline. In most accounts of the inquiry, Berger is a hero who championed Aboriginal rights.[5] However, the prominence of Berger's role did not go uncontested. Even before *Northern Frontier, Northern Homeland* was issued, Georges Erasmus, then leader of the Dene nation, queried Berger's role and defied those who wished to make him the hero of the Mackenzie Valley:

> Some non-Dene have suggested that Judge Berger is our 'last hope.' It is quite true that the Berger Inquiry has happened at an important time in Dene history and that there is great respect for the manner in which Judge Berger has carried out his inquiry. Nevertheless, it is a misunderstanding to see Judge Berger, or any other non-Dene, as our 'last hope.' We have made the Berger Inquiry a success by choosing to use it as a forum to declare our intention to struggle for our national rights, and Mr. Berger in return has contributed to the growth of our collective self-awareness. Whatever the outcome of his report, we will continue to work after he is gone. In the end, we are our last hope. The truth of the matter is that those who see the Berger Inquiry as our last hope are accepting colonialism which has been imposed on us. They are suggesting that only the colonizers can act: the colonized can only 'hope' that someone else will act for them. (Erasmus 181)

Erasmus clearly acknowledges the role that Berger and the Mackenzie Valley Pipeline Inquiry played in providing a national stage for the Dene nation to articulate its vision of self-determination. The Berger Inquiry functioned usefully in publicizing the Dene people's political aspirations and exerting pressure on Canadian leaders to listen to their demands; for the first time in the history of the Northwest Territories, Aboriginal people were actively participating in a government-sponsored, decision-making process. However, Erasmus also questions the tendency to assess history on the basis of the intentions of the powerful, the significance of which Berger identifies but does not problematize. Though Berger urges the government to act responsibly on behalf of Aboriginal groups, he has no suggestions for how Dene, Métis, and Inuit groups may empower themselves, other than simply waiting for recognition from the government.

Erasmus was not the only voice that questioned the central importance placed upon Berger as a remarkable individual; indeed, the question of who speaks for whom was a point of debate that inflected many of the discussions at the Mackenzie Valley Pipeline hearings. Speakers frequently commented on the contentious role of outsiders. For example, Philip Blake, from Fort McPherson, directly confronts his imagined audience by using the pronoun 'you' to underline the sense of responsibility non-Aboriginal Canadians bear for the benefits they have received through their citizenship at the cost of Aboriginal rights: 'We are being destroyed. Your nation is destroying our nation' (qtd. in Watkins 7). Frank T'Seleie of Fort Good Hope also uses the pronoun 'you' strategically: 'This is the first time in the history of my people that an important person from your nation has come to listen and learn from us, and not just come to tell us what we should do, or trick us into saying "yes" to something that in the end is not good for us' (qtd. in Watkins 12). These and other statements from the community hearings indicate that Berger's politics of voice was a point of contention for the Dene, Métis, and Inuit speakers.

An issue that sparked debate amongst the members of the Indian Brotherhood was the role of consultants, who were typically well-paid, White, southern-based researchers (Coates and Powell 105). Media reports focused on the role that young White radicals, such as Mel Watkins, editor of *Dene Nation – The Colony Within* (1977), played in the organization, alleging that these outsiders were using Native spokespeople to advance their own 'Marxist' agenda (Hamilton 143-44). However, though non-Aboriginal advisers played a fairly substantial role in the Berger Inquiry, helping to forge vital links to more southerly networks of support for Aboriginal rights, historical accounts have typically over-emphasized this point, while undervaluing how Aboriginal leaders took the initiative and used White advisers for their own purposes. Coates and Powell argue that for years after Aboriginal leaders had gained control over their organizations and established their own agenda, they were accused of being 'frontmen only' (100). As a result, Coates and Powell suggest, the role of Native organizations has been underrated in many Canadian historical accounts (108). In 1977, Erasmus fired Watkins and other non-Dene advisers. Watkins's dismissal likely was due to a lack of funds following the government's abrupt termination of assistance to the Dene nation and the Indian

Brotherhood (Hamilton 203); nevertheless, the role of outsiders, and who speaks for whom, was a question that drove much of the debate and discussion during the Mackenzie Valley Pipeline Inquiry.

The focus on Berger overlooks the considerable organizational and political activity towards self-government undertaken by Aboriginal groups in the Northwest Territories up to and during the period of the inquiry. Until the early 1970s, Inuit people were considered wards of the state, and only a handful of Dene members had been appointed to the Northwest Territory's commissioner's advisory council. Native communities that wished to become self-governing were expected to 'progress' from one form of municipal body to another – from the status of settlements or hamlets, the most limited forms of local government, to that of villages, towns, and cities. Until 1973, the highest levels of local government for Aboriginal communities in the Northwest Territories were settlements and hamlets, which had very limited authority. The real seat of power remained in offices in Yellowknife and, ultimately, Ottawa (Berger 235). The rigidly hierarchical structure of governance, while paying lip service to the notion of self-government, served to consolidate the federal government's control over the region.

Dene leaders in the 1970s made it clear that a municipal-style government was inadequate as a form of local government. George Barnaby, from the Sahtu Dene community of Fort Good Hope, who became politically active at the time of the Berger Inquiry and has remained engaged in local politics ever since (Kulchyski, *Like the Sound* 172-77), explains how his community achieved control over governing institutions by replacing the municipal council with a community council: 'We [didn't] like that municipal style government, so we developed our *own*' (156). In an interview in 1994, he remembered his frustration with having been the only Dene representative on the territorial council twenty years earlier: 'I told [Justice Berger] that I can't stay in a government like that, doesn't serve the communities, doesn't recognize community rights ... So I said I'm resigning ... and going to work with the Dene Nation to develop a Dene government' (173). As Peter Kulchyski suggests, in the late 1960s and 1970s, a generation of Dene leaders seized the political initiative, achieving in a short period of time a sea change in Aboriginal relations in Denendeh: they established the Indian Brotherhood; they coordinated the virtually unanimous Dene presentation at the Berger Inquiry; they wrote and publicized the Dene Declaration; they took control of the territorial government; and they opened up the process of negotiated land claims (96). The declaration was especially instrumental in establishing a language and politics of Indigenous nationalism that continue to be influential today.

**The Community Hearings**

Quite independently of Berger's report, the hearings at the Mackenzie Valley Pipeline Inquiry played a vital role in animating discussions about the future of the Dene, Métis, and Inuit communities. Even today, researchers from Denendeh continue to consult the transcripts to learn what their members said and to strategize the best approach in ongoing negotiations for land claims and self-government. The community hearings, as well as the commissioned research projects, provided an opportunity for local Dene groups to draw upon the language of the Dene Declaration and to present their case according to a set of interests different from that of the Berger Inquiry. A mapping project, coordinated by Phoebe Nahanni and other Dene community members, provides an instructive example. The immediate aim of the project was to refute the findings by the Arctic Gas company and to stop the construction of the pipeline; but the team took advantage of the momentum for change that the Berger Inquiry galvanized. The transcripts from the Mackenzie Valley community hearings, in tandem with the team's research report, 'The Mapping Project,' written by Nahanni and reprinted in Watkins's collection, *Dene Nation – The Colony Within*, elaborates two goals for this collaborative project: 1) to establish a collective process of research, and 2) to advance land claims negotiations for the Dene nation. These two goals are intimately tied together, suggesting that, for the participants in the mapping project, the politics of 'voice' and of 'land' were mutually constitutive and interdependent.

Over the course of two years, more than twenty Dene participants worked collaboratively in the planning, execution, and evaluation of 'The Mapping Project.' They conducted interviews, travelled to people's traplines, traced the hunting and gathering trails, and recorded the people's stories about the land. The goal was 'to ensure that research involves the Dene from beginning to end' (Nahanni 23). All the recruited field workers for the mapping project were fluent in Dene, enabling the researchers to gather information from a greater number of community members, and representing a significant break from past research on Dene culture and land use. The process of making the maps remained collaborative at every step. First, a group of field researchers attended training workshops in Fort Simpson, organized by the Indian Brotherhood of the Northwest Territories (Nahanni et al. 22,496). Here, the researchers discussed the objectives, purpose, and context of the project, as well as the techniques that could be used in collecting and arranging their findings. Following initial fieldwork, the researchers took the finished maps back to the communities to be again checked by the trappers (22,504). The close ties that Nahanni and the co-researchers maintained with the trappers, hunters, and gatherers ensured the project's collaborative participation.

While the language of legal jurisprudence in 1975 relied upon the 'prior historical use and occupancy' test as the basis for recognition of Aboriginal title and rights,[6] the participants in the mapping project questioned whether land is something that can be parceled out, designated for a specific 'use' or 'occupancy': 'When looking at the sample map shown here, you must keep in mind that, even if you multiply in your imagination to three times the number of lines and routes indicated here, it still represents only partially the extent of use and occupancy of Dene lands' (27). The mapping project makes a strong connection between traditional stories, Aboriginal title, and personal reminiscences: 'From generation to generation our ancestors have passed on information by word of mouth, through legends and by relating personal experiences' (Nahanni 21). Focusing as much on the stories about the land as on the land itself, the researchers moved away from the language of use and occupancy to elaborate their unique understanding of their relationship to the land. This also involved a process of renaming the territory: 'I'd like to point out some place names for you. Before Mackenzie came and claimed the river to be named after him, we called it Deh-cho. This lake we called Sa-too. Most of the places that I know are Slavey place names ... That's where I come from. Simpson we called Lelin Kwen. Trout Lake we called Somba Ke. Nahanni Butte we called Nahaday' (Nahanni et al. 22,519). The research group used the act of mapping to reconceptualize the relationship between Dene people and the land, and between Dene land use and research.

The objective is to show that Dene land is owned by Dene: 'The maps clearly show what the Dene have been saying all along – that we have been here for hundreds and thousands of years; this is our land, our life. This is the most graphic demonstration that we Dene own 450,000 square miles of land' (Nahanni 27). Dene-controlled research is at the heart of this assertion of territory. This time, the goal is to advance the Dene land claim, not to further knowledge for 'a group of consultants from the south'

(Nahanni et al. 22, 495). As these statements indicate, the Dene researchers were committed to both ensuring a collective process of research and asserting Dene jurisdiction over the land. The mapping project also initiated dialogue among community members about the future: 'Quite apart from the value of the ultimate product of this research project, equally vital was the potential of the research experience in informing and promoting discussion amongst our people concerning our past and possible future paths of development' (Nahanni et al. 22, 495). The process of research – involving many participants, from different generations and regions, discussing the past and the future of the Dene nation – comprises the lasting legacy of the project. Indeed, the Berger Inquiry opened up space for Dene groups such as Nahanni's to imagine how filing a land claim, negotiating a self-government package, or conducting a land use research project could follow a different set of criteria and serve a different set of interests from that of previous studies, or from the Berger Inquiry itself. Today, mapping projects in Denendeh continue to play an active role in local politics. Extensive mapping has become a way of resisting the federal government's pressure to parcel out land and designate it for this or that use. As the regions of Denendeh continue to struggle for viable self-government and land claims agreements, community negotiators have an ever-increasing bank of research to construct their arguments.[7]

As Nahanni's community mapping project demonstrates, the Mackenzie Valley Pipeline hearings initiated a vibrant local politics that reoriented how land research is conducted, for whose interests, and to what ends. *Northern Frontier, Northern Homeland* was also successful in drawing attention to the urgent necessity to resolve land claims in the north. Yet Berger did not anticipate the backlash against himself and the Aboriginal communities in Denendeh once the inquiry was over. The aftermath of the Berger Inquiry, with its messy collusions, divisions, and complicities, points to the inadequacy of simplistic notions of 'coming to voice' that ignore larger issues of power.

## Land Claims and the Dene Nation after Berger

In response to *Northern Frontier, Northern Homeland* in 1977, the then Minister of Indian Affairs and Northern Development, Jean Chrétien, declared with annoyance: '[Berger's] mandate was to build a pipeline – not stop a pipeline' (qtd. in Hamilton 182). As it turned out, an economic downturn at the end of the 1970s made energy 'mega-projects' impossible to sell. The grandiose pipeline of the Mackenzie Valley became an unprofitable proposition, and the oil and gas companies abandoned their plans. Despite these factors that led to the termination of the project, the Liberal government retaliated primarily against the Dene nation for having brought their pipeline dreams to an end.

Berger appeared not to foresee that the Dene would ultimately pay for the government's losses. He insisted that the federal government would fulfill its moral and political responsibilities, noting that 'a solemn assurance has been given' to settle land claims (Berger 263). Immediately following the publication of Berger's report, however, the federal government cut all funding to the Dene nation and the Indian Brotherhood. In 1980, Imperial Oil proposed to expand its sixty-year-old Norman Wells field and to build a twelve-inch oil pipeline to Zama, Alberta. Compared to the Mackenzie Valley proposal, the project was modest, covering a shorter distance as well as carrying a smaller volume of gas (Hamilton 203). The Dene people expressed the same concerns at the environmental hearings that they did at the Berger Inquiry. This time, though, the Dene had fewer resources and little leverage to oppose the project. In 1985, the pipeline was built with no settlement of the Dene land claims.

Berger also was punished for his actions. Following the inquiry, Berger returned to the British Columbia Supreme Court but continued to actively speak out for Aboriginal rights. He made a number of public statements in which he argued in favour of enshrining Aboriginal rights within Canada's new constitution of 1982. The Canadian Judicial Council launched an investigation of Berger, and Chief Justice Laskin issued a sharp criticism: 'Judges are expected to abstain from participation in political controversy. To a large degree, Judge Berger was re-activating his Mackenzie Valley Pipeline Inquiry, a matter which was years behind him and should properly be left dormant for a political decision, if any, and not for his initiative in the midst of a sensitive political controversy ... Judges have no freedom of speech and one who feels compelled to speak out is best advised to resign from the bench' (qtd. in Hamilton 206). In early 1983, Berger resigned and returned to private practice, but faced criticism for the same reason: judges should not return to work as advocates.

Berger's report, which urged the federal government to resolve land claims in Denendeh before building a pipeline, did not comment on the federal government's policy of 'extinguishing' Aboriginal rights and title in exchange for land settlements. Whether extinguishment is an acceptable condition of a land claims agreement was and continues to be hotly debated in Denendeh. In 1984, the agreement with the Inuvialuit people, whose territory comprises the Mackenzie River delta, included an extinguishment clause that concludes with grim finality: 'Canada will provide the Inuvialuit with rights, privileges and benefits in return for extinguishment of all aboriginal claims, rights, title and interests to the Inuvialuit in the NWT and Yukon, and to the adjacent islands and waters' (qtd. in Hamilton 247-48). After 1984, pressures mounted on the Dene nation to accept extinguishment, and internal divisions became increasingly marked. In 1990, the Dene nation rejected an Agreement in Principle because it included an extinguishment clause. Disagreements over this decision reinforced divisions among the five regions of Denendeh, each of which took a different approach to the bitter equation of settling land claims and extinguishing Aboriginal rights. After the dissolution of the Agreement in Principle, the federal government approached regional chiefs and offered more modest, localized agreements. Settlements with the Gwi'chin Dene in 1992 and with the Sahtu Dene in 1994 included extinguishment clauses.[8] In 2003, the Dogrib First Nation completed a comprehensive claim negotiation that 'exhausts' their title. The federal government's 'new' policy of exhaustion, in effect since 2002, states that Aboriginal rights do not extend beyond that which is described in the agreement. Kulchyski has argued that exhaustion has the same or worse effect as extinguishment because the agreement both creates and 'exhausts' Dogrib rights. No other source of authority can be referred to in making the case for Dogrib rights (Kulchyski, *Like the Sound* 100).

The Dene people's declaration of nationhood was a radical challenge to the legitimacy of the Canadian state in 1975 and self-government remains one of the most important tools for Aboriginal peoples to assert their rights. The Dene, Métis, and Inuit negotiators continue fiercely to defend their justifications. However, the negotiations often occur on unequal ground, with the government attempting to define the terms and conditions of the agreements. Kulchyski describes self-government as a paradox: 'the name "self-government" has been given to State-sponsored institutional changes among Aboriginal governments, changes that work largely in the interests of totalizing power. At the same time, the concept of self-government has reached the national agenda as the result of agitation and persistence from Aboriginal activists because it bears the promise of representing a site of resistance' (230). In other words, self-government, as conferred upon Aboriginal communities by the government, is always already contained and managed by state apparatuses; yet self-government, as fashioned by community land negotiators, is a useful tool for Aboriginal communities to achieve a sense of autonomy. As the story of the aftermath of the Berger Inquiry in Denendeh makes clear, the question of self-government is both a dream of independence for Aboriginal communities and a mechanism by which the federal government has attempted to assert control over Aboriginal communities.

In the decades following the Mackenzie Valley Pipeline Inquiry, in this climate of both opposition and complicity, Hugh Brody self-consciously addresses the politics of voice and representation that remain implicit in Berger's report. Brody highlights how acts of 'coming to voice' can be co-opted and used for different purposes. In Berger's report, speaking for others remains a largely self-evident process of relaying people's views; in Brody's work, the politics of representation shape his creative and critical production. Brody's anxiety about the potential fallout of his (mis)translations both compounds the problem of speaking for others and generates some innovative approaches.

## Hugh Brody's Strategies of Representation

In contrast to Berger, Brody appears to have little faith in governmental actions or good intentions of leaders. Having worked for a range of employers, including the federal government, non-governmental agencies, universities, band councils, and plaintiffs in land claims proceedings, Brody negotiates on an ongoing basis the question of whose interests he is representing. In films and books produced over several decades, Brody repeatedly expresses doubt about the legitimacy of his research in First Nations communities. In the preface to *Maps and Dreams* (1988), Brody explains how the book came to be. In the late 1970s, the Union of British Columbia Indian Chiefs hired Brody to conduct a 'use and occupancy' study of Athapaskan territory. The purpose of the land study was to gather evidence for a public hearing to oppose the construction of a natural gas pipeline along the Alaska Highway by the Northern Pipeline Agency. Worried about the impact his work might have on the people he hopes to help, Brody explains, 'I was haunted by a thought that must have bothered many researchers: you might find out five or even ten years later whom you were really working for' (*Maps* xxiii). In other words, he was concerned that his work may be re-interpreted and used by the very developers he is committed to opposing. Throughout his work, there is a palpable sense of unease and disquiet about the problem of speaking for a community, and his 'own need to be clamorous on behalf of Indians' (x). He uses a variety of strategies of representation, as if he were searching for a way to both emphasize his distance from the communities he is representing and suggest the possibility of intersubjectivity with politically transformative potential. His own voice, shifting from strident to virtually silent, reflects his ambivalence about his role as mediator. In the following sections, I investigate Brody's strategies of representation – juxtaposition, self-reflexivity, the failure of cultural translation, genre-switching, and reported speech – and show how Brody creates a dynamic text in which points of view, antagonistically arranged, generate productive sites of collision and dispute.

## The Poetics and Politics of Juxtaposition

> I hope to devise a form which in musical terms could be called 'contrapuntal.' A method of composition in which, if all goes well, each individual voice lives a life of its own.
>
> – GLENN GOULD, 'THE IDEA OF NORTH'

In 1969, Hugh Brody made his first major trip to Canada. In the years that followed, over the course of his career as social anthropologist, ethnographer, land claims researcher, and advocate for Aboriginal rights, Brody has sought ways to contest the Canadian government's agenda of assimilation. His main 'anti-assimilation' strategy is to resist the cohesive point of view by highlighting multiple 'ways of seeing.'[9] The attention to point of view and visual modes of knowing emerges from Brody's work as a documentary filmmaker. His films include *On Indian Land* (1988), an historical overview of the Gitksan land claim and the *Calder* decision; *Hunters and Bombers* (1990), about the conflict between the Innu people and the military base of Goose Bay over the issue of low-level military flying; *Time Immemorial* (1991), the story of the Nisga'a land claim up until the early 1990s; and *The Washing of Tears* (1994), a film about cultural loss and recovery among the Mowachaht and Muchalaht First Nations, who were forced to relocate from their territory to a reserve near Gold River on Vancouver Island in the 1960s and 1970s. The genre of the documentary film is well suited to Brody's explorations of the poetics and politics of juxtaposition. Brody exploits the form of the interview to signify abrupt changes in narrative voice. Documentary genres are particularly adept at the strategic deployment of a wide range of modes of speaking, resisting a smooth sublimation of voices. In Brody's films, each voice 'lives a life of its own' (Gould). In his books as well, Brody shows a preoccupation with point of view, often prefixing statements with the tags 'in his view,' or 'from their point of view.' A major strain in Brody's work is the demonstration of 'White' explanations of cultural change being 'sharply at odds with [Indians'] own view of themselves,' as well as the difficulty and political necessity of Aboriginal speakers 'express[ing] their long-neglected points of view' (*Maps* 260). Brody creates a contrapuntal textual score, in which, through the juxtaposition of a series of incommensurable perspectives, he emphasizes Aboriginal difference in defiance of assimilationist governmental policy. He engages in 'procedures of collage,' as James Clifford describes it (*Predicament* 10), in which the goal is 'not to blur, but rather to juxtapose' (*Routes* 12).

Juxtaposition is the core of Brody's work, and influences the representation of cross-cultural interactions in his ethnographies. For example, in *Hunters and Bombers*, Brody juxtaposes the voices of the 'hunters' – the Innu people who live in and around Goose Bay – and the 'bombers' – the American pilots who test their low-flying fighter jets over the 'empty' landscapes of the subarctic. None of Brody's films uses voice-over narration; instead, Brody tacks between six or seven spokespeople in each film, offering no explicit commentary on their different perspectives. In this way, Brody moves in a 'continuous dialectical tacking' between points of view (Geertz 10). One of the purposes of the juxtapositional strategy is to challenge ethnocentrism and to show how certain cultures' points of view have been historically marginalized.

In the book *Living Arctic* (1987), a cross-cultural ethnographic study of the peoples of the North, Brody creates two narratives in juxtaposition. The first, on the right-hand side of the page, is a series of ethnographic essays on Dene and Inuit social practices. The second, on the left-hand page, is a set of quotations from what he calls 'the peoples' own voices' (249) in large blocks of text. Brody culls these quotations from various sources, including Berger's *Northern Frontier, Northern Homeland* and the Mackenzie Valley community hearings. Though the essays follow conventional paragraphing, Brody centres the quotations from Aboriginal speakers in diamond formations on the left-hand page. The example below reproduces the arrangement of a quotation from Richard Nerysoo, who spoke to the Berger Inquiry in Fort McPherson in 1977:

> It is very clear to me that it is an important
> and special thing to be an Indian. Being an Indian
> means being able to understand and live with this world in a
> very special way. It means living with the land, with the animals,
> with the birds and fish, as though they were your sisters and
> brothers. It means saying the land is an old friend and an
> old friend your father knew, your grandfather knew,
> indeed your people always have known ... we see
> our land as much, much more than the white
> man sees it. To the Indian people
> our land really is our life.
>
> Richard Nerysoo
> *Fort McPherson, 1977 (9)*

Brody uses statements about land such as Nerysoo's to underline the fundamental clash in cultural perspectives in the North. This is similar to Berger's set of oppositions, based on the premise of the 'Northern homeland' versus the 'Northern frontier.' Both Berger and Brody use juxtapositional strategies, and here it is important to remember that Brody was one of the primary writers of *Northern Frontier, Northern Homeland*.

What are the political and aesthetic implications of Brody's juxtapositions, both visual and textual? On the one hand, maintaining a strict separation between 'the peoples' own voices' and the main narrative in *Living Arctic* reinforces binary oppositions between 'Native' and 'White' perspectives. Rather than interacting with other voices, in conversation or argument, Brody displays the quotations in isolation. Brody's placement of the quotations invites the reader to decontextualize the quotations, suggesting that the 'Native voice' is transhistorical, static, and unchanging, even though the speakers express a deep-rooted sense of belonging to a specific place. Brody aestheticizes the testimonials, as if they are illustrative, in both senses of the word, of the main text. He further aestheticizes the quotations by interspersing them with photographs of Inuit people and Arctic landscapes. This visually reinforces the connection between image and Aboriginality, potentially contributing to a static representation of Aboriginal difference.

On the other hand, it is also possible to read the quotations on the left-hand side of the page as ironically commenting on, or even speaking at cross-purposes to, Brody's essays. Brody's juxtapositional poetics create an indeterminate space in the fold of the book, leaving it up to the reader to decide what kind of relations the two discourses produce. Brody's texts, which assert the incommensurability of 'White' and 'Native' epistemologies, often dramatize the failure of cultural translation. This failure in establishing a 'common sense' highlights the fragility of the binary oppositions that Brody carefully constructs. The juxtapositions in *Living Arctic* are like a series of quantum leaps that are unpredictable in their effect or meaning. In other books as well, such as *The People's Land* (1975) and *Maps and Dreams* (1988), Brody highlights the ruptures of communication and the impossibility of cultural translation in the severely divided social spaces in the North.

## Failures in Cultural Translation

> The good translation gets you far enough into the other world to begin to see what you are missing. You take your translation device ... and you watch it run out of meaning. You watch it fall apart. That's my notion of cultural translation.
>
> – JAMES CLIFFORD, 'INTERVIEW WITH BRIAN WALLIS' (QTD. IN CRUIKSHANK, *SOCIAL LIFE OF STORIES* 98)

Brody shows the difficulties of cultural translation in the divided world of a colonial settlement in the Eastern Arctic in his ethnography, *The People's Land*. The text is a denunciation of a governmental administrative framework, ostensibly in place to serve the interests of Inuit communities but in fact perpetuating a colonial socioeconomic order. In a similar vein to Frantz Fanon's chilling portraits of a colonial city 'strewn with prohibitions,' in a 'world without spaciousness' for the colonized subject (*The Wretched* 37, 38), Brody describes a Manichean split that bars the possibility of dialogic exchange between White and Inuit communities. Despite their expressed humanitarian intentions, colonial governmental agents – the settlement manager, the missionary, the RCMP officer, the teacher, the medical officer – operate autonomously from and share little in common with the people they are supposed to serve. Brody structures *The People's Land* to mimic the 'dividing line' (Fanon, *The Wretched* 38) of the settlement: the first half of the text records the perspectives of the White community, the second half documents the perspectives of the Inuit community, and the middle chapter narrates the failure of cultural translators to establish lines of communication between the two *blocs*. The text dramatizes its own foundering upon the impasse of the colonial world 'cut in two' (Fanon, *The Wretched* 38), which offers little possibility for dialogue.

Brody shows on numerous occasions how versions of history, narrated by representatives of either side of the colonial divide, contradict one another. As one Inuk[10] man says to Richard Travis, the settlement manager, 'I do not believe what you say, because what you say is never true' (*The People's* 111). There is little or no trust placed in the truth value of utterances made across the social divide. Brody recounts the story of a White male teacher accused of soliciting sexual relations with Inuit boys in the settlement. The Whites' version of the events emphasizes the Inuit's feelings of violent outrage and indignation; the Inuits' version stresses the Whites' unfair condemnation of the teacher. Brody reveals that, in the Inuit people's view, part of the reason the teacher was condemned by the Whites was because he had violated the propriety of the 'dividing line' of a colonialist social order, by maintaining engaged and, to some extent, positive relations with the community. Attak, a member of the Inuit community, says: 'Perhaps he [the teacher] will come back to the settlement one day ... There are so few Whites whom one can talk with and become friendly with' (13). Brody repeatedly points to the ways in which simple conversation is barred in the colonial context.

On numerous occasions, Brody expresses the hope that, in his role as mediator, he may facilitate discussion on the sharply divided settlement of rich and poor, employed and unemployed, White and Inuit. However, there is little possibility for reciprocity or even conversation here. As a White researcher employed by the Department of Indian Affairs and Northern Development, Brody is implicated in the hostile relations of the settlement. Brody more than once refers to his intense feelings of awkwardness as an 'intruder' (5, 10), to his anxieties about misrepresenting people or their issues, and to the atmosphere of suspicion that easily flares up into controversy and misunderstanding in the settlement. Words such as 'irritation,' 'hostility,' 'apprehensiveness,' 'anger,' 'dismay,' and 'suspicion' dominate the text. Brody repeatedly dramatizes his failure to fully understand his subjects' point of view: 'Faltering and nervous, afraid of saying the wrong thing or of saying things wrongly, I avoided taking conversational initiatives' (10). Brody represents himself as subject to the 'nervous conditions'[11] of the settlement, caught between feelings of solidarity with the Inuit community and feelings of intrusion:

> During field-work, there are times when a feeling of despondent pessimism makes conversation even with one's best friends seem impossible. Uneasy, and feeling so little confidence, it seemed either foolish or pointless to be with those who had helped me the most: the Eskimo language seemed too difficult for me, and I felt I would irritate patient friends. (157-58)[12]

Brody's methodology is comparable to Clifford's description of a 'hermeneutics of "vulnerability,"' 'stressing the ruptures of fieldwork, the divided position and imperfect control of the ethnographer' (*Predicament* 43). Brody is not exempt from the 'nervous conditions' of the settlement; he is beholden to the same colonial order that precludes reciprocal relations between Whites and Inuit.

The middle chapter of *The People's Land*, which narrates the failure of the government-appointed settlement manager, Richard Travis, to establish communicative relations between the two domains, is most telling of Brody's anxieties surrounding questions of representation. Despite his initial good intentions to work collaboratively with the local government, Travis becomes incapable of establishing meaningful dialogue with the Inuit community council. Can Brody, as researcher for the Department of Indian Affairs and Northern Development, hope to do any better than Travis? Travis's genuine desire to help and his misjudged efforts to do so resonate with Brody's own fears about the effect his research may have on the people he studies. One of the most damning moments in the chapter is when a member of the Inuit community poses a question, which, according to Brody, 'summarized the whole painful situation': '"I want to ask you one thing," the man asks Travis. "What the hell are you doing here?"' (*The People's* 111). The question could easily be directed at Brody, struggling with his double role as representative of the Department of Indian Affairs and Northern Development and 'visiting social scientist' (71).

Equally worrisome for Brody, who as an outsider feels a parallel to Travis, is Travis's ignorance about his deteriorating relations with his interpreters and translators and their own slipping status in the estimation of the community. The chapter recounts the struggle for authority between the local government (that is, the community council, largely made up of Inuit members) and the federal government, represented by Travis. Isaac Tullik, the chairman of the community council, translates for Travis since the settlement manager does not speak Inuktitut. By the end of Travis's first year, however, relations between him and the council are approaching a crisis, mostly because of Travis's policies on welfare. Travis was notorious for his single-minded efforts to reduce welfare payments to the community. Brody writes:

> The body of Travis's critics was beginning to include his interpreters, and few were willing to interpret for him. The chairman of the council, Isaac Tullik, was also the chief interpreter ... Because he translated all of Travis's important decisions ... many Eskimos had begun to think that their council chairman was hand-in-glove with the settlement manager. This unfavourable opinion was aggravated by Tullik's dual role: as interpreter, he was obliged to say things in Eskimo that confused and annoyed the community, and then, as council chairman, he felt obliged also to explain why the settlement manager had spoken as he did. As the tensions between the community and Travis increased ... [Tullik] tried to identify himself with the faction of the council that was most hostile to Travis. But the public continued to be suspicious of Tullik and hostile towards him. (110)

One year later, at another meeting between Travis and the community council, a number of people fiercely and openly condemned Travis. Tullik's solution is to simply stop translating. At this meeting,

> nothing was translated for [Travis's] benefit ... One woman pointed out that Travis could not understand what was being said. One of the councillors replied that he couldn't understand anything anyway, so there was no point in interpreting for him ...
> [When] Travis spoke ... , all was interpreted into Eskimo, but the interpreter did not translate into English the comments and discussion from the floor. Travis spoke into a curious void, and he had no idea of the effect his words might be having. (116)

Cultural translation founders upon the Manichean divide of the settlement. By refusing to translate, Tullik, despising Travis and the paternalism he represents, purposely fails to establish relations of understanding or to create a 'common sense.'

After the resignation of Travis, the community council voted to apply to become a hamlet, which granted the council more autonomy by rendering redundant the direct supervision of a settlement manager. Yet, as Brody observes, the overarching paternalism of the settlement system would remain in place: 'they [the Inuit] are told that through their participation in local government, they will shift control from the Whites to themselves. In practical terms, the message is clear enough: if you (Eskimos) adopt these political methods, constitute the necessary elected bodies, demonstrate adequate leadership qualities, and all this by following a number of relatively uncomplicated procedural rules, then we (Whites) will turn the government of local affairs over to you' (120). The paradox of a colonial government shepherding in self-government suggests that the version of self-government described above is just another version of assimilation or 'political incorporation' (123).

Brody, unwilling to intervene inappropriately in community affairs, is tentative in imposing his views, preferring to stay quiet and to 'avoid taking conversational initiatives' (10). This silence is symptomatic of other elisions in the text. For example, he does not describe the process of transcribing interviews or conversations, he does not reveal the degree to which he has intervened editorially, nor does he include his own questions or his half of the conversation when quoting from someone. In short, Brody omits details about the process of making the ethnography. Of what political or ethical import, then, is Brody's staging of the failure of cultural translation? Do Brody's self-conscious probings about the limits of representation change the relations of authority in ethnographic discourse, or does the *staging* of the breakup of ethnographic authority function as a way to reconsolidate that very authority? The difficulty of locating Brody's voice in *The People's Land* remains a troubling problem that partially undermines his use of self-reflexive techniques.

### Genre-Switching: Maps, Dreams, and Dream Maps

Brody describes *Maps and Dreams* as 'a book of anecdotes as well as a research report, its structure being the result of an attempt to meet two different needs. The problem is one of audience' (*Maps* xxiii). *Maps and Dreams* shows the stresses and strains of this multiple address. Part report and part memoir, the chapters alternate between social scientific analysis and personal narrative. The even-numbered chapters, re-writings of a land use and occupancy study, a report which Brody prepared for the Union of British Columbia Indian Chiefs at the Northern Pipeline Agency public hearings just two years after the Mackenzie Valley Pipeline hearings (1977), 'give the detailed, at times technical, findings ... that must stand the test of scrutiny ... in uncomprehending or hostile courtrooms' (xxii-xxiii), while the odd-numbered chapters are recreations of field notes from Brody's eighteen-month stay on a reserve in northeast British Columbia in the territory of the Dunne-za First Nation. The odd-numbered chapters, Brody says, 'bring to life unfamiliar points of view' (xxiii) by 'follow[ing] the routes selected by the people' (xx).

For the purposes of underlining his thesis of cultural clash, as well as highlighting his shifting roles as hired researcher and independent writer within the framework of the alternating chapters, Brody continually shifts genre modes – the first-hand ethnographic account, the social scientific analysis, the realist docudrama, the testimonial, the reported legend, the parable, the polemic, the historical document – creating a rich diversity of genres. Most striking is Brody's palimpsest of maps that graphically manifests the region's clash of economic interests. Like the Dene mapping project coordinated by Phoebe Nahanni and others that I discussed in the previous section of the chapter, Dunne-za men and women from nine reserves in the area created the maps by drawing their hunting, gathering, and fishing routes in Dunne-za territory on top of a standard Ordnance Survey grid (Huggan 64). Writes Brody: 'Hunters, trappers, fishermen, and berry pickers mapped out all the land they had ever used in their lifetimes, encircling hunting areas species by species, marking gathering locations and camping sites – everything their life on the land had entailed that could be marked on a map' (*Maps* 147).

Throughout the text, Brody points to the enormous gaps between Aboriginal and non-Aboriginal conceptions of how maps work, how maps chart land, and how land builds dreams. Brody uses the metaphors of 'maps' and 'dreams' in counterpoint to show that when 'dreams collide[,] new maps are made' (xx). He juxtaposes the incommensurable points of view of the pipeline developers and Athapaskan hunters. For the pipeline companies, the frontier is 'development' and 'progress', while the hunters' maps are a nostalgic dream of the past. For the Dunne-za hunters, in contrast, the pipeline dreams of grandeur threaten genocide, while their 'dream maps' provide vital information for community survival.

The maps show that land is not *terra nullius* but rather is deeply inscribed with conflicting histories. Mapping 'empty' land inevitably cuts across someone else's map. 'Cutlines, wellside access roads, pipeline rights-of-way now run everywhere across the country' (132), while traplines run directly into ploughed fields or grazing land. In highlighting the extent to which developers have already surveyed and evaluated much of the land, Brody writes: 'Were a map to be drawn showing all the seismic lines that have already been cut through the region's forests, extensive areas would appear as solid black' (236). The hunters' areas could also be represented as solid black, but their routes remain invisible to empirical/imperial eyes. Atsin, one of Brody's primary informants, comments derisively on the mapping project: 'Crazy white man. He never understands. Too many, too many,' a statement Brody explains as follows: 'Atsin meant that he could never, even in a hundred interviews, mark down all the places he had hunted and travelled' (12).

Again, recalling the Dene mapping project, the Dunne-za dream maps show an intensive 'use and occupation' of land, while at the same time undermining the assumption that land can be quantified and parceled up in discrete categories. In the final odd-numbered chapter, entitled 'A Hearing,' Brody describes the reception of a dream map at the Northern Pipeline Agency community hearings. Near the end of the proceeding, two residents of the reserve bring in a bundle of moosehide that contains 'a magnificent dream map' (266). Dunne-za dreamers believe that the map is a glimpse of both animals' and people's 'trails to heaven.' For the Dunne-za people, the dream map refutes the justifications for the appropriation of land that the officials had offered at the inquiry. The 'thousands of short, firm, and variously coloured markings' on the map demonstrate that all the land is 'used' and 'occupied' by the Dunne-za communities (267). But is the map intelligible to the officials who are paid to operate under radically different frames of reference?

> Many of the Whites who spent the day in the Reserve hall said they were deeply moved [by the dream map]. The chairman repeatedly thanked the people for their words and generosity, and thanked the elders for sharing their wisdom. Yet discussion of the dream map petered out, and the officials hurried into their bus, anxious to drive back to town. The people of the Reserve were puzzled. Where had their visitors gone? The meeting was just getting under way. (268)

The series of sharp oppositions that accompany the 'maps' and 'dreams' of the hunters and industrialists also play themselves out in the differences between the even-numbered and odd-numbered chapters. As *Maps and Dreams* progresses, the differences between the chapters become increasingly stark. Brody is unable or unwilling to establish some common ground between the two modes of address or to create a common logic that would place the two discourses within a manageable frame. Increasingly, the narrative voice vacillates between the 'objective' voice of the expert witness and the 'subjective' voice of the disoriented visitor. While the even-numbered chapters become increasingly insistent about the 'irrefutable detail' of data on Dunne-za land use (148), the odd-numbered chapters expose Brody's profound disorientation in unfamiliar spaces. The odd-numbered chapters stage an increasing sense of confusion and misunderstanding; Brody mistrusts his own tentative interpretations of events or issues on the reserve; the anecdotes stop, start, and switch direction rapidly without comment. Highly detailed, packed with minute observations of things, people, and activities, the stories are fragmented and inconclusive.

In one of the most disjointed and tentative of the odd-numbered chapters, entitled 'A Funeral,' a fight breaks out between two women at a burial ceremony. Brody comments that 'the significance of the argument was obscure' (81); indeed, he never discovers or discloses the reasons behind it. Near the end of the chapter, after having spent the day digging the grave and preparing for the funeral, Brody writes: 'it suddenly struck me that I did not know whose funeral it had been' (82). Brody only finds out at the end of the day the identity of the deceased. The unknown, unnamed woman in the coffin haunts the narrative as an absence. If the lives of Athapaskan hunters are strange to Brody, the lives of women on the reserve are even more remote. Brody's focus on the clash of 'Native' and 'White' worldviews, between 'objective' and 'subjective' epistemologies, blinds him to other intersecting social relations. His explanations of conflict, within the terms of ethnicity, paper over other axes of difference.

In the odd-numbered chapters, women appear and disappear mysteriously, washing clothes (4, 136) or preparing food (76, 266), remaining virtually absent from the even-numbered chapters. Brody explains why he was not able to collect more data on women's land use: '[I]t was the men who explained the system, and who on the whole took control of the research ... Women drew maps and made direct contributions of all kinds to the project. But their contribution is not adequately expressed here' (196-97). The text's representation of women, who appear infrequently and remain generally silent, is further evidence of cultural untranslatability.

**Reported Speech**

In *Maps and Dreams,* Brody includes little direct quotation from his 'informants.' Instead, he uses indirect or reported speech. In *Speech Genres and Other Late Essays* (1986), M.M. Bakhtin argues that reported speech offers the possibility of articulating and making explicit the double-voicedness that is a condition of all language. By using reported speech,

Brody can reframe the voices of his informants 'speaking for themselves' and draw attention to the partial and provisional ways that he, as mediator, can represent them. In so doing, Brody evokes the silences, repetitions, and transgressions of the told-to process.

One of Brody's primary Dunne-za interlocutors is Joseph Patsah, whose main characteristic is untalkativeness. When Brody first meets him, Joseph 'hardly seemed to notice our arrival. Even when we were within a few yards he no more than glanced at us, then turned to rekindle the fire ... His face was impassive, almost rigid; his occasional looks hardly more than quick, sharp glances. Had it not been for these movements I might have thought him deaf or merely indifferent to our presence' (*Maps* 5). When Joseph does speak, Brody does not transcribe his words, preferring instead to paraphrase: 'It is difficult, perhaps impossible, to render his [Joseph's] speech in written English. It is so firmly rooted in oral and Athapaskan modes as to defy a written version ... Since such poor justice to the power of the spoken word is done by the writing of it, especially verbatim, I give here only the main outline of Joseph's narrative' (6, 7). Brody's admission, that a verbatim transcript is inadequate to convey the speaker's intent, is unusual in an ethnography, especially one produced after the advent of tape recorders in the 1960s.

The most direct forms of transcription in *Maps and Dreams* are the hunting, trapping, and gathering maps of the community members. Brody reports that members of the reserve community used the maps as starting points for more stories:

> By the time we came in, he [Atsin] had already cleared the floor space ... and had made a surface for the maps – a sheet of old cardboard.
>
> There, in the darkness of a cabin lit only by the bit of light that shone through a tiny frame window, with three people crowded shoulder to shoulder on the floor, Atsin began to explain how he had lived. Stories. (11)

Brody does not re-tell Atsin's stories. As a way of explaining his paraphrasing of the stories generated from the maps of three hunters – Atsin, Robert, and Joseph – Brody again draws attention to the limitations of 'direct' transcription: '[I]t is impossible to render verbatim all that they eventually said. I had no tape recorder and memory is imperfect. But even a verbatim account would fail to do justice to their meaning' (44).

Rather than directly transcribing the stories that supplement the testimonial maps, Brody uses the mode of reported speech. Reported speech as a technique is effective in managing multiple tellers, conveying the sense of what anthropologist Julie Cruikshank calls the 'layered tellings'[13] of told-to narrative. Reported speech incorporates other voices and discourses that both inform and move beyond the immediate context of the personal conversation. Reported speech is also effective in reflecting the chain of storytellers that have contributed to Dunne-za dream maps and have passed on vital information about hunting. Brody calls the Athapaskan hunters' and gatherers' descriptions of land use as 'individual map biographies,' a research methodology that he helped pioneer and that continues to be influential in the gathering of data for land claims cases. While drawing the maps, people would tell stories, legends, and personal experiences that certain places would inspire. 'Individual map biographies' are thus highly personal translations of land. Not only do they translate land, but they also translate a people's way of expressing their historical and ongoing relationship with the land.

If cultural translation is difficult between Brody and his 'informants,' it is even more so between oil companies and reserve community members at pipeline hearings. Brody highlights the elisions, mis-translations, and 'nontranslations'[14] that take place in formal procedures of consultation. The last odd-numbered chapter of the book, 'A Hearing,' begins with the arrival at the reserve of a 'busload of officials ... specialists on social and economic impacts, a secretary to oversee proceedings ... men from the West Coast Transmission ... the press, and representatives of the Union of Chiefs' (262). Armed with a stack of maps, reams of reports, and a ton of recording equipment, the officials run the hearing on their own terms. Their speeches in 'tortured bureaucratese' are only partially translated into the language of the Dunne-za people (259). Brody shows that consultation often consists of government and industry representatives arriving together at a reserve and announcing their plans: 'These community hearings were characterized by the Northern Pipeline Agency as an opportunity for the Indians and others to respond to the terms and conditions which they, at the agency, had already drafted' (260). The chain of interpreters, translators, and transcribers, along with their 'tangle of equipment' (262), show that the fanfare of a public hearing is little more than a game of broken telephone to the officials. Yet for the Dunne-za members of the reserve, the proposed pipeline threatens their very survival. Brody uses the mode of reported speech to show that even though each member of the reserve has had the chance to speak, it is unclear whether the oil companies will adjust their plans accordingly. In representing the Dunne-za people's presentations, Brody again avoids direct transcription. Instead, he offers the testimony through the interpretive static of the third-person voice:

> When the chairman did at last ask the Indians to offer their points of view, Joseph began to talk ... Here, at last, was an Indian voice. After every few sentences, Joseph paused and let the interpreter translate. In English, the words were not easy to grasp, and its being rendered in the third person made the sense no clearer. But the points were not lost:
>
>> He was saying in our country there was no such thing as money before the white man came; our only way to make a living is to hunt and there is no such thing as money to get from one another and big bulldozers that come over, go across our country.
>> He is saying as long as there is the sun that goes over, that he shall never stop hunting in this country and wherever he likes to do, as long as the sun is still there.
>> He is saying the white man pushed his way into our country, that he stakes up all the land and a long time ago there was no people and then now there is so many ...
>> He is saying if the pipeline goes through, the game will never be here and is there no way that we can stop this pipeline from going through and when the game goes away how would the people make their survival for meat?
>> He says if the white man makes more roads, what if they get on my trapline and if they cut all the trees down, where would I go for hunting and where would I get the fur? (263-64)

Brody's re-creation of the interpreter's reported speech resists the sound-bite approach in testimonial discourse and draws attention to the framing devices that are involved in public hearings. By 'failing' to translate the fullness of testimonial, Brody highlights the multiple mediations that shape the process of 'consultation'. Joseph Patsah's statement to the public hearing, which passes through a labyrinth of ventriloquists, productively unsettles the caricature of the eloquent Native informant.

To some extent, Brody attempts to fail at the job of cultural translator. In so doing, he sabotages the official processes that are themselves deeply implicated in imperial projects. In 1991, as I discuss in Chapter 5, Brody's resistance to his role as cultural translator culminated in the complete erasure of his report as expert witness from *Reasons for Judgment,* by Chief Justice Allan McEachern of the Supreme Court of British Columbia, in the Gitk'san-Wet'suwet'en land claim dispute, *Delgamuukw v. British Columbia.* Given McEachern's retrenchment of colonial land policy, I would suggest that this excision was not entirely a negative outcome. Yet the need for advocacy remains. How then to produce politically transformative work without inciting erasure and dismissal? Brody does not offer any definite answers to this question; yet his continual shifts in representational strategies, in modes of address, and in employment help transform the ground upon which the case for or against Aboriginal rights is articulated.

## Conclusion

The difficulty and necessity of speaking for others are central concerns in the work of Thomas Berger and Hugh Brody. The extent to which a representative may speak for, with, about, or against a community is determined in part by the role(s) assigned to that representative. At the same time, there are opportunities to challenge these roles. As a commissioner for a public inquiry, Berger was limited by the terms of his appointment. Yet within that appointment, he successfully redirected the inquiry, drawing attention to the unresolved land claims in Denendeh and the need for greater local autonomy. His commission, which travelled to many remote communities in the Northwest Territories, was groundbreaking in its attention to the 'homeland' of the people who were likely to accrue few benefits from the energy megaproject. Through his process of consultation, Berger recognized and valorized Aboriginal people's voices. *Northern Frontier, Northern Homeland* indicates how powerfully these voices shaped Berger's findings. At the same time, Berger's validation of Aboriginal people 'coming to voice' paradoxically reasserts the need for federal intervention. For Berger, it is up to government leaders to listen to the voices of disadvantaged communities and initiate change. Meanwhile, the role of the communities themselves in this program for social change is left unclear.

Dene, Métis, and Inuit presenters at the community hearings disputed Berger's politics of voice, which emphasized the authenticity of the community voices while downplaying the commission's role in mediating those voices. The hearings provided an arena for Inuit, Dene, and Métis groups to design longer-term research projects that extended well beyond the scope of the inquiry itself. As much as the presenters at the hearings were focused on the urgent task of opposing the pipeline, they were also concerned with how to advance land claims and negotiate for greater jurisdictional independence. The presenters also made links between the politics of land and the politics of representation. For the researchers working on the Dene mapping project, coordinated by Phoebe Nahanni and others, initiating dialogue among far-flung Dene community members and designing a genuinely collective and collaborative process of research was just as important as collecting evidence for future land and resource negotiations.

Brody also explores the problem of speaking for others in text and film, revealing the complexity of the relationship of identity and representation. He is particularly concerned with the tendency of spokespeople to efface the relations of mediation that accompany their acts of ventriloquism. He develops a number of representational strategies to negotiate his shifting, and sometimes colliding, roles of civil servant, band council employee, and independent researcher and writer. Some of these strategies include juxtaposition, self-reflexivity, genre-switching, and reported speech. He is the first to admit that these strategies do not resolve the problem of representation. Indeed one of his tactics is the failure of cultural translation, which draws attention to the provisionality of all acts of representation, and the inevitably compromised nature of using official channels to produce social change.

The Berger Inquiry represented an important turning point in First Nations politics, with the language of both self-government and of 'voice' emerging with renewed political force. Inuit, Dene, and Métis community workers became politicized through their participation in the inquiry, devising new tools in the struggle for greater autonomy over land, resources, jurisdiction, and development. It was this generation of Dene leaders that created the Indian Brotherhood, took control of the territorial government, wrote the Dene Declaration, and launched negotiated land claims. In the following chapter, I investigate how the Oka crisis in 1990 sharpened the debate over voice and land in mainstream media and in southern universities, and how the terrain of these debates continues to shift and change.

# 'There Is a Time Bomb in Canada'    3
## The Legacy of the Oka Crisis[1]

> There are two voices in the pages of this book, mine and Donald Barnett's. As-told-tos between whites and natives rarely work, when they do, it's wonderful, when they don't it's a disaster for the Native. Don never intended it to be a disaster for me. The first *Bobbi Lee* was a reduction of some two hundred pages of manuscript to a little book. What began as a class to learn how to do other people's life history, turned into a project to do my own. We had disagreements over what to include and what to exclude, disagreements over wording, voice. In the end, the voice that reached the paper was Don's, the information alone was mine.
>
> – LEE MARACLE, PROLOGUE, *BOBBI LEE, INDIAN REBEL*

In the prologue to the revised edition of *Bobbi Lee, Indian Rebel* (1990), Lee Maracle identifies the editorial control that the recorder, Don Barnett, had maintained in the first edition, published in 1975. Maracle's anger at Barnett's editing is palpable. By obscuring his own role, she argues, Barnett has reproduced the historically asymmetric relations of address in 'as-told-tos between whites and natives' (19). He also downplayed the process of collaboration in compiling the recorded testimonial life story. In 1990, Maracle does not re-write but rather re-frames the first version with new introductory material and an epilogue. Although Maracle does not change its content, she radically alters her life narrative through the act of re-telling and re-framing the story.

Maracle's challenge to Barnett, the 'absent editor,'[2] marks a shift in the production of told-to narratives from 1975 to 1990. Increasingly, First Nations narrators, recorders, translators, and editors took more active roles in the making of these collaborative texts. As Maracle suggests, Aboriginal writers no longer depended upon editorial shepherding to set their words in print.[3] The first few years of the 1990s also witnessed an increase in the number of novels, autobiographies, play scripts, short stories, and poetry collections published by Aboriginal authors, heralding a renaissance in Aboriginal writing in Canada. To some extent, the event that ignited this cultural renaissance was the standoff at Kanehsatake during the summer of 1990, an historic moment whose transformative effect is acknowledged by Maracle in 'Oka Peace Camp – September 9, 1990,' one of the introductory texts that frame her revised life narrative.

The standoff at Kanehsatake, which resulted from the municipality of Oka, Quebec, attempting to develop land on Mohawk territory, has become a double-edged event in Canadian history. While strong support for the Mohawk nation across the country revitalized social movements for change in Aboriginal communities, the representation of the 'Oka crisis' in the media reinforced Manichean stereotypes of violent Natives versus besieged settlers, while eliding the historical roots of the conflict. In this chapter, I examine how two Aboriginal artists – Abenaki filmmaker Alanis Obomsawin and Coast Salish/Stolo writer Lee Maracle – use strategies of the told-to narrative to engage with the Oka crisis, challenging the stark 'parallel voices' that have modelled the event (Valaskakis, 'Parallel'). Obomsawin has made a quartet of films about the standoff at Kanehsatake in order to explore how the community's perspectives have shifted over the course of time; and Maracle, across a number of genres, including life narrative, the novel, and poetry, has explored possibilities for doublevoicedness in what appear to be singly authored works. Both artists, within the limits of their chosen media, manipulate forms of the told-to narrative – interview, quotation, and collage – to re-tell and re-frame the events at Oka. While highlighting the asymmetric relations of power that were visible in the images of the barricades, Obomsawin and Maracle construct complex, doublevoiced, composite productions that trouble reified notions of identity, difference, and representation. Their 'told-to narratives' are twice-told narratives, in which they rewrite or re-present the conflict in ways that avoid stereotypical media oppositions.

As a result of the layered viewpoints in their work, these artists offer valuable critical tools in rethinking debates around the politics of representation that risk falling into stasis, or becoming reduced to individualized questions of who speaks for whom. Following the standoff at Kanehsatake, vigorous debates that were already unfolding in the mainstream media and in Canadian literary studies gathered momentum. Aboriginal writers joined with writers of colour in condemning systemic racism in publishing, institutions, and the media; however, in a similar vein to the misrepresentation of the Oka crisis, the writers' demands for change were often misunderstood as a form of identity politics driven by 'the delicate gymnastics of authenticity' (Weaver 9). Obomsawin and Maracle, both of whom have been productive as artists for close to forty years, have played active roles in demanding change in representational structures in Canadian institutions, cultural centres, galleries, film houses, and publishing houses. Their contributions to the politics of voice, as well as their trenchant critiques of competing notions of subjectivity, offer ways of rethinking these debates that avoid inert concepts of identity and difference. The emergence of a Native literary canon in Canada, composed of novels for the most part – Maria Campbell (1973), Beatrice Culleton Mosionier (1983), Jeannette Armstrong (1985, 2002), Tomson Highway (1989, 1998) Lee Maracle (1993, 1996), Thomas King (1993), Eden Robinson (2000), Joseph Boyden (2005, 2008) – has led to the misleading assumption that singly authored texts are instances of 'literary sovereignty' while told-to narratives exemplify 'literary colonization.' But Obomsawin and Maracle, far from dismissing told-to narrative forms, seek new ways of imagining cross-cultural collaboration and sovereignty in this 'post-Oka' historical moment.

## Alanis Obomsawin's Technique of Multiple Tellings

> In 1990, when the crisis occurred in Kanehsatake, it really became a turning point for all people in the country. Because that kind of stealing land or taking over land is not possible anymore ... But up until then it was. So I've seen a lot of changes politically. I think it's going to go on for many other generations to come. We've made a lot of progress. You know, when you see these stands you think there is no progress – but it's not true.
>
> – ALANIS OBOMSAWIN (QTD. IN CIZEK [DIR.])

> There are many stories to Kanehsatake, Oka, or Kahnawake during the crisis – thousands of stories.
>
> – ALANIS OBOMSAWIN (QTD. IN PICK, 'STORYTELLING AND RESISTANCE')

In *Kanehsatake: 270 Years of Resistance* (1993), the first film of her quartet and the one that focuses most explicitly on the events of the standoff, Obomsawin creates an alternative, yet strangely echoing narrative to the one I remember unfolding on my television screen during the summer of 1990. In *My Name Is Kahentiiosta* (1995), *Spudwrench* (1997), and *Rocks at Whiskey Trench* (2000), Obomsawin revisits the conflict and explores its afterlife in the communities of Kanehsatake and Kahnawake. The four films replay the events from different vantage points, as if searching for a way to cut through and re-imagine the overdetermined images of the standoff. Not only does Obomsawin seek to rearrange the Manichean relations of Native vs. settler, warrior vs. citizen; she also challenges the binary oppositions of oral vs. written, the seer vs. the seen, inside vs. outside, the past vs. the present. The stories from within and across the four films exemplify Obomsawin's technique of multiple tellings; that is, she strives to re-position and re-frame the standoff in ways that unsettle the oppositional aesthetics created by the media, as well as providing new ways of interpreting the language of critical and cultural studies on Aboriginal issues through the 1990s.

In *Kanehsatake*, Obomsawin documents the events of the standoff with her own camera, but juxtaposes clips from other sources to create a subtle dialectic of images, viewpoints, and ideological frames. Among the varied records, dating from different historical periods, are colonial archival writings and drawings; Mohawk speeches, writings, and wampum; and other journalists' reports of the standoff (TV broadcasts, interviews, newspaper headlines, and photographs). By combining these excerpts with her own images and interviews from the standoff, Obomsawin provides an historical context that was lacking from dominant media coverage. But at the same time that this collage documentary *supplies* an historical context, it simultaneously draws the viewer's attention to the *partiality* of historical documents that purport to represent Mohawk and settler histories. For example, Obomsawin reads the available archive of visual material from the eighteenth, nineteenth, and twentieth centuries – drawings, engravings, and paintings, as well as stills from the dioramas of the McCord Museum in Montreal, showing Native peoples travelling by canoe, making food, building a wigwam, and so on – against the grain of their colonial and racialized contexts. Despite the original intent of the drawings – anthropological, scientific, religious, or political – in Obomsawin's work they contribute to building a counter-ethnography of Mohawk presence in the area.

Obomsawin adjoins these colonial-ethnographic images and writings with oral and record-making histories as a way to expand script-centric notions of historical 'evidence'. Reading wampum, for example, which Obomsawin does in a voice-over at one point in *Kanehsatake*, provides a history of the Mohawk people's resistance to imperialism using a unique form of record-making that works at the interstice of orality and writing.[4] In conjunction with images of the wampum and its accompanying narratives, Obomsawin quotes from a speech by Joseph Onasakenrat, the first Mohawk chief who was known to read and write and who, along with other people of his community, was imprisoned in 1868 when he resisted the removal of his people from Kanehsatake to Ontario. In a speech in 1868 at the age of twenty-three, Onasakenrat stated: 'We will never go there. We will die on the soil of our fathers.' Onasakenrat's speech, the wampum, and even the colonial archives powerfully assert the historical context of the land dispute, disrupting the immediacy of the 'crisis.' Although the press, government, and army focused on the urgency of disarming the Mohawk warriors and dismantling the roadblocks, Obomsawin's film situates the conflict in a longer story of land dispute, as the subtitle of the film, *270 Years of Resistance*, suggests.

Obomsawin's borrowings of polysemic material suggest that the standoff of 1990 was not an isolated event. Rather, it was a repetition of history that sprang from a vicious and longstanding contest over land between the Mohawk nation and the settler nation-state that remains unresolved today. Through Obomsawin's careful historical contextualization, the standoff can be understood as the most recent incident in a history of resistance against governmental, corporate, and municipal attempts to shrink or eliminate the Mohawk land base. The standoff was the latest in a series of standoffs over the same disputed land – in 1721, 1868, 1959, 1969, and 1990[5] – which show how the Mohawk people have endured and defied a state of siege for 270 years. Obomsawin's point in retelling the story of the latest standoff from a variety of viewpoints in a series of four films is to draw attention to this cyclical history.

The lack of attention to the historical roots of the conflict situated the 'Oka crisis' (as the nomenclature suggests) as an aberrant event in Canadian history, not continuous with ongoing colonial policies. *Kanehsatake* demonstrates that government spokespeople consistently attempted to contain the crisis as a temporary dispute over a relatively small patch of ground. The media, military, and governments worked in tandem to emphasize the aggressive actions of the Mohawk warriors while simultaneously obscuring the governments' own role in producing the discord. Even though the Canadian government had been in active negotiations with the Mohawks over unresolved land issues for the greater part of the last century, including the months and weeks leading up to the standoff, federal government representatives repeatedly performed a sense of surprise and miscomprehension at the Mohawk people's demands during the negotiations. For example, Prime Minister Brian Mulroney described the community negotiators' land claim proposals as 'bizarre', while Tom Siddon, minister of Indian Affairs and Northern Development, called them 'hard to understand' (qtd. in Kalant 175). At the same time that the government downplayed the ongoing negotiations with the Mohawk nation, it also asserted that an agreement was already in place. Amelia Kalant, in her analysis of media representations of the Oka crisis in *National Identity and the Conflict at Oka* (2004), explains that Mulroney's federal government had presented what it called a 'framework agreement' to the Kanehsatake negotiators in 1989-90. Under this proposal, Canada would buy the land under dispute and give it to the people of Kanehsatake – on the condition that the Mohawk people relinquish their title to the land. Though the offer was rejected by the community because of the extinguishment clause, 'the federal government continued to refer to this framework agreement during the standoff, leading to the erroneous perception that the protesters were violating an agreement' (Kalant 11). In this manner, Kalant argues, the government representatives tried to position themselves on the side of rationality, logic, and peace, and the Mohawks on the side of irrationality, chaos, and violence.

Obomsawin's *Kanehsatake* stands as a negative afterimage of the version of the standoff promulgated on television and in newspapers during the summer of 1990. Obomsawin presents a collage of the media coverage of the crisis, in French and in English, including newspaper headlines, army press releases, governmental public statements, and clips from television coverage – but subtly alters their political import. In filming spokespeople delivering statements to the press, Obomsawin uses an oblique and slightly decentred camera angle to encompass the microphones from other broadcasters and to record the reactions of people standing beside speakers. In this way, Obomsawin documents the media context of speakers' statements and reminds her viewers of the media's role in producing the conflict. This technique also draws attention to the asymmetries of the coverage, in which government and army spokespeople often have more visible microphones in front of their faces than the Mohawk spokespeople do. As James Winter convincingly demonstrates with reference to specific examples of the coverage, the media tended to accept at face value the statements made by the government and military, while actively questioning and debating statements made by Mohawk spokespeople (227-40).

Obomsawin encourages her viewer to acknowledge the layers of mediation that inform her images, as well as the interplay of speaker and audience that shapes the reception of the images. A finely crafted scene in *Kanehsatake* exemplifies Obomsawin's technique. The shot opens with a group of armed warriors silently watching a CBC report, entitled 'Native crisis', on a television that is perched on a rock in the open air. The subject of the report is whether or not the Mohawk people have a 'large number of modern weapons' in the Treatment Centre, in the heart of the Pines, where the protesters set up their living quarters during the seventy-eight-day standoff. The announcer introduces the on-site journalist, Tony Ross, whose voice can be heard on the TV but who cannot be seen on the screen. As Ross makes his report, Obomsawin's camera cuts to Ross himself, who is delivering his report into a walkie-talkie, a few steps away from the warriors. For the warriors sitting in front of the TV, with firearms across their laps, the irony is sharp: it is the journalist who has the authority to answer the questions about the arms, and he does not invite the warriors to contribute to the conversation. In any case, the question of how many and what kinds of arms the people have at their disposal is not the kind of discussion the warriors wish to join; indeed, the very topic precludes the possibility of addressing Mohawk perspectives on the standoff. When interviewees such as Ellen Gabriel, Frank Natawe, Minnie Garrow, and others had the chance to speak at press conferences, they would re-tell the history of the land dispute at Kanehsatake – not the 'current event' that the media representatives were interested in producing. As Winter argues, 'the news story' must be fueled by the urgency of 'now'; for the Mohawk people, the story that needs to be told began over two centuries ago (208).

Obomsawin's technique of re-viewing media representations, used in all four films, highlights how the dominant media's editorial process, which narrowly focuses the news consumer's attention on the 'current event', bears a certain responsibility in perpetuating colonial and racist stereotypes. In *My Name Is Kahentiiosta*, Obomsawin re-presents the coverage of the Mercier Bridge blockade, which was erected by the Mohawk community on the Kahnawake reserve as an act of solidarity with Kanehsatake on 11 July. Yet, rather than using live coverage of the race riot that occurred in Chateauguay, Obomsawin creates a montage of headlines from the front covers of Quebec newspapers, including 'Mob hurls rocks at Mohawk cars' in the *Gazette,* 'CETTE FOIS C'EST SERIEUX!' in *Le soleil,* and 'SURRENDER – OR ELSE' in the *Sun*. Accompanying these headlines are images of Chateauguay residents burning a Mohawk effigy and throwing rocks at Mohawk people's cars, as the residents of the Kahnawake reserve, fearing an imminent attack by the army, attempted to evacuate women, children, and elderly people. The headlines, in French and in English, as well as the images, mobilize readily available stereotypes of hot-headed Québécois sovereigntists and of tough governments defying Indians (Kalant 191). None foregrounds the perspectives of the people trapped in their cars, an elision Obomsawin corrects in the fourth film of the series, *Rocks at Whiskey Trench*. In drawing attention to the media representations of the riot, Obomsawin emphasizes the editorial procedures that decontextualize and binarize the images. The pressure to sell stories results in simplified headlines and dramatic images that disavow the historical complexities of the overlapping, fraught relationships between French and English, between settlers and First Nations, and between Quebec and Canada.

In contrast to the newspaper and TV coverage at the time, Obomsawin's films explore the dense interrelationships between Quebec, Canada, and the First Nations, suggesting that the federal government was using the conflict to portray not only the Mohawk but also the Québécois claims of sovereignty as 'bizarre' and 'hard to understand.' The conflict became a rare opportunity for the federal government and the nonseparatist, Liberal government of Quebec, led by Robert Bourassa, to express mutual support. As Kalant argues, with the help of the English-language press, the two governments capitalized on the warrish images to inflame anti-separatist feeling and to blame both First Nations and Québécois nationalists for endangering national unity. This became clear in the coverage of the Mercier Bridge blockade. In English-language, federalist-leaning newspapers such as the *Gazette,* images of Chateauguay residents throwing rocks and cursing *'les sauvages'* portrayed this community, a stronghold of Quebec separatism, as racist and intolerant, as if in contrast to more moderate, federalist sympathizers. Minister of Indian Affairs and Northern Development Tom Siddon, ostensibly criticizing First Nations separatism, implicitly censured Quebec separatism, which was on the rise again in the wake of the failure of the constitutional talks at Meech Lake: 'the government of Canada and the government of Quebec cannot agree to the balkanization of Canada which would see the First Nations become independent sovereign states' (qtd. in Kalant 182).[6] However, as the Mohawk nation's demands for land claims resolution and recognition of their sovereignty did not include plans to secede from Canada, it is likely that Siddon was addressing Québécois sovereigntists as much as First Nations sovereigntists. At the same time, Siddon aligned the government of Quebec with the Canadian government against the future possibility of First Nations secessionists.

For their part, Québécois sovereigntists either discredited the Mohawks' demands for sovereignty as self-serving schemes to secure economic gain, or they condemned the violent extremism of the warrior blockade as a way to assert the mature rationality of current expressions of Québécois nationalism (Kalant 182). Gilles Duceppe, member of the Bloc Québécois, stated in parliament: 'Indians insist on "self-determination" for reasons based on economic and political realities, while the Quebec nation has a sovereignty project which was developed on the basis of historic conditions' (qtd. in Kalant 182). In suggesting that Aboriginal sovereigntists are motivated by economics and politics, while Québécois sovereigntists are motivated by history, Duceppe echoes Marx's assertion that non-European peoples 'have no history.' He also ignores the Mohawk nation's struggle for recognition of its ancient and ongoing traditions of governance (for example, as demonstrated by the Great Law of Peace of the Rotinohshonni or Iroquois confederacy).[7] Furthermore, he brackets the fact that the Mohawk people are part of the First Nations of this continent.

In *Kanehsatake*, Obomsawin shows that the Mohawk version of history is delegitimized through the army's manipulation of evidence – evidence that hinges upon the competing authorities of the oral, the written, and the image. The film explores the tension between the state-sanctioned, legally binding power of writing, the certifying power of spoken testimony, and the power of the image to produce eye-witness accounts (the latter being one of the most highly valued forms of evidence in Western legal discourse). There are a number of scenes in *Kanehsatake* that explore the interplay of writing, speaking, and seeing. For example, one unidentified Mohawk warrior, who was detained under suspicion of concealing weapons, tells Obomsawin that a soldier extinguished a cigarette on his stomach in an effort to get him to confess that the Mohawks had cached large reserves of weapons. It is because the weaponry remained unseen that the soldiers attempted to make the warrior's body 'reveal' the alleged crime. 'Finally I had enough. Two, three hours of getting beaten on, and I signed it,' he declares. 'An empty sheet?' asks Obomsawin. 'Yeah,' he confirms, suggesting that his signature will be used to create a fake confession. The rules of war often demand meticulous (if spurious) documentation. Another charged moment that draws attention to the asymmetries between writing, speaking, and seeing follows the severe beating of Randy Horne, whose code name during the conflict was Spudwrench, and whose life story became the basis of the third film in Obomsawin's series. As Spudwrench later testified, in the middle of the night, as he was standing guard at one of the barricades, five soldiers jumped him and hit him on the head twenty-five times with a heavy object. The purpose of the foray, according to a French-language telecast that Obomsawin translates in a voice-over in *Spudwrench*, was for the soldiers 'to see with their own eyes what was going on' behind the barricades. Spudwrench sustained life-threatening injuries and needed to leave the camp immediately for medical attention, but the Mohawk side was suspicious that the army would not hold to its promise to escort the wounded warrior to a hospital without interrogation. 'Can I have that [promise] in writing?' asks Mohawk spokesperson Robert Skidders, known as Mad Jap during the conflict. Major Alain Tremblay responds: 'I cannot do that, and you know that. You're going to have to take my word.' Tremblay, in suggesting that Skidders 'knows' that he can't provide a written confirmation, is drawing on the common-sense understanding of the power of writing to legally bind and legitimize oral statements. On the other hand, by offering his 'word,' Tremblay is evoking the power of the oath to guarantee integrity, faith, truth, loyalty, and commitment.

The war of who sees, versus who is seen, is a fascinating subplot in *Kanehsatake*, and draws attention to the politics of 'inside' and 'outside' that informed the language of the standoff, and which Obomsawin's film seeks to disrupt. In defiance of the army's attempts at constant surveillance of the camp, the blockaders erected an enormous white tarpaulin. 'This manoeuvre,' Obomsawin comments in a voice-over in her typically understated way, 'proves to be very annoying to the army.' The army first uses a crane to see over the curtain, and later uses helicopters to circle above the treatment centre twenty-four hours a day. At nightfall, the army harasses the warriors with spotlights. 'The only reason they are doing this is because they cannot see,' says Mad Jap, while being blinded with a spotlight. In the next scene, the army's helicopter launches a flare that lands a few feet away from a group of people, including children, sitting around a campfire. The cold glare of the spotlight contrasts with the warm light of the fire; the grinding sound of the chopper becomes a menacing counterpoint to the sound of Kahentiiosta, who sings a lullaby to her frightened child. Obomsawin's coverage of the army's helicopter surveillance asks the viewer to consider the schism in the possible kinds of documentation that are produced 'inside' and 'outside' the barricades.

In *Kanehsatake*, Obomsawin uses a politics of reversal to challenge notions of 'inside' and 'outside' that became deeply entrenched in the simplified images of the standoff. Although most TV coverage showed the Mohawks guarding the roadblock and the army working to dismantle it, Obomsawin reverses this dynamic by clearly documenting the army busy at work tightening their noose around the treatment centre. Following the lifting of the Mercier Bridge blockade on 29 August, the army set about sealing off the treatment centre from the outside world. Obomsawin's film shows the army systematically cutting off the community's lines of communication, such as phone lines and cellular phone signals, as well as stopping or slowing down deliveries of food and medicine. While watching the soldiers wade up to their waists in the Lake of Two Mountains near the treatment centre to build razor-wire fences, one of the warriors comments: 'Just the idea that of putting razor wire in the water – come on guys, get real. I don't think they have really clued into the fact that we aren't going anywhere.' For him, sealing the community inside the barricades underlines the army's failure to understand the reason the people had built the barricades in the first place: to declare their passionate, historically grounded title to the land around the Pines, which they were not going to leave undefended.

In addition to physically sealing off the treatment centre, the army took steps to prevent media coverage by confiscating film, barring journalists from entering the 'controlled zone,' and interrupting broadcast signals. Obomsawin managed to leave the treatment centre with her film only because the president of the National Film Board and a lawyer met her at the barricades one day before the rest of the community left the treatment centre (Grant 18). Walter Skea's quantitative study of newspaper coverage of the crisis confirms that aside from a few reporters who were on the Mohawk side of the barricades, the vast majority gained their information from government briefings and the Canadian army. The army, which replaced the Sûreté du Québec (SQ) on 20 August and remained in place until the end of the conflict on 26 September, had an obvious media advantage over the Mohawks: they were located outside of the barriers, a position that enabled their release of daily or twice-daily press statements. The army's willingness to speak to journalists on a regular basis created the illusion that information was circulating freely. However, the seemingly continuous television coverage of the standoff – the twenty-four-hour CBC news channel had recently been created (Blundell 334) – concealed the army's enforcement of censorship (Valaskakis, *Indian Country* 38). In addition to limiting the Mohawk people's already minimal contact with outside reporters, after 1 September, the army also prevented them from approaching the barricades, as *Kanehsatake* demonstrates.

Throughout the film, people frequently talk about the 'inside' and 'outside,' revealing an anxiety about who has the authority to define the distinction. Soldiers carefully monitor the movement of protesters coming and going from the Oka Peace Camp, situated outside the barricades. 'This is a controlled area and you can't go in,' says one officer to a group of people at the Peace Camp. 'You told us to go here, go there, where can we go? This is Canada, a free country for everyone,' retorts one woman. Soldiers with machine guns, standing at the intersection of 'inside' and 'outside,' symbolize the brute force that is needed to buttress this dividing line. The division is a war zone, as Mohawk warrior Psycho suggests: 'From here on in I guess we are going to be burying each other. Because we won't move.' In other parts of the film, debates about 'inside' and 'outside' take on metaphorical and historical significance. 'If this is "civilized," I would rather stay on this side of the barricade,' says Chicky from inside the barricade, looking towards the razor-wire fence. Chicky's comment reverses the 'savage'/'civilized' dichotomy in discourses on Indian identity and racial difference that have shaped representations of Native North America.

In documenting the army's role in reifying the 'inside' and 'outside' and by showing how social actors on both sides of the barricades come to believe in the distinction, it might appear that Obomsawin's film falls into the trap of the standoff: to the Manicheism of the dominant media, Obomsawin offers a Manicheism of her own, in which she justifies the Mohawk people's actions but not those of the soldiers. But as I have shown, Obomsawin fractures point of view by transecting and overlaying highly variable and conflicting sources. Moreover, Obomsawin's interviews reveal a broad range of differences within both settler and Mohawk communities. She provides a cross-section of both Oka and Kanehsatake communities, interviewing women, children, youth, and elderly people, and drawing attention to the wide range of participants behind the barricades, including Clan Mothers, Warrior Society members, Native Americans from the United States, traditional healers from Mexico, and French- and English-speaking journalists. While most of the media coverage emphasized the warriors' aggressive, masculinist, gun-toting body language, Obomsawin's interviews depict the male warriors as soft-spoken, thoughtful, and responsive to the community's calls for calm. Valaskakis has argued that the Oka crisis brought to light and exacerbated many fractures within the Mohawk community. Mohawk people at Kanehsatake 'still struggle over the alliances and ideologies of Mohawks who support the band council and those who endorse the traditional government of Mohawk Nation Office or the Iroquois Confederacy' (*Indian Country* 62). Other splits include 'traditionals who support different interpretations of Deganawida's Great Law and the Longhouse religion; ... Mohawks who promote the approach of the warriors and those who advocate peaceful, legal, or traditional methods to achieve land and treaty rights, sovereignty and self-determination; ... [and] Mohawks who support economic development through gambling, cigarette sales and smuggling and those who reject these enterprises' (62). Yet during the Oka crisis, the identity formations that departed from the masked, male warrior did not receive the same degree of media exposure.

Though there were competing visions about land, nation, and sovereignty among the Mohawk people, both the federal and provincial governments isolated one version of Mohawk nationalism, and then rendered it criminal and illegitimate (Kalant 179). The participation of the Mohawk Warrior Society at the roadblocks became a focus of media coverage. As Kalant points out, the Warrior Society, which represented a subgroup of the protesters, had been in the news not long before the Oka crisis in allegations of cigarette-smuggling operations occurring at Akwesasne, a reserve that straddles the borders of Quebec, Ontario, and New York. Harry Swain, a reporter for the *Gazette* (and again it is worth pointing out the federalist perspective of this English-language, Montreal-based newspaper), maintained that the members of the Warrior Society 'mix two things – a very successful set of criminal enterprises with a devoutly held ideology which says they are a separate nation. It is a potent combination of cash, guns and ideology' (qtd. in Kalant 174). Thus, the Oka crisis took place in a media context in which Mohawk criminality, violence, and nationalistic fervour were already linked (Kalant 165).

The most interesting way that Obomsawin disrupts the oppositional aesthetics of the standoff is through the mode of the quartet, which reviews the conflict through different perspectives and over the passage of time. Together the four films, released between 1993 and 2000, instantiate Obomsawin's technique of multiple tellings, in which stories from *Kanehsatake* are retold in new interpretive frames. In *My Name Is Kahentiiosta, Spudwrench,* and *Rocks at Whiskey Trench,* the face-off between the army and the warriors fades into the background, enabling other stories to surface. No longer a 'current event', subject to the pressures of producing the urgency of the moment, the standoff comes in and out of focus in the next three films. The main spokespeople in the sequels – Kahentiiosta, Spudwrench, and members of the Kahnawake community, respectively – struggle to articulate the ambivalent legacy of the standoff: Oka opened up opportunities to renew Aboriginal social movements for change, but also created misunderstandings, fears, and, from some non-Aboriginal individuals and communities, a defensive rejection of the language surrounding self-determination and sovereignty. As Obomsawin herself has said (to visual artist Robert Houle): 'The events at Oka created more racism on the one hand, but also caused more people to want to understand' (qtd. in Houle 210).

In *My Name Is Kahentiiosta,* Kahentiiosta creates an alternative mapping of Mohawk land that disavows the politics of 'inside' and 'outside' that informed the standoff. 'There are no borders within the region of Mohawks,' she says in the opening sequence. 'We have brothers and sisters in the whole territory.' In blurring the boundaries between the pockets of Mohawk land in the reserves of Kanehsatake, Kahnawake, and Akwesasne, Kahentiiosta is defying the colonial history of dividing and shrinking Mohawk territory. She is also confronting the media, governmental, and military claims that the standoff was led by a small group of 'terrorists' or 'criminals' who held the majority of the community members hostage. Moreover, by referring to Mohawk 'brothers and sisters,' Kahentiiosta is challenging the media's representation of gender relations during the conflict, which mobilized images of hyper-masculinity on both sides of the barricades.

*My Name Is Kahentiiosta* reveals the active role that women played in the conflict, departing from the macho images of warriors and soldiers, and showing how gender and language complicate the 'native vs. settler' story. Kahentiiosta's narration focuses on the aftermath of the conflict, when the protesters were brought to the courthouse in the nearby town of St. Jerome. Kahentiiosta, who showed up for her arraignment wearing a camouflage tee-shirt and trousers, was the cause of considerable annoyance for the authorities, who insisted that she change into street clothes. The authorities were particularly troubled by the gender implications of her symbolic defiance of the rule of law in Canada and Quebec. When she refused to follow court procedures, she recalls, the guards and army personnel threatened her in specifically gendered ways: 'They said they would release all the women except me. "You're going to be the only woman left here. Soldiers are going to beat you up or rape you."' But Kahentiiosta was unmoved by these threats, answering: 'I am here for a reason – not just to do what you want me to do.'

Kahentiiosta's challenge to the court, which she says is 'not our court,' both engages with and sidesteps the kinds of confrontations associated with the politics of language in Quebec and draws attention to a number of interlocking historical ironies. She relates that she is detained four days longer than the other women because the prosecutor representing the Quebec government would not accept her Mohawk name:

> I gave them my name, Kahentiiosta ... But they didn't like my name – they wanted a Canadian name, I guess. So I just looked at my lawyer and didn't say anything else ... [The judge] wanted an English name – a Canadian name so that they can check to see if I have a record ... "You could get out today if you give us an English name." "You've taken enough from us ... No, I want this name on the record. If [you] don't respect it then we will have to deal with it later. I will stay here till whenever."

In using 'Canadian' and 'English' interchangeably, and rejecting both as the basis of her own identity, Kahentiiosta is echoing the language of Québécois sovereigntists who also do not recognize federal, English-speaking institutions; at the same time, by not speaking in French, she is undermining Québécois settler claims to nationhood. Like many Québécois people before her, Kahentiiosta is contesting the identity formations associated with Canada and the language of English. Ironically, she is disciplined for asserting her right to use a non-English, non-Canadian name in a province that has a history of affirming citizens' rights to conduct public proceedings in French and under Quebec jurisdiction. But at the same time, her refusal (or inability) to speak in French draws attention to both Canada's and Quebec's complicity in policies of language suppression, their deceitful appropriation of 'indigeneity' in their formulations of settler nationhood, and their policies that have resulted in keeping Indigenous and settler populations as separate and unequal. In an interview (2002), Obomsawin echoes some of Kahentiiosta's sentiments, suggesting that First Nations' struggle for historical justice in Quebec has played handmaiden to the more dominant story of Québécois nationalism: 'in Quebec our people are quite separate from the rest [of Aboriginal people in Canada] ... it has become more and more difficult for Aboriginal people because of the province's political situation' (qtd. in Gagnon and Fung 90). Obomsawin also implies that *Kanehsatake* was not well received in Quebec because some journalists objected to her portrayal of Québécois nationalism in the film: 'When it [*Kanehsatake*] came out in French in 1993, the French-language press really put it down in general. That's about all I can say, they just didn't like the film. Of course that wasn't the case for everyone ... but many French-language reporters argued with me about certain aspects of the film. For instance, some journalists were angry because they didn't think I should have included the rock-throwing scene' (90). As discussed previously, the rock-throwing scene not only revealed the roots of racism in the settler imagination but also was used by governments and the English-language presses to portray the Québécois sovereigntist movement in a negative light.

In contrast to her ambivalent relationship with Québécois national institutions (that is, the courtroom), Kahentiiosta asserts the importance of the standoff in revitalizing the struggle for Aboriginal rights: 'We were here not just for ourselves, we were here representing all the Indian people who had been watching the takeover of their land for centuries. This time we were resisting.' The film *Spudwrench* expresses a similar hope in the standoff becoming the impetus for renewed efforts to secure Mohawk land rights and sovereignty. *Spudwrench* contextualizes the land issues within the larger story of cultural renewal, which increasingly plays a role in shaping community ties in Kahnawake. The film shows that the 'Oka crisis,' now about six years in the past, has left its legacy of pain, physically manifested in Spudwrench's crooked fingers and sore back. However, Oka also has contributed to the revitalization of cultural practices and of the Mohawk language on the reserve. The film opens with a scene from the Kahnawake community centre, where people are performing the 'Oka dance' and 'Oka song.' These performances continue to develop new variations and verses. Pointing to a tree behind her, one woman says she planted it in 1991 'for the support of the people in Oka': 'The people will teach their children what happened the summer of 1990. We ask the tree for strength.' The young tree becomes a metaphor for the youth in Kahnawake. As the camera cuts to Stephanie Horne, a young girl playing beside a river, Spudwrench's wife talks about 'our Oka baby' who was behind the barricades during the conflict: 'She was almost one in Oka ... She kept everyone going. She was always smiling.'

Obomsawin not only moves forward in time from 1990 in imagining a future for the Mohawk nation in Quebec, but also backwards in telling the community stories that circle around the story of Spudwrench. Randy Horne chose his code name, 'Spudwrench', to reflect his life work as an ironworker. Along with many other men from his community over the past six generations, including his grandfather, father, and son, Spudwrench helped build some of the tallest buildings in the United States, including the Empire State Building, Rockefeller Center, and the twin towers of the World Trade Center, returning to the reserve every weekend. Obomsawin creates a collage of voices that show the intimate connection between family, community, and place in the minds of Kahnawake residents: 'There's nothing like Friday after work, 'cause that's when we go home. This is our family. All Kahnawake.' 'It's our lifestyle, it's our livelihood. Just like our fathers and grandfathers.' 'I was born and raised here. And I always loved it here ... I wouldn't sell it, I wouldn't give it away, and the rest of the people also feel the same way. Right here in Kahnawake. That's the only thing we have left. We'll never give it up.' Obomsawin does not always identify or show the speaker, rather allowing the statements to flow one into the other as a testimony to the spirit of collectivity at Kahnawake.

*Rocks at Whiskey Trench* continues the theme of cultural revitalization at Kahnawake: near the beginning of the film, children at school recite their lessons in the Mohawk language and the community gathers for a feast in the long house. However, the bulk of the film is interviews with people in tears remembering the events on 28 August 1990, when the community decided to evacuate the youth and the elderly from the reserve because they had received threatening messages from the army to end the blockade on the Mercier Bridge or face the consequences. However, instead of being attacked by the army at the reserve, as they had feared, they are attacked by civilians throwing rocks as they passed through the 'Whiskey Trench', a narrow off-ramp from the bridge with steep walls of concrete on either side. Meanwhile, officers of the SQ, instructed not to intervene, ostensibly in order to avoid escalating a potential situation, stand on the sidelines. Randolph Lewis comments that 'Perhaps more than any of her [Obomsawin's] other films, *Rocks at Whiskey Trench* provides a scathing indictment of white Canadian racism' (Lewis 114-15). In interviews conducted almost a decade after the event, the people of Kahnawake relive their experiences of being pelted with rocks the size of grapefruits and being cut with millions of pieces of glass from their smashed car windows. *Rocks at Whiskey Trench* underlines the degree to which the community remains haunted by the racial violence. During the interviews, the film continually cuts to the rock-throwing and effigy-burning footage. The repeated return to the same disturbing images provides a visual picture of a community suffering from post-traumatic stress, unable to forget the events of that day. Kahnawake resident Alwyn Morris, Olympic gold medalist in kayaking, explains how the damage continues: 'The fact that it happened here, in this country, suggests some very deep down problems from a social standpoint. How long is that wound going to take to heal? I don't know. Maybe not in my lifetime.' Although some Church-based groups have initiated healing circles to promote reconciliation, involving both Chateauguay and Kahnawake residents, the film suggests that the longer history of land appropriation festers in the wounds. As in the film *Kanehsatake*, Obomsawin gives her audience a history lesson on the land at Kahnawake, graphically demonstrating how Mohawk land, granted to the Jesuits specifically for the settlement of the Iroquois people in 1716, has been shrunk down by more than two-thirds by the development of settler agriculture, the St. Lawrence seaway, the Mercier bridge, a web of highways, and suburban sprawl.

Randolph Lewis, in *Alanis Obomsawin: The Vision of a Native Filmmaker* (2006), the first book-length monograph on Obomsawin's work, uses the term 'cinema of sovereignty' to describe Obomsawin's thirty-year trajectory of filmmaking. In spite of the painful incidents of racial violence that the films document, *Kanehsatake, My Name Is Kahentiiosta, Spudwrench*, and *Rocks at Whiskey Trench* imagine a future for the Mohawk people and express the hope that the goals of self-determination, sovereignty, and land claims resolution will lead to more just relations with the Canadian nation-state. As Kahentiiosta comments: 'Now it's the land issue all over Indian country, not just Kanehsatake anymore. There's going to be a lot of negotiating.' She adds that since the standoff, 'we've been helping other nations' (*My Name Is Kahentiiosta*). Similarly, in Robert Houle's words, Obomsawin's films express a certain optimism that '[Cree Member of the

Legislative Assembly of Manitoba] Elijah Harper's interventionist "No" to Meech Lake, and the Mohawk Summer of 1990, were a "Yes" to an honourable and significant place at Canada's constitutional negotiating table for the First Nations' (210).

While Obomsawin's films suggest that Oka has the potential to become a watershed for renewed dialogues, they do not imply a simple progression from assimilation to self-determination. Even though Obomsawin declares her solidarity with the Mohawk people in every frame, her films avoid prescribing what kind of sovereignty might be imagined, or how this sovereignty might be achieved. Although the first film of the series focuses on establishing the historical contexts of Mohawk land rights and traditions of governance, notably through an interpretation of the wampum of 1721, Obomsawin does not discuss how or to what extent contemporary social movements draw upon, for example, The Great Law of Peace of the Rotinohshonni which, for some critics such as Taiaiake Alfred, becomes the basis for enacting Kanien'kehaka (or Mohawk) nationhood (Alfred, *Peace* xvii-xix; xx-xxiii). Yet in highlighting the rich diversity of the communities of the Mohawk nation, Obomsawin's films encourage viewers to imagine land claims in new ways, ways that would, among other things, include women at the negotiating table, preserve a concept of community participation, imagine an alternative to constantly responding to predetermined governmental frameworks, and link the political with the personal. Obomsawin remains committed to cross-cultural perspectives and addressing more than one audience. Her strategies of reversal, juxtaposition, and dispersed narrative voice counter the polarization that characterized the conflict.

## Lee Maracle's Doublevoicedness

As in Obomsawin's work, the acts of re-framing and re-positioning are integral to Lee Maracle's representational strategies. Over the course of her writing career, Maracle has re-packaged, re-released, and re-presented her writings in a variety of ways, often disavowing the framing perspective in earlier instances. This reflects the doublevoiced quality of her writings.[8] Even when she is writing singly authored texts, her writing moves in two or three directions at once, operating in a range of registers and reflecting her self-revisions over time. The title of her collection of poetry, *Bent Box* (2000), highlights her interest in framing and re-framing. Maracle's techniques of re-presentation mirror her shifts in political engagement with two discourses that emerged following the Oka crisis in 1990: the politics of voice and the politics of Aboriginal sovereignty. Both of these discourses have defined her engagement as writer and activist in the Canadian cultural scene.

In the second edition of her told-to life narrative, *Bobbi Lee, Indian Rebel*, published in 1990, Maracle refuses to maintain the fiction of Barnett's invisibility as recorder, transcriber, and editor of her taped autobiography. In the new edition of *Bobbi Lee*, Maracle challenges the inequalities that often structure told-to narratives and exploits the dialogic possibilities that the collaborative text offers. She deletes the foreword and introduction by Barnett, and adds a new foreword (by Jeannette Armstrong), a prologue, an epilogue, and the introductory piece, entitled 'Oka Peace Camp – September 9, 1990,' which acknowledges the role that Oka played in bringing to the forefront the politics of voice in Canadian cultural debates. She also deletes Barnett's subtitle to the life narrative, 'Struggles of a Native Canadian Woman,' with its implication of a generic narrative of resistance, as well as its absorption of 'Native' as a qualifier of the noun 'Canadian.' Maracle does not change the body of the narrative; nevertheless, her autobiography undergoes significant transformations as it interacts with the new framing texts.

As the epigraph to this chapter suggests, a recorder's good intentions to collaborate fairly with a teller are not enough to overcome the historically asymmetric relations of address in told-to narratives. This power imbalance is particularly ironic with respect to the genre of the testimonial life narrative. *Bobbi Lee* was part of 'Life Histories from the Revolution,' a series of narratives recorded, edited, and published by Barnett and the Liberation Support Movement (LSM) from 1966 to 1975. Based in Burnaby, British Columbia, LSM published about fifteen life histories, mostly from Africa (Kenya, Angola, Mozambique, colonial Rhodesia, and South Africa). The series' political orientation is comparable to what John Beverley calls *testimonios* – a form of told-to narrative that is 'linked closely to national liberation movements and other social struggles inspired by Marxism' (*Testimonio* x). According to Beverley, who has written extensively on the genre in the Latin American context, *testimonios* are meant to correct the unequal relations in ethnographic life histories by emphasizing the narrator's control over the life story. *Testimonios* enact a 'powerful textual affirmation of the speaking subject' while simultaneously erasing 'the function and textual presence of the "author," which by contrast is so central to all major forms of bourgeois writing since the Renaissance' ('The Margin' 96, 97). For Beverley, the process of compiling a *testimonio* is an act of solidarity that has politically transformative effects.

Yet there are a number of contradictions that complicate Beverley's theory of *testimonio*. Though he downplays the role of the author-writer as a mere 'compiler' or 'activator' (97), he nevertheless suggests that the compiler is crucial to give voice to the 'previously voiceless, anonymous' subject (98). Even though he wishes to show that the narrator is in control of the narrative, Beverley ends up asserting the indispensability of the recorder in bringing the narrative to light in the first place. To some degree, Beverley's privileging of the narrator over the recorder serves to camouflage the role of the author rather than to eliminate it. Moreover, by switching the critical emphasis from the recorder to the narrator, Beverley reasserts a binarized relation between recorder and narrator, thereby limiting the potential forms of intersubjectivity that the told-to interaction creates.

Don Barnett's introduction to *Bobbi Lee,* which appeared in the first edition of 1975, makes some of these contradictions apparent. Deleted from the revised edition, the introduction creates and sustains subalternity:

> The vast majority of peasants and workers in the super-exploited hinterland of the imperialist system are illiterate ... Their 'backwardness' condemns them to literary silence, as well as poverty, disease and a short life. Our objective is to provide a medium through which these classes can *speak* ... [and] *be heard* by those of us who comprise imperialism's privileged and literate metropolitan minority. Their recounted lives throw our own into sharp relief, while at the same time they offer us fresh perspectives on the processes of repression and revolution from a unique vantage point: *from below*. (Barnett [ed.] xi; emphasis in original)

Though Barnett and Maracle at one time might have been speaking a common language of anti-capitalist, anti-imperialist resistance, Maracle makes clear that that moment of commonality has since splintered and fallen apart. In spite of the best of intentions, *Bobbi Lee* has failed to become the shared resistance story that the two interlocutors had first envisioned. According to Kathleeen Donovan, Barnett's 'blatantly elitist agenda places emphasis on what colonized people can do *for* the dominant culture. In addition, Maracle most certainly was not illiterate. The narrative reveals that she was widely read in the literature of social revolution and was an articulate and forceful speaker for the rights of Native people' (Donovan 39-40). Indeed, Barnett's elitism is palpable as he plays 'the god-trick of seeing everything from nowhere' (Haraway 189), of giving voice to the voiceless while dismissing the formative role of his editorial intervention. By suggesting that he has conferred literacy upon an 'illiterate' subject, Barnett renders his own intervention indispensable. At the same time, by suggesting that the life story was a collaborative project between equals, he asserts the authenticity of (his recording of) Maracle's words. By italicizing the words *speak* and *be heard*, Barnett produces the effect of immediacy while obscuring the power relations at work in the text.

Even though Maracle deletes the introduction, she does not permit the reader to forget that this confessional narrative emerges from her volatile and emotionally charged relationship with Barnett. She acknowledges his role by reproducing the dedication that opens the first edition of *Bobbi Lee*. Here she honours Barnett's life and unexpected death in 1975, the same year *Bobbi Lee* was published: 'We all loved him deeply. Our love must not be wasted in sorrow but rather must manifest itself in our willingness to take up the struggle for proletarian socialism with the same determination and unwavering tenacity that so characterized Don' (Maracle, *Bobbi Lee* 17-18). However, in the prologue that follows the dedication, Maracle distances herself from the 'we' above: 'I respected Don, at the time almost liked him, but not quite. I didn't, couldn't tell him everything. There were too many obstacles in my path' (18). Her feelings of respect have changed into a burdensome sense of indebtedness: 'He did inspire me to get command of my voice. He believed I had great potential, but was quite raw' (19). The colonial and gendered implications of being 'raw' material for Barnett's 'Life Histories from the Revolution' series are not lost on Maracle: 'I remember Don once said his wife was "almost an intellectual." It scared me into silence. Now I see it as so much white male narcissism that kept him arrogantly rooted in autocratic behaviour' (19).

Maracle acknowledges the ambivalence of having both learned from Barnett and resisted his authoritative interpretations of anti-capitalist, Marxist struggle: 'his idea of political struggle was riddled with arrogance, something I loathed, but knew I too was full of' (18). Maracle stages a series of self-revisions over time: 'I was a very distorted child *at the time* of the first book' (19, my emphasis). In the epilogue, she distances herself from her previous writing selves: 'I am sitting in my room mulling over the ancient manuscript from which *Bobbi Lee* was born. My misspent youth, the craziness of internalized racism, my own confusion and the holes rent in my memory had come back at me like cruel bill collectors wanting their pound of flesh' (199). The epilogue is an appeal to the future, to what she is writing towards: 'This epilogue is intended to fill in the missing pieces that came alive in my memory through the long process of unravelling that began in 1975 ... The rest [of those memories] are inserted here on the final pages I will ever write about Bobbi' (201). Fragments of the life of Bobbi nevertheless re-appear in *Sojourner's Truth and Other Stories,* also published in 1990, as well as *Sundogs* (1992), *Ravensong* (1993), and the revised edition of *I Am Woman* (1996). Moving from one version of the life story to another, the reader senses that Maracle has left open gaps in the life narrative. The story of Bobbi's life is not a smooth chronology; rather the thread of the narrative appears and disappears as Maracle retells the story in fiction, poetry, sociology, polemic, and even told-to narrative.

In the revised edition, Maracle calls into question the 'I' of the original *testimonio* – the coming-to-voice of the subaltern subject. In Linda Warley's reading, the new edition gives Maracle 'more textual control over her life narrative,' inscribing 'a different "I"' (Warley 66). The new edition provides Maracle with the means to take part in, but also take apart, the mediating structures that constitute her textualized voice. She redraws the lines of collaboration between herself and Barnett the editor, not by rewriting her story in her own words, but by resituating her voice within different historical and political contexts. In the new edition, Maracle maintains an antagonistic, interventionist relation to all framing voices, including her own. She speaks doubly, beginning again and again in different registers of voice, thus disputing what Beverley and Barnett assume to be the immediacy of the testimonial voice. Indeed, her testimonial voice is highly mediated: it is multiple, changeable, historically situated, and collectively defined. As a result, her text becomes double-voiced in Bakhtin's sense. For Bakhtin, 'heteroglossia' emerges from rigidly hierarchical social relations; Maracle suggests that doublevoicedness emerges from the experience of living as a Native woman in painfully divided Canadian social spaces. Her new edition highlights tensions between voices, rather than implying perfect understanding between speaking 'partners' (Bakhtin, *Speech* 68). Bakhtin likewise refutes the myth of equality in conversational exchange. For Bakhtin, social context, with its many imbricated hierarchies, shapes acts of communication between interlocutors.[9]

The Oka crisis becomes the larger social and political context that informs Maracle's post-1990 writing. In *Bobbi Lee,* as in the novel *Sundogs,*

Maracle uses the image of the razor-wire fences at Kanehsatake as a reminder of the sharp contrasts between Euro-Canadian and First Nations social realities; but the 'Oka crisis' also functions to open up new horizons of what can be said and published in Aboriginal writing in Canada. In 'Oka Peace Camp – September 9, 1990,' Maracle aligns herself with the Mohawk warriors at Kanehsatake. For Maracle, the razor-wire fences made visible the fact that First Nations do not live in a 'post'-colonial world: 'after centuries of the colonial state pressing on our villages, taking life after life, we are finally fed up' (Maracle, *Bobbi Lee* 6). The novel *Sun Dogs*, also set in 1990, pursues the idea that moments of crisis in the relationship between Aboriginal and settler groups in Canada – from Elijah Harper's 'No' in parliament to the Mohawk people's 'No' at the barricades – can become catalysts for changing that relationship. In an interview with Jennifer Kelly conducted in 1994, Maracle emphasizes how the standoff at Kanehsatake created a sense of energy and purpose in Aboriginal communities: 'It [the standoff] was a moment of awakening, a moment of recognition that we were not destroyed, that you cannot destroy culture ... [or] the spirit of people' (J. Kelly 77). Kanehsatake became the catalyst for Aboriginal cultural producers to address a larger audience. Maracle explains:

> *Gatherings*, the journal that came out of En'owkin International School of Writing, was brought out on the heels of 1990, when we found out there are literally hundreds of writers in the country that haven't the opportunity to publish. *Writing the Circle* [edited by Jeanne Perreault and Sylvia Vance] came out in 1990; [Marie Annharte Baker's] *Being on the Moon* came out just after 1990; Duncan Mercredi's poetry came out just after 1990; *Sundogs* was mostly 1990 ... There are a lot of healing societies and healing work being done in our communities as a result of 1990 – all kinds of communities are dealing with the effects of the residential school system, post-1990; the federal government finally came out with a self-government package, which wasn't good enough for us, but that's post-1990. (J. Kelly 78)

By introducing her life narrative through the lens of Oka, and by rehearsing the events of Oka in her novel *Sundogs*, Maracle is underlining the role that the standoff has played and continues to play in reinvigorating talks on land claims, sovereignty movements, treaty-brokering, and other negotiating deals. Despite the 'threat of annihilation' that the standoff posed for the Mohawk people (Maracle, *Sundogs* 134), Oka creates feelings of empowerment for Marianne, the main character in *Sundogs*: 'We are coming alive after a long period of numb existence, paralyzed survival' (141). She expresses her feelings in cultural nationalist terms, as a people taking control of its own destiny: 'We are no longer victims, but people who have made a decision, established a direction for ourselves after what seemed like a century of floundering' (145). Marianne's personal and political empowerment is explicitly linked to her growing awareness of the possibilities of sovereignty in Aboriginal politics. However, as a young woman growing up in multiethnic, racially divided social contexts in Vancouver, Marianne does not have a straightforward relationship with an Aboriginal national identity. Unlike other members of her family, Marianne cannot speak Salish languages and has little or no knowledge of traditional Salish cultural practices. Even though she is living on Coast Salish land, the colonial takeover has barred her from having, or even imagining, a relationship to territory. She also feels disconnected from the men who identify themselves with the Okanagan nation and who organize the Peace Run in support of the Mohawk people. These men speak the Okanagan language, live on Okanagan territory, and engage in Okanagan spiritual and cultural practices. In fractured, disjointed syntax, Marianne questions what sovereignty could mean for her: 'sovereignty – the impossible dream. Equality, solidarity with all creation – a pipe dream. Drum songs and pipe dreams' (206).

Like Frantz Fanon, who warned that the dream of national consciousness may become 'an empty shell, a crude and fragile travesty of what it might have been' (*Wretched* 148), Marianne expresses a degree of uncertainty and ambivalence about the efficacy of the rapidly growing sovereignty movement in securing social justice for Aboriginal people in Canada. Her feelings are conflicted about Elijah Harper's successful termination of the Meech Lake Accord, an agreement that would have reinscribed the myth of the 'two founding nations' (the French and the English) in the Canadian constitution. Unlike her family and friends who are elated in response to Harper's act of defiance, Marianne is not convinced that his stand will amount to much: 'Elijah won. We won ... Indescribable jubilance fills everyone. Between ... huge guffaws is my tiny sliver of doubt' (Maracle, *Sundogs* 120). Marianne's cynicism is heresy within her social circles. Her co-worker Saul, with 'a grand salute' to Elijah, declares that 'Canada will never be the same' (121). Marianne's questioning of this pronouncement 'stops the joyous laughter' and breaks the fragile sense of optimism that had emerged among her friends. She derails the Elijah celebrations at her home as well, resulting in her 'complete alienation' from her family (113). Scanning the people gathered together in her family's home, she asks herself: 'who are these people I call my own?' (112). Her sense of dislocation heightens as family members and friends experience a growing sense of euphoria: 'Emotions, paradoxical and contrary, argue in parallel lines inside me all day' (119).

These 'paradoxical and contrary' emotions reflect not only Marianne's reaction to the Oka crisis, which she watches nightly on her television screen during the summer of 1990, but also her developing love affair with Mark, her boss at work. Maracle continually switches from the political story to the love story and back again in order to underline Marianne's uneven relationship with concepts of Aboriginal sovereignty. Both stories unfold in mercurial, emotionally charged ways. Marianne rides a roller-coaster of emotions – ecstasy and fear, hope and distrust – as her relationship with Mark takes unexpected turns and as the drama of Harper and of Oka reaches climaxes and anti-climaxes. This is because Marianne has few resources at her disposal to take control of the telling of either story: the older, more experienced Mark controls the terms of the love relationship, while the TV holds the story of Oka hostage.

For Marianne, as for Obomsawin (as well as for Jordan Wheeler, who speaks of the 'time bomb in Canada' threatening to detonate during the crisis), Oka risks becoming no more than a media circus of 'info-tainment' if the framing perspectives of the mainstream media remain in place (Wheeler 37). By having her characters learn about the events primarily by watching TV, Maracle highlights the media context of both Harper's and the Mohawk people's acts of resistance. However, the novel opens up a space of response to the monolithic media representations of the 'failure of Meech Lake' and of the 'Oka crisis'. In watching Harper in the televised session of the legislature, the characters dialogically interact with and respond to the monologism of the TV. Maracle stretches out the time of the narration of Harper's historic 'No' over a number of pages in order to show how the characters' reactions to the televised event are more important than the event itself. The character Momma continually talks back to the TV: 'She'll talk for Elijah, kick at the Prime Minister and the ten foolish Premiers, rail at the whole country and re-articulate the genocidal plot theory ... Rita and I [will] ... try to catch a little of what is being said' (Maracle, *Sundogs* 103). Later, during the Oka crisis, Momma smashes the TV with a rock while the premier of Quebec is speaking, indicating her intense frustration with the media representations of the event, and recalling the violence against the Kahnawake residents at the Mercier Bridge blockade (143). Oka becomes a harbinger of profound change in the relations between First Nations and Canada, as well as a warning of the high cost that First Nations are paying in the process of change.

The media issues that Maracle explores in *Sundogs* raise the question of who speaks for whom – who has the legitimacy to speak on behalf of the Mohawk people and who does not get a chance to address a national television audience. The question of voice and representation has been a major preoccupation in Maracle's writing. Over the past three decades, she has played a key role in connecting with Aboriginal writers and writers of colour in demanding to be seen, heard, and included in institutions, media representations, and Canadian cultural policy. It was at the Third International Feminist Book Fair in Montreal in 1987 that Maracle asked Anne Cameron to stop using sacred stories from Aboriginal communities on Vancouver Island, and to 'move over' to make room for First Nations writers to publish their work (Maracle, 'Moving Over' 10). Maracle also participated in three other key conferences in Vancouver that foregrounded cultural race politics and feminism: Women and Words / *Les mots et les femmes* (1983); TELLING IT: Women and Language across Cultures (1988); and Writing thru Race (1994).

In the late 1980s and 1990s, debates over the politics of 'voice' and representation were becoming increasingly heated in a broad range of arenas. Of particular concern were the material conditions of the publication, distribution, and circulation of texts: who gets published, which presses get funding, and who becomes an 'author.'[10] Aboriginal writers strategically connected these disputes over 'voice' to disputes over land, resources, and cultural property. Ironically, the debate over the appropriation of voice has become just as divided as the social inequalities that caused the disputes in the first place. To the charge of 'racism' in the publishing industry, the dominant White society and its media outlets have responded, typically, with charges of 'censorship.' The debate then hardened into starkly opposing positions, reinforcing the lack of dialogue that caused the problems initially. Marlene NourbeSe Philip, in analysing a particular dispute over voice and representation in 1989 with respect to the Women's Press, argues:

> As often happens around issues such as these, the debate quickly assumed a dichotomous nature with the pro-censorship forces arrayed against the

anti-censorship hordes. Racism was the issue that detonated the explosion at the Women's Press; to the exclusion of any other issue, censorship has become the issue that has monopolized the media's attention ... Censorship in all its myriad forms became, in fact, the privileged discourse. (NourbeSe Philip 209)

In contrast to the 'privileged discourse' of censorship, racism in the publishing industry and the lack of opportunities for writers of colour to publish their work became what NourbeSe Philip calls the 'disappearing debate': 'There was no discussion about how to enable more Black women to get into print, or how to help those small publishing houses committed to publishing work by Black authors, or any of the many tasks that must be undertaken to make the writing and publishing world truly non-racist' (213). Valaskakis also expresses impatience with how debates over the appropriation of voice have unfolded in First Nations studies. Defensive responses from White writers to the issue of appropriation have misread the problem at hand. Centring the debate on the 'struggle over who can represent whom, who can tell the stories of others – and how they should be told – tends to focus on issues of censorship and political correctness, masking the lived experience and problems of people of colour and people of the First Nations; neglecting the relationship between representation, appropriation and access, and social and political formations which position people of colour and Native North Americans as other and unequal' (Valaskakis, 'Parallel' 285). The relations between 'representation, appropriation and access' become obscured by the ideology of 'the freedom of the imagination' that animates censorship debates. This ideology, in turn, underpins constructions of the author in print-capitalist economies. The author-function remains veiled by the mystique of creativity and imagination. Meanwhile, the 'social and political formations' that confer author-status on a select few are ignored.

The dominance of the censorship issue in media coverage of the 'voice appropriation' debate resulted in the question of cultural representation becoming an individualized issue of what a particular author is 'allowed' to write. Timothy Findley and Neil Bissoondath were among the high-profile Canadian writers who, in penning a series of letters to the editor of the *Globe and Mail*, were said to invoke the two poles of 'the tyranny of the state over the individual' versus 'the transcendent genius of the Romantic author and his unfettered imagination' (Coombe 76). Meanwhile, the institutional, structural, and material issues that Maracle and

NourbeSe Philip attempted to highlight became sidelined. In response to Jennifer Kelly's question, 'What's your position in the "appropriation" debate?' Maracle resists the question's implicit assumption of a single, unchanging response that delineates a definite 'position'. She replies: 'I don't think there's such thing as appropriation of voice and I really resent the fact that someone came up with that term, because it isn't what we were talking about ... I have said consistently over six years now that you can't appropriate anybody's voice' (J. Kelly 82). By rejecting the very notion of one person appropriating another's voice, Maracle is questioning the role of the individual's choice in the debate. Instead, she turns the focus on the role of institutions and of the book market in perpetuating inequalities. Furthermore, the very concept of 'voice appropriation' implies that the writer has a singular voice that another can take over; instead, in her practice of writing, Maracle remains committed to doublevoiced, composite texts, such as told-to narratives.

Since *Bobbi Lee*, Maracle has used different forms of the told-to narrative to open up debates over voice and representation. In 'Rusty,' a textualized oral narrative in *I Am Woman* (43-61), Maracle takes on the role of the recorder, writer, and editor. Instead of remaining a silent recorder, as Don Barnett did, Maracle goes to some lengths to show that as a listener she played a formative role. The text is a compilation of a variety of kinds of writing, including question-and-answer interview, transcription, internal monologue, and poetry. Maracle includes her questions to Rusty, as well as her own commentary on her interlocutor's story. This Native-to-Native, woman-to-woman told-to narrative aims to reconfigure the told-to interaction and to change or at least mitigate some of the asymmetries of ethnographic life narratives; however, Maracle acknowledges that the great distances between herself and Rusty make conversational exchange difficult. She is acutely aware of her own privileges as a writer who has the critical tools to address the injustice of Rusty's story. Though the collaboration begins with two people 'battering down the walls that separated them and erecting an arc – a bridge – to unite them,' it ends with Rusty's suicide, when 'the walls became reinforced with steel' (Maracle, *I Am Woman* 43). In between, Maracle presents herself as a reluctant recorder/editor, fearful that the schisms between her and Rusty are too great to overcome: 'I was wishing I could get up and leave the room without hurting Rusty, but I couldn't, so I stayed' (48). Rusty's tragic story clearly implicates Maracle and/or Bobbi: 'I would have cried, Rusty, but for the fact that 'tis I who will be hearing your story in the darkness of my room' (61).

Maracle poses questions to herself, weaving parts of her own / Bobbi's life narrative into the text in response to Rusty's story, and abruptly shifting from first-, second-, and third-person narrative voice. The result is an explicitly dialogic testimonial life narrative that reveals the volatile, intersubjective relationship between recorder and teller in told-to narratives.

In much of her writing, Maracle maintains her double focus, as if addressing more than one audience. Maracle draws attention not only to the yawning gaps between Euro-Canadian and Aboriginal understandings of the history of this continent but also, as the told-to narrative 'Rusty' suggests, between Aboriginal people differently aligned in relation to the disparities of class, gender, and levels of education. At the same time, she insists on the need for talking across these gaps to change them: *'The life of Bobbi Lee,'* she concludes in the new preface to her autobiography, *'is why we must talk'* (*Bobbi Lee* 11, emphasis in original). Many critics have commented upon how Maracle's writing tacks back and forth between various perspectives. Lynette Hunter, in a stylistic analysis of Maracle's work, draws attention to the writing's 'double focus' (68), 'mixed register,' 'repetition' (70), and 'double bind' (71). Susie O'Brien describes how Maracle 'alternates between accommodating and alienating narrative strategies' in the short story 'Eunice' (83), while Judith Leggatt, commenting on the novel *Ravensong*, explores the 'fears of cross-contamination' of the Salish and Euro-Canadian populations who 'seldom interact,' and who 'view [each] other with suspicion' (164). Sudden and sharp switches between building 'bridges' across cultural gaps, and sabotaging bridges that others have endeavoured to build, make up the texture of Maracle's writing. The bridge, as well as the half-constructed bridge, is a recurrent image in her writing. The novel *Ravensong* is set in two communities, White and Native, separated by a river, and connected by a bridge that becomes the site of a suicide of one of the main characters. In 'Ramparts Hanging in the Air,' a personal response to the emotionally and politically charged conference TELLING IT: Women and Language across Cultures (1990), Maracle writes: 'We all struggled to build bridges at the TELLING IT conference. Too bad they weren't located in the same spot directly across from each other' (Maracle, 'Ramparts' 171). Maracle is referring to the difficulty of building connections between women in feminist communities that are fractured along the fault lines of race, class, and sexuality.

The TELLING IT conference, held in Vancouver in 1988, like Women and Words (1983) and Writing Thru Race (1994), brought to the forefront debates around voice, representation, and access in which Maracle has played an active role. The Telling It Book Collective, of which Maracle was a part, rejected simple oppositional articulations of identity, instead exploring a spectrum of differences between women. The resulting text – which Daphne Marlatt, member of the editorial collective, calls a 'transformation' rather than a 'transcription' of a conference (Marlatt 9) – uses told-to narrative conventions to create a layered texture of voices. The text combines papers, panel discussions, and readings from the conference with various framing texts written after the conference by members of the editorial collective. The result is a dialogic, collective text that explodes singular notions of voice that are usually associated with 'identity politics.'

On the question of 'identity politics,' Obomsawin is much more direct than Maracle. As she says, she makes films to provide Aboriginal people with the means to speak and be heard: 'The basic purpose [of my films] is for our people to have a voice. To be heard is the important thing, no matter what we're talking about ... that it's OK to be an Indian, to be a Native person in this country' (qtd. in Pick 78). However, this forthright objective – comparable to Barnett's – belies the complexity of 'voice' and representation in her work. In making the four films on the 'Oka crisis,' as a non-Mohawk, Aboriginal, French- and English-speaking, Québécoise, Abenaki woman, Obomsawin is positioned in the interstice between 'insider' and 'outsider,' embodying the multiple perspectives she creates in her social realist films. Like Maracle, Obomsawin began her career in what may be called the position of a 'Native informant' in the late 1960s. She describes how, in her first film assignment at the National Film Board (NFB), she was asked to be a 'consultant' on a film 'about Indians' but was discouraged from questioning or changing the genre of the ethnographic film:

> When I began making films in 1967 it was very difficult ... [T]here were people working there [at the NFB] who were used to making films *about* Indians, and now they had an Indian person working alongside them. My presence didn't please everybody ... The first film I worked on wasn't really my idea ... Some people at the NFB ... asked if I would be a consultant on a film about women making hook rugs in Standing Buffalo, Saskatchewan. I accepted the job, but quickly realized that I was never going to do that again because I was just being used to meet people. (Gagnon and Fung 91)

Obomsawin's own films, which she has written, directed, and produced, unsettle the relations of authority that the ethnographic film creates. Nevertheless, throughout the 1970s and 1980s, she continued to contend with barriers in distributing and circulating her work to Aboriginal audiences. Following this anecdote, she relates that the Department of Indian Affairs and Northern Development actively suppressed her work and refused permission to have it distributed to residential schools. Obomsawin's fearless engagement with some of the most dangerous confrontations between Aboriginal and non-Aboriginal people in Canada also risks more subtle forms of marginalization. As a filmmaker who is known to tell the story of conflict '[c]learly seen from the Native point of view,' as a review of *Is the Crown at War with Us?* puts it (Loreto par. 2), Obomsawin's work sometimes mistakenly is categorized as dealing exclusively with Native concerns. For example, when *Kanehsatake* aired on CBC television on 31 January 1994, CBC arranged a panel discussion with representatives from the Canadian Armed Forces, the SQ, and the federal and provincial governments to ensure that her film's perspective would be 'balanced' by other points of view. Today, Obomsawin has achieved national recognition for her extraordinary career: having become a member of the Order of Canada in 1983, she was promoted to the rank of Officer in 2001 and received the Governor General's Award in Media and Visual Arts that same year. She is most proud of the educational potential of her work, indicating her commitment to institutional change: 'fighting for inclusion of Aboriginal history in the educational system – that's always been my big thing' (qtd. in Gagnon and Fung 91).

The effect of Maracle's and Obomsawin's double-voiced representations is to disrupt those dichotomies – White/Native, rich/poor, colonizer/colonized – that the artists simultaneously force their audience to acknowledge. By speaking in two or more registers and using strategies of the told-to narrative, Maracle and Obomsawin open up debates about sovereignty and the politics of voice. Both have played active roles in demanding change in institutions, media representations, and publishing to ensure that the words and actions of Aboriginal people are recognized and valorized. Their explorations of multiple Aboriginal subjectivities in cross-cultural contexts offer ways of re-thinking debates about the politics of representation that avoid fixed identifications. For Maracle and Obomsawin, Kanehsatake marked a turning point in Aboriginal cultural politics that rejuvenated demands to resolve land claims and to establish nation-to-nation relations. Yet like Cree poet Beth Cuthand, in her poem 'Post-Oka Kinda Woman,' Maracle and Obomsawin avoid readily accessible images of resistance, and raise questions about the kind of sovereignty First Nations social movements should imagine and work towards realizing:

> Here she comes strutting down your street.
> This Post-Oka woman don't take no shit.
> She's done with victimization, reparation,
> degradation, assimilation,
> devolution, coddled collusion,
> the 'plight of the Native Peoples.' (Cuthand 132)

For Obomsawin and Maracle, as for Cuthand, the 'post-Oka kinda woman' rejects the narratives of victimization entrenched in Canadian history. But she also remains suspicious of 'coddled collusion': 'You wanna discuss Land Claims? / She'll tell ya she'd rather leave / her kids with a struggle than a bad settlement' (133). Cuthand is suggesting the need to maintain critical distance from land claim agreements that threaten to reinscribe a colonial status quo – such as those that include extinguishment or 'exhaustion' clauses, or those in which the relationship between corporate rights and Aboriginal rights becomes blurred, as I discuss in the next chapters. Similarly, Obomsawin and Maracle engage with debates about Aboriginal sovereignty without prescribing a singular definition of what sovereignty 'is.' Instead, both artists draw attention to the diversity of Aboriginal communities and the fractures of gender, class, and social opportunities that need to be addressed in order for sovereignty to become an effective, decolonizing tool. It is the multivoicedness of Maracle's and Obomsawin's work and the careful ways in which they draw attention to the mediations that produce different registers of 'voice' that, until now, have not received adequate attention. Their work provides a vital reminder of the need to continue to push for change institutionally, as well as to shift the kinds of questions critics pose in addressing Native cultural production in Canada.

# 'My Story Is a Gift'
# The Royal Commission on Aboriginal Peoples and the Politics of Reconciliation

# 4

> My story is a gift. If I give you a gift and you accept that gift, then you don't go and throw that gift in the waste basket. You do something with it.
>
> – ASSEMBLY OF FIRST NATIONS, *BREAKING THE SILENCE*

In January 1991, a few months after the violent end of the seventy-eight-day standoff at Kanehsatake, the embattled Mulroney government struck the Royal Commission on Aboriginal Peoples (RCAP) and asked the four Aboriginal and three non-Aboriginal commissioners[1] to 'make recommendations promoting reconciliation between aboriginal peoples and Canadian society as a whole' (Canada, 'The Commission's Terms' 699). Choosing a majority of Aboriginal commissioners was meant to make visible the federal government's commitment to 'break the pattern of paternalism which has characterized the relationship between aboriginal peoples and the Canadian government' (699). Like the Truth and Reconciliation Commission (TRC) in South Africa (1996-2001),[2] RCAP contributed to an emergent politics of reconciliation that has become, in recent times, heavily implicated in state policy among some neo-liberal democracies struggling to deal with the legacy of intra-national colonization and longstanding social inequities. This shift to 'reconciliation' demands careful attention: reconciliation for whom, and to what? Can reconciliation mean more than an absolution of guilt for those who have benefited from social inequalities and an enforced forgetting for those who have paid a high cost for those privileges? In this chapter, I investigate how RCAP converted testimony into report and argue that the commission missed an opportunity for creating the conditions for reconciliation. This is not because, as many critics have argued, its vision of self-government was wrong-headed or divisive, its recommendations impractical, or its call for governmental change ineffectual. Rather, I am interested in how RCAP, with its emphasis on recommendations, incrementally distanced itself from the testimony, containing and managing it within strictly controlled editorial practices. As a result, the commission did not elicit the active participation of witnesses in the remaking of a shared history. To put it another way, the report's modes of textualization did not necessitate listeners or readers to engage 'in the second person,' in Gillian Whitlock's evocative phrase, a position that would acknowledge their implication in the history of Canadian-Aboriginal relations.

Nevertheless, RCAP played a crucial role as catalyst in telling, recording, and disseminating subsequent community narratives. Some participants in these hearings took further steps of their own, going on to publish their stories in different forms and in new modes of circulation. Along with my analysis of RCAP's strategies of entextualization – its translation of testimony into report – I also analyse the collective life narrative *Night Spirits: The Story of the Relocation of the Sayisi Dene* (1997), which describes the forced relocation of the Sayisi Dene First Nation from its ancestral territories to Churchill, Manitoba, in 1956. In *Night Spirits,* co-authors Ila Bussidor, former Chief of the Sayisi Dene nation, and Üstün Bilgen-Reinart, a Turkish Canadian journalist, re-frame the contents of RCAP's report, initially prepared by Virginia Petch (1995), and begin a process of recording, compiling, translating, and editing stories from the Sayisi Dene community.

In this chapter, as in other chapters, I am bringing together texts of different genres (formal governmental report and collective life story), produced under different terms of authorship (a commission of governmental appointees on the one hand and a community-driven initiative on the other), and guided by different aims (to craft recommendations for the federal government versus to remember the past and imagine a new future for the Sayisi Dene nation). Clearly, the underlying conditions of production of these projects diverge significantly, resulting in discrepancies in form, style, genre, and content. My purpose in connecting these projects is to explore the deep imbrications of text and context, and to suggest that what can be imagined in Aboriginal cultural production is connected to what is unfolding in larger political and social discourses. *Night Spirits* may not have come to be without the impulsion of the RCAP community hearings; yet as an independent, community-led undertaking, it was able to depart from the normative textualizing practices used in RCAP's report. For example, in contrast to RCAP's report – which demonstrates appropriate concern for protecting the anonymity of Sayisi Dene interviewees – *Night Spirits* highlights the collective and deeply personal nature of the testimonial project. Though the collaborative relationship between Bussidor and Bilgen-Reinart is complicated by the historical legacy of mistranslation between Sayisi Dene people and non-Indigenous groups, the text suggests the possibility of developing a cross-cultural, collaborative relationship in the context of demanding social and political change. The shift to what Carole Boyce Davies calls a 'multiply articulated text' puts the onus on the listener to respond and take responsibility for the past. RCAP's tendency to cut out the 'you' is reversed in this publication, thus encouraging the listener to remain accountable to history in a newly crafted politics of reconciliation.

## The Politics of Reconciliation in RCAP's Report

The ongoing Indian Residential Schools Truth and Reconciliation Commission, struck in 2008, and the formation of British Columbia's Ministry of Aboriginal Relations and Reconciliation in 2005, are part of the current global proliferation of discourses of reconciliation. Recent commissions in places such as South Africa, Australia, and Canada are suggestive of what Pauline Wakeham calls the 'increasing co-optation of discourses of reconciliation by a hegemonic network of institutions and agents – ranging from government agencies, to museums and institutions of national culture, and to the mainstream media' ('Discourses of Reconciliation' par. 1). According to *The Concise Oxford English Dictionary*, two senses of the verb to reconcile are: '1. Make friendly again after an estrangement; 2. Make acquiescent or contentedly submissive to (something disagreeable or unwelcome).' These definitions make clear a number of assumptions. The term 'reconciliation' suggests a return of order between two equals, thereby downplaying power asymmetries, and naturalizing an imagined past of unity, cooperation, and friendliness. It also produces an illusory sense of resolution that conveniently brackets ongoing colonial injustices. Along with apology, forgiveness, and atonement, reconciliation suggests a religious (specifically Christian) context that potentially further entrenches social hierarchies and power imbalances between confessor (victim or perpetrator) and confessee (government). Literary critic Deena Rymhs points to a number of contradictions in discourses of reconciliation: on the one hand, the shift to reconciliation risks eroding the wronged party's agency by assigning a victim's role to Aboriginal people. On the other, it 'call[s] on indigenous communities to "heal" despite continued poverty, differences in education, and a hostile criminal justice system' (Rymhs, 'Appropriating' 119). While reconciliation prioritizes the expiation of the colonizer's sense of guilt, it places the onus upon the colonized to end longstanding conflicts. The result is that 'reconciliation's successes have been more illusory than real' (119).

Despite these ongoing problems with the term, there are a number of advocates who struggle to articulate a politically progressive and nuanced interpretation of reconciliation. In an oft-cited speech to the South African Parliament on 7 January 1994, Nelson Mandela, one of the key architects of the South African Truth and Reconciliation Commission, said that 'True reconciliation does not consist in merely forgetting the past' (qtd. in Lloyd 236). The Aboriginal Healing Foundation, mandated by the government's 'Statement of Reconciliation' in 1998 in response to RCAP's recommendations, has taken Mandela's insight as a point of departure in its collection of essays, *From Truth to Reconciliation: Transforming the Legacy of Residential Schools* (2008). Many of the contributors insist that no reconciliation can take place without change in the social inequities that divide Aboriginal and non-Aboriginal groups in Canada. Fred Kelly, residential school survivor and Anishinaabe elder, argues: 'If reconciliation is to be real and meaningful in Canada, it must embrace the inherent right of self-determination through self-government envisioned in the treaties, and it must be structured to accommodate the cultural diversity and regional differences in concepts, approaches and time frames of the First Nations in Canada' (F. Kelly 22-23). Furthermore, reconciliation must follow a process of 'truth-telling,' understood here as a process of creating space and legitimacy for first-person accounts of individual experiences. Stan McKay, a member of the Fisher River Cree nation in Manitoba, and a spiritual leader, teacher, and activist, advocates 'the telling of individual stories and respectful listening to the stories of others as a route to expand and transform the dialogue' (101). In the exchange of stories, the 'you' or addressee is obliged to respond as well as take responsibility for what she or he hears. Thus the manner in which RCAP transformed the 'raw material' of the testimonies into recommendations played a critical role in determining the degree to which the commission successfully initiated a politics of reconciliation.

Following McKay and others, I argue that more than RCAP's recommendations, it is the *process* that the commission engendered – holding 178 days of public hearings in more than 100 communities, listening to testimony from over 1,000 witnesses, synthesizing the material from more than 200 research reports, and producing a report of more than 3,500 pages[3] – that may hold the potential for initiating acts of reconciliation, grounded in a politics of difference. In Alan Cairns's words, 'the simple fact of the Commission's existence and its legacy will transform the political and intellectual context of future discussions on Aboriginal / non-Aboriginal relations in Canada' (117). Yet in order for reconciliation to be more than a case of amnesia, it must prioritize a politics of difference; and testimony, with its emphasis on multiple voices, is aligned with such a politics. However, the tendency of RCAP's report is to subsume the testimony within a dominant narrative of progress – from assimilation to self-government, from loss to recovery, from mutual mistrust to reconciliation. This narrative of progress limits the degree to which the commission was able to grapple with the contradictory processes of testifying, witnessing, and responding. It should be noted that a coherent, unified structure is hardly surprising in a governmental report; as Cairns reminds us, 'all royal commissions are massive mobilizations of facts and analysis in a particular direction; ... a unanimous report, such as that of RCAP, is the product of compromises that the royal commission version of cabinet solidarity prevents the commissioners from divulging' (120). Notwithstanding the real challenges the commissioners faced in organizing the immense amount of data submitted to the commission, the story of progress necessitates culling incongruities, particularly those found in the transcripts of the community hearings. The need to preserve the report's narrative resulted in the paraphrasing, bracketing, or elimination of testimony that did not fit with the commission's story of improvement.

Cairns argues that one of the concrete benefits of the report is that it provides a 'forum for Aboriginal voices, for letting people speak' (118); however, what I have observed in the report is a strong predilection for translating the hearings into third-person paraphrases, or offering short 'text bites' of testimony presented within a tightly controlled editorial frame. There is a drive to isolate the testimony from its context, to downplay current conflicts,[4] and to anesthetize blunt expressions of raw pain.

According to Peter Kulchyski, in contrast to *Northern Frontier, Northern Homeland* by Thomas Berger, which 'remains worth reading for richness and variety of voices,' RCAP's report is 'more bureaucratic in inflection' (*Like the Sound* 237). Though quotation is extensive, the majority of the citations come from the elected leadership; community voices are less prominent. Dale Turner, in *This Is Not a Peace Pipe: Toward A Critical Indigenous Philosophy* (2006), also remarks upon the bureaucratization of the language of RCAP's report, and argues that one reason for this modulation in the 'voice' of the report was the commissioners' concern to target its primary audience: governmental bodies that hold the power to implement the recommendations (72, 75-79). He further states that when it came time to write the report, the non-Aboriginal members of the commission (who had greater legal and political expertise) took charge, imposing a filter that subtly altered the message from the hearings (76).[5] He maintains that through this process, 'the commission's legal and political imagination [was] firmly embedded in the idea that the sovereignty of the Canadian state was not to be questioned'; as a result, the commission's vision of a nation-to-nation relationship 'ultimately set aside Aboriginal understandings of nationhood' and minimized the Aboriginal voices that were so prominent in the hearings (79).

An example of this minimization of the voices from the community hearings can be found in *People to People, Nation to Nation: Highlights from the Royal Commission on Aboriginal Peoples* (1996), a summary of the report geared towards a more general readership. Here the authors separate the testimony from the analysis by visually presenting clips from the hearings in the left- and right-hand margins of the text. In a similar vein to Hugh Brody's *Living Arctic* and its presentation of excerpts from the community hearings at the Mackenzie Valley Pipeline Inquiry, *People to People* places the testimony on the page in such a way that it functions primarily as an illustration of the main text. Gillian Whitlock's analysis of the textualization of testimony in *Bringing Them Home: Report of the National Inquiry into the Separation of Aboriginal and Torres Strait Islander Children from Their Families* (1997), the report from the Human Rights and Equal Opportunity Commission (HREOC) on the 'Stolen Generations' of Aboriginal children in Australia,[6] is applicable to *People to People*. Whitlock observes that *Bringing Them Home* maintains 'careful demarcations between authorized and unauthorized narrators.' She argues that 'the place in the limelight for unauthorized indigenous narrators is always a carefully defined performative act' (209). A similar mode of representing testimony within carefully demarcated analytical frames is evident both in *People to People* and in RCAP's report.

The transcriptions from the RCAP community hearings stored on the CD-ROM *For Seven Generations: An Information Legacy of the Royal Commission on Aboriginal Peoples* (1997) show that the commissioners were engaged in a more dynamic exchange with the presenters than is apparent in the report. During the hearings, the commissioners and speakers acknowledged their friendship, shared history, and remembrances of various rallies, marches, sit-ins, fish-ins, land claims proceedings, self-government negotiations, public hearings, and other political actions. The NFB documentary film *No Turning Back* (1997), directed by Greg Coyes, presents video clips of the community hearings that demonstrate the extent to which the commissioners established active, responsive discussions with speakers and audience members. They shake hands with or embrace the presenters, sometimes visibly moved by the testimony. But this sense of interaction between speaker and listener is not as evident in the report.

Although speakers at the community hearings frequently challenged the commissioners to act upon their findings, criticisms of the commission are muted in the report. In *No Turning Back,* a speaker confronts the commissioners with their responsibility to both listen and respond to the people's concerns (though again it should be noted that the commissioners had no means to enforce their recommendations): 'I can only hope that the concerns that have been tabled to you will result in some positive changes for all Aboriginal people, and not become just a collection of transcripts that are collecting dust in some federal warehouse.' This kind of challenge is fairly common in the transcripts of the community hearings, yet few are included in the report. The erasure of the 'you' may indicate the commissioners' fear of a defensive response from non-Aboriginal Canadians. Or it may reflect their concern that they would be perceived as politically biased in favour of the testifiers, potentially compromising their legitimacy. Whatever the reason, the report carefully effaces signs of interaction between testifiers and commissioners.

The tendency to bracket off and limit the impact of the testimony is evident in the section of the report that deals with the legacy of residential schools, arguably the most emotionally charged issue dividing Aboriginal and non-Aboriginal people today. The chapter demonstrates a preference for archival research over testimony, for history over the here and now. It includes only two quotations from the community hearings, both of which emphasize the need for individuals to psychologically 'move on.' For example, Marius Tungilik's long and impassioned statement at the Rankin Inlet community hearing, delivered on 19 November 1992, is reduced to a fragment that reinforces the report's overall trajectory of progress and healing: 'We need to know why we were subjected to such treatment in order that we may begin to understand and to heal' (Canada, *Looking Forward* 384). This particular statement, which emphasizes understanding, healing, and the need to look forward to the future, contrasts sharply with the rest of Tungilik's testimony, which poignantly describes the suffering he endured in residential school – sexual abuse, physical beatings, hunger – and the emotional toll these experiences have caused. Tungilik describes with honesty the confusing mix of emotions that resulted from his abuse, as well as his struggle to break out of a cycle of abuse and to come to terms with his role in perpetuating trauma within his own family. The report also excises the more politically charged passages in Tungilik's testimony, in which he demands the Church to recognize and compensate the victims of residential schools, and calls upon survivors to confront their past: 'I strongly feel that it is time for the church to face up to their wrongdoing and to help foot the bill in helping the people they have wronged. I also feel it is high time for former students of the residential schools to come out and deal with problems that they have been forced to live with for the past 25 to 30 years.'[7] It is worthwhile to note that the commissioners acknowledge that the residential school question was larger than could be adequately addressed by the commission: 'Given the range of subjects contemplated by our terms of reference, it was not possible for the Royal Commission to perform these social and investigative functions to the extent necessary to do justice to those harmed by the effect of Canada's residential school system' (Canada, *Looking Forward* 384). The main point of the chapter is to call for a public inquiry, 'with sufficient funding to enable those affected to testify' (383). As I write, the Truth and Reconciliation Commission, with a five-year mandate consistent with many of the recommendations of RCAP, is undertaking a process of community hearings.[8] Yet RCAP's decision to postpone the public inquiry for a later time is an example of the commissioners' tendency to defer engagement with direct testimony, testimony that potentially interferes with the commission's working definition of reconciliation as resolution and progress.

The strength of the chapter 'Residential Schools' lies in its careful study of government memos, documents, and correspondence, mostly from the end of the nineteenth and beginning of the twentieth centuries, which provide an invaluable historical record for understanding Canada's policies of assimilation.[9] Ironically, even though the chapter includes extensive quotation from official records held in the national archives as well as in the Department of Indian Affairs and Northern Development, the author (the chapter credits John Milloy as primary researcher) admits that these sources are partial and incomplete. For example, they 'almost completely' efface allegations of abuse, particularly of sexual abuse (377). The chapter quotes from the director of education in British Columbia, who admitted in 1990 that the files are compromised by this denial: 'The sad thing is we did not know it [sexual abuse] was occurring. Students were too reticent to come forward. And it now appears that school staff likely did not know, and if they did, the morality of the day dictated that they, too, remain silent. DIAND [Department of Indian Affairs and Northern Development] staff have no record or recollection of reports – either verbal or written' (377). The use of euphemisms and of vague language is reflective of the double-bind of the chapter: though DIAND has 'no record or recollection of reports' of sexual abuse, the analysis relies on these sources. At the same time, the chapter leaves aside the testimony delivered at the RCAP public hearings, testimony that unambiguously describes the abuse that survivors witnessed or experienced.

In contrast to 'Residential Schools,' the chapter entitled 'Lessons from the Hearings' in Volume Two (*Restructuring* 436-48) is made up almost entirely of quotations from the community hearings; however, the extent to which the testimony echoes a predetermined argument also becomes evident. Most of the quotations demonstrate the importance of territory and nation for Aboriginal peoples. In a similar manner to the presentation of Dene, Inuit, and Métis voices in Berger's *Northern Frontier, Northern Homeland*, long citations from the community hearings are presented one after the other, as if they 'speak for themselves.' In striking contrast to the rest of the report, little analysis and few intrusive interpretive frames are used.

The emphasis on land and territory dovetails with the report's central vision of moving from an era of assimilation to one of Aboriginal nationalism, the culmination of the narrative of improvement that the commissioners wish to install. In *People to People*, the commissioners state the importance they attribute to the development of Aboriginal nationalism:

> The main policy direction, pursued for more than 150 years, has been wrong ... Canadians need to understand that *Aboriginal peoples are nations,*

that is, they are political and cultural groups with values and lifeways distinct from those of other Canadians ... To this day, Aboriginal people's sense of confidence and well-being as individuals remains tied to the strength of their nations. Only as members of restored nations can they reach their potential in the twenty-first century. (Canada, *People to People* x-xi, emphasis in original)

The commissioners proposed that sixty to eighty First Nations (made up of over 1,000 Aboriginal communities) would become united by means of constitutionally entrenched treaties. Hundreds of recommendations flow from the report's central vision of self-government, relating to the resolution of land claims, the establishment of modern treaties, and the creation of an Aboriginal order of government to work alongside provincial and federal governments. New legislation, such as an *Aboriginal Nation Recognition and Government Act*, an *Aboriginal Treaties Implementation Act*, and an *Aboriginal Parliament Act*, would entrench nation-to-nation relations (Cassidy, 'The Final Report' 4).

There is no doubt that self-government is a key tool in the assertion and protection of Aboriginal rights. As Fred Kelly argues, reconciliation can take place only within a context of just self-government agreements, the honouring of treaties, and the timely processing of land claims (22-23). However, the report's at-times unqualified endorsement of self-government creates some instances of editorial intervention that reveal the commissioners' selective hearing at the public consultation sessions. Because RCAP consistently prioritizes national-level politics over community politics, with many of the 440 recommendations geared towards creating or transforming national-level institutional structures, testimony from non-elected community members, especially those critical of self-government, did not play as significant a role in the report (Kulchyski, *Like the Sound* 236). Furthermore, for Cairns, the organizing framework of RCAP reveals a preference for landed Aboriginal nations over urban populations: 'By concentrating on the landed nation, and denigrating the urban experience, the commission risked placing itself on the wrong side of history,' since demographics show that urban Native communities are growing more quickly than rural and on-reserve communities (130). According to Cairns, a more 'balanced support for both routes to the future would have better reflected emerging realities' (131).

While critique is subdued in the thousand-page dissertation on self-government that makes up Volume Two, *Restructuring the Relationship*, many Aboriginal women spoke critically about self-government during the hearings. However, their opinions were placed in the chapter 'Women's Perspectives' in Volume Four, *Perspectives and Realities*. Excerpts from the community hearings in this chapter reveal women's concerns about self-government in the context of band council politics, accountability, sexual discrimination, and the problems women encountered when relocating to reserves following the Bill C-31 reinstatements in 1985.[10] Although officially recognized by Bill C-31, some women have reported that the amendment has created divisions between individuals and fostered discrimination. For example, women like Florence Boucher (below) had difficulty in securing housing and community services when they were finally allowed to move back to the reserve:

> I can't have a home on the reserve ... The reserves at present could possibly house us, the Bill C-31 minority people, but refuse to ... I will probably have a resting place when the time comes, but why should I accept to be buried on reserve land after I die, when I could also enjoy sharing all the services that are being kept away from me today ... [The problem is] coming from ... Chief and Council. I know they are really against Bill C-31s. They have, I guess, no use for [us]. (Florence Boucher, Lac La Biche, Alberta, 9 June 1992. Qtd. in Canada, *Perspectives* 43; ellipses in original)

Also in 'Women's Perspectives,' the commission cites Lynne Brooks, director of Status of Women Council of the Northwest Territories, who asks, 'Why do women feel such ambivalence towards the idea of self-government? The answer is clear to women ... We have to change our priorities. We must have personal and community healing' (*Perspectives* 76; ellipsis in original). This text-bite clearly reinforces the report's narrative of 'healing' and hope for a brighter future. It cuts out the more controversial statements in Brooks's testimony. For example, in the next sentence, in the transcript of the hearing in Yellowknife on 7 December 1992, Brooks states: 'A mere transfer of power will change nothing but the faces of leadership.' Brooks then elaborates her critique of what she calls a 'male-dominated Aboriginal structure' of leadership (which, she states, is the result of a 'male-dominated European structure'). She relates a number of stories that illustrate the difficulties faced by women who become involved in band and territorial politics. Among other anecdotes, Brooks tells a story of a woman who worked on the campaign for Ethel Blondin, the first Aboriginal (Dene) woman to be elected to the Parliament of

Canada. The husband of this woman vehemently opposed her involvement in politics: 'She was pregnant and the only earning member of her family. Throughout the campaign, she was repeatedly beaten by her husband for daring to be involved in politics and for daring to support a woman in politics. She told no one until long after the campaign. She hid her bruises and she refused to give up. How can we expect women to get involved under such circumstances? How many men would involve themselves in politics if they had to pay such a price?'[11] The placement of Brooks's truncated testimony in 'Women's Perspectives' underscores her point that women's criticisms are not fully taken into account in electoral politics, just as they are somewhat marginalized in RCAP's discussion of self-government.

Mohawk legal scholar Patricia Monture-Angus also questions the commissioners' assumption that the benefits of nation-to-nation relations will necessarily 'trickle down' to the community level. Monture-Angus is concerned with how self-government (as currently implemented in Canada) reinforces social hierarchies *within* Aboriginal communities (on the basis of gender or class, for example). For Monture-Angus, the report's version of self-government risks reinforcing colonial structures of the Canadian nation-state, conferring benefits upon an elite, landed class dissociated from the majority of Aboriginal people. She argues that self-government risks preserving colonial relations: 'Colonialism is no longer a linear, vertical relationship – colonizer does to colonized – it is a horizontal and entangled relationship (like a spider web). Now, sometimes the colonized turn the colonial skills and images they learned against others who are less powerful in their communities, thus mimicking their oppressors' (11). Ultimately Monture-Angus rejects the term 'self-government' altogether: 'I now understand that both self-government and self-determination have become too elitist and too political in the worst sense of the word to assist me in thinking myself out of my oppression' (11). Instead she argues for what she considers a much larger, yet at the same time more intensely personal idea – independence. Based on her reading of Paulo Freire, she argues that 'independence' best reflects her notion of 'self-determination' as a way of 'deciding if and when you are living responsibly. Self-determination is principally ... about our relationships' (8). One of her aims is to 'create or reclaim relations of connection' (11):

> Maintaining good relationships with your family, clan and nation, but the rest of the living world as well (by which I mean the environment

and all things around us), means that you are fulfilling one of your basic responsibilities as a human being. It is this web (or the natural laws) that is the relationship that has been devastated by colonialism. (9)

Her key terms – relationships, responsibility, relations of connection – establish the importance of the listener responding to and accepting a sense of responsibility for what he or she hears. By prioritizing testimony in the dynamic relationship between speaker and listener, a politics of reconciliation may emerge.

Gillian Whitlock, in her analysis of the use of testimony in *Bringing Them Home*, offers an alternative conceptualization of reconciliation to that of progress. Drawing on studies of testimony in Holocaust-related research,[12] Whitlock stresses that the 'second person', who is fundamental to the testimonial contract, becomes the witness, thereby affirming the experience and trauma of the first person (200). While acknowledging that the speaker who voices trauma undergoes a transformative process, Whitlock explains that her interest is in 'how the testimonies actively elicit that "implication"' of non-indigenous Australians, who are 'called upon to be witnesses of the self as well as witnesses to the trauma of stolen children' (199). If non-Indigenous audience members tune in to their own reactions as witnesses and acknowledge historical responsibility for their privileges, then perhaps a process of reconciliation can begin. For Whitlock, then, 'testimony is at the heart of this struggle' for reconciliation (201).

Testimony from the transcribed community hearings has played and will continue to play a vital role in strengthening community networks among Aboriginal groups. To this day community workers, land claims negotiators, politicians, and activists continue to use the arguments in the report as levers to initiate change and make demands upon governments. Most importantly, RCAP was successful in bringing about an historically significant paradigm shift from 'Canadian Indian policy' to 'First Nations relations in Canada' (Posluns 86), a change that enacts a dynamic and relational conceptualization of Aboriginal-settler history. For Marlene Brant Castellano, former co-director of research for the commission and Mohawk educator, this shift to a relational understanding of history also signals a philosophical shift towards Aboriginal epistemologies: 'the genius of the report is that it states clearly and consistently that "everything's related" thereby reflecting an understanding basic to Aboriginal systems of knowledge' (2). It is precisely this relationality that I am interested in exploring, because it invites the 'second person' to take responsibility for the past in discourses of reconciliation. The *process* of RCAP remains important, visionary, ambitious, and far-reaching, especially in light of the formative role the commission played as a generating force in telling, recording, and publishing community stories.

The process of testifying at the community hearings has inspired further textual projects. Even though Monture-Angus 'experienced the Commission as a non-Aboriginal space' (11), she claims that the commission instigated her to publish her own vision of 'First Nations' independence' (as opposed to self-government) in *Journeying Forward: Dreaming First Nations' Independence* (1999): 'This book was first ... completed as a discussion paper for the Royal Commission on Aboriginal People[s]. It has evolved considerably since then' (11). Other publications have similarly emerged from the RCAP hearings. Nancy Wachowich, author-editor of the told-to narrative *Saqiyuq: Stories from the Lives of Three Inuit Women* (1999), acknowledges that '[t]he original impetus for this project came from the Royal Commission on Aboriginal Peoples' (ix). RCAP's request to the Innu First Nation for a community-based research project was part of the impulsion for *Gathering Voices: Finding Strength to Help Our Children* (1995), a collective life history that documents the Innu First Nations' People's Inquiry into the deaths of six children in a house fire in 1992 (Innu Nation et al. 139). Finally, *Night Spirits: The Story of the Relocation of the Sayisi Dene* (1997), discussed in detail below, was compiled partly in response to Virginia Petch's report for the commission (Bussidor and Bilgen-Reinart xxi). The goal of these book projects is to repackage, re-frame, and reissue testimony from the community hearings and alter the relations of authority that RCAP had established. Testimony, because it resists the through-line of a singular narrative, offers a starting point to imagine a model of reconciliation that evades the assimilative embrace of a coerced amnesia. Yet testimony, no matter how powerful or articulate, can only be conveyed or transmitted within the constraints of its framing devices. The possibilities of reconciliation depend upon how and why testimony is represented, and through what kinds of explanatory frames.

### *E'thzil:* Mistranslation and Nontranslation in *Night Spirits*

The collective testimonial life story *Night Spirits,* co-authored by Ila Bussidor and Üstün Bilgen-Reinart and narrated by thirteen other Sayisi Dene spokespeople, initiates a shift in both publication and reception of First Nations told-to life narratives in the 1990s. *Night Spirits* is an example of the 'collective life history,' which 'moves beyond the sense of a *dually authored* text to a *multiply articulated* text' (Boyce Davies 4, emphasis in original): 'These narratives can be read as individual stories ... or they can be read collectively as one story refracted through multiple lives, lives that share a common experience' (4). A collective life history defies linear arrangement and chronology, interweaving stories as recurring and spiralling fragments. Whereas the dually authored life story was the dominant mode of told-to narratives in the 1970s and early 1980s,[13] publications in the 1990s included greater numbers of collectively produced Aboriginal life stories.[14] In these latter texts, multiple recorders and narrators exchange places, thereby limiting the editorial control of the recorder, as well as transforming the role of the listener. In *Night Spirits*, the listener or 'second person' plays a role in the transformative relations that testimony potentially engenders; however, mistranslation or nontranslation threatens to disrupt communication. The impossible necessity[15] of testifying and witnessing pull the project in multiple directions, creating a layered, complex text. *Night Spirits*, a formally innovative, collective life story, comments self-reflexively upon the fraught process of entextualization and on the difficulty of reaching a 'you' who can respond to the stories.

The struggle to get a response from the listener drives the explicitly politicized agenda of *Night Spirits*. The story begins in 1956, when the federal government deemed it necessary to relocate the Sayisi Dene First Nation from its vast ancestral territories in northern Manitoba to the town of Churchill, about two hundred kilometres away. The ostensible reason was to offer better social services to the community; however, relocations from the 1950s, 1960s, and 1970s should be understood as part of a broader policy of assimilation, as RCAP's report explains (Canada, *Looking Forward* 251ff). Arriving on the shores of Hudson's Bay at the approach of winter without adequate housing or other supplies, and far from their hunting grounds, the Sayisi Dene people struggled to survive near-impossible conditions. Three years later, they were relocated to Camp-10, a settlement beside a large cemetery on the outskirts of Churchill; and in 1967, they were moved again to Dene Village, a further ten kilometres outside of town. In 1973, the people relocated themselves to Tadoule Lake, about two hundred and fifty kilometres west of Churchill, where they continue to live today.

Though Sayisi Dene representatives have told and retold the story of the relocations many times to government officials, settlement managers, researchers, social workers, and journalists, their presentations have not resulted in a clear acknowledgement of governmental responsibility for the loss of virtually an entire generation from 1956 to 1977. In this period, over three-quarters of the 117 deaths, which represented one-third of the community, were classified as 'violent', resulting from the abysmal living conditions in each of the Churchill camps (Bussidor and Bilgen-Reinart 146-47). Reams of letters, interviews, transcripts from public hearings, and sociological studies document the people's forty-year protest. From 1956 onwards, community leaders repeatedly wrote to the Department of Indian Affairs, demanding more suitable spaces for living than the shores of Hudson Bay, Camp-10, or Dene Village (72). The bibliography shows that *Night Spirits* is closely tied to the people's political struggles for social change. *Night Spirits* has provided ammunition in their ongoing battles with the federal government. These include the demand for compensation for the relocation;[16] territorial disputes with the borders of Nunavut;[17] a self-government agreement;[18] and land claims negotiations.[19]

Virginia Petch's report for the commission, 'The Relocation of the Sayisi Dene of Tadoule Lake,' inspired Ila Bussidor to collect, transcribe, and translate fuller accounts of her community's relocation. Petch, an independent researcher and anthropologist who has worked with the Sayisi Dene people and other groups in northern Manitoba since 1985, based her report primarily upon historical records, such as memos and letters from the Hudson's Bay Company and the Department of Indian Affairs. Though she conducted personal interviews of community members from 1990 to 1994, in an effort to protect the privacy of those she interviewed, she does not reproduce those conversations. Instead she paraphrases the community members' life stories, including what could be Bussidor's life story,[20] reporting that this band member 'believes that in order to begin the healing process she must tell her story and many others must follow suit' (Petch, Section 5.0).

In 1993, Bussidor appeared before the RCAP public hearings in Thompson, Manitoba, demanding a special community hearing at Tadoule Lake. For Bussidor, it is imperative for the commissioners to hear the story of the relocation from the people themselves:

> My name is Ila Bussidor, a former Chief of the Sayisi Dene First Nation ... My people were moved by the federal government from Little Duck Lake to Churchill in 1956. This relocation destroyed our independence and ruined our way of life. After fifteen years of neglect and despair in Churchill, we could begin to count the dead. More than one hundred of my people, one-third of our population, died in the Churchill Camps

because of this unplanned, misdirected government action. This didn't happen a thousand miles from here, or a hundred years ago ... It happened to my people, my family, thirty to thirty-five years ago. It seems like only yesterday, and it affects us still today ...

The Sayisi Dene are requesting the Royal Commission to hold a public hearing in Tadoule Lake. You are the people who will be reporting to the government. It is crucial that you hear first hand from the people who hold that story, a story not documented, but a living memory. There are no words to describe that urgency of this request on behalf of the five surviving elders, who personally witnessed the first Treaty payments. (Bussidor, 'Presentation')

Bussidor's insistence that the commissioners come to Tadoule Lake shows the need for re-telling stories independently of Petch's report. This is not to say that Petch's report inaccurately or inappropriately represented the Sayisi Dene people's stories. Rather, Bussidor's direct address to the commissioners, using the pronoun 'you,' asserts the need for the commissioners to engage more directly as witnesses in affirming the testimonies of the community. Bussidor's statement also reflects the importance she places on the collective nature of the project. It is not enough to report second hand the stories of the aftermath of the relocation; it is urgent for each member of the community to relay his or her own experiences. Bussidor further underlines this urgency as time is running out for the older survivors of the relocation. For Bussidor, a public hearing at Tadoule Lake would finally open up a space in which her community could challenge the Canadian government's benign interpretation of the relocation. A community hearing would also provide a much-needed forum for individuals to begin acknowledging their experiences, which had remained silenced for decades.

For Bussidor, telling the story of her people through the third-person voice of a formal report cannot initiate the kind of change that occurs in the process of making a collective life history. Bussidor tells the reader in meticulous detail the process of researching, transcribing, translating, and editing community members' stories. Many of the thirteen narrators are personally connected to Ila Bussidor, including her sisters, aunts, grandmother, cousins, and husband. The linked genealogy of the narrators provides a model for the web-like, nonhierarchical structure of the text. In 1990, Bussidor asked Bilgen-Reinart, a journalist and former broadcaster with the Canadian Broadcasting Corporation (CBC), to help her collect her community's testimonial life narratives; and from October 1994 to February 1996, Bussidor and Bilgen-Reinart conducted interviews. As a community-based project of remembering, *Night Spirits* challenges the history of told-to narratives in which a non-Aboriginal writer transcribes the words of an Aboriginal teller. Instead, Sayisi Dene community members share the responsibilities of writing, telling, recording, translating, and editing. Much of the text is made up of the narrators' recollections of the past. Betsy Anderson, an elder and Bussidor's grandmother, establishes the interpretive frame of the book in her role as principal narrator of the first two chapters. In these opening chapters, she provides a short autobiographical sketch, a history of the Sayisi Dene nation, and a series of legends. Anderson's stories underpin the rest of the text, providing a cultural framework for the community stories that follow.

A sense of political urgency permeates *Night Spirits*. 'Every story is a tool we can use if we want to. That is what our elders say,' Bussidor writes (Bussidor and Bilgen-Reinart 8). The transformative processes of telling, listening, translating, and transcribing stories are as important as the stories themselves in this text. Underlining this notion of stories as tools for political change is the narrators' frequent address to 'you': the listener/reader is put in the hot seat. The opening lines of Bussidor's chapter 'My Story' establish Bussidor's direct address to her audience: 'This is the story of my family and my people. I want to share the memories and the traumas of my childhood with you' (3). Similarly, in her presentation to the RCAP community hearings in Thompson, Bussidor highlights the lack of reciprocity in the I/You relationships of her childhood in the Churchill camps. Using the public hearings as an opportunity to challenge her listeners' passivity, Bussidor states:

> In the classrooms of the schools, we faced unimaginable racism and discrimination, in our tattered clothes, dirty faces and unkempt hair. No one saw the terror in our eyes, or knew of the horrors we experienced at home, after school, the abuse, physical, mental, emotional and sexual. Many of us relied on the trash cans behind the stores and hotels for food. (Canada, *Looking Forward* 436-37)

Bussidor is confronting Churchill's non-Sayisi Dene society – including White, Inuit, Métis, and Cree communities – with their silent denial in the face of suffering. Like Bussidor, many of the narrators in *Night Spirits* remember visiting the town dump to look for food. The frequent references in the text to the city's garbage underline the narrators' repeated point that what 'you' threw out, 'we' were forced to consume for survival.

The strategic address of the 'you' in *Night Spirits* is something that Bussidor's collaborator, Bilgen-Reinart, struggles to come to terms with. Like Hugh Brody, she expresses ambivalence about her role as 'second person' and the unwitting effects of her intervention. When Bussidor asked her to participate in the project, Bilgen-Reinart expressed her anxiety about the impending responsibility:

> My first impulse was to pull back. I knew some of the heart-breaking injuries my friend and her people had suffered. But to enter their experience, to re-live those nightmares with Ila, and to navigate a joint project with her, seemed perilous. (Bussidor and Bilgen-Reinart xiv)

Bilgen-Reinart's initial reluctance to participate in the project is reflective of her fear of becoming the witness – a position that would in turn necessitate a reckoning with her own self. Dori Laub, co-founder of the Video Archive for Holocaust Testimonies at Yale, comments on the necessity for the witness to engage with the teller's story: 'as interviewer I am present as someone who actually participates in the reliving and reexperiencing of the event. I also become part of the struggle to go beyond the event and not be submerged and lost in it' (Laub 76). To compensate for her feelings of discomfort, especially in the early stages of the project, Bilgen-Reinart suggests that her own participation was minimal, focusing instead on the activities of her co-author:

> We put our tape recorder on the little table beside the bed, and Ila began the interview [of Betsy Anderson, her grandmother]. They spoke in Dene ... Granny Betsy talked about what she had lived, what she had seen, what she had lost ...
>
> The next day, and the day after, and the day after that, it was Ila who did the talking into the tape recorder. For hours and hours, she re-lived the years in Churchill. We had closeted ourselves in the one-room ATCO trailer that served as the resource classroom of the local school. Ila's older sister Sarah Cheekie came into that trailer too, eager to tell her story. (xiv) [ ...]

> By the end of that first week of interviewing, Ila was exhausted. She told me she had felt depressed after I left because we had re-awakened too many painful memories. But she continued to do interviews in Dene. She interviewed the elders, she taped her older sister and brothers, and she transcribed and translated those interviews. (Bussidor and Bilgen-Reinart xvi)

Bilgen-Reinart describes the effects on Bussidor of the draining work of memorializing losses – losses at once national, communal, familial, and personal – before she describes her own role and personal reactions. However, Bilgen-Reinart's self-construction as a passive listener and observer is not maintained throughout the project. Her participation as listener soon forces her to take a more active role.

When the collaborators visit Dene Village, where the Sayisi Dene people were moved for a second time in 1967, and where Bussidor's parents died in a house fire, Bilgen-Reinart is obliged to accept her role as witness. Dene Village is a treeless site on the outskirts of Churchill, with no direct access to water. Bilgen-Reinart had agreed to accompany Bussidor, along with other community members, on their first return trip to Dene Village in two decades, observing, 'Ila dreaded the trip. She was tense and edgy as we made our travel arrangements. "I know I have unfinished business there," she told me' (xvi). Upon reaching Dene Village, Bussidor does not leave the truck, and Bilgen-Reinart is compelled to walk around the abandoned site alone:

> I crossed the lane to get to the remains of the home of Ila's parents, Artie and Suzanna Cheekie: a square-shaped cement foundation just like the others ... As I quietly gazed around the foundation, I saw something that made me freeze: a piece of charred beam still attached to the cement, its black stubby end sticking out of the snow – the only evidence of the fire that had destroyed the house ... I heard moans, screams, whispers, and a howling wind. In a January blizzard, were there children huddling inside these concrete walls? (xxviii)

The passage could be read as a meditation on the paradoxical role of the witness. A story without a witness is virtually incommunicable: it is little more than charred remains, a burnt-out shell, 'moans, screams, whispers, and a howling wind.' It is the witness's responsibility to affirm the existence of the fugitive pieces. Dori Laub's insights on the role of the listener in the transmission of trauma are useful here: 'the interviewer-listener takes on the responsibility for bearing witness that previously the narrator felt he [sic] bore alone. It is the encounter and the coming together between the survivor and the listener, which makes possible something like a repossession of the act of witnessing. This joint responsibility is the source of the reemerging truth' (Laub 85). This 'joint responsibility' provides a provisional definition of reconciliation based on the interactive process of testimony.

However, as much as the acceptance of this 'joint responsibility' of the teller and listener is transformative, Laub insists that massive psychic trauma 'precludes its registration' (qtd. in Caruth 5). Put another way, Cathy Caruth speaks of 'a peculiar paradox: that in trauma the greatest confrontation with reality may also occur as an absolute numbing to it' (Caruth 5). The charred beam that makes Bilgen-Reinart 'freeze' in her tracks is a symbol of the impossible necessity of witnessing trauma. Standing alone in this desolate place, Bilgen-Reinart becomes aware of her own stake in witnessing this story. As Caruth reminds us, witnessing an event occurs only 'at the cost of witnessing oneself' (10). In acknowledging the dangers of trauma's contagion, of the 'traumatization of those who listen' (10), Bilgen-Reinart simultaneously must acknowledge her own complicity in perpetuating (at least up until that point) the silence that surrounds the relocation. This acknowledgement of the high investment and risk of witnessing is the first step in taking responsibility for history's violence, which in turn provides the ground upon which a politics of reconciliation may be built.

Still, it is not easy for Bilgen-Reinart to maintain this heightened and dangerous state of awareness, and she continues to encourage the Sayisi Dene people to tell their own stories with as little of her own intervention as possible. Bussidor, meanwhile, insists that Bilgen-Reinart remain active and engaged as a listener. Bussidor's and Bilgen-Reinart's differing approaches to collaboration are evidence of Laub's understanding that 'the process of testimony [is], essentially, a ceaseless struggle' (Laub 75).

While Bilgen-Reinart emphasizes the importance of the victims directly confronting and describing their trauma, Bussidor is more interested in reconstructing a community-based history that does not revolve exclusively around the relocations. Bilgen-Reinart's stress on the importance of facing the past reveals her assumptions about how to deal with traumatic experiences. She emphasizes the importance of speaking the trauma as a way to advance towards healing: 'Before healing can begin, the injury has to be described. This is a dark story. We're telling it in hope' (Bussidor and Bilgen-Reinart xix). Her introduction describes Bussidor's exhaustion, depression, fear, and pain in making *Night Spirits*, reflecting her understanding of the purpose of the life story project: to retell the story of loss. In contrast, Bussidor speaks of an even more distant past, one she remembers as comforting, loving, and safe. Without shying away from the harrowing details of her past, Bussidor collects and recollects memories of another time that she says she wishes to 're-live':

> I want to tell you about the loving memories of my mother and my father before they were destroyed by what we call 'fire-water' in my native tongue, Sayisi Dene. I want to go back to when I was a little girl and relive the time when my father would come home from his trap line and lift me up in his big, strong arms, kiss me, and swing me up in the air. I want to feel again my mother's tenderness as she cared for me and my brothers and sisters. I want to feel her arms around me as she rocked me back and forth, softly singing a lullaby in Dene. I felt safe, very loved, and protected then. (3)

For Bilgen-Reinart, the purpose of remembering the past is to face up to the violence of settler history; for Bussidor, the work of memory reconnects her to her parents and helps her imagine another life that might have been. In other words, she is attempting to install a Sayisi Dene–centred account that is not determined by her community's colonial experiences.

Yet the work of the testimonial can never be completed. Despite Bussidor's careful work of memorialization, her parents, Suzanna and Artie Cheekie, who died in the house fire in 1972 in Dene Village, remain a ghostly absence that haunts *Night Spirits*. They can only be 'heard' through their creased photographs or through their voices as 'night spirits.' The text's epigraph connects Suzanna Cheekie with the night spirits that hear the smallest whisper but whose utterances cannot be understood: 'When I was a little girl, every night at bedtime, my mom ... would tuck us in and tell us we had to be quiet or *e'thzil* would hear us. The word *e'thzil* means "night spirits." Night spirits are the spirits of dead people' (n.p.).

The 'night spirits' are symbols of what Bussidor and Bilgen-Reinart fail to collect, or what the narrators cannot or will not recollect in the testimonial life story project. Though the collective testimonial enables the co-authors to honour both the memory of the dead and the survivors of the Churchill camps, they are aware of the limitations of the genre. The complex interactions between interviewer and witness create gaps in the story that cannot be bridged easily. To some extent, *e'thzil* stands for the unrepresentability of the trauma of the relocation. In Laub's words: 'There are never enough words or the right words, there is never enough time or the right time, and never enough listening or the right listening to articulate the story that cannot be fully captured in thought, memory and speech' (Laub 77). As spectres that are both there and not there, *e'thzil* powerfully suggest the risk involved in the exchange that underlies acts of testifying and witnessing trauma; the substitution of roles has unpredictable and potentially explosive effects.

*E'thzil* highlight not only the impossible necessity of witnessing trauma but also the difficulties of translation, mistranslation, and nontranslation in imperial-colonial contexts. The unintelligibility of these spirits is symbolic of the cultural and linguistic misunderstandings that caused the forced relocations in the first place. According to the narrators of *Night Spirits*, failure of communication between cultural groups led directly to the initial relocation of the Sayisi Dene community in 1956. This breakdown in exchange is not an isolated historical event; a series of misunderstandings have repeated themselves over the period of contact. Mistranslation or nontranslation in the history of the relationship between the Sayisi Dene people and the Canadian government haunts the text. It is within a context of historical miscommunication that Bussidor becomes both a testifier and a witness to her community's stories.

The story of mistranslation or nontranslation begins with the Sayisi Dene First Nation signing an adhesion to Treaty Five in 1910, for which negotiations carried on no longer than a few hours (Bussidor and Bilgen-Reinart 26). Betsy Anderson is one of the few who remembers the signing of the treaty. Her comments indicate that the lack of translation was a deliberate strategy to swindle land from the Sayisi Dene people: 'I remember that the treaty was signed without proper translation. The Dene didn't fully understand what was in it. We just assumed it was a peace treaty ... If we had been told that we were signing away our land for the amount of five dollars a person, there was no way our people would have agreed' (27). The treaty was signed with three X's.

The process of relocating the people to the rocky shores of Hudson's Bay near Churchill also exemplifies the government's will to make unilateral decisions without consultation. In July 1956, a couple of months before the relocation, the supervisor of Indian affairs for the region, R.D. Ragan, visited the 'Duck Lake Band' to discuss the intended move. 'After a very full discussion it was unanimously and amicably agreed by the Duck Lake Band still at this Post that they would move to the mouth of the North River,' Ragan wrote in a departmental memo (qtd. 45). However, as Bussidor and Bilgen-Reinart point out, the Dene spoke no English, and Ragan and his officials spoke no Dene: 'In view of the immense communication problems faced by both sides, what Ragan meant by a "full discussion" is anyone's guess' (45).

With a symptomatic lack of cultural sensitivity to Sayisi Dene beliefs, in 1959, the Department of Indian Affairs relocated the community again, this time to Camp-10, a site adjacent to the Churchill cemetery. Eva Anderson, a Dene elder who lived in Duck Lake and in the Churchill camps, recalls:

> It was very disturbing to our people because we were now to live a few steps away from mass burial grounds. If our people were in charge and if someone had listened to our voices, a different site may have been selected instead of next to a graveyard. Our people the Sayisi Dene had always respected the spirits of the dead. A burial ground is a sacred place, not to be disturbed, it's a resting place for our relatives who are gone to the spirit world. The white people (Indian Affairs, the government people), who made the decisions for our people, did not acknowledge our culture and traditions. Everything about our ways as a people was overlooked right from the beginning. That is why they placed us right in the middle of a burial ground to live for the next decade. (61)

Like Bussidor, Eva Anderson implies a connection between ghosts and the failure of communication. Ghosts, as entities that exist ambiguously at the threshold of death and life, of memory and forgetting, become the governing metaphor of the text to represent the continual reinscription of miscommunication in the Sayisi Dene First Nation's relationship with the Canadian State.

The story of how many Sayisi Dene children were removed from their families and communities for either residential schools or foster care in the 1960s and 1970s follows the same pattern of lack of communication and mistranslation. Mary Yassie describes how Children's Aid apprehended her sister's two children:

> One day someone from the Children's Aid came over to our house and made my parents [the children's grandparents] sign forms without letting

them know what they were signing. They were home alone and no one was there to translate for them. They were tricked into signing adoption forms for their two small grandchildren. One day they came and took those two children away and we have never seen them to this day. We don't know what happened to them. If my parents had a translator they would never have signed forms like that. (104)

Four of the main narrators of *Night Spirits* – Mary Yassie, Eva Anderson, Betsy Anderson, and Ila Bussidor – suggest that a lack of translation was one of the main causes of the compounding community tragedies. What is especially chilling about the stories of abducting Sayisi Dene children for residential school and foster care is the extent to which Canadian social institutions – hospitals, schools, government departments, correctional services – worked in tandem to facilitate the children's removal. Several stories describe children being sent to residential schools directly from hospital visits. Caroline Yassie states: 'in 1951, when I was ten years old, I was sent out to a hospital to get treatment for tuberculosis. From the hospital, government people sent me to residential school. The next time I saw my parents, I was sixteen years old' (36). Similarly Sarah Cheekie, who sustained a near fatal injury after trying to break into a pawnshop, never returned from the hospital following her treatment; she was sent directly to residential school (81). Both sisters were apprehended in a secret manner. The denial, silence, and miscommunication that characterize the legacy of the relocations also affect the accounts of those community members who attended residential schools, suggesting the high cost of trauma and its potential for repetition.

The fearsome potential for repeating traumas is an issue that the narrators of *Night Spirits* often discuss. In 1973, the Sayisi Dene people chose a new site on Tadoule Lake to relocate themselves. With help from Phil Dickman, a community worker in Churchill, as well as from Ronnie John, a hunter who had remained on Sayisi Dene territory at the time of the first relocation, the majority of the community members left Dene Village for good. The community carried out this relocation without the support of the Department of Indian Affairs and Northern Development, which claimed – with a total lack of acknowledgement of the effects of its own policies – that too much money had already been spent on relocating the Sayisi Dene people (126). Although this self-relocation is an extraordinary success story, demonstrating the resilience of the Sayisi Dene people, it has not laid *e'thzil* to rest. The narrators speak candidly about the social challenges their new community continues to struggle with, including alcohol and drug abuse and family violence. Many describe the extent to which their suffering continues to the present day. Ila Bussidor says: 'The pain from the relocation stays with us, no matter how hard we try to go forward. The damage is something we may never repair – as is evident in my community today. I am left with scars that will remain with me for the rest of my life, just like everyone who lived through and survived that nightmare' (5).

In *Almost Home: A Sayisi Dene Journey* (2003), a documentary film on the current challenges facing the Tadoule Lake community, Sayisi Dene interviewees echo Bussidor's sentiments as they struggle to release themselves from the ghosts of Dene Village.[21] As if to visually represent the haunting presence of the past for the Sayisi Dene people, *Almost Home* intersperses footage from Dene Village in 1971 with more recent coverage. A notable scene in the film (echoing an important episode in *Night Spirits*) shows Bussidor visiting the remains of her parents' burned home in Dene Village. She comments: 'Every time I go to Churchill, and it's not very often, I've always gone to Dene Village. And I don't know what draws me back there because there's really nothing there except the cement foundations and the memories of my parents ... I always want to go there and pay my respects to them in the very spot that they died.' During this visit, Bussidor is accompanied by her nephew, Dan Clarke, now a young adult and living in the Toronto area, who was given up for adoption by Bussidor's sister when he was a baby. Instead of remaining in the truck as she did the first time she returned to Dene Village with Bilgen-Reinart, Bussidor acts as a guide for her nephew. She stands with one hand on the concrete foundation and one hand on Dan, who is silently weeping. Bussidor has taken on the role of witness, offering Dan solace by listening to his story.

The candour with which the narrators of *Night Spirits* as well as the interviewees of *Almost Home* speak of their continued struggle with social problems and psychic trauma contrasts with the representation of the self-relocation in RCAP's report. While the report acknowledges that 'the Commission's interviews with residents of Tadoule Lake reveal that social and economic problems have not disappeared' (Canada, *Looking Forward* 437), it reinforces a narrative of progress from 1956 to 1995, with the securing of a self-government agreement for the Sayisi Dene (Bussidor and Bilgen-Reinart xii). The report's advancement of self-government as a cure-all is not entirely appropriate for the Sayisi Dene people, who, despite their achieving of self-government and their signing of a land claims agreement, have continued to dispute the Nunavut border. In *Almost Home*, we learn of Bussidor's continued efforts to resolve the land rights issue, as she travels to Winnipeg to attend the Assembly of Manitoba Chiefs' General Assembly to discuss the disputed territory. While the commissioners acknowledge that the Sayisi Dene people's 'traditional lands have been included within the boundaries of Nunavut,' an act of land appropriation that 'adds to the Sayisi Dene's sense of grievance' (Canada, *Looking Forward* 438), the report's support of self-government without critical distinction impedes its ability to acknowledge the complexities of competing claims. Thus the historical pattern of non-communication between the Sayisi Dene First Nation and the federal government continues with the publication of RCAP's report, despite the commissioners' recognition of past wrongs and their strong condemnation of the relocation.

As a formally innovative collective life history, *Night Spirits* attempts to place the process of testimony back in the centre of the story of the relocation. The diffuse structure of the text enables the co-authors to share author-ity among the narrators, writers, translators, and editors. Instead of translating community stories into third-person accounts or smoothing over the divergent voices into coherent recommendations, as in RCAP's report, *Night Spirits* highlights the gaps and silences that resist sublimation in testimonial projects. *E'thzil* haunt the text, troubling relations of communication and confronting readers with their own silent complicity in the face of tragedy and suffering. The emphasis in *Night Spirits* is on the transformative effects of researching, transcribing, translating, and editing community members' stories. Indeed, just as the process that RCAP enacted is arguably more effective than the report itself in shifting Aboriginal relations in Canada, the process of compiling *Night Spirits*, for the Sayisi Dene participants, became the initiator of a larger movement for social justice and recovery.

The practice of making a collective life history involves a simultaneous process of witnessing another's suffering and acknowledging one's own stake in this act of witnessing. Reconciliation is dependent upon the listener coming to terms with her own risk, privilege, and complicity in the act of witnessing. The impossible necessity of witnessing is related to the search for an active conceptualization of reconciliation. Although discourses of reconciliation can be deployed cynically by nation-states to quell social unrest and silence dissent, an alternative politics of reconciliation may spring from within a state-sanctioned structure such as a royal commission, particularly if such an institution recognizes the role of community stories and the importance of responding to them. Testimony, irreducibly plural, offers the possibility of reconciliation through a politics of difference. For some Sayisi Dene community members, participation in the RCAP public hearings at Tadoule Lake broke a forty-year silence about the tragic effects of the relocations; likewise, for some readers, *Night Spirits* offers a starting point to respond to a history that they themselves ignominiously have benefited from. In studying the role of the 'second person,' we might contribute to and advance an alternative mode of reconciliation and take the first step in transforming historical consciousness – for speakers and listeners, victims and perpetrators, insiders and outsiders.

# 'What the Map Cuts Up, the Story Cuts Across'
## Translating Oral Traditions and Aboriginal Land Title

# 5

> Well, for most of the time when I was watching, law was running quite free of the economy, doing its errands, defending its property, preparing the way for it, and so on ... But ... on several occasions, while I was actually watching, the lonely hour of the last instance actually came. The last instance, like an unholy ghost, actually grabbed hold of law, throttled it, and forced it to change its language.
>
> – E.P. THOMPSON, 'EIGHTEENTH-CENTURY ENGLISH SOCIETY'

In 1997, the Supreme Court of Canada decision *Delgamuukw v. British Columbia* determined that courts of law must admit oral traditions as evidence. 'The laws of evidence must be adapted in order that they [oral histories] can be accommodated and placed on an equal footing with the types of historical evidence that courts are familiar with, which largely consists of historical documents,' wrote Chief Justice Antonio Lamer. Otherwise, 'an impossible burden of proof' is placed on groups that do not have written records (*Delgamuukw* [SCC] par. 87). For Aboriginal plaintiffs in particular, the use of oral traditions offers a chance to contest colonial and racial assumptions about the 'vanishing Indian' or the 'noble savage' that inform the official history of contact. However, despite the legal recognition of oral traditions as evidence, profound difficulties of transcription and translation remain. Given that the rules of evidence have been developed over centuries in English common law, historically barring oral history as 'hearsay', placing oral history on 'equal footing with' standard forms of proof is a complex and fraught process. Furthermore, reading oral traditions for hard evidence of territorial ownership ignores how Aboriginal people view their relationship to the land, and how this relationship is expressed through the act of storytelling. Examining the 'content' of traditional narratives in isolation from the circumstances of the recital misses the point that storytelling is an embodied performance, a series of situated tellings, a moment or event in which interlocutors mutually shape meaning through communication. As I have attempted to demonstrate in *First Person Plural*, the interaction between teller and audience constitutes the story itself. Performing, translating, and writing oral traditions are dependent upon the contexts of (re)tellings.

An examination of the *Delgamuukw* trial heard in the British Columbia Supreme Court – whose verdict, rendered in 1991, was found to contain 'palpable errors' of judgment by the Supreme Court of Canada six years later (*Delgamuukw* [SCC]: par. 7)[1] – highlights the major challenge facing community land claims negotiators: to use oral traditions in ways that re-think the concepts of evidence, ownership, and Aboriginal title to land. Legal discourse decontextualizes 'pieces' of evidence as moveable text; yet oral history often resembles a web-like series of linked stories. What emerged from the trial was the need for the court to learn *how* to listen to the evidence. Listening requires responding to and taking responsibility for what one hears; responsibility underlines the need for the court to develop an ethics of interpreting oral history.

In this chapter, I read the 1991 *Delgamuukw* land claims trial in conjunction with two collections of textualized oral narrative, each of which explores the relationship between oral traditions, land, and Aboriginal title and offers ways of envisioning the negotiation of a land dispute as an ethical process of 'response and response-ability' (Blaeser, 'Writing' 54). In reading *Delgamuukw* alongside *Write It on Your Heart: The Epic World of an Okanagan Storyteller* (1989), told by Harry Robinson and edited by Wendy Wickwire, and *Life Lived Like a Story: Life Stories of Three Yukon Elders* (1990), written by anthropologist Julie Cruikshank in collaboration with Athapaskan storytellers Angela Sidney, Kitty Smith, and Annie Ned, I propose that a principle of collaboration offers strategies for addressing the problem of translating oral traditions into statements of Aboriginal title in the courtroom. I am aware that such a proposal might strike my reader as somewhat naïve, given the deep incommensurability of courts of law and storytelling exchanges: legal discourse asserts its authority by maintaining a sharp demarcation between 'evidence' and 'hearsay', while hearsay, an out-of-court statement by someone other than the witness, is one way of describing the transmission of oral history through a chain of storytellers that stretches back in time. Yet I am committed to reading the transcripts from the *Delgamuukw* trial in tandem with these collections of textualized oral narrative with a view towards articulating how legal discourse may operate differently, or how new forms of collective agency may arise in the larger pursuit of Aboriginal land rights. In *Write It on Your Heart* and *Life Lived Like a Story*, collaboration functions as a methodology, as an ethics, and as a performative practice. Robinson's storytelling practice, shaped by his listener's responses, attends to the ethical dimensions of land disputes. Collaborative authorship in *Life Lived Like a Story* functions to broaden narrowly legalistic definitions of Aboriginal rights by foregrounding the role of negotiation and exchange. Within the narratives themselves, the storytellers provide contexts for understanding the stories, creating an active form of communication with their audience. Both texts use the principle of collaborative authorship to show how the act of recording oral narrative is a two-way process, continuously moving back and forth between many tellers and listeners, over many years, and even over many generations.

Thus collaborative authorship in *Write It on Your Heart* and *Life Lived Like a Story* offers a conceptual framework by which to re-read the *Delgamuukw* case. Again I am compelled to underline that my purpose is not to downplay how social and historical contexts constitute the material background of texts, or how social power informs our textual interpretations. Indeed, legal texts such as the ones studied here make explicit how multiple state apparatuses, embedded in colonial legislation, severely circumscribe the degree to which Aboriginal communities can enact self-government, steward their lands, and determine their own futures. As Cheryl Suzack reminds us in 'Law Stories as Life Stories' (2005), social critique cannot overcome its 'conditions of production' (117). Yet common law is based upon the processes of giving testimony, responding to witnesses, and cross-examining evidence, and these multiple enactments of dialogic interaction should be exploited to their capacity. In this I am following the lead of the Gitksan and Wet'suwet'en plaintiffs, who sought to transform the courthouse into their feast hall and who argued forcefully for the ongoing connections between their stories, territories, land title, and rights of jurisdiction. The significance of this risk must be remembered and used to fuel the ongoing struggle for Aboriginal rights through legal avenues.

### The Struggle for Aboriginal Title and Rights: Historical Contexts

In *Reasons for Judgment: Delgamuukw v. British Columbia* (1991), Chief Justice Allan McEachern ruled that no Aboriginal title or rights had existed prior to European settlement. McEachern went on further to say that, even if Aboriginal rights had existed, they had been extinguished by the assertion of sovereignty by Great Britain: 'It is the law that aboriginal rights exist at the "pleasure of the crown," and they may be extinguished whenever the intention of the Crown to do so is clear and plain ... The plaintiffs' claims for aboriginal rights are accordingly dismissed' (McEachern ix). As startling as McEachern's categorical denial of Aboriginal rights may appear, it was not inconsistent with legal precedents. One of the central tasks facing any First Nation engaged in a land claims suit has been to prove 'Aboriginal title' to the land; yet, until recently, the courts have recognized Aboriginal title only at the precise moment of extinguishing it. As anthropologist Dara Culhane has observed, 'Legal and political recognition of Aboriginal title and extinguishment of Aboriginal title have been inextricably interdependent and mutually defining. The assertion of dominance and the surrender of autonomy must occur at the same instant' (86). As discussed in Chapter 2, although the policy of 'extinguishment' was ostensibly replaced in 2002 by the policy of 'exhaustion,' the basic premise has remained the same.[2] The required interdependency of recognition and extinguishment gives Aboriginal title ambiguous status in relationship to Crown title and private ownership of land. In contrast, the Gitksan and Wet'suwet'en plaintiffs in the *Delgamuukw* trial argued that Aboriginal title should describe a communal holding of land, that Aboriginal title should be considered inalienable, and that Aboriginal title should underlie Crown title.

Though in 1997 the Supreme Court of Canada criticized McEachern's reasoning and affirmed the existence of Aboriginal title, the legacy of the decision continues to be debated fiercely among legal scholars of Aboriginal rights.[3] The *Delgamuukw* case was launched in 1987 after the Gitksan and Wet'suwet'en First Nations sued the provincial and federal governments for ownership of and jurisdiction over 58,000 square kilometres of their traditional territories in northwest British Columbia. After 374 court days, the trial ended on 30 June 1990, and McEachern released his reasons for judgment on 21 March 1991. The plaintiffs appealed the decision, and in 1997, ten years after the trial began, the Supreme Court released its landmark decision, which affirmed the existence of Aboriginal title. It is important to note that the judges of the Supreme Court did not review the evidence; instead, they ordered a new trial. As a result, even though *Delgamuukw* has been lauded as a significant victory for Aboriginal plaintiffs, this optimism is somewhat misplaced, since to date the case has not been retried and the ownership and jurisdiction of the land remain unresolved. More generally, Peter Kulchyski has cautioned against imposing a linear narrative of progress in the ongoing battle for Aboriginal title and rights in Canada:

> There is no clear, evolutionary logic in the historical development of Aboriginal rights. In spite of after-the-fact stories that have tried to imply a consistent logic in the approach to Aboriginal rights, there was a basic incoherence, an instability and set of contradictions embodied in the approach of various British and Canadian administrations ... The recognition and affirmation of Aboriginal rights cannot be seen as an outcome of a progressive liberalization of society ... It is a history of sustained, often vicious struggle, a history of losses and gains, of shifting terrain. (*Unjust* 9-10)

Using Kulchyski's insight as a starting point, I will demonstrate how Aboriginal rights have been both affirmed and renounced in a few, key, legal documents from 1763 to *Delgamuukw*. The Royal Proclamation of 1763 offers a good example of the simultaneous recognition and denial of Aboriginal rights that Kulchyski describes. It at once asserts British dominion over First Nations' territories *and* offers the possibility of constructing a strong case for Aboriginal rights and title. This founding document of Aboriginal-Canadian relations, ratified by more than twenty-four First Nations' representatives at the Treaty of Niagara in the summer of 1764,[4] recognizes Aboriginal title to land at the same moment that it denies that title:

> And whereas it is just and reasonable, and essential to Our Interest and the Security of Our Colonies, that the several Nations or Tribes of Indians, with whom We are connected, and who live under Our Protection, should not be molested or disturbed in the Possession of such Parts of Our Dominions and Territories as, not having been ceded to, or purchased by

Us, are reserved to them, or any of them, as their Hunting Grounds. (*Royal Proclamation*, Part IV S Preamble)

The Royal Proclamation recognizes the existence of 'Nations or Tribes of Indians' and their right to the land, which is based on prior occupancy. Aboriginal title here underlies Crown title, and Aboriginal rights exist independently of the Crown's recognition of those rights. In other words, the Crown has not created Aboriginal rights. Today, Aboriginal legal teams continue to refer to the Royal Proclamation in constructing their arguments for the *sui generis* nature of Aboriginal title.[5] However, while the proclamation deems it 'just and reasonable' to recognize the prior occupancy of First Nations, it is also significant that the proclamation sees this recognition as 'essential' to 'Our Interest and the Security of Our Colonies.' Ultimately, 'peace with the Natives' here serves the purpose of colonial expansion. Another ambivalence in the proclamation lies in the Crown's stated intention to protect Aboriginal peoples, a perceived responsibility that later became known as the Crown's 'fiduciary duty.' Today, Aboriginal groups use fiduciary duty as leverage to compel government to act in their best interests. However, fiduciary duty also has justified the historically entrenched discourse of paternalism, which implies that Canada knows best what Aboriginal interests are, and how they should be met. This establishes the historical precedent of Canada acting without consulting with First Nations.

The land claims case known as *St. Catherine's Milling and Lumber Co. v. The Queen* (1888) illustrates how 'fiduciary duty' can be used to deny First Nations the right to participate in legal decisions that affect them directly. The case was, essentially, a dispute between the provincial and federal (Dominion) governments over who had the right to collect royalties from logging. It had little to do with Aboriginal rights per se, though the two governments mobilized strategic definitions of Aboriginal rights to make their respective cases. Well before the *St. Catherine's* case, Treaty 3 (1873) had established Anishinaabe interests to the land. However, the two governments both argued that the treaty process had resulted in the surrender of Aboriginal title. The Dominion argued that Aboriginal title underlies Crown title, but, through the treaty process, the title had been surrendered to the Crown. The province argued that Crown title underlies Aboriginal title, and, through the constitution, the right of economic development had been transferred to the province. In the end, the judges agreed with the province (Kulchyski, *Unjust* 21-22).

Despite the fact that the *St. Catherine's Milling* decision revisited the terms of Treaty 3, an agreement negotiated with Anishinaabe leaders, no Anishinaabe representatives were present in the courtroom (21). Thus, the court granted the province the right to profit from treaty land without consent or consultation with First Nations. Here the Crown's fiduciary duty to protect Aboriginal interests became a capricious shelter. Indeed, it became a convenient way to deny the collective or communal nature of Aboriginal title: title becomes a 'personal or usufructary right,' 'dependent upon the good will of the Sovereign' (27). In other words, the court deemed Aboriginal title to be a 'burden' upon the underlying Crown title, a burden the Crown could take up or put down at its pleasure. This escape clause on Aboriginal title has remained embedded in legal understandings of Aboriginal title since 1888. Even the *Delgamuukw* decision of 1997, which in many ways affirms Aboriginal title, maintains the right of the Crown to suspend Aboriginal title.[6]

In more recent Canadian legal history, the simultaneous recognition and denial of Aboriginal rights has continued to swing upon the volatile pendulum of legal proceedings and governmental legislation. For example, many scholars recognize the decision of *Calder v. British Columbia* (1973) as an important 'advance' in securing Aboriginal title and rights. An oft-quoted statement from the *Calder* decision establishes Aboriginal title as 'communal' and based on prior occupancy: 'the fact is that when the settlers came, the Indians were there, organized in societies and occupying the land as their forefathers had done for centuries. This is what Indian title means and it does not help one in the solution of this problem to call it a "personal or usufructuary right"' (69). This definition of Aboriginal title repudiates that of the *St. Catherine's Milling* decision. However, while all seven members of the Supreme Court agreed on the *existence* of Aboriginal title, they were divided on the question of whether that title had been extinguished by the Crown's declaration of sovereignty, and, due to a legal technicality, the case was dismissed (60-62).

Despite *Calder*'s affirmation of the existence of Aboriginal title, in 1991, in the *Delgamuukw* decision, McEachern denied that Aboriginal title or rights had existed prior to European settlement. In ruling against the Gitksan and Wet'suwet'en plaintiffs, McEachern insisted, numerous times, that he was constrained by legal precedent: 'Our courts ... labour under disciplines which do not always permit judges to do what they might subjectively think (or feel) might be the right or just thing to do in a particular case ... As will become apparent, the case is framed, as it had to be, for strict legal remedies' (McEachern 2, 3). McEachern makes clear that his judgment is 'legal,' if not 'right' or 'just.' Six years later, however, the Supreme Court of Canada determined there were errors in the decision, arguing that McEachern had not given enough weight to the oral histories. In Stan Persky's words, 'the court ruled, unanimously and more forcefully than ever before, that Native people in Canada have a unique claim to their traditional lands, that provinces don't have the power to arbitrarily extinguish Aboriginal title, and that future courts must accept valid Native oral history as a key ingredient in proving such claims' (Persky 2). The 1997 decision shows that it is *possible*, legally speaking, to argue for Aboriginal title without simultaneously bringing about its extinguishment or exhaustion, by establishing the existence of Aboriginal rights independently from the Crown's recognition of those rights.

This is precisely what the Gitksan and Wet'suwet'en set out to do in their trial: to forge a decolonized, self-determined notion of Aboriginal title. They argued that Aboriginal title, existing by virtue of prior occupancy, underlies Crown title, thereby shifting the burden of proof in land disputes to the Crown. The Gitksan and Wet'suwet'en also argued that Aboriginal title is inalienable; that is, it is not possible to buy or sell it. In this interpretation, Aboriginal title becomes a stronger claim to land than private ownership. If Aboriginal title is not held by individual landowners who lay claim to specific pieces of land, but rather represents a form of communal ownership, then Aboriginal title could be practised as 'title held by nations to broad territories' (Kulchyski, *Unjust* 11). By emphasizing the sovereignty of the Gitksan and Wet'suwet'en First Nations, the plaintiffs argued that Aboriginal title itself is a type of Crown title. Because land title is meaningless without the right to control its practice, the plaintiffs claimed 'jurisdiction' over the disputed territory. Importantly, they also claimed jurisdiction over the representation of their oral traditions and the testimony of the elders.

The *Delgamuukw* trial was the first land claims trial in Canada that called upon Aboriginal elders, scholars, House Chiefs, and other community members as expert witnesses, rather than relying solely on 'outsider' witnesses. In the words of Peter Grant and Neil Sterritt of the Gitksan and Wet'suwet'en legal team: 'A critical distinction between *Delgamuukw* and other cases was that *Delgamuukw* was founded first and foremost on the evidence of the Gitksan and Wet'suwet'en people themselves' (Grant and Sterritt 295). The Gitksan and Wet'suwet'en people took a chance in presenting the evidence in their own way, resisting and transforming established procedures for giving evidence, which they saw as weighted against oral traditions in the first place. As Julie Cruikshank argues, the Gitksan and Wet'suwet'en seized the opportunity 'to state their relationship to land on their own terms' and to 'control the representations of their culture' ('Invention' 34). In so doing, the plaintiffs transformed the courtroom into their feast hall and used the trial as a means of enacting their land title and right of jurisdiction.

## Oral Traditions in the Courtroom: *Delgamuukw v. British Columbia* (1991)

The Gitksan and Wet'suwet'en legal team argued that, in performing their oral traditions, they were enacting both *title to* and *jurisdiction over* land.[7] 'My power is carried in my House's histories, songs, dances and crests,' stated Ken Muldoe, who held the Gitksan name Delgam Uukw at the time of the trial; 'It is recreated at the Feast when the histories are told, the songs and dances performed, and the crests displayed' (Gisday Wa and Delgam Uukw 7). In both Gitksan and Wet'suwet'en cultures, each community member is associated with a House, and each House owns and has jurisdiction over a given territory. The expressions of ownership of these territories are Gitksan *adaawk,* Wet'suwet'en *kungax,* and ceremonial regalia (Monet and Skanu'u 26; Cruikshank, 'Invention' 35). Although complex and difficult to define, especially in an English translation, *adaawk* and *kungax* may be understood as performances in a feast hall that formalize the institutions of a House – owned territories, crests, songs, names, major events, and relationships with other Houses (Napoleon 126). Gyologyet (Mary McKenzie), a Gitksan House Chief with jurisdiction over three large territories, describes the importance of *adaawk* as it relates to her knowledge of her territory: '*Adaawk* in Gitksan language is a powerful word describing what the house stands for, what the chief stands for, what the territory stands for ... And it's the most important thing in Gitksan ... Without *adaawk* you can't very well say you are a chief or you own territory' (qtd. in Monet and Skanu'u 28). Gyologyet states that *adaawk* 'tells, in a feast hall, ... who are the holders of fishing places, creeks and mountains that belong to each House of the Chiefs' (McEachern 356). In performing *adaawk,* the Chiefs assert territorial ownership and ancestral connections to land. In the view of the plaintiffs, *adaawk* and *kungax* – neither of which had been performed outside the feast halls up until the trial – provide clear evidence of title and rights to the disputed territory.

However, the Gitksan and Wet'suwet'en legal team faced a difficult challenge to present the elders' testimony as statements of land ownership in ways that the court would accept. First, neither *adaawk* nor *kungax* express land ownership through concrete descriptions of land boundaries. The Gitksan and Wet'suwet'en witnesses defied the province's 'colour-coded maps' that sought to define land in units (Gisday Wa and Delgam Uukw 63). Second, the descriptions given in *adaawk* and *kungax* are mostly of travels through the land, not settlements upon it. According to Gyologyet, *adaawk* is 'not a story, it's just how people travelled is *adaawk*' (qtd. in Monet and Skanu'u 28). In linking the acts of telling and travelling, and de-emphasizing story content as the primary maker of meaning, Gyologyet here accentuates the act of storytelling as an enactment of land title. She associates the passing on of stories, from one generation to another, with travelling the land. Travel, land ownership, and the exchange of stories are thus closely related concepts, as seen in Gisday Wa's description of the Wet'suwet'en *kungax* 'as a song, or songs about trails between territories' (McEachern 57). The performative and narrative dynamism of *adaawk* and *kungax* imbue place with fluidity and movement that defy Euro-Canadian legal understandings of land ownership. Richard Benson, who testified that he hunted and trapped throughout Gyologyet's territories during the 1930s and 1940s, similarly suggests a connection between the act of travelling and the act of storytelling:

> I travel all the way through these place. ... [W]hat I travel through, that's what I am telling. You see, I walk through, I trap through here. I walk all the way through and I know all these place and these mountains ... I am telling what I already been – I walk through and I see these creeks and I walk through there and I know where they are and I know who it belongs to. (McEachern 361)

For Benson, travelling the land shows the court that he knows the land and who owns it. His insistence upon the importance of travel in understanding land ownership contrasts with the Crown attorneys' focus on territorial boundaries.

Third, *adaawk* and *kungax* are highly performative oral genres that enact meaning through recitation and through feasting. 'By attending the feasting of any Chief, even if it is my own feasting, I hear the Chiefs repeat or tell of the *adaawk*,' says Gyologyet; 'This is the importance of the feasting, that these *adaawks* are told' (356). Listening to the *adaawk* at the feast hall confirms and enacts a House's claim to territory; speakers and listeners reaffirm ownership of one another's territories through the performance. Public telling and community knowledge of *adaawk* and *kungax* are key conditions in establishing the legitimacy of the narratives; retellings of *adaawk* increase the stories' power. As Delgam Uukw states, 'The histories of my House are always being added to. My presence in this courtroom today will add to my House's power ... Through the witnessing of all the histories, century after century, we have exercised our jurisdiction' (Gisday Wa and Delgam Uukw 8). By remembering and performing *adaawk* and *kungax* in the courtroom, as if it were a feast hall, the Gitksan-Wet'suwet'en witnesses were enacting their title to land. Regardless of the outcome of the trial, Delgam Uukw implies, repeated tellings in the courtroom expand the Houses' histories while increasing the narratives' authority.

The court, however, remained suspicious of the plaintiffs' presentation of evidence. This was not surprising to the Gitksan and Wet'suwet'en: the probability that the court would not appreciate the significance of the performances remained a source of anxiety. Many, in fact, had opposed the legal team's strategy of performing *adaawk* and *kungax* in the courtroom, a place symbolic of Canadian colonial dominance. For example, the former Delgam Uukw, Albert Tait, had tried to discourage the Chiefs from performing *adaawk* or wearing regalia and crestblankets in the courtroom, claiming the court would not award due respect to these cultural statements of sovereignty and territorial jurisdiction. If the court ruled against the Chiefs wearing their regalia, he argued, 'the shame of the disrespect will be costly to erase' (qtd. in Monet and Skanu'u 22).

In order to give serious consideration to the plaintiffs' evidence, the court needed to consider *how* to listen to *adaawk* and *kungax*. However, McEachern's *Reasons for Judgment* reveals that the courthouse process, despite its reliance on the acts of testifying, questioning, and debating, is not dialogic enough to take into consideration the interactive exchange that lies at the heart of *adaawk* and *kungax*. Unlike the Gitksan and Wet'suwet'en legal team, McEachern was concerned only with the content, not the context, of the testimony. Seeking to base his decision solely upon what he himself could 'see' and understand through the transcribed texts of witnesses' testimony, McEachern adopted a positivistic perspective that was ill-suited for decoding the kinds of evidence offered by the Gitksan and Wet'suwet'en witnesses.

'Hearing' oral traditions as evidence of Aboriginal rights in a court of law is a challenge, even for listeners more sensitive than McEachern. The many layers of mediation that make up court documents render interpretation a fraught process. During the trial, interpreters translated the testimony told in Gitksan or Wet'suwet'en, spelling out words letter by letter, while stenographers recorded these translations in shorthand. At the end of each day, court employees converted the shorthand back into prose, producing transcripts to be consulted by the judge and lawyers for the purpose of cross-examining witnesses, an exercise that took place sometimes months after the witnesses had given their initial testimony. The continuous process of decontextualizing and recontextualizing the court testimony had a profound effect on how the stories generated meaning. Leslie Pinder, a legal consultant for the plaintiffs in the *Delgamuukw* case, has described the process by which legal teams gather evidence from testimony, highlighting the dangers of decontextualization: 'In court cases, we word-search transcripts to reassemble evidence; it doesn't resemble anything that was said, by anyone. We cut the words, even our written words, away from the environment, and hold them up as pieces of meaning, hacked up pieces of meaning' (11-12). Moveable text, cut and pasted into new contexts, warps and changes the possible range of meanings that a testimony produces.

Pinder's graphic description of the violence of interpretation, in which re-membering testimony is closer to dismemberment, is particularly relevant to the problem of translating Aboriginal oral traditions and languages. The courtroom, a symbol of Euro-Canadian dominance over Aboriginal epistemologies and languages, is saturated in colonial discourses that virtually foreclose the possibility of accurate or fair interpretations of *adaawk* and *kungax*. Moreover, the transcripts emerge from the severely binarized relations of legal contest, in which the Crown and the plaintiffs attempt to annihilate one another's arguments by whatever means necessary. In the cross-examinations, the Crown lawyers sought to discredit the reliability of *adaawk* and *kungax*. The plaintiffs' lawyers, on the other hand, asserted that *adaawk* and *kungax* were definitive statements of land title, even though some of the stories do not appear to describe territory at all. The performative dimension of *adaawk* and *kungax* has been excised from McEachern's *Reasons for Judgment*, leaving subsequent readers with little choice but to recreate his focus on text without context. And, finally, the perceived strangeness of *adaawk* and *kungax* reflect assumptions about 'primitive' and 'civilized' societies that are deeply embedded in English common law.

Though McEachern officially admitted oral tradition into the courtroom, his *Reasons for Judgment* shows that he was not convinced of its validity. His response to the testimony of Antgulilibix (Mary Johnson), a Gitksan Chief claiming ownership of and jurisdiction over a large portion of the territory under dispute, reveals the sharp distinction he consistently made between the issues of land ownership and oral history: 'Mrs. Johnson ... did not have a clear understanding of the boundaries of her House, but she spoke comprehensively about its legends. When asked about the *adaawk* of her House of Antgulilibix she related several stories which I would have classified generally as mythology' (McEachern 57). For McEachern, territorial boundaries belong to the realm of visible proof and concrete evidence, while 'legends' exist beyond time or place or measurement. He concluded, 'I am unable to accept *adaawk, kungax* and oral histories as reliable bases for detailed history'; '[T]he *adaawk* are seriously lacking in detail about the specific lands to which they are said to relate' (75, 58).

It is true, at least to a non-Gitksan listener, that Antgulilibix's *adaawk* does not appear to provide a detailed history about 'specific lands.' The *adaawk* told to the court on 9 June 1987, for example, is about a brother and two sisters who are travelling and cannot find anything to eat; eventually, the brother, Wildim waax, starves to death. He returns to his mourning sisters in the form of a grouse, giving up his life a second time to feed his sisters. The transcription below, by Leslie Pinder, is in verse form to signal the pauses in Antgulilibix's performance:

> And not long after he [Wildim waax] died,
> they [the sisters] heard the drumming grouse,
> and the elder sister lay down near the log where the grouse drums.
> Whenever a grouse is drumming,
> he always comes back to the same spot where he drums,
> an old log covered with moss, and it's soft.
> So the elder sister hid herself underneath the moss beside the log,
> but she missed the grouse.
> Then the young sister lay down.
> She caught the grouse and they killed the grouse,
> so they sat down and they both cried.
> They remember their brother that's just died
> and they compose a dirge song. (Pinder 5)

The story offers many possibilities of interpretation. It can be read as a nationalist allegory in which a brother sacrifices his life for his family/nation and the survivors compose an anthem in his honour. Alternatively, the story may evoke a social taboo, in which the reabsorption of the brother into the bodies of the sisters is the expression of a prohibited desire. It may also be a sociohistory, documenting a famine from the past, or a moral parable, teaching respect for the dead and the interdependence of human and animal life. Finally, the story could be a statement of Aboriginal title, building upon the nationalist allegory of sacrifice and renewal. The grouse, which used to be a human, always drums at the same place; in the story, this place becomes the location of the feast house. According to Gyologyet, the stories in *adaawk* 'tell the owner and the location of the Feast House' (McEachern 356). Wildim waax's reabsorption into the sisters' bodies cements the family's claim to territory and community. The sisters' dirge song memorializes the brother's sacrifice, and generations of singers remember and re-create his claim. The *adaawk*'s authority comes through a long chain of singers, including Antgulilibix.

When the plaintiffs' lawyer, Peter Grant, asked Antgulilibix to sing the dirge song referred to in the *adaawk*, McEachern interrupted Grant and asked if a performance was necessary. When Grant insisted, McEachern responded:

> *Court:* I don't want to be skeptical, but I have some difficulty in understanding why the actual wording of the song is necessary. ...
> *Grant:* The song is part of the history, and I am asking the witness to sing the song as part of the history, because the song itself invokes the history.
> *Court:* How long is it?
> *Grant:* It's not very long. It's very short.
> *Court:* Could it not be written out and asked if this is the wording? Really, we are on the verge of getting way off track here, Mr. Grant. Again, I don't want to be skeptical, but to have witnesses singing songs in court is, in my respectful view, not the proper way to approach this problem ...
> *Grant:* It's a song which itself invokes the history and the depth of history of what she is telling ... It is necessary for you to appreciate –
> *Court:* I have a tin ear, Mr. Grant. It's not going to do any good to sing it to me. (qtd. in Monet and Skanu'u 42)

After much discussion between McEachern and Grant, Antgulilibix finally sang the song. Grant asked her to translate the Gitksan song into

English. She translated the song word by word, here represented in verse form to distinguish each word phrase:

> They [the sisters] sing about the grouse flying, flying,
> how the grouse flies, those are the first words.
> And another word says,
> 'I will ask for you to tell him to give it to me.'
> That means when the first sister grabs
> just the tail end of the grouse.
> And another word says,
> 'It will make noise underneath your wings.'
> That means when you hear the drum,
> when the grouse drums and it makes a loud noise.
> And then another words [sic] says
> how the grouse gave himself up to die for them
> to help them save their lives.
> So that's the end of the song.
> And today the young lady that caught the grouse
> stood at the foot of our totem pole that we restored in 1973,
> and she is holding the grouse with tears in her eyes. (qtd. 42)

McEachern's response to Antgulilibix's translation is to question again the legitimacy of the oral traditions in a court of law. 'All right now, Mr. Grant, would you explain to me, because this may happen again, why you think it was necessary to sing the song? This is a trial, not a performance' (qtd. 42). Yet performance is the whole point of *adaawk*.

It is easy, and perhaps tempting, to denounce McEachern's abrupt impatience and cultural insensitivity as personal failings. Yet in so doing, we risk bracketing the thornier question of how the process of land claims hearings is itself embedded in colonial and ethnocentric assumptions. As Pinder writes with crushing irony, 'In what he [Judge McEachern] says and believes he represents the best of what we have to offer' (Pinder 4). The discursive limits of land claims trials have produced McEachern's inflexibility. Significantly, the Gitksan and Wet'suwet'en were not asking McEachern to extract the 'meaning' of *adaawk*. Antgulilibix's story and song about the grouse who sacrifices his life for his sisters are clearly difficult performances to reconcile with land claims proceedings; her *adaawk* can be interpreted in many ways and told for different purposes. The purpose here was to show the court how *adaawk* functions as part of the chiefs' territories, systems of land ownership, and jurisdiction. Following the oral performances, the plaintiffs asked expert witnesses to provide context and analysis.

Key to the plaintiffs' case was the expert testimony of anthropologists, who submitted reports comprising over 1,000 pages of evidence. Much of their discussion addressed *how* the court should consider evidence in land claims trials. For example, Hugh Brody questioned the requirement that Aboriginal peoples 'prove' their use and occupancy of land: 'We do not apply these criteria [in defining Canada's national borders]. We do not draw boundaries around our territories by using and occupying them' (Brody, 'The Nature' 7). Brody also reviewed anthropological theory, arguing that, until recently, anthropology has ignored 'how people regard themselves.' The 'heart' of his report, Brody writes, is to 'recognize and then break free from Euro-Canadian ethnocentricity' (7). McEachern, however, was not swayed. Brody's argument that versions of history depend upon point of view and politically asymmetric relations of power ultimately led to the exclusion of his report from McEachern's *Reasons for Judgment*.

In contrast to his reaction to the anthropologists who testified on behalf of the plaintiffs, McEachern wrote approvingly about the historians who presented evidence: 'Generally I accept just about everything they [the historians] put before me because they were largely collectors of archival, historical documents. In most cases they provided much useful information with minimal editorial comment. Their marvellous collections largely spoke for themselves' (McEachern 52). In McEachern's view, written documents, such as records from Hudson's Bay Company traders or memos from the Department of Indian Affairs, 'speak for themselves,' while stories from oral history do not. Yet as discussed in previous chapters, the claim that something 'speaks for itself' can mask the workings of numerous mediators whose own authority depends upon maintaining the effect of the direct address. McEachern's favourable response to the archival documents shows that the rules of evidence in common law turn upon a series of culturally loaded binary oppositions, such as writing vs. speech, fact vs. opinion, data vs. hearsay. Though live speech may be required to legitimize and authenticate written evidence, written documents continue to carry the weight of 'fact,' as well as the weight of 'civilization.' For example, McEachern referred to the alleged absence of writing in Gitksan and Wet'suwet'en cultural traditions to delegitimize their evidence.[8]

In order to win a land claim in a court of law, Aboriginal plaintiffs have to prove that: 1) the people are grounded historically in the lands and resources claimed; 2) they use and occupy the land (the land cannot be 'abandoned'); 3) they have an ongoing involvement in those lands; 4) the way they use the lands and resources is consistent with traditional uses; and 5) they are an organized society (Culhane 111-24; Oman 138). In consideration of what Aboriginal people have to prove in order to secure their title, engaging in the land claims process in the first place forces them to accept, to some extent, assumptions about 'primitive' societies. For example, in the *Delgamuukw* trial, the Crown argued that the Gitksan and Wet'suwet'en people had relinquished their Aboriginal identity and therefore their Aboriginal title to land if they had driver's licences or held wage-based jobs. McEachern writes: 'Witness after witness *admitted* participation in the wage or cash economy. Art Matthews Jr. (Tenimyget) ... [is] the head saw filer at the Westar sawmill ... Pete Muldoe (Gitludahl) has followed a variety of non-aboriginal vocations including logging on the lands claimed by another chief; Joan Ryan (Hanamuxw) teaches school in Prince Rupert' (McEachern 56; my emphasis). Having to prove that the people have an ongoing, current, dynamic relationship with the land today, while at the same time proving that they use the land 'traditionally,' puts the plaintiffs in a double bind. When one elder said he had a 'registered trap line' to prove that he used the land currently, the Crown lawyers argued that his implicit acceptance of the idea of registering a trap line showed that he no longer had an 'Aboriginal' relationship to the land, that he had submitted to government regulation, and that he therefore had the same kind of relationship to the land as a non-Aboriginal trapper. Argues McEachern, 'The evidence satisfies me that most Gitksan and Wet'suwet'en people do not now live an aboriginal life. They have been gradually moving away from it since contact' (McEachern 56).

The criterion of proving that the Gitksan and Wet'suwet'en societies were 'organized' reveals most clearly the ethnocentric and racist basis of the court process. The Crown tried to show that the Gitksan and Wet'suwet'en people were not 'organized' before contact. By deploying a crude primitive-versus-civilized binary opposition, the crown argued that Gitksan and Wet'suwet'en societies were so 'unorganized' before contact that they could not be said to exist. As one member of the plaintiffs' legal team, Yaga'lahl (Dora Wilson) writes, 'The genealogies that were spread out on the walls some days in the courtroom were really something to see. We had to put these on charts, pages and pages of these, and yet we were told we didn't exist. Didn't exist. They don't know where we came from. If we didn't own the land, what were we doing there?' (Yaga'lahl 202).

During her presentation of the genealogy charts in court, Yaga'lahl said, 'I'm right here in front of you. Look at me, listen to me talk. How can you deny that I exist if I am right here?' (qtd. in Monet and Skanu'u 77).

If the people do not exist, then the next logical step is to assume that the land is uninhabited. Under the traditions of English common law, uninhabited land, or *terra nullius*, automatically becomes Crown land. It was therefore crucial that the plaintiffs demonstrated concrete proof of their presence in the land. Yet, as we have seen, the Gitksan and Wet'suwet'en speak of their lands in terms of travel and mobility, avoiding strict delineation of the land into so many square kilometres. McEachern viewed the mobility of the Gitksan and Wet'suwet'en as an indication of their lack of connection to the land in question. 'Even in their aboriginal pursuits ... the plaintiffs do not seem to consider themselves tied to particular territories. I need only mention witnesses such as Pete Muldoe, Stanley Williams and Alfred Mitchell, who described hunting and trapping, when they were young, and more recently, on many, many different territories' (McEachern 56). McEachern commented that in general, there has been considerable mobility among Aboriginal peoples of the region (56-59). He concluded that this mobility invalidated the plaintiffs' argument for land title because it casts into doubt whether the present inhabitants of the land were direct descendants of those who had lived in the region over the centuries (59-61).

The lesson to be learned by the *Delgamuukw* case is that meaning in oral storytelling is not only conveyed by the words but also by the contexts of tellings and retellings. In *Write It on Your Heart* and *Life Lived Like a Story*, the stories are shaped by a complex interaction between two or more interlocutors, from different cultural backgrounds, necessitating the participation of a host of translators, transcribers, editors, and publishers. These collections of recorded oral narrative, removed from the antagonistic relations of the courtroom, enable the reader to explore in greater depth the circumstances surrounding the telling as well as the shifting relations of authority between recorder, teller, translator, and editor. In arguing for collaboration as a model for land claims negotiation, I hope to trace a connection between story and land not compromised by the narrow confines of legal discourse; at the same time I acknowledge that, to some extent, these collections are informed by the same discourses of anthropology and of law that have asserted settler rights over Indigenous rights in legal decisions, including in the *Delgamuukw* trial. My aim is to address the ethical responsibility of communication that should guide the resolution of land claims disputes, but that land claims proceedings rarely accommodate.

## Harry Robinson and Wendy Wickwire: *Write It on Your Heart*

> The stories is worked by Both of us you and I.
>
> – HARRY ROBINSON, LETTER TO WENDY WICKWIRE
> (QTD. IN ROBINSON, *NATURE POWER*)

Harry Robinson's stories provide a starting point for addressing the question of ethics in the resolution of land claims. Discussion of ethical responsibility is conspicuously absent from McEachern's *Reasons for Judgment*. In contrast, Robinson's stories reflect upon the 'response and ... response-ability' of telling and recording oral narrative in cross-cultural contexts: as Kimberley Blaeser suggests, 'the oral involves an active exchange when it incites response and a sense of response-ability in the listener' ('Writing' 54; 66n). Robinson's ostensible reason for telling stories to Wickwire in English was to reach a wider audience, and he repeatedly encouraged Wickwire to publish his stories (Wickwire, Introduction, *Living by Stories* 29-30); but I would submit that he was also motivated to set the record straight on the historical foundations of Aboriginal and non-Aboriginal relations in Okanagan territory. His 'contact narratives' establish the conditions of his collaboration with Wickwire. It was vital for Robinson to establish a working, communicative relationship with Wickwire in order to explore the intimate connection between oral traditions, land, and Aboriginal title – not to advance a formal land claims proceeding, as the Gitksan and Wet'suwet'en storytellers were doing, but to establish an ethical teller-listener interaction with Wickwire, which would in turn impel an acknowledgment of the unextinguished and inalienable nature of the Okanagan people's land rights.

Harry Robinson, a traditional storyteller from the Okanagan First Nation who learned most of his stories in childhood from his grandmother, Louise Newhmkin, was born in 1900 and worked most of his life with horses and cattle, running his own ranches with his wife, Matilda Johnny, for close to fifty years. In 1971, shortly after Matilda's death, a hip injury forced Robinson to sell his ranches and slow down physically; it was only at this time that Robinson began telling the stories he had learned from his grandmother and other community members (*Write* 20-21). Wickwire, who was born in Nova Scotia and lived in Merritt and Lytton for ten years while she was doing research for her doctoral thesis, was introduced to Robinson in August 1977, by some mutual friends, Randy Bouchard and Dorothy Kennedy. Using a reel-to-reel tape recorder, Wickwire recorded and later transcribed and edited Robinson's stories. In an interview in 1993, Wickwire described their close relationship, which developed over a period of years: 'I'd make him dinner ..., go to a rodeo with him, or go on a car trip, or something, and we'd always have a great time. Hanging out, we kind of became like father and daughter' (Wickwire, 'Interview').

Aware of the historical prominence of White recorder-editors and the extent of their interventions in 'transcribing' oral traditions, in her introductions to Robinson's stories, Wickwire is quick to highlight Robinson's authorial role, while downplaying her own part as recorder, transcriber, and editor. Though, as she explains, her relationship with Robinson was founded upon mutual respect and trust, the storytelling sessions were, for the most part, a one-way process: 'As his hearing was slightly impaired, two-way exchanges were somewhat strained. He was more relaxed in a one-way telling situation than he was in trying to decipher my end of the conversation' (Introduction, *Write* 14). Implying that her own role in recording the stories involved turning on the tape recorder while Robinson told a seemingly inexhaustible stream of stories, she casts herself in the role of facilitator, re-creating the great 'wealth' of the speaker's narratives (11). 'Except for pauses to smoke his Players cigarettes or to suck on peppermints, he spoke without interruption for several hours at a time,' Wickwire writes (Introduction, *Nature* 8). Her mediation in textualizing the recorded accounts is similarly presented as minimal. Because Robinson was a bilingual speaker of both his native Okanagan language and English, and 'had translated his own stories to perform them in English,' the intervention of a translator was not required, and 'editing was unnecessary' (17). Moreover, Wickwire states that she has not changed any of Robinson's words, 'except where the pronouns become confusing' (Introduction, *Write* 15). '[P]resent[ed] ... exactly as told' (15), the stories have a high authenticity value, claims Wickwire, because of the allegedly minimal number of editorial changes. Wickwire's emphasis is on the extraordinary talents of Robinson as a storyteller, shifting the reader's attention away from how the collaborative process between teller and listener prompted and shaped the stories that emerged.

Despite Wickwire's near self-effacement as a recorder-editor, there are clues in the tape recordings that Wickwire was not always a silent listener. Her tape recordings, transcribed in part by Blanca Chester, who helped to prepare *Nature Power: In the Spirit of an Okanagan Storyteller* (1992) for publication, indicate that Robinson told stories in direct response to Wickwire's questions. According to Chester (who also publishes under the name Blanca Schorcht), particularly in the earlier stories, Wickwire asked many questions (Schorcht 2). In addition, the story collections themselves suggest that Robinson's choice of stories is influenced by his interaction with his audience, an issue Wickwire discusses at some length in the introduction to their third collection, *Living by Stories: A Journey of Landscape and Memory* (2005). Robinson took care in providing context for Wickwire by telling stories that commented upon cross-cultural and cross-lingual communication. Despite her presentation of the narratives with little contextual background, Robinson in effect provided contexts for understanding the stories within the stories themselves.

A case in point is the relationship between the languages of Okanagan and English, which emerges, in Chester's transcriptions, as a topic of extensive discussion between the interlocutors. As Robinson says to Wickwire, 'some of them Indian word – I can't turn into English. Seems to be they got no mate' (qtd. in Chester 16). In the following dialogue in Chester's article, Robinson and Wickwire discuss the differences between *ha-HA* and *Shoo-mish*. Both are Okanagan words relating to forms of spiritual power. Wickwire is searching for a clearer distinction between the two terms:

> *WW:* So if you were going to talk about that word [*ha-HA*], how would you talk about it?
> *HR:* *ha-HA*. Well, it could be …
> *WW:* Does it mean a person?
> *HR:* No. No person. *ha-HA*.
> Well, in other way, God the *ha-HA*.
> God was a *ha-HA*.
> He nothing else.
> *WW:* Could a sweathouse – could that be that?
> *HR:* A sweathouse.
> No, no sweathouse.
> Is the steambath, the sweathouse.
> *WW:* But what about that *Shoo-mish*?

> *HR:* That's one of 'em.
> See, we didn't get to this yet.
> I was going to tell you.
> But we going by the number.
> *WW:* But Harry, a person who has that –
> If a person has that then is he this? (16)

While Wickwire searches for ways to define and classify *ha-HA* and *Shoo-mish*, Robinson resists decontextualizing the words from the stories. Immediately following the conversation, Robinson tells a story about a medicine man who has the power to become invisible. Presumably, this story explains the difference between *ha-HA* and *Shoo-mish*, though Robinson uses the terms interchangeably. Wickwire again asks Robinson to distinguish the two words:

> *WW:* So you call it two things. You call it *Shoo-mish* and
> *ha-HA*. You call it both things?
> *HR:* Well, that's his power.
> And that's his *Shoo-mish*.
> Now, that's in English.
> We say that's his power.
> But in the Indian, we'll say his *Shoo-mish*.
> *WW:* And also, what about that *ha-HA?*
> *HR:* Well, because his *Shoo-mish* was a *ha-HA*.
> *ha-HA* his *Shoo-mish*. (20)

While Wickwire attempts to define and distinguish *ha-HA* and *Shoo-mish*, Robinson collapses the difference between the two terms, highlighting instead the differences between Okanagan and English. When Wickwire again asks for clarification, Robinson tells another story about invisibility, this time about a tiny insect that can move very quickly, and thus seems invisible. Invisibility appears to play a role in both *Shoo-mish* and *ha-HA;* likewise, stories about the unseen elude Wickwire's efforts to define terms within recognizable categories of knowledge in the English language.

Though Wickwire says that Robinson was 'hard of hearing' and did not like to be interrupted, Chester's transcriptions suggest that Robinson is answering her questions. However, his preferred mode of response is narrative. Robinson's strategy of telling more stories in response to Wickwire's queries shows that Robinson uses narrative as a form of explanation. As Chester notes: 'For Robinson, stories are a familiar way of explaining and teaching. To Wendy, however, the stories often appear unrelated to the questions she asks' (13-14). In a conversation with Chester, Wickwire comments on Robinson's use of story as explanation: 'If he looked at me and felt that he wasn't explaining himself, he got this very tormented look. He sort of would lapse into a story as his way of trying to explain it' (21). Wickwire speculates that Robinson uses stories in the same way that Western academics use dictionaries or lexicons (21).

If Robinson explains things to Wickwire through narrative, then it follows that Robinson's choice of stories emerges from his discussions with Wickwire. For example, Wickwire says that Robinson told her many 'power stories'. As Wickwire herself points out, this is not only because Robinson knew many power stories but also because Wickwire asked questions about concepts of power, such as *ha-HA* and *Shoo-mish:* 'Harry knew I was very interested in native power, so he told me many power stories' (Introduction, *Write* 16). Robinson encourages Wickwire to listen to the stories if she wants answers to her questions. He suggests that once a listener or reader develops some familiarity with the stories, she or he can grasp their explanatory power. Time and patience are needed to assimilate the stories' meanings:

> So, take a listen to these, a few times and think about it, to these stories, and what I tell you now. Compare them. See if you can see something more about it. Kind of plain, but it's pretty hard to tell you for you to know right now. Takes time. And then you will see. (Wickwire, Introduction, *Nature* 19)

Robinson encourages Wickwire to listen to the stories a few times because, he suggests, his stories are highly self-referential. One story provides contextual information for understanding others; they interconnect in web formations. Wickwire notes that Robinson told some stories many times over, as if to emphasize different angles of the story relevant to the discussion at hand. For example, an important recurring story in Robinson's repertoire is his creation story. Wickwire reports that Robinson told the creation story 'many times throughout our years together, sometimes in full, sometimes in fragments' (Introduction, *Nature* 13). The retellings show readers how 'Harry approached a story freshly each time he told it'

(18). Each performance is relative to the immediate context of telling, and interpretation of the stories is dependent upon the listener's and teller's interaction.

By redirecting her questions about the stories to still more stories, Robinson is making a bid for control over the representation of his stories. The active role he takes in interpreting his stories runs counter to ethnographic or participant-observation traditions of fieldwork, in which the anthropologist would provide background for the stories. It also runs counter to the process of delivering 'expert witness' testimony in the courtroom. In the *Delgamuukw* trial, storytellers did not get the chance to use dialogue to create interlocking stories. Instead, they were expected to tell stories that contain definitive statements of Aboriginal title. Meanwhile, anthropologist expert witnesses were expected to clear up any ambiguities by extracting 'the meanings' of the stories. This type of analytical process is anathema to Robinson's narrative mode of explanation, emerging from conversation with his audience.

A significant part of the exchange between Robinson and Wickwire revolves around their different roles in the making of recorded oral narrative. His stories ironically comment upon the historically asymmetric relations of authority between White recorders and Native storytellers. He is especially concerned with the power of printed copies of treaties or land agreements that have justified the expropriation of Aboriginal land. Robinson connects his interaction with Wickwire to historical relations between Aboriginal speechmakers and non-Aboriginal transcribers in Okanagan territory. In this way, he fleshes out an ethics that might guide the act of recording oral traditions in cross-cultural contexts, especially when land rights are at stake. Though Robinson's stories were not subjected to the same kind of legal processes of decontextualization and delegitimization that *adaawk* and *kungax* were in the *Delgamuukw* trial, they can be read as meta-narratives that comment upon the power relations between cultures labeled 'oral' and 'literate', and their divergent claims to land.

Robinson's creation story, which he told to Wickwire on numerous occasions, parodies the importance that Canadian law has placed upon mere paper and writing in the crucial question of land title and rights. In the story, God or the 'Big Chief' creates the first five peoples of the world – Chinese, Hindu, Russian, Indian, and White. God gives each of the first peoples a written document and throws them to the far corners of the world: 'Wherever you landed, that's yours. / Then you open up the paper / and that'll tell you what you going to do' (*Write* 41). This paper functions as a statement of land title. After distributing land and its accompanying document to the Chinese, Hindu, and Russian ancestors, God has only one piece of paper for the Indian and White ancestors, who are twins. God puts the paper under a rock and tells the twins not to touch it. But once God leaves, the younger White twin steals the paper when the older Indian twin, Coyote, is not looking. When God returns and asks where the paper is, the younger twin denies having taken it. This stolen piece of paper becomes the basis of Canadian law and 'legal' seizures of Aboriginal land.

Robinson suggests that, as a result of this betrayal, theft is inherent in legal definitions of Aboriginal land title. The law will always fall short of becoming an effective guarantor of justice in Canadian society. Instead, the law asserts its own truths:

> [T]he white man, they got the law.
> Then they mention on the law,
> And he says not to tell lie.
> Lie is bad.
> In the court you take the Bible,
> You kiss this Bible to say the true,
> Not to tell a lie.
> They know that much because they got the law. (*Write* 46)

Robinson implies that the only time a person is required to tell the truth in Canadian society is when that person is in court, with a hand on the Bible. Both the Bible and the court are powerful symbols of dispossession for Aboriginal people in Canada. In the name of the Bible, Canadian governments and churches have instituted colonial programs, such as residential schools, that have profoundly disrupted First Nations communities throughout Canada; in the name of the law, Aboriginal title has become extinguished at the moment of its recognition. Moreover, the Bible and the court embody non-Aboriginal perspectives upon land title. In land claims proceedings, as Kulchyski comments, 'the languages of Aboriginal peoples, not just the verbal patterns and "translatability" but the very grammar implied in the cultural forms, have not been addressed by the courts. Sweetgrass is not burned to cleanse, pipes are not shared. Instead the dominant cultural form presents itself as Truth: bibles are produced' (*Unjust* 2). For the courts, 'land title' means nothing unless it is printed on paper; for Robinson, in contrast, paper will never record true title to land. His stories are written not on flimsy pieces of paper but in the land, or 'on your heart.' They are 'land speaking,' in the evocative phrase of Okanagan writer Jeannette Armstrong: 'It is said in Okanagan that the land constantly speaks. It is constantly communicating. Not to learn its language is to die. We survived and thrived by listening intently to its teachings – to its language – and then inventing human words to retell its stories to our succeeding generations' (Armstrong, 'Land' 176). The close connections between land, oral traditions, and social belonging have clear political implications in this era of using oral traditions and Aboriginal languages in land claims negotiations, and Robinson repeatedly stresses these connections in his stories to Wickwire.

When God finds out about the theft, he expels the younger twin to a distant place across a great expanse of water. God lets him keep the paper, telling him that it is 'going to show you how / you going to make it to get back here' (*Write* 49). Once he returns, he must tell his older brother what the paper says:

> That paper, it'll tell you what to do.
> But you have to tell the Indians ...
> You're the one that's got to tell him all what's on there.
> You have to tell him.
> You have to let him know.
> I suppose to let you know, the both of you
> But you hide it and you take it.
> All right.
> But when you get back, you have to show him,
> show him what's on that paper. (50)

The younger twin is supposed to show the paper to his brother, but he fails to do so: 'he don't tell the Indians the whole story. / He hiding some' (50). Since then, the White ancestor's descendants have maintained control over the land through the paper and the legal system. Robinson repeatedly returns to the scene of the two twins, the first lie, and the case of the hidden document, showing how this initial lie has recurred many times in the history of Aboriginal and non-Aboriginal relations in Okanagan territory. His story suggests that the promise of resolving land disputes in a just manner lies in interlocutors developing a sense of ethical response and responsibility for their interaction, though the combative model of land claims trials cannot easily assimilate such a dialogic process.

Immediately following the telling of the creation myth, Robinson tells another story – this one about events in the relatively recent past (1929) – that again dramatizes the conflict between dominant society's paper documents and Aboriginal title to land. By telling another story on the heels of the first, Robinson is using one story to explain another, contextualizing one within the other, and forming, according to Wickwire, 'a longer, loosely knit but continuous story-cycle' (Introduction, *Write* 17). Within this 'continuous story-cycle' of interlocking narratives, Robinson grafts more recent stories onto the 'text' of the older ones. In telling a new story, he draws his listeners' and readers' attention to how the story is a contemporary version of a much older story. Robinson recalls that contractors wanted to build a road through the reserve. Even though the contractors promised to pay the Okanagan community for the use of land and gave the band a written document stating their intention to pay, the band never received this payment:

> See?
> They build this road in 1929.
> Went through the reserve.
> And they said to the Indian, ...
> 'Then, when we got the money
> then we'll pay you for your land
>     for the road going through.'
> All right.
> The Indians say, 'All right.'
> They write it down.
> And when did they pay?
> They never paid 'em yet.
> They never did pay. (*Write* 46)

Robinson highlights how Canadian law upholds or ignores the authority of written documents depending upon political expedience. While Canadian law enforces the supremacy of written documents over oral traditions, the act of writing the promise down on paper enables the road contractors to conveniently forget that promise. For Robinson, in contrast, oral stories are more reliable records of people's relationship to land because stories passed down through the generations live longer than paper.

Robinson stages the stories in local landscapes not only to document Okanagan title to land, but also to create a shared world in which he can establish relations of exchange with Wickwire. With an intense precision, Robinson situates his stories in local Okanagan geographies, explaining through story the existence of a physical feature of the region. It is of the utmost importance that Robinson communicates how his stories are literally grounded in local landscapes. In this way, Robinson rewrites the history of contact and communicates with Wickwire his version of Canadian and Okanagan histories. For example, in the story 'Helped by a Wolverine,' Robinson describes the very copse of trees in which one of the characters stands. He clearly wants Wickwire to remember this particular spot:

> And he keep going towards Merritt,
>   where the highway is now ...
> And then he go down towards Merritt.
> And when he get so far down,
>   and when you go down that road from the summit
>     and you go down towards Merritt
>       and you see the bunch of poplars on the side of the road.
> Down, you know, below from the road in places,
>   the poplars, there and there, like a bunch of them.
> He come to that place. (147-48)

'That place' is an exact spot that Robinson and Wickwire had passed by during the day; now, at night, Robinson tells the story that revolves around this particular place. The narratives build through the characters' (and his own and Wickwire's) travels through land. He connects the time of the narrative and the distance of the travels. In this way, Robinson provides local contexts for Wickwire to understand the stories.

If Robinson can show Wickwire how his stories connect to specific places, he may convince her of Okanagan title to land. The story 'Coyote Plays a Dirty Trick' is especially significant in establishing Okanagan presence in the region[9] because its traces can be 'read' in Okanagan bedrock. In the story, Coyote sends his son up to the moon so that he can abduct his son's two wives. But Coyote's Son manages to return to earth with the help of an old spider couple who live on the moon. When Coyote's Son lands, he walks on bedrock and leaves the imprint of his footsteps on the ground. These marks can still be seen today:

> That's this place.
> That was in Lytton.
> That's in Lytton.
> Then Young Coyote, he says,
> > 'Now this is my country.
> > This is my place.' ...
> And Young Coyote, he walk
> > and there's supposed to be rock,
> > > supposed to be bedrock.
> Looks like a bedrock.
> Flat, right on the ground.
> He walk on there.
> And now today,
> > if anybody know where that is
> > > they could still see the tracks
> > > > that was marked on the rock. (106)

Some years ago, as Robinson details, Canadian Pacific Railways (CPR) wanted to pass over the rock where Coyote's Son landed. Okanagan communities in the region insisted that CPR take a detour to miss the rock:

> And the Indians over there,[10] they know where that is.
> Then when they survey the railroad, that CPR,
> > And they [Indians] tell the white man,
> > > 'Looks like your surveying, your line is right on our history' ...
> > They told 'em all about it
> > > and they told 'em just a part of that story.
> Not all.
> Just a part of that story ...
> > 'We want you to miss it.
> > You can work your surveying from up somewhere,
> > and not to hit this part here.
> > If you miss 'em, it'll be better.'
> All right, they do that.
> And now today it's still there. (106-7)

For Robinson, telling stories demonstrates Okanagan title to land. However, the kind of title to land that the stories describe is not easy to assimilate into notions of private property. Indeed, Robinson suggests that

Aboriginal title is not an individual property right. The confrontation with CPR demonstrates that private property is not an appropriate way to describe Aboriginal title to land; rather, Aboriginal title is more aptly described as a communal holding of land that is inalienable because it underlies Crown title.

Like the story 'Coyote Plays a Dirty Trick,' 'Prophecy at Lytton' is precisely situated in a local landscape, and both stories have left traces of their events in bedrock. In 'Prophecy at Lytton,' a young boy makes a blue and white blanket out of bird feathers and presents it as a gift to God. God then turns the blanket into a blue and white rock. According to Robinson, the rock is still somewhere near Lytton: 'Up to the hillside, that way, / That's where that is. / And this rock is there' (191). However many years ago, it was buried by some Okanagan people, in order, Robinson suggests, to block its sale. For Robinson, this act of burying the rock asserts the inalienability of Okanagan land title:

> When this rock disappeared, it might be before 1800,
>     something like that ...
> And the Indians at that time, they say, ...
>     'We better hide that rock.
>     We going to sunk 'em in the ground.
>     Because the white people came, and they might find 'em ...
>     They'll pack 'em away.
> They could steal that from us ... ' (192-93)
>
> But they never tell the young people, the young Indian.
> They tell some.
> But later on, they just quit telling 'em.
> And they don't tell 'em anymore ...
>
> Supposing they figure,
>     if they let the young people know,
>         and nowadays, that they could tell the white people,
>             and they could sell it.
> They going to get the money from the white people for that rock.
> They might ask $500 or something like that.
> And the white people will give 'em that money. (194)

Neither land nor story, in Robinson's view, can be bought or sold. Land is inalienable from community use; stories are 'inalienable' from the storytelling interaction. Robinson tells Wickwire how he learned about this rock without having seen it:

> [N]obody know today about that [rock].
> But I know.
> And my wife know.
> Because I learned that from her father.
> And I learn the same story from my grandmother.
> And so she learned that from her father.
> And also we learned that from Mary Narcisse.
> Mary Narcisse was living until 1944 until the age of 116.
> That's how we know that. (194-95)

The stories have been passed through generations and only exist through the act of telling. Even the rock exists only insofar as it is passed on as a story. To remember the stories, Robinson needs a community of tellers and listeners: 'Sometimes we need two, three of us. And tell the stories for maybe a couple of hours, the old people' (Wickwire, Introduction, *Nature* 8). The stories launch still more stories when many storytellers and listeners are present. Though this sense of interlocking stories is somewhat de-emphasized in Wickwire's collections, which accentuate the stories themselves over the process of storytelling, Robinson and Wickwire both demonstrate that a mutually respectful collaborative process – whether openly acknowledged or not – is necessary to enact ethically engaged storytelling and textualizing practices. What Robinson also implies, in his stories that provide metacritical commentary on the question of land rights and the land claims process, is that the establishment of a storytelling *exchange* (telling and listening) must precede any agreement on paper, which in any case must not compromise the inalienability of a people's title to land.

The relationship between land and storytelling, as well as between land jurisdiction and authorship, is further explored in Julie Cruikshank, Angela Sidney, Kitty Smith, and Annie Ned's *Life Lived Like a Story*, which highlights more explicitly the interactive setting of storytelling. Following the arguments of Cruikshank and other scholars, I emphasize the importance of paying careful attention to *context*, particularly the contexts of (re)tellings in textualized oral traditions. Julia Emberley, in her analysis of *Life Lived Like a Story*, argues that Cruikshank's emphasis on context renders static her multiplicitous, dialogic, collaborative text by reasserting the primacy of the 'accurate transcript' (Emberley 188). In fact, Cruikshank agrees, pointing out that an over-emphasis on context, often found in ethnographic overviews, 'smoothes out contradictions in an effort to present a comprehensive picture' (Cruikshank et al. 4). Yet I would suggest that *de*contextualized readings pose a greater danger of concretizing events or concepts by removing them from the interactions of history and place (as demonstrated by McEachern's misreading of Gitksan and Wet'suwet'en oral traditions, for example). I would further suggest Cruikshank manages the tension quite effectively between providing a context and drawing attention to the falseness of 'comprehensive picture[s]' through her development of the concept of collaborative authorship.

The theory and practice of collaborative authorship, as formulated by Cruikshank, have become highly influential in Native literary studies and oral historical research.[11] Collaborative authorship exploits the flexibility and intersubjective potential of recorded oral narrative while avoiding any easy definitions of collaboration as the reconciliation of cultural differences. The tension between 'collaboration' and 'authorship' enables the recorded oral narrative to accommodate a diverse range of objectives and audience.

### Collaborative Authorship: *Life Lived Like a Story*

In *Life Lived Like a Story*, the claim to 'collaborative authorship' does more than add three names to the title page. Both collaboration and authorship are of crucial importance in understanding the process of both telling and listening to Athapaskan oral narrative in cross-cultural contexts. Collaborative authorship not only shapes Julie Cruikshank's editorial decisions but also inflects the three elders' storytelling practices. Not only do the stories themselves represent wealth; they also act as expressions of land ownership. Like the *Delgamuukw* transcripts and *Write It on Your Heart*, *Life Lived Like a Story* offers a compelling exploration of the connections between oral traditions, land, and Aboriginal title. Yet the stories do not describe territories in so many square kilometres. Rather, travelling through land is 'proof' of belonging to that land. *Life Lived Like a Story* redefines land *as* story: land becomes a set of social relations, not a thing in itself.

The text does not suggest collaboration is a 'solution' to the problem of cultural representation. Indeed, the objectives of the four authors are, at the outset, at odds. Collaborative authorship signals both the divergence and the convergence of agendas among the four authors. Cruikshank began recording stories in Yukon and Alaska in 1974 in an effort to document social change in the region over the past two generations. However, in response to her questions about the gold rush or the building of the Alaska Highway, Athapaskan/Tlingit storytellers Angela Sidney, Kitty Smith, and Annie Ned recited long lists of place names, recounted complex genealogies, and told hundreds of traditional stories and songs (Cruikshank et al. 2). Like Wickwire, Cruikshank was at first not sure how these place names and traditional narratives were answers to her questions. To resolve this sense of discrepancy, Cruikshank felt impelled to re-envision her research project: 'Under their [the elders'] tutelage my interests have shifted away from an oral history committed to documenting changes in social reality and toward an investigation of narrative forms for talking about, remembering, and interpreting everyday life' (x). Collaboration, therefore, based on the notion of exchange, is a renegotiation of the purpose, direction, form, and content of the research. As a methodology, collaboration provides an alternative to 'participant observation' approaches in anthropology, while, as an ethics, collaboration is a principle of intersubjectivity in which both Cruikshank's and the elders' contributions are recognized and rewarded both economically and socially. Collaboration foregrounds the interpenetrating contexts of tellings and re-tellings, defying separation of audience, setting, and narrator. A collaborative approach also stresses the mediating layers of textualized oral narratives – transcription, translation, editing, and publishing.

The text takes seriously Sidney's claim that 'my stories are my wealth' (36). Her statement became the basis of the collaborative authorship 'contract' between the four authors. Each storyteller has published at least one book of stories under her own name; the bibliography lists four publications under Sidney's name, two under Smith's, and one under Ned's.[12] These books of stories, published by the Council for Yukon Indians and the Yukon Native Languages Project, have been distributed to family members as well as to local community stores, schools, libraries, band council offices, and radio stations (14). Cruikshank, acknowledging that the publication of *Life Lived Like a Story* by a university press may help her own career but will not significantly benefit the storytellers or their communities, thus substantiates her claim to collaborative authorship by facilitating the dissemination of the material in different forms and to different audiences.

The decision to publish multiple versions of the stories was not only an ethical choice by Cruikshank to ensure reciprocity. The concept of multiple publications is important to the elders' storytelling practices as well. In *Life Lived Like a Story,* authorship is not understood as an act of singular creation by one individual. As Ned insists, 'Not *you* are telling it: it's the person who told you that's telling the story' (278). Throughout her cycle of stories, Ned emphasizes the importance of 'get[ting] the words right' in order to do justice to past storytellers or oral authors (267). Before she begins telling a story, she explains where and from whom she first heard the story:

> Now I'm going to tell a story about long time ago. This is my two grandpas' story, Big Jim's and Hutshi Chief's. I'm telling this story not from myself, but because everybody [old] knows this story. This is not just my story – lots of old people tell it! Just like now they go to school, old time we come to our grandpa. Whoever is old tells it the same way. (279, square brackets in the original)

Ned continually emphasizes that she is telling the story 'the same way' that she heard it. This does not mean that every telling of the story creates the same meanings. 'Oral testimony is never the same twice, even when the same words are used, because the relationship – the dialogue – is always shifting. Oral traditions ... have social histories, and they acquire meaning in the situations in which they are used' (Cruikshank, *Social* 40). Each telling of the 'same' story is like a publication and carries with it the responsibility of a form of copyright. The chain of intermediaries that passes on the story, and the circumstances surrounding the re-tellings, constitute the story itself. Here, 'authorship' becomes a collective responsibility shared among four people. But even the named four authors inadequately describe the collective nature of authorship in oral modes. Sidney, Smith, and Ned set themselves, Cruikshank, and the story in a web of relationships, a network of people, places, and events. When telling a story, the elders' identities stretch backward and forward in time as they relate their stories and those of others who are long dead. No story is authored by, or 'belongs' to, one person exclusively. This is a common claim in Native North American storytelling practices. The interaction between storyteller and audience 'removes the teller from the role of author to the role of mediator. The story is passed along from those who came before' (Wong 95). As Bakhtin suggests, using the speech of someone else makes possible 'various types, subcategories and forms of authorship' (*Speech* 104). The shift from 'author' to 'mediator' contests the links between private property and individual genius that are entrenched in notions of authorship in print-capitalist economies.[13]

This model of authorship tells us something about Athapaskan notions of property. In expressions of Athapaskan land ownership, the principle of exchange is more important than the principle of accumulation. Similarly, the act of passing through land, rather than delineating units of land, affirms one's belonging to a place. Cruikshank recounts that a Tagish community land claims negotiator, frustrated with the difficult task of constructing a one-to-one relationship between land and territory, once said, 'How can you own a piece of land? It's like saying you can own a cloud!' (qtd. in Cruikshank, *Social* 17). Land is something in motion, like water or wind; it is closer to a verb than a noun. The Athapaskan and Tlingit conception of territory, based on exchange and travel, not on possession and accumulation, is similar to Gitksan and Wet'suwet'en concepts of land ownership. However, as we have seen in the *Delgamuukw* case, fluid concepts of land ownership do not easily translate into the language of the court.

What Cruikshank calls the 'layered tellings' of Sidney's story, 'Kaax'achgóok,' demonstrate that relations of exchange constitute the story itself. Cruikshank uses the phrase 'layered tellings' to describe how a storyteller is able to use a single narrative to convey a range of meanings: 'What appears to be the "same" story, even in the repertoire of one individual, acquires multiple meanings depending on the location, circumstance, audience and stage of life of both narrator and listener' (*Social* 44). 'Kaax'achgóok' is the story of a hunter who, along with his companions, is blown off course in a boat by a storm; however, by navigating by the sun on the summer solstice the following year, Kaax'achgóok is finally successful in returning home (Cruikshank et al. 5). Each telling of the story is comparable to a separate publication in Athapaskan oral traditions; each performance is historically situated as the audience and meanings shift. Sidney, who describes herself as a Tagish and Tlingit woman of the *Deisheetaan* (Crow) clan, and who is fluent in Tagish, Tlingit, and English (21), first told the story in 1945 at a feast to mark the return of her son, Pete, from the Second World War. In 1974, she told the story to Cruikshank, explaining that Cruikshank needed to hear this story first before she could understand the rest of her life story. In 1988, Sidney told the story again to commemorate the opening of the new Yukon College (*Social* 42). For each of these tellings, Sidney explains why she is telling the story; her emphasis on the event of communication underscores the highly situational and performative nature of her stories.

In the 1974 telling of 'Ḵaax̱'achgóok' to Cruikshank, Sidney begins by identifying who first told her the story, why she is retelling it, and how she claims the right to pass it on:

> I was ten when I heard this story first.
> My auntie, Mrs. Austin, told me the story the first time.
> Later I heard my father tell it to the boys.
> This is that song I gave to Pete.
> I'm going to tell how we claim it. (Cruikshank et al. 139)

The story is accompanied by a song that is considered cultural property in Tlingit traditions. This is the same song that, as I discussed in Chapter 1, Tlingit storyteller A.P. Johnson requested Richard and Nora Dauenhauer to strike out of the record, since it cannot be performed or disseminated without explicit permission (Dauenhauer and Dauenhauer, *Haa Shuká* 333n).[14] Sidney is likewise unambiguous on this point: 'you should not sing songs that belong to other nations' (Cruikshank et al. 39). When Sidney first sang it in 1945, her father's cousin contested her right to perform it. As Sidney says, '[The chief], Patsy [Henderson] told my mother, "It's not you fellows' song, that song. You can't use that song." He asked Johnny Anderson about it, and Johnny Anderson said, "No, it's not *Deisheetaan* song"' (136). Sidney acknowledges that her *Deisheetaan* clan does not own the song: 'Well, that's right, it's *not* our song' (136). She then travelled about a hundred kilometres from Carcross, Yukon, to Skagway, Alaska, to speak to two elders in order to confirm her right to sing the song (Cruikshank, *Social* 38). The elders told her that Ḵaax̱'achgóok, the main character in the story, had given the song to her clan in exchange for his brother, who had been detained as a prisoner during a conflict between the two communities. The visit to Skagway verified Sidney's guardianship of the story: 'He [Ḵaax̱'achgóok] gave us that song ... [H]e gave it to us in place of his brother. That's why we use it. That's why I use it! That's why I gave it to Pete when he came back from the army, because he just went through what happened to Ḵaax̱'achgóok. He drifted away in the ocean, but finally he came back' (Cruikshank et al. 136).

Sidney's narrative frame suggests not only that Tlingit clans claim ownership of songs, but also that some songs establish links between territories and act as assertions of land title. However, Sidney does not speak of land as an object that she or her community possesses; rather, she emphasizes travelling through land as her way to affirm her connection to place. Her linking of modes of telling with modes of travel is evident when, in 1985, she told Cruikshank the circumstances of her son's return from the Second World War:

> My son Pete was in the war: I got Old Man to get little radio so we could listen to hear where they're moving the troops so we would know where he is. Five years he's gone – just like that K̲aax̲'achgóok story I told you.
>
> Finally, it's getting over, war. Pete sent a message: he sent a letter home, airmail ... We start counting the days ... we gave him five days to cross the ocean ...
>
> When he landed in New York he sent a telegram again ... From there, we counted the days again. We gave him four days to come to Vancouver ... From there when he gets on the boat, we counted [the days] again. We give him four days to land in Skagway. From the time he got the boat from Vancouver we're counting the days again. (135-36)

Like K̲aax̲'achgóok, the hunter in the story, Pete was out of contact for a long time but eventually returned home, travelling by ship, train, and ferry and announcing his imminent return by radio, letter, telegram, and map. Here Sidney links modes of travel with modes of communication. Doing so underlines the links that she repeatedly makes between travelling the land and telling stories, mediated through technologies of communication and navigation, and recalling K̲aax̲'achgóok's ingenuity in ascertaining the summer solstice in order to plot his journey home.

While place in *Life Lived Like a Story* acts as an 'immediate catalyst' for telling stories (Sands, 'Narrative' 11), it is not necessarily a specific location. Place has narrative movement, like a story. For Sidney, stories begin with clan history; each clan belongs to a specific place and traces journeys from there. Belonging to a clan does not require living within a defined set of boundaries. In one section of her clan history, or *Shagóon*, Sidney describes a recent visit to Angoon. Angoon is the village where her *Shagóon* begins and the location from which she traces her songs, stories, and histories (Cruikshank et al. 37). Taken as a whole, the *Shagóon* resembles a series of travelogues. In describing her fifty-six-hour journey by car and boat, Sidney makes constant reference to the means of communication – phone and telegram – that the travellers used to contact communities along the way. She recalls her feelings about the trip to Angoon:

> Well, they talk about us, those people in Angoon. They never see us but they know we're up here from way far back. They know part of them are up here. They've been calling us, 'Come back, come back.' They want to see us. (146)

Calling 'come back, come back' is perhaps a song of lament for a dispersed nation. Yet the sense of melancholy over displacement is tempered by the recreation of the community through story. The acts of calling, singing songs, or telling stories re-establish the links between community and territory. Speaking those connections through story and song is a form of community building. By talking about one another, even if they are well out of earshot, the nation solidifies its common stories and territories.

Sidney speaks of songs as if they were signposts on journeys across territory. The following story recounts the initial departure of her ancestors from Angoon a long time ago:

> When they're ready to take off, they made a song: 'Shove it out now!' This is the song they pushed them out with ... [T]hat's the song they separated on ...
>
> Before they started out again, they made another song: 'Way out to the sky I aim my boat.' Then that group split three ways: some went out to deep water, and some went to Yakutat. [Some] came up the coast and went up Chilkat River. (40)

Sidney's songs, composed in verb phrases, emphasize the narrative movement of place. These songs reveal the close interconnection between 'legends' and 'specific lands' – a relation that McEachern could not imagine or discern from Antgulilibix's testimony.

In a manner comparable to that of the Gitksan and Wet'suwet'en witnesses and Harry Robinson, all three storytellers in *Life Lived Like a Story* associate telling stories with travelling through very specific landscapes. When travelling in Cruikshank's pickup truck, Annie Ned often interrupted conversations to sing songs connected with geographical locations outside the window. For Ned, many of the songs belong to particular clans that occupy specific territories established by ancestral travel: 'You don't know this place, so I will sing a song to you to tell you where you're going. This is Big Jim's song. It's just like he cries with this song' (277). Similarly, Kitty Smith recorded 230 place names, in both Southern Tutchone and Tlingit, while travelling in Cruikshank's truck. Some of her stories are made up entirely of place names (Cruikshank, *Social* 18). Likewise, Angela Sidney travelled with Cruikshank by car, boat, and railway in order to map Tagish and Tlingit place names on topographic maps. As they travelled, Sidney 'attached specific stories, songs and events to features of the landscape' (22), beginning a process that would culminate in the publication of *Place Names of the Tagish Region, Southern Yukon*, issued in 1980 by the Yukon Languages Project. Sidney often begins stories with openings such as the one for 'Wolf Story,' which carefully establishes a local landscape:

> This story happened *here*, at *this* head of Tagish Lake someplace ...
> behind that big white rock.
> Up toward Ten Mile, *Tsux̱x'aayí*.
>
> There's a big rock there on the beach.
> That's where this story happened.
> *Ḵaax̱ Teiyí* – 'sawbill duck rock,' they call it in Tlingit.
> *Tsós Tsei'e'* in Tagish language.
> There's another story that that rock was once a man who married a woman ...
> Anyway, this is where it happened. (88, my emphasis)

The rock in the story becomes the nexus of a series of interlocking stories. The close connection between travel, place, and storytelling in *Life Lived Like a Story* defies any sense of land or territory as a bounded unit quantifiable in definitive measurements. Although there is no doubt in the storytellers' minds about who owns the land or the story, the concept of ownership does not necessarily match notions of private property. For example, in recounting her family history, Annie Ned describes the territory of Nùłatà, her first husband's paternal grandfather, clarifying that '"owning" the lake did not mean that *Nùłatà* or his Wolf kinsmen made exclusive use of the lake, but rather that he was in a position to invite others to come to hunt and fish there' (273). In discussing Michel de Certeau's insight – 'What the map cuts up, the story cuts across' (qtd. in Cruikshank, *Social* 1) – Cruikshank comments upon the problem of reifying oral traditions as assertions of land ownership in court battles for Aboriginal title: 'Community land claims negotiators are faced with the difficult task of reconciling the state's narratives about land as bounded units to be owned and operated for profit with their own spatial understanding that stories crosscut maps' (16). These stories, as J. Edward Chamberlin argues in another context, do not provide 'a revelation of ownership in any simple-minded sense, because these stories didn't establish possession of the place. On the contrary, they showed how the people were possessed by it – owned and occupied, as it were, and answerable to it by means of their stories and songs' ('From' 127). Response to, and responsibility for, the land is a more appropriate description than land ownership.

In *Life Lived Like a Story*, exchange is the central metaphor by which the three storytellers attempt to convey concepts of ownership of both land and story. The storytellers show the fine distinctions between giving and throwing away, taking and stealing, owning and using. In 'Wolf Story,' Angela Sidney sketches an ethics of potlatch, in which giving things away increases wealth. Potlatch is a 'redistribution system' that turns on a concept of common, not private, property (Cruikshank et al. 10). In *Potlatch Papers* (1997), cultural critic Christopher Bracken suggests that one of the main reasons for outlawing potlatch at the end of the nineteenth century was that it defied capitalist notions of wealth as accumulation. As a result, potlatch represents a significant challenge to Canadian legal definitions of property. Sidney's story is about an unsuccessful hunter:

> The man hunts every day – ...
> They've got a little bit of grub, but they're stingy with it.
> They eat just a little bit at a time.
> He hunts, hunts, hunts, but he kills nothing. (88)

Wolf, through his own example of generosity, teaches the hunter that stinginess is the cause of bad luck in hunting. Wolf addresses the man:

> 'I'm Wolf ...
> I killed all those caribou for you. You can have it,
> And I give you my snowshoes, too.
> From now on your luck is going to change.
> You're going to have good luck.' ...
> And he gave him his bow and arrow.
> 'I'll give you everything that I use to keep myself going ...
> I'm going to leave you in the morning and you can have all
> that meat.' (89)

The next morning, the man packs the meat and returns home, and the family has enough to eat for the rest of the winter, suggesting that Wolf's gift has helped re-establish equilibrium in the social relations of the community.

All three storytellers carefully distinguish the act of giving something *to* someone, within the context of a social relationship, from the act of throwing something *away*, to no one. Kitty Smith's story 'Mountain Man' is about a woman who not only received many gifts from a female relative, but also stole from caches. As a result of causing an imbalance in her society's relations of exchange, she risks becoming outcast or 'throw[n] away' (233). Smith's story is an exploration of the tensions between stealing, taking, giving, and throwing away:

> They say she was *stealing* some kind of cache – nobody likes that.
>
> One lady loved her though –
> her auntie or her half-sister, I'm not sure.
> She *gave* her lots of things –
> Snare, some knife, sewing things, rabbit snare –
> She *gave* it, you know, everything.
>
> 'They're going to *throw away you!*
> You're going to go by yourself.
> They talk about you all the time.
> You *steal,* they say that you steal,' she tells her. (233, my emphasis)

The woman is abandoned, but walking alone she comes across an elderly couple who needs assistance in securing food. The woman becomes an excellent hunter and provides for the couple, and, like Wolf, restores the balance between taking and giving.

As if using 'Mountain Man' as a conceptual framework or 'cultural scaffolding' (Cruikshank, *Social* 70) to explain her own life experiences, Smith draws attention to another form of stealing – land appropriation. The loss resulting from this stealing – that is, the loss of land rights – has yet to be recuperated. She relates how she once defied a 'bigshot government man,' the former commissioner of the Yukon territory (Cruikshank et al. 251). The commissioner had asked Smith to extinguish her fire, thereby presuming jurisdiction over the territory. Smith recalls her words to the commissioner (though she didn't know at the time who he was):

> Me my Grandpa's country, here. My Grandma's. My roots grow in jackpine roots all. That's why I stay here. I don't go to your Grandpa's country and

> make fire. No. My Grandma's country I make fire. Don't burn. If I be near your Grandma's country, it's all right you tell me. (251)

Later, in relating the incident to her grandson, she adds:

> I'm bigshot, too. I belong to Yukon ... I'm born here. I branch here! The government got all this country, how big it is. He don't pay 5 cents, he got him all. Nobody kicks me out. No, sir! My roots grow in jackpine roots. (252)

Like the woman in 'Mountain Man,' the government has taken more than its share. It has claimed land title to 'all this country' and has given little in return; yet unlike the woman in the story, it has made few amends. Indeed, instead of compensating Native peoples for this appropriation, in a bizarre reversal of the traditional narrative, it is the government that has attempted to banish Native peoples from their own land (through the reserve system and other practices).

The lessons of maintaining balance in relations of exchange in the elders' stories inform the practice of collaborative authorship in the text. Although stories are 'wealth' in *Life Lived Like a Story*, in relating a story to an audience, the teller passes on the burden of response and responsibility to the listener. Structurally, *Life Lived Like a Story* creates a dialectical movement between voices in the text. In tacking back and forth between the layers of the text – from Cruikshank's essays, introductions, appendices, and notes, to the storytellers' life histories, traditional narratives, and songs – the reader can detect both a fine distinction between voices and their dialogic interaction. Each telling of a story, whether in speech or in writing, generates another story. Both linkages and distances are produced as tellers, listeners, translators, and readers mediate, and meditate upon, the 'wealth' of possible meanings that the storytelling interaction creates.

### Redefining the Territory: Collaborative Authorship in the Courtroom

Oral traditions are fundamentally different from the discourse of evidence or proof. Storytelling is an embodied performance, not an archive of documents. *Adaawk* and *kungax*, as dialogic and performative storytelling genres, do not translate easily into the language of fact; they require receptive listeners. However, the discursive limits of the courtroom virtually preclude dialogic exchange. While in 1997 the Supreme Court of Canada found 'palpable errors' (*Delgamuukw* [SCC]: par. 7) with Judge McEachern's decision, stating that oral history must be 'accommodated and placed on an equal footing with' (par. 87) standard forms of evidence, the decision offered few clues about how to better 'hear' oral traditions in the courtroom. If oral traditions are genuinely to challenge current definitions of 'evidence', 'title', 'ownership', and 'land use', the battle for Aboriginal rights will require a much more intensive process of negotiation than the current antagonistic model allows.[15]

I have proposed in this chapter that the principle of 'collaborative authorship' may provide a model for negotiating land disputes. What might this suggestion look like in a hypothetical land claims case? It is of critical importance that researchers from a range of disciplines engage with legal discourses and put them in dialogue with other discourses that might help fashion a new ethics of land claims negotiation. A new ethics of land claims negotiation would depend upon the court actively responding to the evidence and acknowledging the interconnections in oral history that complicate the usual process of presenting evidence for cross-examination in decontextualized text-bites. It would depend upon the court considering *how* to listen to the evidence. It would also demand that the court consider its role in reproducing colonial discourses that fuel a variety of state apparatuses that seek to control and manage Aboriginal communities. Also critical is a revised notion of 'authorship' that acknowledges that oral traditions used as evidence in land claims trials are cultural property, that they are interconnected, and that they delineate a claim to territory, land title, and jurisdiction. During the *Delgamuukw* trial, the Gitksan and Wet'suwet'en plaintiffs made the case that the performance of their *adaawk* and *kungax* enacted their land title and jurisdiction. In ratifying their responsibility to their lands, the Gitksan and Wet'suwet'en witnesses took enormous risks in transforming the colonial space of the courtroom into their feast hall. Their principled actions should be remembered and carried on to energize the ongoing struggle for Aboriginal rights. The aim, in the words of E.P. Thompson, is to 'force it [the law] to change its language' so that new forms of collective agency may emerge.

In moving from a land claims trial to collections of textualized oral narrative in this chapter, and recovering the possibility of alternative readings of the testimony presented at the *Delgamuukw* trial, my aim is to attend with care to the role of socio-historical context in the material background of texts. In producing alternative interpretations of *adaawk* and *kungax*, I hope to honour the wishes of Yaga'lahl (Dora Wilson), who stated that the trial will become a 'victory' insofar as 'we have it [our oral history] written in black and white now for anyone to see in those transcripts, in those 374 volumes of transcripts' ('The Time of the Trial' 11). In practising contextually grounded readings, I am using a storytelling ethics of connection to illuminate the role of the listener or reader in determining the story itself, while simultaneously warning against an idealized conception of the storyteller / listener interaction. Such an idealization risks ignoring the conditions that restrict aboriginal communities from practising in an unhampered manner their land title, jurisdiction, self-government agreements, or even their right of copyright in relating their oral traditions. Finally, juxtaposing the transcripts from *Delgamuukw* with *Write It on Your Heart* and *Life Lived Like a Story* serves the larger purpose of this book: to fashion an interdisciplinary methodology that links texts, histories, and critical approaches that, for the most part, have been analysed in isolation from one another.

# 6
## 'I Can Only Sing This Song to Someone Who Understands It'
## Community Filmmaking and the Politics of Partial Translation

> The artfulness of the ethnographic object is an art of excision, of detachment, an art of the excerpt. Where does the object begin and where does it end? This I see as an essentially surgical issue. Shall we exhibit the cup with the saucer, the tea, the cream and sugar, the spoon, the napkin and placemat, the table and chair, the rug? Where do we stop? Where do we make the cut?
>
> – BARBARA KIRSHENBLATT-GIMBLETT, 'OBJECTS OF ETHNOGRAPHY'

> All art is, I suppose, a kind of exploring. Whether or not it's true of art, that's the way I started filmmaking. I was an explorer first and a filmmaker a long way after.
>
> – ROBERT FLAHERTY (QTD. IN PAUL ROTHA, *ROBERT J. FLAHERTY*)

> The Inuit style of filmmaking takes lots of teamwork. We work horizontally but the usual Hollywood film works in a military style. Our team would be talking, 'how are we going to shoot this?' with my art directors down to my sound man. We put the whole community to work.
>
> – ZACHARIAS KUNUK, 'THE PUBLIC ART OF INUIT STORYTELLING'

The film *Atanarjuat, the Fast Runner* (2001), based on what the filmmakers say is part of the 'continuous stream of oral history' in Igloolik Inuit storytelling traditions ('Atanarjuat' par. 2), opens with Kumaglak's refusal to sing a song to a mysterious stranger. He insists that 'I can only sing this song to someone who understands it.'[1] Kumaglak's statement is a kind of manifesto that shapes the politics and poetics of the film: to respond to and contest the history of appropriation in recording Inuit songs. Kumaglak will not sing because he does not know how the listener will receive, re-tell, and re-use the song for his own purposes. His suspicions prove to be well founded: the 'up North stranger' murders him, enabling Kumaglak's son, Sauri, to become the leader of the group and to steal the song as his own anthem. The incident suggests that the song's power lies in its performance, and the relations of address cannot be separated from the song itself. Taking the song out of one context and recontextualizing it in another profoundly affects the range of meanings that it can generate.

As a film that explicitly highlights the fact that it is Inuit written, produced, directed, and acted, *Atanarjuat* seeks to challenge the long history of outsiders collecting Inuit oral traditions. The co-founders of Igloolik Isuma Productions say that they are 'deliberately re-appropriat[ing] ... ancient knowledge from Southern museums and books' ('Bringing' par. 3). Making the film involved a range of community elders, storytellers, recorders, translators, filmmakers, and crewmembers. The goal in representing a well-known, local legend on film was not to exhibit the characteristics of Inuit social life as ethnographic curiosities, but to remember family histories (Kunuk, 'I First' 13), to (re)learn Inuktitut (including 'Old Inuktitut,' as co-founder Paul Apak Angilirq calls the language that his elders spoke when they lived on the land [Angilirq, 'Interview' 19]), to experiment with aesthetic forms that draw upon oral traditions, and to assert the deep historical roots of Igloolik Inuit culture in the region. It was not purely a coincidence that the filmmakers began shooting *Atanarjuat* in the same month and year (April 1999) that Nunavut came into being (Saladin D'Anglure 227): they used techniques of 'community filmmaking' to contribute to larger projects of cultural, artistic, and social revitalization in Igloolik. *Atanarjuat* uses strategies of autoethnography, partial translation, and collaborative, cross-cultural production to create mediated Inuit voices that counter ethnographic traditions of apprehending a singular cultural essence. A comparison to historical constructions of Inuit stories and songs in text and film, and particularly to Robert

Flaherty's *Nanook of the North* (1922), shows how *Atanarjuat*'s collaborative filmmaking production opens up for negotiation hierarchical relations in both textmaking and filmmaking.

A consideration of the convergence of the making of the film with the formation of Nunavut reveals that, as an expression of cultural nationalism, *Atanarjuat* self-consciously places itself at the forefront of the current Inuit cultural renaissance. The last minutes of *Atanarjuat*, which may be described as metadramatic scenes,[2] reveal some instances in the making of the film, and model how a locally based company like Isuma can generate work and provide training for a wide range of Igloolik residents. The Isuma film, *Nipi (Voice)*, also made in 1999 – and made at a time when the making of *Atanarjuat* was forced to halt due to shortfalls in funding – provides a platform for the filmmakers not only to warn against the dangers of perpetuating colonial-bureaucratic relations in the new territory, but also to insist upon the development of a locally-focused arts and culture policy as part of Nunavut's priorities. *Nipi*'s underlying message is that Nunavut's future leaders should look beyond their dreams of resource development and seriously acknowledge forms of cultural, artistic, and community revitalization as a way to progress from assimilation to self-determination. Nunavut's commitment to make space within its institutions for *Inuit Qaujimajatuqangit* (IQ) – 'that which Inuit have long known' or 'an Inuit way of doing things' – is dependent upon the participation of its elders, artists, and cultural workers to stitch together 'the past, the present, and future knowledge, experience, and values of Inuit society' (IQ Task Force 2002, qtd. in A. Henderson 191). I discuss how and for what reasons Isuma's films put into practice both the content and process of *Inuit Qaujimajatuqangit* and how such an approach enables the filmmakers to craft an insurgent, critically informed politics of cultural nationalism.

### Nanook and After: *Atanarjuat* as a Counterethnographic Film

In Chapter 1, I argued that the history of collecting Aboriginal oral traditions has reinforced the notion of the ethnographic fragment. *Atanarjuat* responds to the long history of recording Inuit oral traditions and deploys a number of strategies to reinvent the process of recording, translating, and circulating oral texts. In particular, as Kumaglak's opening statement suggests, the film challenges historical constructions of Inuit songs as decontextualized oral 'poems', removed from the contexts of performance and reception. From the 1910s and 1920s, transcribed Inuit songs, initially collected by anthropologist-explorers such as Franz Boas, Diamond Jenness, and Knud Rasmussen,[3] and later collected in anthologies by writers and literary critics, including George W. Cronyn, Jerome Rothenberg, and John Robert Colombo,[4] garnered interest as oral verse, appealing to Romantic ideas about the oral origins of 'literature.' In many of these literary anthologies, editors have retranslated, rearranged, and re-presented the songs without knowing the languages in which they first were performed. While some of the editors provide contextualizing information in headnotes or footnotes, the songs themselves are generally presented as freestanding lyric poems. The 'art of excision' (Kirshenblatt-Gimblett 388) in the making of the literary ethnographic fragment hides the mediated nature of textualized oral performances that *Atanarjuat*, in both film and book forms, continually stresses.

It is precisely this decontextualization of Inuit oral traditions that the filmmakers of *Atanarjuat* are determined to challenge and reverse in their slow-paced, three-hour film. Isuma, which means 'to think' in Inuktitut, was co-founded in 1990 by Zacharias Kunuk, originally a carver, who bought his own video camera in 1981 and who worked for the Inuit Broadcasting Corporation (IBC) before co-creating Isuma; the late Paul Apak Angilirq (commonly known as Paul Apak), who also worked for IBC and who initiated the plan to make the feature film based on the Atanarjuat legend; Paulossie Qulitalik, an elder, actor, and cultural adviser; and Norman Cohn, an independent videographer who first met Kunuk in 1985 as the seminar leader of a video art training program in Iqaluit. *Atanarjuat* should be situated within Isuma's larger oeuvre of documentaries, dramas, and 'docudramas,' many of which stress the pedagogical value of carefully recording Inuit traditional skills related to travelling, hunting, sewing, igloo-making, and preparing food. One of the main purposes of *Qulliq* (*Oil Lamp*, 1993), for example, is to provide enough information to the viewer to learn how to tend a *qulliq*, a stone lamp whose fuel is seal oil (Evans 45). Similarly in *Atanarjuat*, the slow pace of the filming, in which the camera lingers upon people's faces, clothes, tools, and activities, encourages the viewer to pay close attention to the manner in which the Inuit people in the precontact era developed innovative technologies to survive and thrive in the Arctic. The slow pace also conveys effectively the social contexts within which the drama unfolds.

Isuma productions in general, and *Atanarjuat* in particular, converse with and revise ethnographic traditions of filmmaking in the North, of which the most popular and well-known example is Robert Flaherty's

*Nanook of the North* (1922). Like many other visitors to the region in the early twentieth century, Flaherty locates 'authentic' Inuit culture in the historical past, a move that anticipates, with regretful certainty, the culture's disappearance in the present.[5] Although he first travelled to the North in search of iron ore for the railway magnate Sir William Mackenzie and acknowledges in the opening credits of his film the financial support of the French fur-trading company Revillon Frères, Flaherty downplays the encroachments of the modern world. Instead, he presents the hardships of Nanook and his family as an epic battle between 'Man and Nature'. The title cards that accompany the silent film perpetuate the romance of the North as the final frontier: 'The mysterious Barren Lands – desolate, boulder-strewn, wind-swept – illimitable spaces which top the world'. Flaherty implies that the *terra nullius* of the Arctic offers an 'illimitable' range for the southern artist's imagination; Flaherty is free to paint this *tabula rasa* as he pleases. In Flaherty's vision, the inhospitable climate also determines the 'character' of the Inuit people: 'The sterility of the soil and the rigor of the climate no other race could survive; yet here, utterly dependent upon animal life, which is their sole source of food, live the most cheerful people in all the world – the fearless, lovable, happy-go-lucky Eskimo'. As much as Flaherty expresses admiration for the resilience of the Inuit people, his condescension is equally palpable.

The argument that *Atanarjuat* directly engages with and revises Flaherty's adventure romance is disputed by a number of critics, including Shari Huhndorf, who, in citing a significant number of reviews that have described the film in ethnographic terms, suggests: 'These interpretations render *Atanarjuat* meaningful solely in relation to European narrative conventions, or by explaining its purpose as translating Inuit culture for outsiders' ('*Atanarjuat*' 822). Yet, I argue, *Atanarjuat* is not an *anti*ethnographic film. Instead, it may be described as a *counter*ethnographic film. That is, it makes ethnographic references as a way of echoing, parodying, or critiquing colonial ethnographic traditions while at the same time foregrounding Inuit perspectives. Further, I would argue that *Nanook* functions as an intertext for *Atanarjuat*. There are a number of scenes from *Atanarjuat* that deliberately replay images from *Nanook*.[6] In Monika Siebert's words, 'The visual allusions [to *Nanook*] pile up – dogs get kicked, raw meat gets eaten, knives and sled runners get licked, igloos go up, and the camera lingers over the detail of tattooed faces and handcrafted tools' (538). Citing Kunuk's lecture 'The Public Art of Inuit Storytelling' (2002), Arnold Krupat argues that Kunuk offers 'if not an invitation, at least full permission to compare his film to *Nanook* and not necessarily as an antidote to *Nanook*, despite the fact that postcolonial critics, myself included, see it as very different from *Nanook*' (Krupat, '*Atanarjuat*' 619). The Isuma filmmakers are in conversation with Flaherty's work: for example, like Flaherty, the Isuma filmmakers focus on what southerners would see as the 'illimitable spaces' and beauty of the tundra. Even more striking is the parallel between the two films' preoccupation with the details of everyday Inuit life in the precontact period, as Siebert notes. However, *Atanarjuat* distinguishes itself from *Nanook* by emphasizing the characters' affective relationships to the people, landscapes, and objects that surround them.

A moment that exemplifies *Atanarjuat*'s deliberate re-viewing and re-presenting of *Nanook* occurs when Atanarjuat pulls up to the shore in his kayak in the same manner as Nanook does in Flaherty's film. The visual parallel between the two landings on the beach is striking, yet the effect is significantly different. In *Nanook*, Flaherty uses the moment to exploit ideas of cultural otherness for comic effect: from inside his kayak, Nanook pulls out Nyla, his wife in the narrative; a baby; an older woman, Cunayou; and a puppy. The inclusion of the puppy underlines the parallel that Flaherty repeatedly draws between the characters and animals.[7] In *Atanarjuat*, the setting, camera angle, and action of the kayak-landing scene are virtually identical; but instead of pulling his family out of the kayak, Atanarjuat meets his wife, Atuat, on shore and listens to their baby kicking inside her womb. The organic image of Atanarjuat feeling for movement within Atuat contrasts sharply with the slapstick routine of pulling people and animals out of the kayak. While Flaherty's scene is filmed for comic effect, the close-up shot of Atanarjuat and Atuat creates sympathy for the characters and further individualizes them.

There are some overlaps between *Nanook* and *Atanarjuat* in the process of filmmaking, and some of Flaherty's methods continue to influence contemporary ethnographic film. Flaherty worked closely with members of the Inuit community and was able to make this film only because he had developed a relationship with Alakarialak, the actor who played Nanook, and his family. Developing his own form of participant-observation ethnography, Flaherty prioritized face-to-face interactions, developed personal relationships, and lived in the Arctic for an extended time period (Evans 8). He describes his reliance on the Inuit in carrying out the project and his sense of partnership with his subjects: 'In many travelogues you see, the film-maker looks down and never up to his subject ... He is always the big man from New York or from London. But I have been dependent on these people' (qtd. in Calder-Marshall 95). Flaherty developed and printed rushes on location and screened them with the help of Alakarialak and other Inuit people, a strategy that provided instant feedback and involved the community in the process. In this practice, his strategy is comparable to that of the Isuma filmmakers, who also involve and train local participants.

On the other hand, Flaherty's dependence upon local community members reasserted class hierarchies and preserved the hierarchical relation between director and crew. Though he strived, within the ideological limits of the day, to 'show them [the Inuit], not from the civilized point of view, but as they saw themselves, as "we, the people"' (Flaherty, qtd. in Calder-Marshall 76-77), the attempt to represent Native people's own perspectives must be examined closely. In this book, I have uncovered the power plays involved when editors, writers, filmmakers, commissioners, and other figures that control the conditions of textual or filmic (re)production insist that they are 'allowing' a narrator to 'speak in his or her own voice.' Notwithstanding the historical context in which Flaherty was making his films, Flaherty maintains ethnographic control. Frances Flaherty, the filmmaker's wife, describes Flaherty's relationship to the Inuit film crew:

> He had the Eskimos to help him – Nanook and three others: Wetaltook, Tookalook, and Little Tommy. They did everything for him. They brought water for developing the film, chiseling six feet down through river ice and bringing it in barrels sloshing with ice and deer hair that fell into it from their fur clothing. They strained it and heated it. They built a drying reel out of driftwood ... [while] Bob printed his film, frame by frame, by the light of the low arctic sun. (qtd. in Calder-Marshall 17)

Though Flaherty relied upon help from the Inuit, the key roles of the auteur – writing, directing, and editing the film – remained under his control. Despite his intentions to fairly represent the Inuit people, Flaherty's perspective is saturated with southern misconceptions, particularly the stereotype that 'primitive' people are somehow fundamentally opposed to change and technological innovation. At times, Flaherty risked the lives of his Inuit collaborators in order to capture a desired image from the romanticized past. While he was filming Nanook and his companions hunting the walrus with harpoons – a style of hunting that had not been practised for years in the area since guns had become available – the hunters asked Flaherty for help: 'repeatedly the crew called to me to use the gun – but the camera crank was my only interest then and I pretended not to understand' (R. Flaherty, 'How' 59). Flaherty, filming the great hunters of the North, was himself a hunter of images, as William Rothman observes (35). Although Flaherty does not reveal his own presence in the film, his subjectivity as explorer shapes the film's perspective. A revealing drawing of the making of the film, attributed to Wetaltook (sometimes spelled Wetallok), shows Flaherty standing alone in the middle of the set, visibly taller than the others, directing the action, as the others watch him, as if waiting for the next set of instructions.[8] Whether Wetaltook is gently mocking Flaherty's presumption of authority is unclear, but the drawing gives us clues about the asymmetries of Flaherty's 'dependence' upon local communities.

The making of *Atanarjuat*, in contrast, followed a more collaborative, cross-cultural, community-based process; in Kunuk's words, 'We did it in the Inuit style' ('The Public' par. 10). *Atanarjuat*'s creation of mediated Inuit voices avoids Flaherty's focus on the individual hunter battling nature. While Flaherty says that 'the making of a film is the elimination of the non-essential' (qtd. in Rotha 5), the Isuma filmmakers suggest that providing social context is key to understanding Inuit cultural life. Sally Berger, a curatorial assistant for the video program at the Museum of Modern Art in New York, once asked Kunuk what he thought about *Nanook;* Kunuk simply replied, 'Too fast.' For Berger, Kunuk's laconic response highlighted 'the limitations in drawing parallels between contemporary Indigenous production and Flaherty's monolithic representation of the "eskimos"' (S. Berger 177). But Kunuk's comment also reveals something about his own filmmaking style, which could be described as 'very slow.' *Atanarjuat* is striking for its extended periods of silence as well as its long, uninterrupted shots of people or activities. In describing one uncut, three-minute sequence in which Atanarjuat calms his dog team, film critic S.F. Said suggests that in conventional filmmaking practices, '[t]he scene would most likely have been omitted or cut to three seconds ... But *Atanarjuat* is full of such sequences' (25). The slow pace indicates that the Isuma filmmakers are not interested in creating decontextualized, minimalist images of the North but rather aim to create the effect of an integrated social context.

*Atanarjuat*'s representation of songs brings into focus Isuma's approach in challenging (without rejecting altogether) traditions of ethnographic representation. There are a number of different types of songs in the film: for example, the young men of the community – Aamarjuaq, Atanarjuat, and Uqi – taunt one another with sexually suggestive, rival songs; the young women, Puja and Atuat, both pursuing the gifted hunter Atanarjuat, compete in fast-paced throat-singing or breath songs; Atanarjuat hums a little ditty about the beauty of the day as he returns from a successful hunting trip; and Atanarjuat and Puja sing songs of romantic longing during their caribou hunting trip as Puja casts her love spell. The film integrates the songs into the everyday life of the communities. Different songs are sung for different purposes and reflect a range of composition styles, from spontaneous ad-libs to formal reiterations of old songs. Each genre – the taunt, the boasting song, the breath song, the hunting song, and the seduction song – follows specific norms of performance.

Although most of these songs are translated into English, the central song – the anthem, if you will, the cement of the community, whose words everybody knows but not everybody sings each time – is sung three times in the film but is never translated into English.[9] This is the song that Kumaglak refuses to sing in the opening scene of the film. The subtitled film enables the filmmakers to create two parallel texts that interact and speak to each other in complex ways. The gap between what is spoken and what appears on the bottom of the screen can be manipulated strategically, for a variety of effects, enabling the filmmakers to address different audiences.[10] The book version of *Atanarjuat,* by Paul Apak Angilirq and others, which includes screenplays in both languages (Inuktitut and English), film stills, interviews, personal essays, and ethnographic commentary, adds still more layered tellings to the oral script. The film's strategy of partial translation highlights the space of cultural contact and difference in acts of textualizing orature and orality, resisting the explanatory impetus of the ethnographic monograph or film.

By deploying strategies of incomplete translation in the subtitles and in the bilingual screenplays, the filmmakers explore the uneven relations of address both within Inuit audiences and between Inuit and non-Inuit audiences. Each screening of the film creates its own peculiar possibilities of meaning. Depending on where the film is being shown, the proportion of the audience who understands the song will vary. Clearly, a greater proportion will understand the song when the film is shown in Igloolik or Iqaluit rather than in Toronto or Paris. But the incomplete communication happens not only between those who understand Inuktitut and those who do not. The film also explores the differences in reception of and participation in the song among the Inuktitut-speaking characters. During the first performance of the song, the new, ascendant group within the community, led by Sauri, who defeated his father with the help of the stranger in the opening scene, sings it with gusto. Others, such as Kumaglak's widow Panikpak, mumble the words, stare at their feet, and hide their lack of participation behind their clothes or hair. In the second performance, the relations of power have shifted, and the situation is reversed. It is Panikpak who initiates the singing in order to dispel the evil spirit and expel members of the previously ascendant group.

Although the song, referred to as Kumaglak's 'special *ajaja*' in the English-language screenplay, is not translated in the film, it is translated in the bilingual book version of *Atanarjuat*. Here is Panikpak's performance at the end of the film:

> Aii ya ... ai yai yaa ...
> I can't find my blanket ... ayai yaa
> Aii ya ... ai yai yaa ...
> In the middle of the night,
> when we're sleeping ... ai ya yaa ...
> Aii ya ... ai yai yaa ...
> Trying to make a song ... ai ya yaa
> In the middle of the night
> when everybody's sleeping
> ... ayaii yai yaa ... (Angilirq et al. 193)

'Trying to make a song' suggests that the song has not yet been performed; it is a prologue to its enactment in the future. The song circles in on itself, becoming a song about making a song. Perhaps there is no song beyond its promise, or perhaps there is another song that can only be heard, recorded, or broadcast by 'someone who understands it.'

The discrepancy between the film and book versions, of which the song is not the only example,[11] emphasizes the constitutive role of performance in textualized narrative and song. The differences in who sings, when, and for what purposes underline the relations of address that constitute the song, as well as its role in enacting social hierarchies and power plays. By not always matching the subtitles to the action on the screen and by fading the subtitles occasionally into the snow-covered background, as Shari Huhndorf notes, the Isuma filmmakers are deliberately prioritizing Inuktitut speakers as their main audience ('*Atanarjuat*' 825). The subtitles in *The Journals of Knud Rasmussen* (2006), Isuma's second feature-length drama, cater even less to non-Inuktitut speakers. None of the songs is translated, and many conversations are subtitled as 'chattering.' Much of

Isuma's work has an explicitly educational intent, and by employing techniques of partial translation, the filmmakers are guaranteeing that their primary audience – Inuktitut speakers – hears the language without always being able to rely on the subtitles for the translation. Furthermore, the filmmakers' approach in shooting a scene emphasizes less the importance of memorizing a script; rather, they encourage the actors to respond personally to the situation within which the characters are immersed. Isuma explores a mode of making films that invites a certain degree of spontaneous interpretation of and variation from the script on the part of the actors and crew. For example, in a grant application that Isuma submitted to Telefilm for the *Nunavut* series (1994-95), the producers wrote:

> At Isuma, our 'Final Draft Scripts' are composed of story outlines for each project which describe the Inuit idea of the program and generally what our actors will do. These scripts are based on research with elders who recount true stories orally from their own experience and knowledge of the past: how things were done, and how people behaved. Details of action and specific dialogue are then improvised during filming in an Inuit way, through discussion among cast and crew based on their own experience. (qtd. in Evans 47)

It is the *process* of making the film which is of primary importance at Isuma – a process which, as I will explain further, foregrounds 'an Inuit way' of knowing and doing things (sometimes referred to as *Inuit Qaujimajatuqangit* in Inuktitut) while respecting individual choices and interpretations. The final shape of the film emerges from consulting with elders, researching Inuit practices, and eliciting individual experiences, not solely from previously written screenplays.

For Isuma, video art is above all a social practice, an act of community building and of knowledge exchange. Norman Cohn, who describes how he helped pioneer independent, 'guerilla'-style video art in Chicago and Connecticut (Evans 66-69), comments: 'the invention of low-cost video at the end of the 1960s enabled people from Harlem to the Arctic to use TV as a tool for political and social change in local communities' (Cohn, 'The Art' 27). Isuma's 'community filmmaking techniques' place emphasis on training – in camera work, makeup, sound, lighting, stunts, and special effects. In 1991, Isuma created Tarriaksuk Video Centre, a non-profit television training and equipment centre, which in turn sponsored Arnait Video Productions (Women's Video Workshop) and Inuusiq Youth Drama

Workshop. Isuma's website describes the company's mandate: 'Isuma's mission is to produce independent community-based media – films, TV and now Internet – to preserve and enhance Inuit culture and language; to create jobs and economic development in Igloolik and Nunavut; and to tell authentic Inuit stories to Inuit and non-Inuit audiences worldwide' ('Our Mission' par. 1). The team of filmmakers disrupts the usual hierarchies of film production – producers, directors, writers, actors, camera operators, and food suppliers – and cultivates a more collective, collaborative process. This collaborative process of filmmaking becomes evident in the final minutes of *Atanarjuat,* when the practice of making the film is exposed. Here the actors exchange roles with tailors, cooks, fishers, hunters, child-care providers, and snowmobile drivers, contributors to the film who now have their moment in front of the camera.

A collaborative process was equally important in producing the book version of *Atanarjuat.* The title pages announce that *Atanarjuat* was 'Inspired by a traditional Inuit legend of Igloolik,' with the 'Original story and Inuktitut screenplay by Paul Apak Angilirq,' 'Additional writ[ing by] Zacharias Kunuk, Hervé Paniaq and Pauloosie Qulitalik,' 'English screenplay by Norman Cohn,' and 'Ethnographic commentary ... by Bernard Saladin d'Anglure.' Gillian Robinson edited the book (though the extent of her role is unclear), while Juliana Boychuk translated Cohn's English-language screenplay back into Inuktitut. In addition, Isuma jointly published the book (with Coach House Press), suggesting the company wished to maintain control over the text's reproduction and circulation.

The story of the writing of the film also reveals collaborative technique. The writer, Paul Apak, worked from both written and oral sources, as well as his own childhood memories. 'Paul Apak decided that we would do *Atanarjuat* because we all grew up with this story and once it was taught to you, you never forgot that naked man running out on the ice. We all heard this story and now it was the time to use new technology to put these stories through the TV' (Kunuk, 'The Public' par. 8). Along with reviewing the ethnographic record, Apak and others recorded in syllabics eight versions of the legend narrated by Igloolik community members.[12] These multiple versions were compressed, rearranged, and reduced to one penultimate English version, which was then transformed into Inuktitut and English film scripts by Apak, Kunuk, Qulitalik, Hervé Paniak, and Cohn. During the scriptwriting process, the five writers consulted with elders on what might have been language use, gender relations, and social norms of the time when the Inuit lived on the land before contact. Cohn translated the script into English and comments on the process:

> We discussed every scene, every gesture, every line of dialogue, and wrote two scripts at the same time, arguing and acting things out around the table. Apak wrote the scenes down on one laptop in the old Inuktitut font we got from the school, while I wrote the same scenes in English on the second laptop ...
>
> Apak and I would go home at night and each work on our scenes, trying to fix them up, and then the next day we would make sure they fit together and go on to the next ones. At the same time Apak consulted with other elders, like Emile Immaroitok, a language specialist, or George Aggiak, who knew a lot about shamanism, to make sure the dialogue was right, especially for the olden times when Inuit spoke a more formal, poetic and complex Inuktitut than today. (Cohn, 'The Art' 25)

The final film script is thus a compilation of numerous interpretations of the legend as well as an amalgamation of various storytellers' and writers' knowledges, styles, preferences, aesthetics, and politics. In the final version, Apak changed the traditional story in both subtle and dramatic ways. The most substantial change is the ending. In many of the available written versions of the story, as in the following rendition by Jimmy Ettuk, who in 1964 both drew the legend and wrote the story on the back of the drawing for Terry Ryan (an art collector and former civil servant in the Department of Transport at Clyde River, Baffin Island), Atanarjuat kills his tormentors in an act of revenge[13]:

> In the winter, he [Atanarjuat] built an igloo and invited his enemies. His wife approached in her tattered clothes and he said, "I wanted you to wear tattered clothes." Then he ripped up her clothes even more. All she had left on was a top. Then his other wife came in crying and he said "Let me see your hands." She gave him her hand and he ripped her hand right down the middle. He asked her why she had betrayed him and she replied that she had come to hate him. Then he called his pursuers who wanted to kill him to the slippery lake. He said, "Last spring you made me run on the ice without anything on my feet. I will never forget that." So then, he clubbed all his enemies to death with some caribou antlers while they were trying to run away. (Blodgett 132)

In contrast to Ettuk's story, Apak's version has Atanarjuat threatening to kill his enemies but then declaring, 'Here the killing stops.' Saladin d'Anglure, who recorded four other versions of the legend in 1972, 1987, 1990, and 1991, argues that the film version reflects the influence of ideologies of Christian forgiveness (199, 203), but Isuma's explanation is a little different. Paraphrasing his interviews with the filmmakers, Michael Robert Evans, in *Isuma: Inuit Video Art* (2008), writes: 'Apak, Kunuk, Cohn and the others at Isuma decided on a positive ending because they wanted to emphasize the importance of harmony and working together, a vital Inuit value honed over millennia of cooperation in small bands immersed in a harsh environment. Much of Inuit life is communal, and when someone puts himself above this communal web, he also puts himself outside it' (94). Isuma's change to the legend's ending is revealing not only of the filmmakers' larger goal of affirming Inuit value systems, but also of their aim of revitalizing Inuit oral traditions through their selective transformation. The variations in the textualizations of the legend suggest that Inuit songs and stories are subject to individual interpretation, performance, and cultural change. This is not to say that songs and stories are passed down inaccurately; orature depends upon a certain amount of exact repetition. However, like Ettuk's drawing-*cum*-story, the film *Atanarjuat* is an intercultural fusion that emerges from its particular historical moment. Apak, as any storyteller-writer will do, has decontextualized and recontextualized the legend to suit his own purposes and to speak to his chosen audiences. In this manner, the filmmakers have subtly embedded the present in their representation of the past.

*Atanarjuat*, unlike *Nanook*, draws attention to its own status as a dramatic re-creation of the events and circumstances from the precontact era. The metadramatic scenes of the final minutes of the film reveal the collaborative process of making the film and highlight the film's contemporaneity. The actors inhabit a middle zone between themselves and their characters as they are shown practising traditional skills of cooking, fishing, and hunting. Of the actors' preparation for their roles, the filmmakers have commented: 'They [the actors] are learning new words and learning songs ... And also they are learning about how people went about life at that time ... They will have to know more than just acting' (Angilirq et al. 21). This moment of self-reflexivity marks both the film's proximity to, and distance from, the genre of the ethnographic film. The Isuma filmmakers use autoethnography as a way both to problematize colonial ethnographic explanation and to reclaim the right to describe Inuit cultural practices in their own way. In all of these scenes, the people look directly at the camera, mostly smiling and laughing, giving viewers a sense of the community filmmaking techniques that Cohn and Kunuk describe. Panikpak (Madeline Ivalu) holds a huge, writhing fish in her hands; she is looking at the camera with surprise and delight. Atanarjuat (Natar Ungalaq), naked and bootless, with a long blanket wrapped around his shoulders, dances from one cold foot to the other, waiting for the camera operators, aboard a snowmobile, to prepare the shot. Only Peter-Henry Arnsatsiaq, the actor who plays Uqi, the villain, arriving for rehearsal in his black leather jacket and listening to his headphones, doesn't smile. He stares into the camera almost menacingly and does not divert his path as he advances towards us. He is still playing the part of Uqi, but at the same time, he is also confronting the camera with a persona that threatens the commodified image of Flaherty's 'happy-go-lucky Eskimo', safely contained in the distant past. These memorable scenes give a glimpse of what is at stake in changing static representations of the 'Eskimo'.

It could be argued that the metadramatic scenes at the end of *Atanarjuat*, which reveal the presence of directors, camera operators, and film crew, reinvent another famous scene from *Nanook:* the episode in which the trader plays the gramophone for Nanook and his family. Nanook, either genuinely astonished at 'how the white man "cans" his voice', as the subtitle suggests, or mischievously hamming it up for the camera, bites the gramophone record and bursts into a fit of laughter. His laugh may be a challenge to Flaherty, who tried to efface the presence of the recording devices and to give the impression that the action is going on without intervention. An interesting 'stand-in' for Flaherty, as Rothman points out, is the trader (31). Flaherty aims the camera directly at Nanook, Nyla, and the children, but he brackets the trader's presence. We never see the whole body of the trader, who is consistently positioned at the extreme edge of the camera frame. Like Flaherty himself, the trader escapes the camera's gaze: 'he sees but remains unseen' (Huhndorf, 'Nanook' 140). Also like Flaherty, the trader operates the technologies of voice amplification and hides behind them, masking the play of power that they represent. This erasure of the presence of the recorder is comparable to the way in which *Nanook* masks the violence of colonial relationships. The final scene of *Atanarjuat*, in contrast, unambiguously announces a major shift in the politics of representation: now Inuit people are holding the cameras and making films according to an 'Inuit style of filmmaking' (Kunuk, 'The Public' par. 10).

While *Nanook* is set in an undifferentiated Arctic landscape – in the 'illimitable spaces which top the world' – *Atanarjuat* pays careful attention to the local geography of Igloolik. Indeed for Kunuk, the evocation of precise geography is another way he distinguishes his film from Flaherty's. In 'The Public Art of Inuit Storytelling,' a lecture delivered at Simon Fraser University in 2002, in response to a question from the audience about the legacy of *Nanook* in Isuma's films, Kunuk answered: 'Robert Flaherty did his documentary about 500 miles south of our community ... We are doing ours further north' (par. 35). On the *Atanarjuat* website, viewers can trace Atanarjuat's thirty-seven-kilometre run across the sea ice of the Hecla Strait from Igloolik to Sioraq (or Tern Island). Isuma's publication includes a photograph of a bench-like stone near the settlement of Igloolik, known as the place where Atanarjuat sat during one of his hunting expeditions. Atanarjuat, then, is a local hero who emerges from a recognizable and familiar landscape. Captain George Lyon, part of Admiral William Parry's expedition in 1821-23 to find the Northwest Passage to Asia, once referred to Atanarjuat and Aamarjuaq as 'patrons of the region' (qtd. in Saladin d'Anglure 197). Because the story takes place in a specific locale, it retains the status of a historical epic, commemorating the history of the Igloolik Inuit people's ancestors. Igloolik, then, is not just a settlement created by the federal government in the 1950s as part of a relocation program to facilitate the dispensing of welfare and other social services (Angilirq et al. 29); it is an ancient site, replete with stories of people who have lived there continuously over thousands of years.

In contrast to the specificity of the film's landscape, the film's time frame is fairly open-ended (between five hundred and a thousand years ago); as a result of this historical non-specificity, it has been argued that, like ethnographic films of the past, *Atanarjuat* recreates a pre-colonial world that, until the metadramatic final scenes, appears to be unaffected by the present.[14] Set long before any of the modern tragedies stemming from a century of aggressive colonization in the North, the film could be interpreted as avoiding difficult questions that implicate southern Canadian viewers, while at the same time supplying familiar, ethnographic images of the Inuit pursuing a lifestyle of long ago. The film's global acclaim suggests that, like *Nanook, Atanarjuat* resonates with a wide-ranging, international audience that has had little or no contact with Inuit culture. Since its première in Igloolik in December 2000, *Atanarjuat* has enjoyed enormous recognition internationally. It has received many prestigious awards, such as the Camera d'Or at the Cannes Film Festival in 2001, Best

Film at various film festivals around the world, and five Genie Awards in Canada ('Atanarjuat' par. 1). Reviews have been strongly positive, including a comment in the *New York Times* that *Atanarjuat* is a 'masterpiece ... that honors the history of the art form [of the documentary] even as it extends its perspective' (Scott par. 3). Beyond its sheer excellence as a film, and without downplaying its well-deserved achievements, why or how does *Atanarjuat* reach such a diverse audience? Does it merely recirculate highly marketable images of the Inuit, or, as I have argued, do the techniques of autoethnography, partial translation, and community filmmaking work to subvert these colonial representations?

I am suggesting that the film's community-based, activist mode of production – designed to strengthen local economies and develop local skills – undercuts a romanticized, primitivist interpretation. In Cohn's words, 'When you start to realize that the process of how things are made is an important part of how they impact on audiences, then the war over process is not a small thing – and that's what we're doing here. We are fighting a guerilla battle over a process of production that we think is politically much more progressive than the conventional process of production' (qtd. in Evans 73). Part of the goal in waging this 'war over process' is to contribute to a larger social movement dedicated to the development of Nunavut's autonomy and the practice of *Inuit Qaujimajatuqangit*. And while the Isuma filmmakers are Nunavut sovereigntists, they are also deeply committed to developing a special role for the community of Igloolik, which is the home of Nunavut's Department of Culture, Language, Elders, and Youth. In the last section of this chapter, I discuss how Isuma both supports Nunavut and maintains its position slightly outside the territory's governing structures in order to maintain its insurgency as a voice of cultural critique.

**From 'the North' to Nunavut**

I have suggested that it is more than a coincidence that the filmmakers began shooting *Atanarjuat* in the same month as the creation of Nunavut in April 1999. Igloolik Isuma Productions, which emerged from the same political crucible as Nunavut, is a good example of how self-government can create the conditions for innovative cultural and artistic projects. Isuma's four founding partners define their company in terms that could be called self-governing and sovereigntist. Their aim is to take control of the means of production and redefine the process of filmmaking: 'Our objective was not to impose southern filmmaking conventions on our unique story, but to let the story shape the filmmaking process in an Inuit way' ('Filmmaking' par. 2). Since 1985, Isuma has produced more than thirty films, which, taken as a whole, suggest the integral relationship between politics and culture, reflected in the titles of two series of films, *Nunavut (Our Land)*, a thirteen-part TV series, and *Unikaatuatiit (Story Tellers)*, a grouping that includes films such as *Nunaqpa (Going Inland)*, *Qaggiq (Gathering Place)*, *Quliq (Oil Lamp)*, and *Saputi (Fish Traps)*. In Evans's words, 'Isuma producers position their organization as a resistance cell ... of colonial Canada' (Evans 30). Their targets of critique include the relocation of Inuit people to artificial settlements in the 1950s and 1960s and conventional filmmaking technques that do not necessarily benefit local economies. Instead, Isuma filmmakers assert their commitment to community-based filmmaking methods by hiring actors, film crew, and supporting staff from the local region. Just as the community contributed to the making of *Atanarjuat*, *Atanarjuat* also contributed to the community:

> Inuit jobs and local spending on *Atanarjuat* pumped more than $1.5 million into the local economy of Igloolik. This film will be the cornerstone of a new Nunavut film industry: job-intensive and Inuit-owned. With Igloolik's 60% unemployment rate and ten times the national rate of suicide, these economic and cultural benefits were and are both deserved and desperately needed. ('Filmmaking' par. 5)

The story of the founding of Igloolik Isuma Productions also reflects the co-founders' sovereigntist, Inuit-centred politics. Isuma began as a breakaway production house that split from the Inuit Broadcasting Corporation (IBC) in 1990. The IBC, which began broadcasting in 1982, was initially created by the Inuit Taparisat (or 'Inuit Brotherhood'), with the goal of preserving the Inuktitut language and offering Inuit perspectives on Canadian media channels. The purpose was also to provide programming that was more locally relevant than the Canadian Broadcasting Corporation's (CBC's) northern services. In many ways, the IBC's mandate is compatible with Isuma's; yet the Igloolik-based videographers pit their work decisively against the IBC, which they see as part of a larger, colonial and southern enterprise to include yet minimize the impact of Inuit perspectives. According to Cohn, the manner in which the IBC manages its budget is a case in point. There is little in the way of local budgeting control, so that IBC's regional production centres (one of which is located in Igloolik) cannot determine how to spend their funds (Evans 125). The process by which the IBC develops its programming also reveals a propensity for top-down control: the IBC favours the creation of short segments, submitted from multiple production centres, which are then cobbled together to form magazine-style programs (126). This is strikingly different from Isuma's more holistic process, which aims to create rich presentations of Inuit cultural practices, in consultation with elders, using long, uninterrupted shots. Finally, though the goal of IBC is to support local productions, its headquarters remain in Ottawa, and its funding comes from the Department of Canadian Heritage; according to Isuma, Ottawa bureaucrats thereby maintain control over its programming. For Apak and Kunuk, IBC eventually became a stifling work environment and, after working for ten and eight years, respectively, they left the organization to found Isuma in 1990 (Angilirq et al. 7).

The struggle to fund *Atanarjuat* provides a concrete example of Isuma's commitment to speak out against ongoing paternalisms in Inuit-Canadian relations. In 1996, Isuma applied to Telefilm, the federal filmmaking granting agency, for the maximum amount of $1 million for English- or French-language films. However, because the proposed film was in the Inuktitut language, Telefilm stated that it was not eligible for either of these funding 'envelopes'; consequently it was relegated to the Aboriginal-language funding envelope, which is capped at $100,000. In response, Kunuk and Cohn wrote multiple letters, pointing out that they were being forced into a 'funding ghetto' (Cohn, qtd. in Evans 130) despite their willingness to compete in the larger funding contests. Eventually Isuma received $537,000 from Telefilm, though the shortfall caused a year-long halt in the making of *Atanarjuat*. The following year, the money came through more smoothly, and, along with support from the National Film Board, the filming began again in April 1999 and was completed the following year (Evans 133). For Kunuk and Cohn, Telefilm's funding structure systematically limits the potential growth of Aboriginal-language filmmaking in Canada and is symbolic of ongoing colonial relations.[15]

The story of Nunavut follows a path similar to that of Isuma in its hard-won struggle against various forms of (neo)colonialism. Although Nunavut officially became a territory on 1 April 1999, the history of Nunavut begins in 1976, when the Inuit Tapirisat of Canada submitted a land claim proposal to the federal government. Signed in Iqaluit on 25 May 1993, after almost twenty years of negotiating efforts, the agreement to establish Nunavut (which means 'our land' in Inuktitut) transformed 350,000 square kilometres of the Eastern and Central Arctic into a new territory controlled by the Inuit, who make up 85 percent of its population. Political scientist George Wenzel argues that 'Nunavut' is more properly understood as 'two Nunavuts': the public Government of Nunavut (GN) and the Nunavut Land Claim Agreement (NLCA). While the GN is a national, political unit created by an act passed in Canadian parliament, the NLCA, managed by the Inuit land claims organization Nunavut Tunngavik Inc (NTI), has an entirely Inuit constituency and acts as partner, adviser, and critic to the GN, particularly on matters relating to Inuit culture and language (Wenzel 239-40). In Wenzel's words: 'Nunavut came into being invested with two different, even opposite, sets of expectations. On one hand, as a federal territory, the GN was expected to have a form and function similar to that of the other two territories ... On the other, the majority of the new territory's citizens expected the government that included the NLCA area and its Inuit beneficiaries would not only represent its political interests, but also have an Inuit approach to governance and reflect the values of its majority Inuit polity' (240). Here Wenzel is underlining the role that the NTI played in galvanizing Nunavut to culturally differentiate itself from the old Northwest Territories.

Since the beginning of the negotiations to form Nunavut in the 1970s, questions of culture and language have played a central role. For example, the Nunavut Implementation Commission (the transitional predecessor to the Government of Nunavut) explicitly mandated that 'the government of Nunavut will undertake to protect and preserve the distinct society which has existed in Nunavut for thousands of years' (qtd. in Huhndorf, 'Atanarjuat' 823). The government of Nunavut has followed suit, expressing its commitment of 'ensuring that Inuit culture and language [are] an integral part of the society' (qtd. in Martin 185). One way in which the territorial government has sought to achieve this goal is by integrating *Inuit Qaujimajatuqangit*, or Inuit traditional knowledge, into governmental policies.

Since 1999, debates over culture in Nunavut have focused upon the perceived ability of the territory to enact, in its legislation and governing processes, the philosophy of *Inuit Qaujimajatuqangit* (IQ). Political scientist Ailsa Henderson explains that IQ, usually glossed as 'an Inuit way of doing things,' is notoriously difficult to define. As a holistic philosophy, IQ encompasses a vast range of ideas and actions, including knowledge of land, kinship patterns, and customary law, as well as the elders' accumulated 'memories, knowledge, stories, and skills' (*Report from the September IQ Workshop 1999*, qtd. in A. Henderson 192). Literary critic Keavy Martin, citing Qikiqtani Inuit Association policy analyst Japetee Arnakak, also suggests that IQ should not be considered primarily as a fixed body of knowledge; rather, it is 'a set of teachings on practical truisms about society, human nature and experience passed on orally (traditionally) from one generation to the next ... It is holistic, dynamic and cumulative in its approach to knowledge, teaching and learning' (Arnakak, qtd. in Martin 185-86).

IQ is a politically charged term, not only because it 'is fundamentally about power, about Inuit taking charge and making positive changes for the future' (A. Henderson 198), but also because it has become an important point of discussion in the Nunavut legislature. Each governmental department is responsible for developing its own IQ-based policies. Paul Okalik, former premier of Nunavut, expresses the commitment of the government 'to include IQ as an integral part of government policy development' (qtd. in Alia 31). For Okalik, IQ integrates his memories of growing up, of listening to stories, and of hunting, as well as providing a cultural 'foundation' to counteract colonial policies of displacement and social fragmentation (qtd. 31). The wide range of issues that falls under the purview of IQ poses a difficulty for incorporating it within bureaucratic structures that favour an 'easy checklist-inspired definition of the concept' (A. Henderson 191).

The extent to which the government is able to practice IQ remains one of the central issues animating public debate in the territory today, as Henderson, in her analysis of detailed surveys and public opinion polls of residents of Nunavut indicates.[16] However, the government's expenditures on culture are somewhat limited, focusing more strongly on economics than on social and cultural concerns. For example, the 2006 budget of the Ministry of Culture, Language, Elders, and Youth ($19 million) was less than 2 percent of the Nunavut government's total budget of approximately $1 billion (Tester and Irniq 50). Furthermore, Frank James Tester and Peter Irniq contend, 'IQ can be both empowering of Inuit and Inuit culture ... or co-opting' (49). Citing David Simailak, Nunavut's Minister of Finance from 2004 to 2007, who references IQ in his budget statement, Tester and Irniq argue that like any other term or philosophy, IQ can be manipulated to 'justify policies that ha[ve] little or no relevance to traditional Inuit culture' (49).[17]

Many of Isuma's goals – producing Inuktitut-language films, prioritizing Inuit points of view, revitalizing cultural traditions, boosting local economies – reveal the practice of *Inuit Qaujimajatuqangit,* and phrases like 'an Inuit way of doing things' appear repeatedly on Isuma's website and in the filmmakers' public statements. Isuma is committed to telling stories in Inuktitut and 'from an Inuk point of view', which became the title of the collective's first production; to this day, *From Inuk Point of View* (1985) has not been subtitled in English.[18] However, Kunuk and Cohn are also aware of the dangers of co-opting Inuit perspectives, as their disputes with the IBC and Telefilm indicate, and Isuma takes seriously its role in critiquing Nunavut's governing priorities and speaking out against the dangers of the new government reproducing the same relations of power that it inherited from the old Northwest Territories. The filmmakers are using their international success to encourage the government to develop a coherent cultural policy and to develop filmmaking in Nunavut. To some extent, Isuma's application of political pressure has been effective: although Nunavut has no arts council, it has contributed to Isuma productions following the success of *Atanarjuat*. In 2003, Nunavut established a film commission called the Nunavut Film Development Corporation (NFDC), which has helped fund several Isuma projects (Cohn, personal communication).[19]

Isuma's active engagement with Nunavut politics is seen in their documentary film *Nipi (Voice)* (1999), in which Inuit elders and politicians reflect upon the predicaments of national consciousness leading up to the creation of the new territory. 'Rapid change from traditional to modern life in Nunavut has concentrated power, wealth and information in a few hands', summarize the video liner notes. The film juxtaposes the views of Nunavut's leadership class – land claims negotiators, trust fund managers, senators, and elected representatives – with those of Igloolik elders, exposing fissures within and among the generations. *Nipi* can be understood as an exercise in *Inuit Qaujimajatuqangit*. In particular, it demonstrates the importance of conversing with elders, whose perspectives differ from community leaders invested in negotiating governance with the federal government or developing Nunavut economically. If, as Keavy Martin argues, *Inuit Qaujimajatuqangit* 'is most readily manifested in the knowledge and memories of Nunavut Elders', then *Nipi* foregrounds the richness of this oral body of knowledge by prioritizing the voices of elders whose lives in part precede the intercession of residential schools, welfare initiatives, and permanent settlements (Martin 185-86).

While the speakers are united in their desire to break from federal control, they envision radically different styles of leadership and vigorously dispute the best path towards decolonization. Some, such as José Husgak, president of the land claims organization Nunavut Tunngavik Incorporated, celebrate Nunavut's economic achievements. Husgak states: 'Managing a business is what we're driving at. So many people knock on our door looking for Inuit partners to make profit with.' As it negotiates its first decade, Nunavut highlights the uneasy and fraught relationship between Aboriginal rights and corporate rights that has become a concern in implementing self-government agreements. It has become imperative to define the nature of this relationship as international pressure mounts for nonrenewable resources in the North. Others, such as Paul Quassa, chief negotiator for the Nunavut land claim, sound warnings about the persistence of colonial policies: 'Now Inuit are ... policy makers. But the way we pictured it in the negotiation process, ... the decisions [would] come more from the Inuit. Looking at it now, it's still not like that. They [the policies] are still run more by the southerners.' Meanwhile, the elders shift the terms of the debate somewhat, describing seasonal and weather patterns in Igloolik, as well as offering advice about how to hunt for walrus. They also comment on changes to Inuit social structures that they have witnessed; in George Kappianaq's words, 'Back then people were only controlled by their elder. They did what he wanted and they listened to him. That's how it was but it's not like that anymore.' Rosie Iqallijuq, another Igloolik elder, diagnoses the problem somewhat differently, suggesting that previous generations were 'listening too much to the system and wanting to control too much.' The film's juxtapositional structure demonstrates 'the two Nunavuts' that Wenzel describes, while at the same time further differentiating a spectrum of points of view within those two halves.

Although Isuma filmmakers are part of a larger social movement in Nunavut to produce culture and art according to the principles of *Inuit Qaujimajatuqangit*, their strategies of partial translation and counter-ethnography emphasize not only the bilingual and culturally composite nature of their project but also the divided nature of their audience. What *Nipi (Voice)* illustrates is that in the shift to self-government, there are no guarantees of more equitable relations of negotiation among interlocutors enmeshed in unequal social contexts. The story of Nunavut is not simply or unproblematically a story of liberation, and Isuma is determined to address the issues and challenges that the territory faces. Isuma aims to open up for debate questions of democracy, power, and economic and cultural development that pertain not only to policies in Nunavut but also in Canada.

Literary and filmic representations of Inuit oral traditions historically have tended to decontextualize Inuit songs and stories from the storytelling exchange and to aestheticize the isolated fragment. The ethnographic fragment gives the impression of being the last remnant of vanishing Inuit lifestyles, thus reinforcing discourses of disappearing primitive cultures, while constructions of the Far North as *terra nullius* further imply cultural disappearance. The objective of the Igloolik Isuma filmmakers is to counter this decontextualization by creating the effect of an integrated social context in their films. *Atanarjuat*'s evocation of the deep roots of the Igloolik Inuit community, reflected not only in the careful attention to local cultural traditions, landscapes, and language but also in Isuma's 'community filmmaking techniques,' counteracts representations of the North as empty land. The many collaborators involved in the process of writing, directing, and producing Isuma films diffuse the control that the recorder/editor historically has maintained in textualizing oral traditions and challenge representations of Inuit orature as isolated ethnographic fragments. The confluence of timing between the making of *Atanarjuat* and the creation of Nunavut, 'the people's land,' accentuates Isuma's insistence upon the human geographies of the Arctic. Isuma has contributed to Inuit politics that have culminated in the formation of Nunavut, and Isuma's aims – developing independent community-based media, working in Inuktitut, revitalizing Inuit culture, creating jobs in the local economy, and initiating training programs in Igloolik and Nunavut – are commensurate with *Inuit Qaujimajatuqangit*, a principle that drives Nunavut's ongoing development of cultural policy. However, the members of the collective do not simply celebrate the territory's apparent securing of political autonomy or take the government's apparent pledge to enact IQ at face value. Instead, Isuma is committed to remaining a vibrant critical force in Nunavut, and it will continue to remind the territory's leaders of the vital role that art and culture play in northern communities.

# Conclusion
## Collaborative Authorship and Literary Sovereignty

In this book, I have examined the degrees of authorship and of collaboration that arise out of the omissions, manipulations, and negotiations encoded in a wide range of texts that purport to be collaborative. Historically, non-Aboriginal recorders and editors have maintained tight control over the process of entextualizing Aboriginal oral forms, transcribing, translating, structuring, editing, introducing, interpreting, and publishing versions of Aboriginal oral expression under their own name. This presentation of a narrative under the name of the collector demonstrates that narrators historically have had little control over the outcome of their participation in the collaborative project. As a result of these historical conditions, some Aboriginal writers and critics have disassociated themselves from told-to narratives. Lenore Keeshig-Tobias, in her essay 'Stop Stealing Native Stories' (1990), exposes the history of non-Aboriginal collector-editors recording and disseminating transcribed oral traditions for their own purpose and professional gain. She draws attention to a continuum between various forms of appropriation – of voice, stories, authorship, spiritual knowledge, cultural artifacts, language, land, resources, and governance. The links she makes between the appropriation of stories, the expropriation of land, and the loss of governance are reflective of a larger discursive shift in First Nations studies since the early 1990s: in recent years, Aboriginal literary critics have sought ways to foreground and prioritize Indigenous sovereignty in their analyses.

To some extent, the emergence of discourses of Indigenous sovereignty has contributed to the assumption that singly authored texts are instances of literary sovereignty while told-to narratives exemplify literary colonization. Yet this book has shown that Aboriginal writers, storytellers, and filmmakers, as well as community land claims negotiators, map-makers, and activists, working with collaborators who may or may not be from the same community or share a similar cultural background, far from dismissing told-to narrative forms, have developed new approaches to textualizing oral traditions that counteract ethnographic traditions and that re-imagine the struggle for Aboriginal sovereignty in dialogic forms. They have engaged in cross-cultural negotiations in order to demonstrate that tribally-centred critical approaches have 'everything to do with intersections and exchanges between inside and outside worlds' (Womack, 'The Integrity' 111). Indeed, it could be argued that Aboriginal sovereignties cannot be well understood except through a process of dialogue since there exists no one-size-fits-all definition that meets widespread acceptance.

Craig Womack, well known as an American Indian literary nationalist, writes about how, for decades, critical studies of American Indian *writing* have been dominated by analyses of *storytelling*, in a cultural-ethnographic mode, leading to claims that 'virtually all Indian writing is based on oral tradition and ceremony' without adequate attention to tribal differences or historical shifts ('A Single' 18). As a result, over the past couple of decades, Aboriginal literary critics such as Womack, Maria Campbell (1992), Kimberly Blaeser (1993), Jeanette Armstrong (1993), Lee Maracle (1992, 1996), Janice Acoose (2001), Kristina Fagan (2004, 2008), Jace Weaver et al. (2006), and Daniel Heath Justice (2008), from a variety of political viewpoints and ideologies, have turned to the language of sovereignty to articulate a sense of independence from the manifold histories of appropriation, and have drawn connections between their literary analysis and the current era of land claims, self-government agreements, and modern-day treaties. Arguments in support of Indigenous literary sovereignty often invoke what Blaeser calls 'tribal-centered criticism' ('Native' 53), emphasizing the importance of transforming social and discursive spaces for Aboriginal people and the need for an activist, socially engaged criticism whose aim is to build knowledge networks within Aboriginal nations, rather than continually responding to and countering dominant Euro-American epistemologies. Anishinaabe literary critic Niigonwedom James Sinclair argues that 'Indigenous centered literary scholarship' relates to 'grassroots Indigenous struggles' and engages with 'specific tenets present in Native literatures (such as elements of tribal community histories, politics, and subjectivities)' (Fagan et al. 20). Each of these writers necessarily has interpreted the concept of 'sovereignty' in significantly different ways, underlining the multiple discursive fractures within constructions of Indigenous nationhood. For example, in a collaboratively authored article made up of a series of position papers, Fagan, Justice, Keavy Martin, Sam McKegney, Deanna Reder, and Sinclair (2009) question how the theory and practice of Indigenous literary nationalism in the Canadian context might differ from related debates in the American context. The co-authors ask: 'Is this somewhat American Indian-led movement applicable in Canadian Indigenous contexts? Can (and should) Indigenous literary self-determining efforts in Canada be localized? Does dealing with different colonial regimes result in different senses of "rhetorical sovereignty?"' (19).[1] The emergence of literary sovereignty as a set of debates has led to productive disagreement and critique since, according to some critics, pressure can build to present unanimous support for sovereigntist positions.[2]

These vigorous debates suggest that Indigenous literary sovereignty is not a monolithic construction; on the contrary, it is a heterogeneous, multiply inflected discursive field. Dale Turner remarks that while it is critical for non-Aboriginal people to recognize the importance of Aboriginal sovereignty, '[t]he precise content of a theory of Aboriginal sovereignty, however, will remain open, as indeed it should; Aboriginal sovereignty is best understood by listening to the diverse voices of Aboriginal peoples themselves' (Turner, *This* 59). To exemplify his point that each Indigenous nation or community has its own sense of what sovereignty means and how it will be honoured, Turner provides a detailed analysis of Iroquoian political philosophy, specifically Iroquoian *Guswentha*, or Two Row Wampum. Like Gail Guthrie Valaskakis, as I discussed in Chapter 1, Turner argues that the *Guswentha* is frequently misunderstood and caricatured as a philosophy of cultural parallelism, without an appreciation of the dynamic function of wampum in rituals of exchange. In early colonial America, though wampum materially represented a morally binding agreement, such an accord was not static; it necessitated regular reaffirmation through formal performances of oratory (47): 'Wampum belts were exchanged in the context of reciprocity and renewal – two central concepts in Iroquoian political thought ... Treaties, such as the early friendship treaties, required constant renewal, and agreements could only be made with the consent of both sides. If one side did not agree, there would be no exchange of wampum belts' (47-48). Turner here is suggesting that Iroquoian principles of reciprocity and renewal demanded substantial back-and-forth dialoguing and exchange.[3]

Part of my aim in *First Person Plural* has been to explore sovereigntist arguments through cross-cultural, collaborative forms of expression that are based on processes of exchange among both Indigenous and non-Indigenous interlocutors. In foregrounding dialogic approaches to Indigenous nationhood, I have attempted to listen to a diverse range of voices in as many modes as possible, investigating how Aboriginal people have used books, films, public hearings, land claims negotiations, the media, and other communicative modes to articulate models of sovereignty to a wide audience. Furthermore, in turning to both collaborative texts and a variety of public forums, I have suggested that 'coming to voice' involves dialoguing with other voices. I should clarify that my point is not to 'water down' strong claims to Indigenous sovereignty or to equate it with postmodern conceptions of heteroglossic, hybridized dialogue, as if Indigenous self-determination were on equal footing with the Canadian nation-state's assertion of sovereignty. Rather, following Turner, I am attempting to construct a sense of dialogic Indigenous sovereignty that is at once on its own terms and reciprocal. In other words, I am hoping to highlight the constitutive role of voices-in-dialogue in the practice of Indigenous sovereignty.

An example of such a dynamic conception of Indigenous sovereignty based on the systematic prioritization of dialogue and exchange can be found in the collective life story *Night Spirits: The Story of the Relocation of the Sayisi Dene*. Beginning as a research report prepared by Virginia Petch for the Royal Commission on Aboriginal Peoples (1991-96), the project soon took on a life of its own when one of Petch's interviewees, Ila Bussidor, travelled to Thompson, Manitoba, to convince the commissioners to come to Tadoule Lake to listen to her community's stories about the devastating after-effects of the relocation in 1956. Bussidor then approached Turkish Canadian journalist Üstün Bilgen-Reinart to collaborate with her to produce a book version of the Sayisi Dene people's multiple dislocations. Bussidor's shift from anonymous 'informant' to 'co-author' is itself an act of self-governance; yet the Sayisi Dene people do not consider their self-government package, secured in 1996, as an end-point in the struggle for their community's sense of autonomy and control. First and foremost, self-government has not laid the community's 'night spirits' to rest. Second, as is the case for many First Nations communities, 'self-government' in

Tadoule Lake is still a far cry from what might be considered 'independence' in the broadest sense, as Monture-Angus argues (8). And third, still to this day, the Sayisi Dene people are trying to resolve their border dispute with Nunavut since they allege that the new territory includes part of their ancestral lands. Thus sovereignty in this text is not synonymous with self-government, understood as a political agreement with the federal government; yet neither is the quest for sovereignty unrelated to the Sayisi Dene people's demands for formal recognition of their land and jurisdictional rights. What is particularly striking about this text is the manner in which the text frames the search for independence through a process of dialogue, appealing to a 'you' – who includes both Aboriginal and non-Aboriginal people in Canada – to listen to the stories and to remain accountable to this history of dispossession.

*Night Spirits* and many of the other texts in this study show that the politics of 'voice' and of 'land' are mutually constitutive and interdependent in discourses of Aboriginal sovereignty. 'The Mapping Project,' coordinated by Phoebe Nahanni in collaboration with a number of other Dene community members for the Mackenzie Valley Pipeline community hearings (1973-75), provides a good example of how the politics of voice and of land are tightly intertwined. For Nahanni, Dene-controlled research is a condition of Dene sovereignty; the researchers were as committed to asserting their land rights as they were concerned with ensuring a collective process of research. Working in the Dene language, the twenty-plus participants launched the debate over sovereignty into the dialogic space of the community hearings. This project, along with many others associated with the Berger Inquiry, offered the Dene, Métis, and Inuit people of the region a chance to develop new approaches to the tasks of filing land claims, negotiating self-government packages, and conducting land use studies.

'The Mapping Project' suggests that Aboriginal people's struggle to exercise jurisdiction over territory, resources, and land title is connected to their efforts to assert control over the representation of stories, songs, and other forms of cultural property. The Gitksan and Wet'suwet'en First Nations broke significantly from the past by asking their elders to act as expert witnesses in the land claims trial *Delgamuukw v. British Columbia* (1987-91). In Chapter 5, I analysed the compelling link between land and storytelling, as well as between land jurisdiction and authorship, and proposed that a principle of collaborative authorship may offer a model for addressing the problem of translating oral traditions into statements of Aboriginal title in the courtroom. I am aware that such a proposal risks a certain naïveté in imagining a court proceeding outside the box of the antagonistic relations of legal discourse – a discourse steeped in culturally deterministic notions of 'primitive' and 'civilized' societies, particularly with respect to legal rights associated with the 'use,' 'occupancy,' and 'ownership' of land. Yet in reviewing the legal history of Aboriginal rights in the courtroom – what Peter Kulchyski calls a 'history of sustained, often vicious struggle, a history of losses and gains, of shifting terrain' – I am not convinced that working strictly within the established rules of the court is the answer (*Unjust* 9-10). In this I am following the lead of the Gitksan and Wet'suwet'en plaintiffs themselves, who took enormous risks in attempting to decolonize the process by which they argued for Aboriginal title and jurisdiction to their territories; in a variety of ways, they sought 'to state their relationship to land on their own terms' and to 'control the representations of their culture' (Cruikshank, 'Invention' 34). Ultimately, they sought to transform the courthouse into their feast hall, and, by reciting their *adaawk* and *kungax*, they used the legal proceeding as further affirmation of their land rights: in the words of Delgam Uukw, 'The histories of my House are always being added to. My presence in this courtroom today will add to my House's power ... Through the witnessing of all the histories, century after century, we have exercised our jurisdiction' (Gisday Wa and Delgam Uukw 8).

The language of identity – of speaking in one's own voice and on one's own terms – powerfully shaped cultural debates in the 1990s in a variety of arenas, and was ignited partially by the intertwined conflicts over voice, land, and representation during the Oka crisis in the summer of 1990. The standoff generated starkly oppositional images in the struggle for Aboriginal sovereignty; in the words of Mohawk warrior Psycho, as reported in Alanis Obomsawin's documentary film, *Kanehsatake*, 'From here on in I guess we are going to be burying each other. Because we won't move.' Both the filmmaker Obomsawin and the writer Lee Maracle have engaged with the Oka crisis, and both declare their solidarity with the Mohawk people in various ways; however, both eschew the oppositional language that infused a great deal of the dominant media representations of the standoff. Far from dismissing told-to narrative forms in their search for a language of sovereignty, Obomsawin and Maracle sought new ways of practising cross-cultural collaboration by re-framing widely circulated images or by relaunching previously published material in new contexts. In circumventing binaristic models of resistance, Obomsawin and Maracle, like Cree poet Beth Cuthand in her poem, 'Post-Oka Kinda Woman,' consistently opt to leave the next generation with 'a struggle [rather] than a bad settlement' (Cuthand 133). All three artists draw attention to potential problems in some models of sovereignty, particularly the embedded gender and class assumptions that risk conferring privileges on a Native elite working within ongoing colonial frameworks.

Insurgent models of sovereignty – ones which break decisively from the colonial past of forced settlement, residential schools, and the suppression of Inuit language and culture – inform both the content of Isuma's films and their unique 'community filmmaking techniques,' which emphasize job training, boosting the local economy, and soliciting Inuit elders' knowledge of cultural traditions. Isuma's history, which began in 1990 when Zacharias Kunuk and Paul Apak left the federally managed Inuit Broadcasting Corporation (IBC) to form their own filmmaking collective, cannot be disentangled from Nunavut's history. Although the Isuma filmmakers could be described as cultural nationalists, having contributed in one way or another to the goal of securing greater autonomy for Nunavut, they also use their position outside Nunavut's governing structures to their advantage, articulating at times a sharp critique of the new territory's priorities. Through films like *Nipi (Voice)*, the Isuma filmmakers warn of the potential for the new government to become virtually indistinguishable from the very establishment that it struggled to overthrow (Evans 128). One issue the Isuma collective is concerned with is the need for Nunavut to develop a comprehensive cultural policy that supports its artists. Although the filmmakers are part of a larger social movement in Nunavut to honour the principles of *Inuit Qaujimajatuqangit* – 'that which the Inuit have long known' or 'an Inuit way of doing things' (IQ Task Force 2002, qtd. in A. Henderson 191) – in the shift to an Inuit-centred politics, there is little in the way of immunity against co-optation. Like any other term, *Inuit Qaujimajatuqangit* can be used to justify policies that have little to do with, or even outright hamper, the vital continuance of traditional Inuit culture. Thus Isuma sees its role as an agent to keep conversations interactive over questions of power, development, and the role of culture both in Nunavut and in Canada.

If the Oka crisis acted as a catalyst in setting off a series of questions along the lines of who can speak for whom, the formation of Nunavut in 1999 created the hope that the just settlement of land disputes in tandem with Aboriginal self-government agreements are key tools in transforming histories of appropriation. Yet the process of decolonization can be slow, with many setbacks along the way, as ongoing disputes over land and property rights (such as Caledonia Hills) make clear. Peter Kulchyski argues that by the early 1980s, 'self-government' became the key term in the government's 'new paradigm for managing Aboriginal peoples' (*Like the Sound* 86); twenty years later, 'a self-government machinery now exists in Canada' (238). At the same time, despite his cynicism, Kulchyski also insists that self-government remains one of the most important concepts for Aboriginal activists to mobilize in order to assert their sovereignty.

None of the transformations in told-to narratives that I have discussed in this book can guarantee the establishment of more equitable relations of collaboration. For example, told-to narratives that involve Aboriginal writers, translators, and editors do not necessarily produce a more fair and balanced partnership among co-creators. The 1991 *Delgamuukw* land claims trial is a case in point. The participation of Gitksan and Wet'suwet'en expert witnesses did not bring about the recognition of Aboriginal title and rights, at least not in the lower court. That said, I have argued that a new approach to collaborative authorship can go a long way in reconfiguring the relations of authority in told-to narratives. In *Life Lived Like a Story*, co-author Angela Sidney states that 'my stories are my wealth,' underlining the importance of acknowledging oral forms of authorship. The multiple publications of the stories, under the names of the storytellers, give weight to the claim of collaborative authorship. At the same time, the storytelling process suggests that stories have value through their dialogic exchange.

Collaborative authorship remains an uneasy and volatile process. Moments of cross-cultural misunderstanding, failures in cultural translation, and static in communication inform the relations of exchange imbricated in unequal social contexts. Collaboration cannot be thought of as a process in which interlocutors successfully overcome or transcend the impediments to their 'free' speech. In every communicative act there is a gap – between teller and listener, between writer and reader, between signifier and signified. However, this gap can be a creative space in which new forms of agency and of voice may arise. Collaboration, understood as an active process of 'alliance building' that manages a 'disarticulation of agendas' (Clifford, *Routes* 87), potentially unsettles the historically entrenched pattern of 'parallel voices' between First Nations and the Canadian nation-state, as well as the binary oppositions of the teller versus the recorder, the oral versus the written. Collaboration may also give rise to a new model for understanding and honouring Indigenous sovereignty, as well as conveying a sense of historical accountability that, as a non-Indigenous person of the 'Second Nations,' I am implicated within. A diversity of forms of affiliation is possible and indeed necessary to recognize the struggle of writing and of telling a more just story of Indigenous presence in North America, through the mode of cross-cultural collaboration.

# Notes

**Introduction**

1 As demonstrated in this Introduction and throughout this book, I use the terms Aboriginal, Native, Indigenous, and First Nations more or less interchangeably, though each appellation has its own inflection, evoking its own particular set of historical meanings and connotations. My guiding principle is to follow the manner in which Native writers, scholars, and cultural workers describe themselves and their communities. The default term I use in this study is 'Aboriginal,' and I use this term primarily to refer to groups within Canada. I use the term 'Indigenous' to make connections between groups across the borders of settler nation-states such as Canada, the US, Mexico, and Australia. I sometimes refer to 'Native writers,' a common descriptor in Canadian literary criticism. Where relevant, I use specific names of communities, such as Cree, Dene, Métis, or Mohawk, and so on. When I am discussing questions of nationhood and sovereignty, I sometimes use the term 'First Nations,' unless I am wishing to include Inuit or Métis people, who are, at least in Canadian law and legislation, categorized separately from First Nations. This last point underlines the reality that many of the terms under discussion flow from colonial legislation and governmental policies and, as such, carry with them histories of exclusion, marginalization, and deterritorialization (Damm 11-12). Nevertheless, it is also clear that Aboriginal people have maintained their own names and used a wide range of labels to suit their community's evolving goals.

2 Important precursors to this study include Barbara Godard's *Talking About Ourselves* (1985), George Cornell's 'The Imposition of Western Definitions of Literature on Indian Oral Traditions' (1987), Margery Fee's essays (1987, 1997, 1999), J.E. Chamberlin's essays (1997, 1999, 2000), Michele Grossman's essays (2004, 2006), and Michael Jacklin's essays (2004, 2007, 2008), that deal with the relationship between oral and written traditions. Susan Gingell's *Textualizing Orature and Orality: Special Issue of Essays on Canadian Writing* (2005) and Renée Hulan and Renate Eigenbrod's *Aboriginal Oral Traditions: Theory, Practice, Ethics* (2008) bring together a wide range of textualizing practices, examining the role of

oral traditions in preserving knowledge, sustaining language and culture, protecting intellectual property rights, and disseminating knowledge in new modes of circulation (such as electronic media). Although Helen Hoy (2001) and Eigenbrod (2005) do not focus primarily on textualized oral narrative, their monographs offer a useful critical framework for discussing the negotiation of insider/outsider positionings in multiply layered texts, particularly for what Eigenbrod calls 'the im/Migrant reader' of Aboriginal literatures in the Canadian context.

3 For example, Gingell organized 'The Oral, the Written, and Other Verbal Media: Interfaces and Audiences' at the University of Saskatchewan (Saskatoon) in June 2008, a conference and festival that brought together storytellers, literary critics, oral historians, and spoken word performers.

4 Susan Berry Brill de Ramírez's *Contemporary American Indian Literatures and the Oral Tradition* (1999) works flexibly at the interface between written and oral narratives, as well as between contemporary and historical oral traditions, though her focus on 'oral novels' reveals her prioritization of contemporary novels that use a literary style labeled as 'oral.' Similarly, Blanca Schorcht's *Storied Voices in Native American Texts* (2003), although including a chapter on Harry Robinson's told-to narratives, focuses primarily on dialogism and orality in contemporary Native American novels. Julie Cruikshank's collaborative work with three Athapaskan elders in *Life Lived Like a Story* (1990) and Greg Sarris's *Keeping Slug Woman Alive* (1993) provide a valuable bridge between anthropological and literary analytical concerns; both are discussed in detail in this study. Kathleen Sands's articles (1997, 1998), as well as her collaborative biography with Theodore Rios, *Telling a Good One: The Process of a Native American Collaborative Autobiography* (2000), have helped me articulate many of the challenges involved in textualizing oral narrative. Brian Swann's scholarly and anthologizing work on translation and re-translations of contemporary and historical Native American oral literatures, particularly *Coming to Light: Contemporary Translations of Native Literatures of North America* (1996) and, with Arnold Krupat, *Voices from the Four Directions: Contemporary Translations of the Native Literature of North America* (2004), provide useful overviews of the relevant debates as well as some important examples of contemporary textualized oral narrative.

5 For examples of critical studies that over-emphasize the role of the recorder in determining the form and content of the told-to narrative, see Krupat's early and influential essay, 'Indian Autobiography: Origins, Type, Function' (1983), David Murray's *Forked Tongues: Speech, Writing and Representation in American Indian Texts* (1991), and Gayatri Chakravorty Spivak's discussion of the historical construction of the 'Native Informant' in *A Critique of Postcolonial Reason: Toward a History of the Vanishing Present* (1999).

6 For examples of critical studies that excessively emphasize the free agency of the teller, see Kathleen Donovan's *Feminist Readings of Native American Literature: Coming to Voice* (1998) and John Beverley's *Testimonio: On the Politics of Truth* (2004).

7 I am certainly not alone in applying Bakhtin's theories of 'speech genres' and of 'heteroglossia' to textualized oral narrative and other composite texts in Indigenous literary studies. Indeed, mixed-blood Choctaw Cherokee literary critic Louis Owens (1992) has noted 'the current tendency of critics to consider Bakhtin as a topical ointment applicable to virtually any critical abrasion'; yet he also confirms that 'Bakhtinian analysis strikes me nonetheless as a valuable tool' (256). Similarly Arnold Krupat, while acknowledging the dangers of overusing Bakhtin, argues that the philosopher's writings offer a way to forge a 'dialogic approach' to the issues informing Native American literary studies. Krupat

writes: '[t]o take Bakhtin's thought seriously ... is to go beyond a vague pluralism or an untheorized commitment to diversity to a recognition that our speech and thought is inevitably implicated in the speech and thought of others' (*The Turn* 28).

8 For an excellent discussion of how various forms of political liberalism have not recognized Aboriginal rights in Canada, in part because of the persistence of the settler mentality, and how a 'generous version of political liberalism' *must* recognize Aboriginal conceptions of political sovereignty both within and against the framework of minority rights, see the Introduction to Dale Turner's *'This Is Not a Peace Pipe': Towards an Understanding of Aboriginal Sovereignty* (2005) as well as his revised monograph, *This Is Not a Peace Pipe: Toward a Critical Indigenous Philosophy* (2006).

9 Labrador-Métis critic Kristina Fagan, in her review of *Reasoning Together: The Native Critics' Collective* (2008), asks: 'How can we work within the "reasoning" mode so valued within the academy while maintaining our responsibilities to our communities and our own experiences?' ('Delicate' 78). In the 'collaborative interlogue' by Fagan et al. (2009), entitled 'Canadian Indian Literary Nationalism?: Critical Approaches in Canadian Indigenous Contexts – A Collaborative Interlogue,' Deanna Reder, a Cree-Métis critic, addresses some of the successes and ongoing challenges of First Nations studies programs at universities (32-35). Literary and cultural critic Michael Jacklin, in his work on collaborative Indigenous life writing from Canada and Australia (2004, 2007, 2008), usefully emphasizes the significance of cultural protocols to both the narrative exchange and the writing and editing process. He makes a convincing case that all academics, including literary critics, should consult with Indigenous communities in crafting their interpretations.

**Chapter 1: 'Where Is the Voice Coming From?'**

1 Assimilation remained the official policy in both Canada and the United States until the late 1960s. In Canada, policies of assimilation included residential schools, forced relocations of communities, and the removal of children from families through Children's Aid. Policies of assimilation culminated in the Liberal government's White Paper of 1969 but continue in different forms today. Every few years, politicians propose legislation that threatens to scrap the *Indian Act* altogether – for example, former Prime Minister Jean Chrétien's Aboriginal Governance Act of 2002, which I discuss in Chapter 4.

2 Other examples of anthologies from the first half of the twentieth century include Margot Astrov's *The Winged Serpent* (1946) and A. Grove Day's *The Sky Clears: Poetry of the American Indians* (1951). The 1970s witnessed a renewal of interest; the best-known and most controversial example is Jerome Rothenberg's *Shaking the Pumpkin* (1972). More recent publications such as A.L. Soens's *I, the Song* (1999), Karl Kroeber's *Native American Storytelling: A Reader of Myths and Legends* (2004), and Brian Swann and Arnold Krupat's *Voices from the Four Directions: Contemporary Translations of the Native Literature of North America* (2004), indicate that interest in the genre continues.

3 The philosophy of Romantic nationalism is usually attributed to Johann Gottfried Herder (1744-1803), who argued that people who share a common language, land, and folklore constitute a nation. He contended that these elements together – language, land, and folklore – not only shape the character of a people but also produce the spirit or soul of a nation (Samper 30). For further discussion of Romantic nationalism, see Fee's essays (1987, 1997, 1999), David A. Samper's '"Love, Peace, and Unity": Romantic Nationalism and the Role of Oral Literature in Kenya's Secondary Schools' (1997), and Glenn Willmott's 'Modernism and Aboriginal Modernity: The Appropriation of Products of West Coast Native Heritage as National Goods' (2004).

4 Clements notes that Curtis's *The Indians' Book* is the 'first truly cross-cultural anthology of Native American verbal art,' drawing on material from eighteen tribes from many parts of the United States and Canada (Clements 185).

5 See Clements for an excellent comparison of museum practices of displaying Native American cultural artifacts, and anthologizing practices of presenting Native American oral literatures (179-98). See also George Cornell's seminal essay, 'The Imposition of Western Definitions of Literature on Indian Oral Traditions' (1987), in which he critiques the interpretation of oral traditions as poetry by literary-minded critics such as Hymes, Tedlock, and Swann (177-80).

6 See Krupat, 'On the Translation,' and Clements (Chapter 1) for more on the differences between 'literary' and 'anthropological' styles of entextualization, especially in the first decades of the twentieth century.

7 Germaine Warkentin's 'In Search of "The Word of the Other"' (1999) explores the many 'communicative' and 'mnemonic artifacts' of Iroquois and other nations of eastern North America (2). She discusses, among other communicative devices, Iroquoian wampum belts, Athapaskan petroglyphs, Blackfoot painting, and Ojibway birch-bark scrolls: 'Perhaps too easily classified as "oral" cultures, the Native peoples of North America possess a rich legacy of material sign-making, attested to in the archaeological record, in the linguistic evidence, and in early North American history as Europeans have recorded it' (4). See also Marie Battiste's analysis of how Indigenous peoples 'have used a wide array of forms and systems of communicating or writing or remembering' (111) in 'Print Culture and Decolonizing the University: Indigenizing the Page' (2004).

8 See Petrone, *First People*, for examples of First Nations writing and speeches in the eighteenth and nineteenth centuries.

9 Andrea Bear Nicholas, in 'The Assault on Aboriginal Oral Traditions: Past and Present' (2008), argues that Leland mistranslated Wabanaki words, collapsed various versions of stories into one, outright fabricated certain elements in the stories, and rendered anonymous the storytellers he worked with (14-17). Nicholas further states these misrepresentations of Wabanaki oral traditions were reproduced in school and university textbooks up until the early 1980s and continue to exert influence in the present (16-17).

10 See Chapter 5 for a discussion of Angela Sidney's telling of the story 'K̲aax̲'achgóok' and its role in the exchange of property.

11 David Stoll, an American anthropologist, argued in his book, *Rigoberta Menchú and the Story of All Poor Guatemalans* (1999), that there was no possibility that Menchú could have seen with her own eyes some of the experiences she claimed to have witnessed in *I, Rigoberta Menchú*. Stoll's assertions sparked public controversy and academic debate over the cultural determinants informing concepts such as eye-witnessing, proof, and subjectivity. Ecocritic Joni Adamson argues that Stoll's 'charges [of inaccuracy] also point to wide cultural differences between the ways the Maya perceive of their books and *testimonios* as "seeing instruments" that help us better understand the present and move intelligently into the future and the way that Anglo-Europeans perceive of their books as a place for a Voice of Authority to pronounce Truth' (151).

12 The notion of a 'too thorough inclusion' is Jennifer Henderson's; she is addressing the interpellation of feminist critique in discourses that claim to be gender neutral (J. Henderson 41). See also Patricia Monture-Angus's *Journeying Forward: Dreaming First Nations' Independence* (1999) on the problem of mainstream representations that include 'the Native perspective' as a way of ultimately dismissing it (28).

13 Despite the text's strategies of juxtaposition and self-referentiality, some readers, such as literary critics Susanna Egan and Heather Hodgson, argue that Wiebe's role as recorder, editor, and author problematically reproduces some of the troubled history of told-to narratives. In particular, Egan objects to Wiebe's adoption of an omniscient voice and his self-effacement as editor (12-14), while Hodgson targets his narrative intrusions, his standardization of Johnson's spelling and grammar, and his placement as first author on the title page (155). Though I am sympathetic to these interpretations, ultimately I concur with Deena Rymhs, who argues: 'Rather than seeing the different genres and narrative modes in *Stolen Life* as masking problems with authorship and story-making, one could view them as actively drawing attention to the problems with voice, authority, credibility, and truth' ('Auto/biographical' 105). She also states that 'Johnson, we must keep in mind, presided over the making of this text. To dismiss or overlook this point is also to dismiss her authority' (105).

14 Another well-known text in Indigenous studies on the question of 'insider' and 'outsider' perspectives on research is Linda Tuhiwai Smith's *Decolonizing Methodologies: Research and Indigenous Peoples* (1999). While exposing the ways in which knowledge *about* Indigenous communities is 'deeply embedded in the multiple layers of imperial and colonial practices' (2), Smith crafts alternative models for research within a broader politics of 'self-determination, decolonization and social justice' (4).

15 In *Tribal Secrets: Recovering American Indian Intellectual Traditions* (1995), Warrior models sovereigntist readings of Native American literary texts, arguing that political discussions and textual analyses should be more integrated in scholarly writing. In the name of 'intellectual sovereignty,' Warrior references primarily Native American writers in order to counteract the history of Euro-Americans and Euro-Canadians writing 'about' Native subjects. Warrior's work frequently has been misinterpreted as excluding the work of non-Native critics; his contribution to *American Indian Literary Nationalism* (2006), 'Native Critics in the World: Edward Said and Nationalism,' responds to these criticisms and makes a compelling case for cosmopolitan approaches to sovereignty.

16 Temagami scholar Dale Turner critiques Alan Cairns's interpretation of the two-row wampum, or Guswentha, arguing that Cairns does not mention 'the three beads of respect, peace, and friendship that bind the two rows together' (*This* 54). These three beads suggest that the Guswentha cannot be dismissed as a philosophy of cultural parallelism; it embodies a vision of cross-cultural interaction between independent nations.

17 *Native American Oral Traditions: Collaboration and Interpretation* (2001), edited by Evers and Toelken, is a collection of essays and contemporary told-to narratives in which collaborators discuss a wide range of challenges and opportunities associated with collaborative work. Each contribution is co-authored by a collector-editor and a storyteller for whom 'the familiar divisions between "scholar" and "Native"' are not applicable or too simplistic' (9).

18 In the Introduction to *Life Lived Like a Story*, Cruikshank describes how, when she began working with Athapaskan/Tlingit elders in the Yukon in 1974, her intention was to produce an oral history that documented the impact of large-scale social change in the region, such as the building of the Alaskan Highway. However, in response to her questions, Angela Sidney, Kitty Smith, and Annie Ned would recite place names, recount complex genealogies, or tell traditional stories and songs (Cruikshank et al. 2). As a result, Cruikshank was obliged to rethink the process and purpose of her research. For more discussion of this issue, see Chapter 5.

19 I am borrowing the metaphor of 'mediation's static' from Laura J. Murray and Keren Rice's interpretation of Greg Sarris's work. In their Introduction to *Talking on the Page: Editing Aboriginal Oral Texts* (1999), Murray and Rice write that 'mediation's static does not have to drown out the telling. Sarris's sophisticated combination of story and argument suggests that it is in fact through awareness of mediation, of the nature of the relation between receivers ... and senders, that tellers can most effectively craft their words, and listeners and readers best hope to hear: the static becomes part of a larger multidimensional story, instead of a mask to an elusive, essential meaning' (xiv).

**Chapter 2: Coming to Voice the North**
1 Berger's report, *Northern Frontier, Northern Homeland*, was published by Canada and the Department of Indian Affairs and Northern Development in 1977. Berger later published a slightly revised version under his own name in 1988. For the most part, this chapter refers to the 1988 publication under Berger's name. Where necessary I have cited 'Canada' to refer to the 1977 report.
2 Peter Kulchyski also expresses admiration for Brody's 'powerful, expressive language,' his 'acute sensitivity to Aboriginal communities,' and his 'extraordinary insight into the dynamics of struggle engaged in by Aboriginal people' (*Like the Sound* 54-55).
3 Hugh Brody is an internationally recognized scholar, anthropologist, land claims researcher, policy adviser, filmmaker, and writer. He has worked with numerous band councils and community land claims research groups over the past three decades. In the 1970s, he worked with the Department of Indian Affairs and Northern Development, and then with Inuit and Indian organizations. He has taught at various universities in Europe and in Canada, including Queen's University, Belfast, and McGill University, Montreal. While this chapter focuses on Brody's work in Canada with First Nations peoples, as a comparative anthropologist, Brody also has studied land use issues relating to the Hai-kom Bushmen in Namibia, Africa, has researched the economic impact of hydro projects on the Nez Perce tribe in Idaho, and has examined the social, economic, and cultural losses due to resettlement of tribal communities in India.
4 An example of a respondent at the Mackenzie Valley Pipeline Inquiry who envisions Aboriginal independence within the context of Canadian federalism is Robert André, from Arctic Red River, whom Berger claims 'represents the concept of native claims held by the majority of the people of Indian ancestry in the Mackenzie Valley': 'We want to survive as a people, [hence] our stand for maximum independence *within your society*. We want to develop our own economy. We want to acquire political independence for our people, *within the Canadian constitution*. We want to govern our own lives and our own lands and its resources. We want to have our own system of government, by which we can control and develop our land for our benefit' (Canada, *Northern* 172; my emphasis).
5 See, for example, Coates and Powell (xi-xvi; 155-59); Hamilton (179-207); Hutchinson; Swayze; and *The Inquiry Film*. The most extreme example of such a reading is Hamilton's *Arctic Revolution* (1994). Hamilton traces the shift of power from Ottawa to the territorial governments from 1953 to 1995. What is striking about this 'arctic revolution,' according to Hamilton, is how colonial agents chose to relinquish their power: 'half a dozen white men ... showed enormous statesmanship in deliberately handing over power to the natives' (xii). Berger is included in this group: 'The Berger drama was ... a spectacular show and focused on one remarkable man, Mr. Justice Tom Berger' (179-80), 'a man of great character and unblemished reputation' (205-6).

6 The land claims decision *Calder v. British Columbia* (1973) established the importance of Aboriginal plaintiffs gathering evidence of their ancestors' 'use and occupancy' of disputed territory. In that decision, six of the seven Supreme Court judges found that Aboriginal title had existed prior to European arrival, based on long-term 'use and occupancy' (Culhane 81).

7 In his documentary film *Ghosts of Futures Past: Tom Berger in the North* (2006), produced for David Suzuki's *The Nature of Things*, Geoff Bowie interviews some mappers from Denendeh who are using a variation of Nahanni's mapping project to resist the federal government's pressure to designate certain lands to be developed industrially. Kulchyski also remarks upon the close connection between mapping and telling stories in Denendeh and describes Bella T'Seleie's 1993 mapping project of Sahtu territory in the vicinity of Fort Good Hope:

> Bella found, through this project, that many of the stories and indeed much of the culture were embedded in those place names. When she talked to elders, they would rarely just point at the map and say 'this is called this'; rather, they would tell the story of how the place came to be, why it was named, and how it related to other places, other stories, different family networks, and more. To do the research properly would take a lifetime, and even then the nature of the project was such that it would never and could never be a 'full' record. (*Like the Sound* 260)

Kulchyski's articulation of the relationship between mapping, storytelling, and territory is remarkably similar to Nahanni's and Brody's (discussed later in this chapter), as well as to Cruikshank's description of Angela Sidney's, Kitty Smith's, and Annie Ned's projects of recording place names (discussed in Chapter 5).

8 Kulchyski argues that regional differences within Denendeh explain why, following the unravelling of the Agreement in Principle in 1990, the Gwi'chin Dene and Sahtu Dene First Nations settled individually, the Dogrib postponed their agreement, and the Dehcho still have not signed a deal. The Gwi'chin Dene, who are geographically close to the Inuvialuit, wanted to settle a claim and achieve the stability and prosperity that the Inuvialuit appeared to be enjoying following their claim in 1984. The Sahtu, who are adjacent to Nunavut and who have a strong majority in their region, are in a position to better assert their autonomy, even within the terms of extinguishment. Dehcho, meanwhile, has a larger non-Native population; as a result, the Dene population is more concerned about what extinguishment might mean (*Like the Sound* 95-96).

9 I borrow the phrase 'ways of seeing' from John Berger. Berger's work is relevant to Brody's in its preoccupation with juxtaposing disparate points of view.

10 'Inuk' is the singular of 'Inuit'.

11 'The condition of the native is a nervous condition': Zimbabwean author Tsitsi Dangarembga borrows this quotation from Jean-Paul Sartre's introduction to Fanon's *The Wretched of the Earth* for the epigraph of her novel, *Nervous Conditions*. Dangarembga explores Fanon's argument that various forms of psychic malaise emerge from stark, Apartheid-like social dichotomies in colonial society. She suggests that these Apartheid-like relations have persisted in postcolonial Zimbabwe.

12 I use the term Inuit or Inuktitut (the Inuit people's language) rather than Eskimo unless quoting directly from *The People's Land*.

13 Julie Cruikshank uses the phrase 'layered tellings' to describe how a storyteller is able to use a single narrative to convey a range of meanings: 'What appears to be the "same" story, even in the repertoire of one individual, acquires multiple meanings depending on the location, circumstance, audience and stage of life of both narrator and listener' (*Social* 44). See Chapter 5 for more.

14 For more on the politics of 'nontranslation' within the context of imperialism, see Cheyfitz, and Godard ('Writing').

### Chapter 3: 'There Is a Time Bomb in Canada'

1 My title borrows from Jordan Wheeler's article 'Voice', which discusses the representation of the 'Oka crisis' in dominant media outlets, and which I discuss in more detail in Chapter 1.

2 The 'absent editor' is Brumble's phrase, which, as I discuss in the Introduction, 'create[s] the fiction that the narrative is all the Indian's own' (Brumble 75).

3 Before the 1970s, it was difficult for Aboriginal storytellers or writers to publish their work under their own name. For example, it took Edward Ahenakew fifty years – from 1923 to 1973 – to publish his told-to narrative, *Voices of the Plains Cree*, which also lists the editor, Ruth M. Buck, on the title page. Examples of contemporary told-to narrative that list Aboriginal storytellers, translators, or editors as authors and/or acknowledge oral authorship include: Beverly Hungry Wolf's *The Ways of My Grandmothers* (1980); Nora Marks Dauenhauer and Richard Dauenhauer's *Haa Shuká/Our Ancestors: Tlingit Oral Narratives* (1987); Freda Ahenakew and H.C. Wolfart's *Our Grandmothers' Lives, As Told in the Their Own Words* (1992); Darwin Hanna and Mamie Henry's *Our Tellings: Interior Salish Stories of the Nlha7kápmx People* (1995); Maria Campbell's *Stories of the Road Allowance People* (1995); Ila Bussidor and Üstün Bilgen-Reinart's *Night Spirits: The Story of the Relocation of the Sayisi Dene* (1997); George Blondin's *Yamoria the Lawmaker: Stories of the Dene* (1997); Nancy Wachowich in collaboration with Apphia Agalakti Awa, Rhoda Kaukjak Katsak, and Sandra Pikujak Katsak's *Saqiyuq: Stories from the Lives of Three Inuit Women* (1999); Nympha Byrne and Camille Fouillard's *It's Like the Legend: Innu Women's Voices* (2000); and Theodore Rios and Kathleen Mullen Sands's *Telling a Good One: The Process of a Native American Collaborative Autobiography* (2000). I discuss some of these texts briefly in Chapter 1.

4 Obomsawin provides a reading of wampum from 1721, which is a declaration of the Mohawks' rights to land on the island of Montreal (Hochelaga), following their expulsion by the French king to their hunting grounds, the site that is now known as Kanehsatake/Oka, on the shores of the Lake of Two Mountains.

5 The first standoff at Kanehsatake occurred in 1721, when the Supulcians received land rights to Kanehsatake/Oka from the French king, whose representatives did not consult with the Mohawks about this land transfer. In 1868, Joseph Onasakenrat, chief of the Mohawk people, resisted the removal of his people to Ontario and was imprisoned; this action incited the second standoff. The third standoff, in 1959, aimed to derail the municipality's plans to raze part of the Pines to lease to a private corporation, Club de golf Oka Inc. Despite the Mohawk people's objections, a nine-hole golf course was completed in 1961. The fourth standoff took place in 1969, when the federal government expropriated disputed Mohawk territory that was part of the original Lake of Two Mountains Seigneury to build the Montreal International Airport at Mirabel. Finally in 1990, during the fifth standoff, the Mohawk people blockaded the road into the Pines to stop the town

of Oka's plan to expand the golf course. See Winter (210-12) for more details on these standoffs.
6 The Meech Lake Accord was a proposed amendment to the Canadian constitution in 1990 that, among other things, recognized Quebec as a 'distinct society'. Since Premier Robert Bourassa indicated his intention to sign the agreement, Quebec would have joined the Canadian constitution (Quebec, under Premier René Lévesque, did not sign the constitution in 1982). The Accord required ratification by all ten provincial legislatures and parliament to come into effect. For ratification, each provincial assembly would have had to unanimously consent to a motion to hold a vote on the Accord. In Manitoba, Elijah Harper, Independent Cree Member of the Legislative Assembly, did not give his consent since the Accord did not recognize Aboriginal people as part of the 'founding nations' of Canada.
7 The Great Law of Peace, a massive oral text at least five hundred years old, was brought to the Iroquois people by a prophet known as the Peacemaker. For more perspectives on the Great Law of Peace of the Rotinohshonni or Iroquois Confederacy, see Gail Guthrie Valaskakis, *Indian Country* (46-49), Patricia Monture-Angus, *Journeying Forward* (32), Dale Turner, *This Is Not a Peace Pipe* (49-55), and Taiaiake Alfred's *Peace, Power, Righteousness* (63-64, 89-90, 101-5). It should be noted that Alfred's explanation of the *Kaienerekowa* (or Great Law of Peace) is rehearsed in different forms throughout the text, and chiefly through his engagement with the Rotinohshonni Condolence Ceremony, which in turn provides the structure and moral compass of his book. In thirteen steps, the Rotinohshonni Condolence Ceremony enacts Kanien'kehaka (or Mohawk) nationhood (xvii-xix; xx-xxiii).
8 Many literary critics have commented upon Maracle's textual doublevoicedness, including Dadey, Hunter, Leggatt, and O'Brien.
9 In *Speech Genres and Other Essays* (1986), Bakhtin challenges the myth of the two 'partners' in a conversation, instead drawing attention to the larger political and social contexts of a discussion:

> Still current in linguistics are such fictions as the 'listener' and 'understander' (partners of the speaker), the 'unified speech flow', and so on. These fictions produced a completely distorted idea of the complex and multifaceted process of active speech communication ... The fact is that when the listener perceives and understands the meaning (the language meaning) of speech, he simultaneously takes an active, responsive attitude toward it. He either agrees or disagrees with it ... augments it, applies it ... and so on ... Any understanding of live speech, a live utterance, is inherently responsive, although the degree of this activity varies extremely. Any understanding is imbued with response ... the listener becomes the speaker. (*Speech* 68)

10 For a detailed discussion of the structural inequalities in Canadian publishing as a result of systemic racism, as well as a precise picture of the politics of representation in and around 1990, see Godard, 'The Politics.'

### Chapter 4: 'My Story Is a Gift'

1 The co-chairs for RCAP were the Honourable René Dussault, Justice of the Quebec Court of Appeal and former Quebec Deputy Minister of Justice (1977-80), and Georges Erasmus, former president of the Dene nation (1973-83) and former National Grand Chief of the Assembly of First Nations (1985-91). The other commissioners were Paul Chartrand, a

Métis professor of Native Studies at the University of Manitoba; J. Peter Meekison, professor of Political Science and Belzberg Chair in Constitutional Studies (Faculty of Law) at the University of Alberta; Viola Robinson, Mi'kmaq, former president of the Native Council of Canada; Mary Sillett, founding member and former president of the Inuit Women's Association of Canada and former vice-president of Inuit Tapirisat of Canada; and Bertha Wilson, who was born in Scotland, and who was the first woman to be appointed to the Supreme Court of Canada (in 1982).

2 The TRC in South Africa was assigned the task of 'establishing as complete a picture as possible of the causes, nature and extent of the gross violations of human rights' during the Apartheid regime from 1960 to 1994 (qtd. in Graham 11). Shane Graham comments that the 'TRC was designed to at least lay the groundwork for reconciliation between the agents and supporters of the former white minority regime and the opponents of apartheid' (11).

3 Canada, Royal Commission on Aboriginal Peoples, *Report of the Royal Commission on Aboriginal Peoples*. 5 vols. Ottawa: The Commission, 1996.

4 Though *Looking Forward, Looking Back*, the first volume of the *Report*, acknowledges that 'the Royal Commission on Aboriginal Peoples was born in a time of ferment when the future of the Canadian federation was being debated passionately' (Canada, *Looking Forward* 2), citing Oka, Ipperwash, and Gustafsen Lake, no further mention is made of these conflicts in the report. This turning away from controversy, along with the commission's decision not to use its powers of subpoena to call for both documents and witnesses, as Anthony Hall argues, are evidence of 'the Commission's determination to avoid an adversarial format' (Hall 72). By eliding high-profile, ongoing conflicts, the commission is suggesting a model of reconciliation that does not include conflict in the present.

5 Turner notes that '[o]f the four Aboriginal commissioners – George Erasmus, Paul Chartrand, Viola Robinson, and Mary Sillett – only Chartrand had a legal background ... Of the three non-Aboriginal commissioners, Bertha Wilson was a former Supreme Court judge, Peter Meekison was a professor of political science and former Deputy Minister of Intergovernmental Affairs in Alberta, and René Dussault was a Quebec Superior Court judge' (157n).

6 In Australia, the HREOC was commissioned to hold a National Inquiry into the separation of Aboriginal and Torres Strait Islander children from their families and communities. The ensuing report, *Bringing Them Home*, records that 'between one in three and one in ten Indigenous children were forcibly removed from their families and communities' between 1910 and 1970 (qtd. in Whitlock 198).

7 For the complete testimony, see Marius Tungilik, Rankin Inlet Public Hearing, NWT, 19 November 1992. In Canada, *For Seven Generations*, CD-ROM.

8 Although the commission is publishing some of the contributions to the community hearings on its website, not all statements can be released. *Truth, Healing, Reconciliation*, a pamphlet explaining the mandate of the commission, states that 'participation is voluntary and participants can choose how they want to share,' either 'in a private, one-on-one interview' or 'through a public discussion' (Indian Residential Schools' Truth and Reconciliation Commission, *Truth* 5). However, the finer print in *Schedule N: Mandate for the Truth and Reconciliation Commission* states that sessions are required to be held *in camera* if unsubstantiated allegations of wrong-doing are made. What emerges from *Schedule N* is that the commission will be held behind closed doors to the extent necessary to protect the anonymity of those who may be implicated in criminal charges.

9 A footnote indicates just what an achievement this careful archival work represents. When researchers asked to examine approximately 6,000 residential school files that are held by the Department of Indian Affairs and Northern Development, they encountered significant resistance: 'The Royal Commission secured access to this documentation only after protracted and difficult negotiations; these were eventually successful, but they seriously delayed completion of the project. Only one member of the research team was allowed to review the material and then only after signing an agreement setting out a detailed research protocol and obtaining an "enhanced reliability" security clearance' (Canada, *Looking Forward* 386n).

10 The purpose of Bill C-31, which was passed on 28 June 1985, was to eliminate sexual discrimination in the *Indian Act* and align it with the Canadian Charter of Rights and Freedoms. Before this date, status Indian women who married non-status men lost their status and were unable to pass their status on to their children. Though the amendment corrected this gender bias, other provisions have created new problems. For example, the children of women who were reinstated after 1985 cannot pass on status to their children; this is known as the third-generation cut-off. Furthermore, on-reserve budgets in housing, education, social assistance, and infrastructure have become over-stretched due to the increase in members requiring services and supports. See RCAP's Volume Four, *Perspectives and Realities* (33-53) for a detailed discussion of this issue, as well as Cheryl Suzack, 'Law Stories as Life Stories: Jeanette Bedell, Yvonne Bédard, and *Halfbreed*' (especially 118-19).

11 For Brooks's complete testimony, see 'Governance, Justice and Family Violence,' moderated by Commissioner Ethel Blondin, Yellowknife, NWT, 7 December 1992. In Canada, *For Seven Generations*, CD-ROM.

12 Whitlock mentions, among other works, Bal, Crewe, and Spitzer; Felman and Laub; and Manne.

13 Examples of the dually produced life narrative from the 1970s and 1980s include Wilfred Pelletier and Ted Poole, *No Foreign Land: The Biography of a North American Indian* (1973); Jean Speare (ed.), *The Days of Augusta* (1973); Rosamond Vanderburgh, *I Am Nokomis, Too: The Biography of Verna Patronella Johnston* (1977); and Margaret Blackman, *During My Time: Florence Edenshaw Davidson* (1982; rev. ed. 1992).

14 Examples of collective life stories from the 1990s and early 2000s are Innu Nation and Mushuau Innu Band Council, *Gathering Voices: Finding Strength To Help Our Children* (1995); Darwin Hanna (ed.) and Mamie Henry (ed., tr.), *Our Tellings: Interior Salish Stories of the Nlha7kápmx People* (1995); Peter Kulchyski, Don McCaskill, and David Newhouse (eds.), *In the Words of Elders: Aboriginal Cultures in Transition* (1999); and Nympha Byrne and Camille Fouillard (ed.), *It's Like the Legend: Innu Women's Voices* (2000).

15 In speaking of the 'impossible necessity' of the shared responsibility of testifying and witnessing to a traumatic past, I am borrowing ideas from Gayatri Chakravorty Spivak's discussion of ethical engagement with subaltern subjects. In her 'Translator's Preface' to Mahasweta Devi's *Imaginary Maps*, Spivak speaks of ethics as 'the experience of the impossible,' which 'sharpens the sense of the crucial and continuing need for collective political struggle' (xxv). She further explains that during a collective struggle, 'full ethical engagement' with each and every subaltern is impossible; yet it is precisely this 'ethical singularity,' where we 'engage profoundly with one person,' which is 'necessary' to fuel a longstanding and effective political movement (xxv).

16 According to Petch, writing in 1994, 'after forty years, no answers to the relocation issue have been given by government and no compensation or apology has been received' (Section 7.0). As reported in the film *Almost Home: A Sayisi Dene Journey*, in 2003 the

government made an offer of compensation but to this day approval is still pending (Lang, Petzold, and Fuller).
17 In RCAP's report, the commissioners acknowledge that the Sayisi Dene First Nation's 'traditional lands have been included within the boundaries of Nunavut' (Canada, *Looking Forward* 438). This dispute is ongoing.
18 In 1995, the Sayisi Dene at Tadoule Lake negotiated a self-government package that includes control over health, education, and community programs (Bussidor and Bilgen-Reinart xii).
19 In May 1996, the Sayisi Dene nation joined nineteen other Manitoba First Nations in signing a tentative agreement with the federal government that granted 23,000 acres (9,000 hectares) of land and $580,000 for economic development to the Sayisi Dene (Bussidor and Bilgen-Reinart 138). However, as mentioned in note 17, the Sayisi Dene First Nation has not yet resolved its contestation with Nunavut's border.
20 Though Petch kept her informants anonymous, there are strong parallels between Bussidor's life story as narrated in *Night Spirits* and Petch's version in Section 5.0 of her report.
21 The filmmakers – Robert Lang, Shelia Petzold, and Michael Fuller – had first met Bussidor in 1971 in Churchill; at that time, they were among a group of five young film students who made a documentary film about the Sayisi Dene people's unjust relocation. In the voice-over of *Almost Home*, Petzold states that Bussidor contacted the filmmakers and requested a new film about her community.

**Chapter 5: 'What the Map Cuts Up, the Story Cuts Across'**
1 I focus on the British Columbia Supreme Court trial (1987-91) because it included the court proceedings and presentation of evidence. The Supreme Court of Canada did not re-examine this evidence; it assessed only the validity of McEachern's reasonings.
2 Through the federal government's policy of exhaustion, established in 2002, negotiated agreements both create and limit Aboriginal rights. In other words, Aboriginal rights do not exist independently of the agreement in question.
3 Though *Delgamuukw* initially was celebrated as a victory of Aboriginal land rights, particularly in media representations immediately following the decision in 1997, prominent legal scholars of Aboriginal rights have also discussed its limitations. Candace Metallic and Patricia Monture-Angus, in 'Domestic Laws versus Aboriginal Visions: An Analysis of the *Delgamuukw* Decision' (2002), argue that Lamer's recommendation to adapt the rules of evidence amounts to 'no more than a bit of tinkering' (par. 24). Val Napoleon, in '*Delgamuukw:* A Legal Straitjacket for Oral Histories?' (2005), contends that although the Supreme Court of Canada declared McEachern in error and ordered a new trial, the process of litigation nonetheless 'filtered and altered' the oral histories of the Gitksan and Wet'suwet'en people, producing 'a distorted legal truth' about oral histories that now powerfully shapes the discourses of Aboriginal rights (125). The most far-reaching critique is that of John Borrows in 'Listening for a Change: The Courts and Oral Tradition' (2001). Borrows focuses on Lamer's qualification that any adaptation of the rules of evidence 'must not strain the Canadian legal and constitutional structure' (*Delgamuukw* [SCC]: par. 82). Borrows objects to this caveat, arguing that if Aboriginal oral histories are taken seriously, 'the very core of the Canadian legal and constitutional structure' may be called into question (25).
4 For more on the participation of First Nations in the ratification of the Royal Proclamation at the Treaty of Niagara, and how Anishinaabe and other elders continue to narrate the specifics of the treaty-making process, see Borrows, 'Wampum at Niagara' (1997).

5 *Sui generis* is a Latin term meaning original; *The Concise Oxford English Dictionary* defines it as 'of its own kind; unique.' In the context of the struggle for Aboriginal rights, *sui generis* suggests that Aboriginal title cannot be included within a larger concept; it is prior to, and cannot be sublimated under, Crown title.

6 Kent McNeil argues that the decision offers future governments and corporations an escape clause by which Aboriginal title may become ineffectual in its practice. In the interests of 'economic and regional fairness,' Lamer ruled, less than severe adherence to Aboriginal title is permissible (*Delgamuukw [SCC]* par. 161). The court's examples of what constitutes 'economic and regional fairness' are startling in their wholesale affirmation of corporate rights: 'The development of agriculture, forestry, mining and hydroelectric power, the general economic development of the interior of British Columbia, ... [and] the building of infrastructure and the settlement of foreign populations' can justify the expropriation of Aboriginal land (*Delgamuukw [SCC]*, 'Infringements of Aboriginal Title'). McNeil argues that the critical issue left out of the *Delgamuukw* decision is self-government, which could give Aboriginal title the teeth that it needs to challenge its inherited colonial definitions (McNeil 20). For this reason, the Gitksan and Wet'suwet'en made the case for both title to and jurisdiction over the disputed territory.

7 In their legal arguments, the plaintiffs stressed the interdependence of *title* and *jurisdiction* of land: 'The uniqueness of the Gitksan and Wet'suwet'en action lies in the statement of claim. Not only are we seeking recognition of title to the territories, but we are further seeking recognition of jurisdiction of our people over their own lands' (Gisday Wa and Delgam Uukw 1).

8 McEachern stated that the Gitskan and Wet'suwet'en cultures are 'primitive' because: 'The absence of any written history, wheeled vehicles, or beasts of burden ... suggest the Gitksan and Wet'suwet'en civilizations, if they qualify for that description, fall within a much lower, even primitive order' (qtd. in Cruikshank, 'Invention' 30n). Cruikshank notes that McEachern repeats this sentiment three times with minor variations to convey that writing, wheeled vehicles, and horses are his criteria for determining the degree of civilization of human populations.

9 In *Our Tellings*, a collection of Nlha7kápmx oral narratives recorded, edited, and translated by Nlha7kápmx community members, the story of Coyote's Son also plays a central role. The Nlha7kápmx First Nation is a close neighbour of the Okanagan people. Darwin Hanna, one of the editors, learned of the centrality of this story in Nlha7kápmx storytelling traditions as he collected the stories: 'I talked to my great-uncle Nathan, who sat me down and told me to ask the elders about Ntl'ik'semtm (Coyote's Son). He said, "If you ask about that one story, the rest will follow naturally"' (Hanna and Henry 12). The story of Coyote's Son functions as a springboard for many other stories. This is perhaps due to the story's close connection to Nlha7kápmx land and territory.

10 In referring to 'the Indians over there,' Robinson may be signifying the Nlha7kápmx people (see previous note for more).

11 For detailed analyses of *Life Lived Like a Story* in literary studies, see Michael Jacklin, 'Making Paper Talk: Writing Indigenous Oral Life Narratives' (2008); Susan Berry Brill de Ramírez, 'Surviving the Colonialist Legacy of the Klondike Gold Rush: A Native Woman Elder's Liberatory and Integrative Storytelling Turn' (2007); Kathleen Mullen Sands, 'Narrative Resistance: Native American Collaborative Autobiography' (1998); Cynthia Wentz, 'Jackpine Roots: Autobiography, Tradition, and Resistance in the Stories of Three Elders' (1998); and Julia Emberley, *Venus in Furs: The Cultural Politics of Fur* (1998: 186-90). *Life Lived Like a Story* has also been used as a model for a number of oral history

projects, including *Saqiyuq: Stories from the Lives of Three Inuit Women* (1999), by Nancy Wachowich in collaboration with Apphia Agalakti Awa, Rhoda Kaukjak Katsak and Sandra Pikujak Katsak, and *Telling a Good One: The Process of a Native American Collaborative Autobiography* (2000) by Theodore Rios and Kathleen Mullen Sands.

12 See Angela Sidney, Kitty Smith, and Rachel Dawson, *My Stories Are My Wealth* (1977). Angela Sidney has also published *Place Names of the Tagish Region, Southern Yukon* (1980), *Tagish Tlaagú/Tagish Stories* (1982), and *Haa Shagóon/Our Family History* (1983). In addition to co-authoring *My Stories Are My Wealth*, Kitty Smith has published *Nindal Kwädindür/I'm Going To Tell You a Story* (1982). Annie Ned is the author of *Old People in Those Days, They Told Their Story All the Time* (1984). All of these texts were recorded and compiled by Cruikshank.

13 For more on the construction of authorship in print-capitalist economies, see Michel Foucault's 'What Is an Author?' (1979), Barbara Godard's 'The Politics of Representation: Some Native Canadian Women Writers' (1990), Norman Feltes's *Modes of Production of Victorian Novels* (1986), and Fredric Jameson's 'On Literary and Cultural Import-Substitution in the Third World' (1996). Each contests, in different ways, the myth of the author as an individual genius, highlighting instead the conditions of producing, publishing, and disseminating texts from historical-materialist perspectives.

14 To read A.P. Johnson's version of the story of Kaax'achgóok, see Richard and Nora Dauenhauer's anthology, *Haa Shuká* (82-107).

15 Please see my article '1997: The Supreme Court of Canada rules that the laws of evidence must be adapted to accommodate Aboriginal oral histories,' forthcoming in *Translation Effects: Literary Translation in Canada*, for a discussion of the legacy of *Delgamuukw* in land claims cases in Canada since 1997. See also Borrows, 'Listening for a Change'; Napoleon; and Drew Mildon, 'A Bad Connection: First Nations Oral Histories in the Canadian Courts' (2008).

**Chapter 6: 'I Can Only Sing This Song to Someone Who Understands It'**

1 The English-language published screenplay does not include Kumaglak's statement. This is the first of many discrepancies between the book and film versions, reflecting the flexible, improvisational technique that the filmmakers use. In this particular instance, the discrepancy further emphasizes the secrecy of the song and draws attention to the film's politics of partial translation that I discuss in detail below.

2 Thanks to Susan Gingell for suggesting 'metadramatic scenes' to describe the final minutes of the film.

3 See Franz Boas, *The Eskimo of Baffin Land and Hudson Bay* (1901), Helen Roberts and Diamond Jenness, *Eskimo Songs: Songs of the Copper Eskimos* (1925), and Knud Rasmussen, *Across Arctic America: Narrative of the Fifth Thule Expedition* (1927).

4 For literary anthologies that include versions of Inuit songs translated as lyric poems, see George W. Cronyn, *The Path on the Rainbow: An Anthology of Songs and Chants from the Indians of North America* (1918); A. Grove Day, *The Sky Clears: Poetry of the American Indians* (1951); Jerome Rothenberg, ed., *Shaking the Pumpkin: Traditional Poetry of the Indian North Americas* (1971); William Brandon, ed., *The Magic World: American Indian Songs and Poems* (1971); John Robert Colombo, ed., *Poems of the Inuit* (1981); and A.L. Soens, ed., *I, The Song: Classical Poetry of Native North America* (1999).

5 See Grace; Huhndorf, 'Nanook'; and Rothman on how Flaherty's film assumes that 'authentic' Inuit culture will disappear.

6 Re-presenting scenes from *Nanook of the North* can be seen in other docudramas by Igloolik Isuma Productions, such as *Qaggiq (Gathering Place)* (1989), *Nunaqpa (Going Inland)* (1991),

*Saputi (Fish Traps)* (1993), and, in particular, the thirteen-part series *Nunavut (Our Land)* (1994-95) which is set in the 1940s.

7 See Rothman on how Flaherty draws parallels between Nanook's family and animals (30-31).

8 To view a reproduction of the drawing, see Rotha (50-51). Wetaltook's name is spelled Wetallok in Rotha.

9 *The Journals of Knud Rasmussen* (2006), Isuma's second feature-length dramatic film, opens with the famous shaman, Avva (sometimes spelt Awa), and his family singing what appears to be the same song that opens *Atanarjuat*. Like the characters in *Atanarjuat*, Avva's family and community clearly identify Igloolik as their home base. The featuring of the song in both films suggests a powerful continuity of culture, language, territory, and community at Igloolik, emphasizing the song's function as an anthem for the region.

10 See Arnold Krupat, '*Atanarjuat, the Fast Runner* and Its Audiences,' for a compelling argument on how the film simultaneously addresses three distinct audiences: 1) a local Inuit audience, which remains its primary audience; 2) a southern audience that is generally responsive to those cultural and artistic forms of expression that challenge the viewer to 'see with a Native eye' and 'to move the epistemological center'; and 3) an audience from southern, metropolitan centres who are 'either unwilling or unable to alter their habits of perception' and thus 'respond to the film's production of the beautiful as a purely formal matter, giving rise to an experience at best to be contemplated or else simply consumed' – without, in other words, taking to heart the film's critique of southern misconceptions of the North (608, 609).

11 Another instance of disjuncture between the film and the book is the rape scene: while Uqi shouts commentary onscreen, his words remain untranslated in the subtitles and screenplay.

12 It is unclear to what extent Apak relied on historical accounts of the legend. Saladin d'Anglure states that the filmmakers drew upon four versions he had recorded in the late 1980s and early 1990s, by storyteller Michel Kupaaq (199), and Apak mentions eight versions that he and his associates recorded, as well as his own memories of the story. To read three versions of the story, including one told by Michel Kupaaq to Therese Ukaliannuk in 1990, see Evans (76-88).

13 See Boas (330-31), Rasmussen, *Intellectual* (298-99), Saludin d'Anglure (199-203), and Evans (76-88) for versions of the legend as a revenge story. Franz Boas published the earliest ethnographic record of the legend of Atanarjuat (titled *Armuckjuark*, the name of Atanarjuat's brother) in 1901, using a version written by a sea captain, George Cromer.

14 For example, Joanna Hearne argues that *Atanarjuat* can be interpreted (among other possible readings) as 'a romanticized vision of primitive simplicity' (321).

15 Later, the filmmakers submitted a new grant application on the topic of Telefilm's unfair funding system. In Cohn's words, 'we want to see if they're willing to finance a video that will expose the very people doing the financing' (qtd. in Evans 28), but the funding application was declined.

16 According to Henderson, most residents of Nunavut say they are happy with Nunavut when they consider the vitality of Inuit culture, values, and language over and above economic issues (A. Henderson 201). 'Cultural vitality' is here understood as the opportunity to 'eat country food, spend time on the land, speak Inuktitut at home, or participate in harvesting activities' (206). In other words, Henderson claims, even for those who have secured higher incomes and stable government jobs in the new territory, the benefits of Nunavut are viewed as having 'nothing to do with money and everything to do with the

ability to lead a life grounded in what might be considered traditional practice' (207). These are some of the issues that *Inuit Qaujimajatuqangit* encompasses.

17 In his budget statement, Simailak uses IQ to justify the removal of trade barriers: 'Consistent with the *Inuit Qaujimajatuqanginnut* ['moving toward understanding of IQ'] principle of *Qanuqtuurniq* ['exploring or discussing ideas'], our government will work with the business community, with Inuit organizations and other stakeholders to continually seek new ways to thrive. That includes identifying and removing barriers to business, removing unnecessary regulations, and enhancing business development programs' (qtd. in Tester and Irniq 50).

18 Kunuk states that *From Inuk Point of View* is aimed primarily at an Inuit audience: 'That's why we never really subtitled it in English' (qtd. in Evans 65). Though *From Inuk Point of View* has not been subtitled, it has only an English-language title. 'Inuk' usually refers to a person of Inuit ancestry; 'Inuit' is the adjective as well as the plural noun of 'Inuk.'

19 The NFDC has funded Isuma in the form of labour rebates, totalling to about $500,000 over five years. It has also helped translate *Before Tomorrow* (2008) into Spanish and has provided travel funds for the filmmakers to present their work in New York City and in Mexico. Cohn expresses support for the NFDC, but also argues that the labour rebate funding structure has created some problems. He explains: 'NFDC budget is about $600,000 per year and the labour rebates are capped at $300,000. This means Nunavut has the strange policy of setting a limit on the number of filmmaking jobs it is willing to create in the territory' (Cohn, personal communication). The NFDC's procedure of limiting the potential for job creation contrasts with Isuma's emphasis on job creation, training, and the support of local economies. Cheryl Ashton, CEO of NFDC, acknowledges the funding challenges in Nunavut, with its relatively small tax base, and states her hope that within five years NFDC will be able to offer a greater range of services, from script development to editing to marketing films (Ashton, personal communication).

**Conclusion**

1 One difference is that in contrast to the American context, strong feminist perspectives more overtly have shaped Aboriginal literary nationalism in Canada. Campbell (1973), Maracle (1996), Armstrong (1998), Acoose (2001), and Cheryl Suzack (2008) are just some of the critics who skillfully interweave Indigenous-nationalist and feminist analyses. It should be noted that Womack, Warrior, and Justice are highly aware of the potential for a masculinist bias in American Indian nationalism, and offer a range of feminist antidotes. See Womack's analysis of Paula Gunn Allen's Indigenous feminism in 'A Single' (21-32), Warrior's critique of Laura Tohe's disavowal of feminist critical approaches in 'Native' (211-13), and Justice's diagnosis of 'the dominance of male perspectives in Indigenous literary nationalism' (in Fagan et al. 26).

2 Justice asks: 'what happens ... when a concept like sovereignty shifts from indigenous empowerment and responsibility and is instead used as a hammer to stifle dissent within the community?' ('"Go"' 154). Justice provides some provocative examples in which mixed-blood identity and Indigenous nationalism have been on a collision course (161-65). See also Warrior's discussion of the work of some Aboriginal critics in which '[t]he need for disagreement and dissent ... [is] seemingly subsumed by adherence, participation, and belonging' (Warrior, 'Native' 213).

3 For more on the primary role of debate and consensus-building in Iroquoian or Rotinohshonni intellectual traditions, see Taiaiake Alfred's *Peace, Power, Righteousness*, Fagan, 'Tewatatha:wi,' and Valaskakis, *Indian Country*.

# Works Cited

Aboriginal Rights Coalition. *Blind Spots: An Examination of the Federal Government's Response to the Report of the Royal Commission on Aboriginal Peoples*. Ottawa: Aboriginal Rights Coalition, 2001.
Acoose, Janice. 'A Vanishing Indian? Or Acoose: Woman Standing Above Ground?' Ruffo 37-56.
Acoose, Janice, Lisa Brooks, Tol Foster, LeAnne Howe, Daniel Heath Justice, Phillip Carroll Morgan, Kimberly Roppolo, Cheryl Suzack, Christopher B. Teuton, Sean Teuton, Robert Warrior, and Craig S. Womack. *Reasoning Together: The Native Critics' Collective*. Norman, OK: U Oklahoma P, 2008.
Adamson, Joni. *American Indian Literature, Environmental Justice and Ecocriticism: The Middle Place*. Tucson: U Arizona P, 2001.
Ahenakew, Edward. *Voices of the Plains Cree*. Ed. Ruth M. Buck. Toronto: McClelland and Stewart, 1973.
Ahenakew, Freda, and H.C. Wolfart, ed., tr. *Our Grandmothers' Lives, As Told in Their Own Words*. Saskatoon: Fifth House, 1992.
Alfred, Taiaiake. *Peace, Power, Righteousness: An Indigenous Manifesto*. Don Mills, ON: Oxford UP, 1999.
Alia, Valerie. *Names and Nunavut: Culture and Identity in Arctic Canada*. New York: Berghahn, 2007.
Angilirq, Paul Apak. 'Interview with Paul Apak Angilirq.' With Nancy Wachowich. Angilirq et al. 17-22.
Angilirq, Paul Apak, Norman Cohn, and Bernard Saludin d'Anglure. *Atanarjuat, the Fast Runner: Inspired by a Traditional Inuit Legend of Igloolik*. Ed. Gillian Robinson. Toronto: Coach House; Igloolik: Isuma, 2002.
Armstrong, Jeannette. 'Land Speaking.' *Speaking for the Generations: Native Writers on Writing*. Ed. Louis Ortiz. Tucson: U Arizona P, 1998. 174-95.
–. *Slash*. Penticton: Theytus, 1985.

–. *Whispering in the Shadows*. Penticton: Theytus, 2002.

–, ed. *Looking at the Words of Our People: First Nations Analysis on Literature*. Penticton, BC: Theytus, 1993.

Asch, Michael, ed. *Aboriginal and Treaty Rights in Canada: Essays on Law, Equality, and Respect for Difference*. Vancouver: UBC P, 1997.

Ashton, Cheryl (CEO, Nunavut Film Development Corporation). Personal communication. 8 June 2009.

Assembly of First Nations. *Breaking the Silence: An Interpretive Study of Residential School Impact and Healing as Illustrated by Stories of First Nations Individuals*. Ottawa: Assembly of First Nations, 1994.

Astrov, Margot. *The Winged Serpent: An Anthology of American Indian Prose and Poetry*. New York: John Day, 1946.

*Atanarjuat, the Fast Runner*. Dir. Zacharias Kunuk. Written in Inuktitut by Paul Apak Angilirq. English subtitles by Norman Cohn. Igloolik Isuma Productions and National Film Board of Canada, 2001.

'Atanarjuat, the Fast Runner.' 2007. <http://www.atanarjuat.com/>. 1 September 2009.

Bakhtin, Mikhail M. *Problems of Dostoevsky's Poetics*. Tr. and ed. Caryl Emerson. Minneapolis: U Minnesota P, 1984.

–. *Speech Genres and Other Late Essays*. Tr. Vern W. McGee. Ed. Caryl Emerson and Michael Holquist. Austin: U Texas P, 1986.

Bal, Mieke, Jonathan Crewe, and Leo Spitzer, eds. *Acts of Memory: Cultural Recall in the Present*. Hanover, NH: U of New England P, 1999.

Barnett, Don, ed. *Bobbi Lee, Indian Rebel: Struggles of a Native Canadian Woman*. Life Histories from the Revolution Series. Richmond: LSM Information Center, 1975.

Bataille, Gretchen, and Kathleen Mullen Sands. *American Indian Women: Telling Their Lives*. Lincoln: U Nebraska P, 1984.

Battiste, Marie. 'Print Culture and Decolonizing the University: Indigenizing the Page: Part 1.' *The Future of the Page*. Ed. Peter Stoicheff and Andrew Taylor. Toronto: U Toronto P, 2004. 111-23.

Bauman, Richard, and Charles L. Briggs. 'Poetics and Performance as Critical Perspectives on Language and Social Life.' *Annual Review of Anthropology* 19 (1990): 59-88.

Benjamin, Walter. 'The Storyteller.' *Illuminations*. Ed. Hannah Arendt. Tr. Harry Zohn. New York: Schocken, 1969. 83-109.

Bennett, John, and Susan Rowley, comps., eds. *Uqalurait: An Oral History of Nunavut*. Montreal and Kingston: McGill-Queen's UP, 2004.

Berger, John. *Ways of Seeing*. New York: Viking, 1973.

Berger, Sally. 'Move Over, *Nanook*.' *Wide Angle* 17.1-4 (1995): 177-91.

Berger, Thomas R. *Northern Frontier, Northern Homeland: The Report of the Mackenzie Valley Pipeline Inquiry*. Vancouver: Douglas and McIntyre, 1988.

Beverley, John. 'The Margin at the Center: On *Testimonio* (Testimonial Narrative).' Smith and Watson 91-114.

–. 'The Real Thing.' Gugelberger 266-86.

–. *Testimonio: On the Politics of Truth*. Minneapolis: U Minnesota P, 2004.

Bird, John, Lorraine Land, and Murray MacAdam, eds. *Nation to Nation: Aboriginal Sovereignty and the Future of Canada*. Toronto and Vancouver: Irwin, 2002.

Blackman, Margaret B. *During My Time: Florence Edenshaw Davidson* [1982]. 2nd rev. ed. Vancouver: Douglas and McIntyre, 1992.

Blaeser, Kimberly. 'Native Literature: Seeking a Critical Centre.' Armstrong (ed) 51-62.
—. 'Writing Voices Speaking: Native Authors and an Oral Aesthetic.' Murray and Rice 53-68.
Blodgett, Jean. *North Baffin Drawings: Collected by Terry Ryan on North Baffin Island in 1964*. Toronto: Art Gallery of Ontario, 1986.
Blondin, George. *Yamoria the Lawmaker: Stories of the Dene*. Edmonton: NeWest, 1997.
Blundell, Valda. '"Echoes of a Proud Nation": Reading Kahnawake's Powwow as a Post-Oka Text.' *Canadian Journal of Communication* 18 (1993): 333-50.
Boas, Franz. *The Eskimo of Baffin Land and Hudson Bay: Bulletin of the American Museum of Natural History* 15 [1901]. New York: AMS Press, 1975.
Borrows, John. 'Listening for a Change: The Courts and Oral Tradition.' *Osgoode Hall Law Journal* 39.1 (2001): 1-38.
—. 'Wampum at Niagara: The Royal Proclamation, Canadian Legal History and Self-Government.' Asch 155-72.
Bowie, Geoff, dir. *Ghosts of Futures Past: Tom Berger in the North*. Toronto: CBC Television, 2006.
Boyce Davies, Carole. 'Collaboration and the Ordering Imperative in Life Story Production.' Smith and Watson 3-19.
Boyden, Joseph. *Three Day Road*. Toronto: Viking, 2005.
—. *Through Black Spruce*. Toronto: Viking, 2008.
Bracken, Christopher. *Potlatch Papers: A Colonial Case History*. Chicago: U Chicago P, 1997.
Brandon, William, ed. *The Magic World: American Indian Songs and Poems* [1971]. Athens: Ohio UP, 1991.
Brill de Ramírez, Susan Berry. *Contemporary American Indian Literatures and the Oral Tradition*. Tucson: U of Arizona P, 1999.
—. 'Surviving the Colonialist Legacy of the Klondike Gold Rush: A Native Woman Elder's Liberatory and Integrative Storytelling Turn.' *Adventures of the Spirit: The Older Woman in the Works of Doris Lessing, Margaret Atwood, and Other Contemporary Women Writers*. Ed. Phyllis Sternberg Perrakis. Columbus: Ohio State UP, 2007. 241-69.
'Bringing Ancient Knowledges Home.' Art Direction. 2007. <http://atanarjuat.com/art_direction/index.html>. 5 September 2009.
Brody, Hugh. *Living Arctic: Hunters of the Canadian North*. London: Faber and Faber, 1987.
—. *Maps and Dreams: Indians and the British Columbia Frontier* [1981]. Vancouver and Toronto: Douglas and McIntyre, 1988.
—. 'The Nature of Cultural Continuity among the Gitksan and Wet'suwet'en of Northwest British Columbia.' Opinion report prepared for the Office of the Gitksan and Wet'suwet'en Hereditary Chiefs in the matter of *Delgamuukw v. R.*
—. *The Other Side of Eden: Hunters, Farmers and the Shaping of the World*. Vancouver and Toronto: Douglas and McIntyre, 2000.
—. *The People's Land: Eskimos and Whites in the Eastern Arctic*. Harmondsworth, UK: Penguin Books, 1975.
—, dir. *Hunters and Bombers*. London: Channel 4; Montreal: NFB, 1990.
—, dir. *On Indian Land*. Hazelton, BC: Gitksan and Wet'suwet'en Tribal Councils, 1988.
—, dir. *Time Immemorial*. Toronto: Tamarack Productions; Montreal: NFB, 1991.
—, dir. *The Washing of Tears*. Nootka Sound: Nootka Sound and Picture; Montreal: NFB, 1994.
Brumble, David. *American Indian Autobiography*. Berkeley: U California P, 1988.
Burgos-Debray, Elizabeth. *I, Rigoberta Menchú: An Indian Woman in Guatemala*. Tr. Ann Wright. New York and London: Verso, 1984.

Bussidor, Ila. 'Presentation by the Sayisi Dene First Nation.' Round 3. Thompson, MN (93.06.01). In Canada, *For Seven Generations*.

Bussidor, Ila, and Üstün Bilgen-Reinart. *Night Spirits: The Story of the Relocation of the Sayisi Dene*. Winnipeg: U Manitoba P, 1997.

Byrne, Nympha, and Camille Fouillard, eds. *It's Like the Legend: Innu Women's Voices*. Charlottetown, PEI: Gynergy, 2000.

Cairns, Alan C. *Citizens Plus: Aboriginal Peoples and the Canadian State*. Vancouver: UBC P, 2000.

Calder-Marshall, Arthur. *The Innocent Eye: The Life of Robert Flaherty*. Baltimore: Penguin, 1970.

Campbell, Maria. *Halfbreed*. Toronto: McClelland and Stewart, 1973.

–, trans. *Stories of the Road Allowance People*. Penticton: Theytus, 1995.

–, Doreen Jensen, Joy Asham Fedorick, Jaune Quick-To-See Smith, Jeannette Armstrong, and Lee Maracle. *Give Back: First Nations Perspectives on Cultural Practice*. Vancouver: Gallerie, 1992.

Canada. 'The Commission's Terms of Reference.' In *Looking Forward, Looking Back. Report of the Royal Commission on Aboriginal Peoples*. Ottawa: Minister of Supply and Services, 1996. 699-702.

–. *Gathering Strength: Canada's Aboriginal Action Plan*. Ottawa: Minister of Indian Affairs and Northern Development, 1997.

–. *Looking Forward, Looking Back*. Vol. 1. *Report of the Royal Commission of on Aboriginal Peoples*. Ottawa: Minister of Supply and Services, 1996.

–. *Northern Frontier, Northern Homeland: The Report of the Mackenzie Valley Pipeline Inquiry*. 2 vols. Ottawa: Minister of Supply and Services, 1977.

–. *People to People, Nation to Nation: Highlights from the Report of the Royal Commission on Aboriginal Peoples*. Ottawa: Minister of Supply and Services, 1996.

–. *Perspectives and Realities*. Vol. 4. *Report of the Royal Commission on Aboriginal Peoples*. Ottawa: Minister of Supply and Services, 1996.

–. *Restructuring the Relationship*. Vol. 2. *Report of the Royal Commission on Aboriginal Peoples*. Ottawa: Minister of Supply and Services, 1996.

–. *For Seven Generations: An Information Legacy of the Royal Commission on Aboriginal Peoples*. CD-ROM. Libraxus. 1997.

Caruth, Cathy. Introduction. *American Imago* 48 (1991): 1-11.

Cassidy, Frank. 'The Final Report of the Royal Commission on Aboriginal Peoples.' *Policy Options* 18.2 (1997): 3-6.

–, ed. *Aboriginal Title in British Columbia: Delgamuukw v. The Queen*. Lantzville, BC: Oolichan Books and Montreal: Institute for Research on Public Policy, 1992.

Castellano, Marlene Brant. 'Renewing the Relationship: A Perspective on the Impact of the Royal Commission on Aboriginal Peoples.' Aboriginal Rights Coalition 1-22.

–, Linda Archibald, and Mike DeGagné, eds. *From Truth to Reconciliation: Transforming the Legacy of Residential Schools*. Ottawa: Aboriginal Healing Foundation, 2008.

Chamberlin, J. Edward. 'Culture and Anarchy in Indian Country.' Asch 3-37.

–. 'Doing Things with Words: Putting Performance on the Page.' Murray and Rice 69-90.

–. 'From Hand to Mouth: The Postcolonial Politics of Oral and Written Traditions.' *Reclaiming Indigenous Voice and Vision*. Ed. Marie Battiste. Vancouver: UBC P, 2000. 124-41.

–. *If This Is Your Land, Where Are Your Stories? Finding Common Ground*. Toronto: Knopf, 2003.

Chester, Blanca [see also Blanca Schorcht]. 'Storied Dialogues: Exchanges of Meaning between Storyteller and Anthropologist.' *SAIL* 8.3 (1996): 13-35.

Cheyfitz, Eric. *Poetics of Imperialism: Translation and Colonization from* The Tempest *to* Tarzan. New York: Oxford UP, 1997.

Cizek, Katerina, dir. *Alanis Obomsawin: Dream-Magic. Horizon: Digital Art + Culture* 9 (2003). <http://www.horizonzero.ca/flashsite/issue9/issue9.html?lang=fr&section=intro>. 21 December 2010.

Clements, William M. *Native American Verbal Art: Texts and Contexts*. Tucson: U Arizona P, 1996.

Clifford, James. 'Introduction: Partial Truths.' *Writing Culture: The Poetics and Politics of Ethnography*. Ed. James Clifford and George E. Marcus. Berkeley: U California P, 1986. 1-26.

–. *The Predicament of Culture: Twentieth Century Ethnography, Literature and Art*. Cambridge: Harvard UP, 1988.

–. *Routes: Travel and Translation in the Late Twentieth Century*. Cambridge MA: Harvard UP, 1997.

Coates, Kenneth, and Judith Powell. *The Modern North*. Toronto: James Lorimer, 1989.

Coetzee, Carli. '"They Never Wept, the Men of My Race": Antjie Krog's *Country of My Skull* and the White South African Signature.' *Journal of Southern African Studies* 27.4 (2001): 685-96.

Cohn, Norman. 'The Art of Community-Based Filmmaking.' Angilirq et al. 25-27.

–. Personal communication (email), 25 May 2009.

'Collaborate.' *The Concise Oxford English Dictionary*. 9th ed. Ed. Della Thompson. First edited by H.W. Fowler and F.G. Fowler. Oxford: Oxford UP, 1995. 258.

Colombo, John Robert, ed. *Poems of the Inuit*. Ottawa: Oberon, 1981.

–. *Songs of the Indians*. 2 vols. Ottawa: Oberon, 1983.

Cook-Lynn, Elizabeth. *Why I Can't Read Wallace Stegner and Other Essays: A Tribal Voice*. Madison: U Wisconsin P, 1996.

Coombe, Rosemary. 'The Properties of Culture and the Possession of Identity: Postcolonial Struggle and the Legal Imagination.' Ziff and Rao 74-96.

Cornell, George. 'The Imposition of Western Definitions of Literature on Indian Oral Traditions.' King, Calver, and Hoy 174-87.

Coyes, Greg, dir. *No Turning Back*. Montreal: NFB, 1996.

Cronyn, George W. *The Path on the Rainbow: An Anthology of Songs and Chants from the Indians of North America* [1918]. New York: Liveright, 1934.

Cruikshank, Julie. 'Invention of Anthropology in British Columbia's Supreme Court: Oral Tradition as Evidence.' *BC Studies* 95 (1992): 25-42.

–. *Social Life of Stories: Narrative and Knowledge in the Yukon Territory*. Lincoln and London: U Nebraska P, 1998.

Cruikshank, Julie, in collaboration with Angela Sidney, Kitty Smith, and Annie Ned. *Life Lived Like a Story: Life Stories of Three Yukon Elders*. Lincoln: U Nebraska P; Vancouver: UBC P, 1990.

Culhane, Dara. *The Pleasure of the Crown: Anthropology, Law and First Nations*. Burnaby, BC: Talon Books, 1998.

Curtis, Natalie. *The Indians' Book: An Offering by the American Indians of Indian Lore, Musical and Narrative, to Form a Record of the Songs and Legends of Their Race* [1907]. New York and London: Harper, 1935.

Cuthand, Beth. 'Post-Oka Kinda Woman.' *Native Poetry in Canada: A Contemporary Anthology*. Ed. Jeannette Armstrong and Lally Grauer. Peterborough, ON: Broadview, 2001. 132-33.

Dadey, Bruce. 'Dialogue with Raven: Bakhtinian Theory and Lee Maracle's *Ravensong*.' *Studies in Canadian Literature* 28.1 (2003): 109-31.

Damm, Kateri. 'Says Who: Colonialism, Identity, and Defining Indigenous Literature.' Armstrong (ed) 9-25.

Dangarembga, Tsitsi. *Nervous Conditions*. Seattle: Seal P, 1988.

Dauenhauer, Nora Marks, and Richard L. Dauenhauer. *Haa Shuká/Our Ancestors: Tlingit Oral Narratives*. Seattle: U Washington P; Juneau: Sealaska Heritage Foundation, 1987.

–. 'Oral Literature Embodied and Disembodied.' *Aspects of Oral Communication*. Ed. Uta M. Quasthoff. New York: de Gruyter, 1995. 91-109.

–. 'The Paradox of Talking on the Page: Some Aspects of Tlingit and Haida Experience.' Murray and Rice 3-42.

Day, A. Grove. *The Sky Clears: Poetry of the American Indians*. Lincoln: U Nebraska P, 1951.

*Delgamuukw v. Canada* [1997] 3 S.C.R. 1010.

Donovan, Kathleen. *Feminist Readings of Native American Literature: Coming to Voice*. Tucson: U Arizona P, 1998.

Egan, Susanna. 'Telling Trauma: Generic Dissonance in the Production of *Stolen Life*.' *Canadian Literature* 167 (2000): 10-29.

Eigenbrod, Renate. *Travelling Knowledges: Positioning the Im/Migrant Reader of Aboriginal Literatures in Canada*. Winnipeg: U Manitoba P, 2005.

Emberley, Julia V. *Venus and Furs: The Cultural Politics of Fur*. London: I.B. Tauris, 1998.

Erasmus, Georges. 'We the Dene.' Watkins 177-81.

Evans, Michael Robert. *Isuma: Inuit Video Art*. Montreal: McGill-Queen's P, 2008.

Evers, Larry, and Barre Toelken, eds. *Native American Oral Traditions: Collaboration and Interpretation*. Logan: Utah State UP, 2001.

Fagan, Kristina. 'The Delicate Dance of Reasoning and Togetherness.' *Studies in American Indian Literatures* 20.2 (2008): 77-101.

–. 'Tewatatha:wi: Aboriginal Nationalism in Taiaiake Alfred's *Peace, Power, Righteousness: An Indigenous Manifesto*.' *American Indian Quarterly* 28.1, 2 (2004): 12-29.

–, Daniel Heath Justice, Keavy Martin, Sam McKegney, Deanna Reder, and Niigonwedom James Sinclair. 'Canadian Indian Literary Nationalism?: Critical Approaches in Canadian Indigenous Contexts – A Collaborative Interlogue.' *Canadian Journal of Native Studies* 29.1-2 (2009): 19-44.

–, and Sam McKegney. 'Circling the Question of Nationalism in Native Canadian Literature and Its Study.' *Review* 41.1 (May 2008): 31-42.

Fanon, Frantz. *The Wretched of the Earth* [1963]. Tr. Constance Farrington. New York: Grove P, 1968.

Fee, Margery. 'Aboriginal Writing in Canada and the Anthology as Commodity.' *Native North America: Critical and Cultural Perspectives*. Toronto: ECW P, 1999: 135-55.

–. 'Romantic Nationalism and the Image of Native People in Contemporary English-Canadian Literature.' King, Calver, and Hoy 15-33.

–. 'Writing Orality: Interpreting Literature in English by Aboriginal Writers in North America, Australia and New Zealand.' *Journal of Intercultural Studies* 18.1 (1997): 23-39.

Felman, Shoshana, and Dori Laub. *Testimony: Crises of Witnessing in Literature, Psychoanalysis, and History*. New York: Routledge, 1992.

Feltes, Norman N. *Modes of Production of Victorian Novels*. Chicago and London: U Chicago P, 1986.
'Filmmaking Inuit Style.' Production Diary. 2007. <http://www.atanarjuat.com/production_diary/index.html>. 5 September 2009.
Flaherty, Frances. *The Odyssey of a Film-Maker: Robert Flaherty's Story*. Putney, VA: Threshold, 1984.
Flaherty, Robert. 'How I Filmed *Nanook of the North.*' *Film Makers on Film Making*. Ed. Harry M. Geduld. Bloomington: Indiana UP, 1971. 56-64.
Flaherty, Robert, dir. *Nanook of the North*. Revillon Frères, 1922.
Foucault, Michel. 'What Is an Author?' [1979]. *The Critical Tradition: Classic Texts and Contemporary Trends*. Ed. David T. Richter. New York: St. Martin's P, 1989. 978-88.
Gagnon, Monika Kin, and Richard Fung, eds. *13 Conversations about Cultural Race Politics*. Montreal: Artextes, 2002.
Geertz, Clifford. *Local Knowledge: Further Essays in Interpretive Anthropology*. New York: Basic Books, 1983.
Gingell, Susan, ed. *Textualizing Orature and Orality: Special Issue of Essays on Canadian Writing* 83 (2005).
Gisday Wa and Delgam Uukw. *The Spirit in the Land: The Opening Statement of the Gitksan and Wet'suwet'en Hereditary Chiefs in the Supreme Court of British Columbia, May 11, 1987*. Gabriola, BC: Reflections, 1989.
Godard, Barbara. 'The Politics of Representation: Some Native Canadian Women Writers.' *Native Writers and Canadian Writing*. Ed. W.H. New. Vancouver: UBC P, 1990. 183-228.
–. *Talking About Ourselves: The Literary Productions of Native Women in Canada*. Ottawa: CRIAW, 1985.
–. 'Writing Between Cultures.' *Langues, traduction et post-colonialisme / Languages, Translation and Post-Colonialism. TTR* 10.1 (1997): 53-99.
Gould, Glenn. 'The Idea of North.' *Glenn Gould's Solitude Trilogy: Three Sound Documentaries*. Toronto: CBC Records/Les Disques SRC, 1992.
Grace, Sherrill. 'Exploration as Construction: Robert Flaherty and *Nanook of the North.*' *Essays on Canadian Writing* 59 (1995): 123-46.
Graham, Shane. 'The Truth Commission and Post-Apartheid Literature in South Africa.' *Research in African Literatures* 34.1 (2003): 11-30.
Grant, Agnes. Rev. of *Kanehsatake: 270 Years of Resistance*, dir. Alanis Obomsawin. *Canadian Dimension* 28.2 (1994): 18-21.
Grant, Peter R., and Neil J. Sterritt. 'The *Delgamuukw* Decision and Oral History.' *Expressions in Canadian Native Studies*. Ed. Ron F. Laliberte, Priscilla Settee, James B. Waldram, Rob Innes, Brenda Macdougall, Lesley McBain, and F. Laurie Barron. Saskatoon: U Saskatchewan P, 2000. 291-313.
Griffiths, Linda, and Maria Campbell. *The Book of Jessica: A Theatrical Transformation*. Toronto: Coach House, 1989.
Grossman, Michele. 'Beyond Orality and Literacy: Textuality, Modernity and Representation in *Gularabulu: Stories from the West Kimberley.*' *Journal of Australian Studies* 91 (2004): 133-47.
–. 'When They Write What We Read: Unsettling Indigenous Australian Life-Writing.' *Australian Humanities Review* 39-40 (2006). <http://www.australianhumanitiesreview.org/archive/Issue-September-2006/home.html>. 3 January 2011.
Gugelberger, Georg M., ed. *The Real Thing: Testimonial Discourse and Latin America*. Durham: Duke UP, 1996.

Hall, Anthony. 'RCAP's Big "Blind Spots." Aboriginal Rights Coalition 66-80.
Hamilton, John David. *Arctic Revolution: Social Change in the Northwest Territories, 1935-1994*. Toronto and Oxford: Dundurn P, 1994.
Hanna, Darwin, ed., and Mamie Henry, ed., tr. *Our Tellings: Interior Salish Stories of the Nlha7kápmx People*. Vancouver: UBC P, 1995.
Haraway, Donna. *Simians, Cyborgs, and Women: The Reinvention of Nature*. New York: Routledge, 1991.
Hearne, Joanna. 'Telling and Retelling in the "Ink of Light": Documentary Cinema, Oral Narratives, and Indigenous Identities.' *Screen* 47.3 (2006): 307-26.
Henderson, Ailsa. *Nunavut: Rethinking Political Culture*. Vancouver: UBC P, 2007.
Henderson, Jennifer. *Conducting Selves: Race and Government in Canadian Settler Women's Narratives*. PhD diss. York U, 1999.
Highway, Tomson. *Dry Lips Oughta Move to Kapuskasing*. Saskatoon: Fifth House, 1989.
–. *Kiss of the Fur Queen*. Toronto: Doubleday, 1998.
Hodgson, Heather. 'Legacy of the Bear's Lip.' *Canadian Literature* 167 (2000): 154-56.
hooks, bell. *Talking Back: Thinking Feminist, Talking Black*. Boston: South End P, 1989.
Houle, Robert. 'Alanis Obomsawin.' *Land, Spirit, Power: First Nations at the National Gallery of Canada*. Ed. Diana Nemiroff, Robert Houle, and Charlotte Townsend-Gault. Ottawa: National Gallery of Canada, 1992. 204-11.
Hoy, Helen. *How Should I Read These?: Native Women Writers in Canada*. Toronto: U Toronto P, 2001.
Huggan, Graham. 'Maps, Dreams and the Presentation of Ethnographic Narrative: Hugh Brody's *Maps and Dreams* and Bruce Chatwin's *The Songlines*.' *ARIEL* 22.1 (1991): 57-69.
Huhndorf, Shari. '*Atanarjuat, the Fast Runner*: Culture, History, and Politics in Inuit Media.' *American Anthropologist* 105.4 (2003): 822-26.
–. 'Nanook and His Contemporaries: Imagining Eskimos in American Culture, 1897-1922.' *Critical Inquiry* 27 (2000): 122-48.
Hulan, Renée, and Renate Eigenbrod, eds. *Aboriginal Oral Traditions: Theory, Practice, Ethics*. Halifax: Fernwood, 2008.
Hungry Wolf, Beverly. *The Ways of My Grandmothers*. New York: William Morrow, 1980.
Hunter, Lynette. 'Standpoint Theory Approaches to Recent Canadian Autobiographical Text.' *La création biographique; Biographical Creation*. Ed. Marta Dvorak. Rennes, FR: PU de Rennes, 1997. 67-75.
Hutchinson, Roger. *Prophets, Pastors and Public Choices: Canadian Churches and the Mackenzie Valley Pipeline Debate*. Waterloo, ON: Wilfred Laurier UP, 1992.
Hymes, Dell. *'In Vain I Tried to Tell You': Essays in Native American Ethnopoetics*. Philadelphia: U Pennsylvania P, 1981.
Indian Residential Schools' Truth and Reconciliation Commission. *Schedule N: Mandate for the Truth and Reconciliation Commission*. 10 June 2009. <http://www.trc-cvr.ca/index_e.html>. 2 July 2009.
–. *Truth, Healing, Reconciliation*. June 2009. <http://www.trc-cvr.ca/index_e.html>. 2 July 2009.
Innu Nation and Mushuau Innu Band Council. *Gathering Voices: Finding Strength to Help Our Children*. Ed. Camille Fouillard. Vancouver: Douglas and McIntyre, 1995.
*The Inquiry Film: A Report on the Mackenzie Valley Pipeline Inquiry*. Toronto: Inquiry Films, 1977.
Jacklin, Michael. 'Consultation and Critique: Implementing Cultural Protocols in the Reading of Collaborative Indigenous Life Writing.' *Indigenous Biography and Autobiography*. Ed. Peter Read, Frances Peters-Little, and Anna Haebich. ANU E Press, 2008. 135-45.

–. 'Critical Injuries: Collaborative Indigenous Life Writing and the Ethics of Criticism.' *Life Writing* 1.2 (2004): 55-83.
–. 'Making Paper Talk: Writing Indigenous Oral Life Narratives.' *ARIEL* 39.1-2 (2008): 47-69.
–. '"What I have done, what was done to me": Confession and Testimony in *Stolen Life: The Journey of a Cree Woman*.' *Kunapipi* 29.1 (2007): 19-33.
Jaimes, Annette M., ed. *The State of Native America: Genocide, Colonization, and Resistance*. Boston: South End P, 1992.
Jameson, Fredric. 'On Literary and Cultural Import-Substitution in the Third World.' Gugelberger 172-91.
Jensen, Doreen. 'Art History.' Campbell et al. 15-26.
Justice, Daniel Heath. '"Go Away, Water!": Kinship Criticism and the Decolonization Imperative.' Acoose et al. 147-68.
Kalant, Amelia. *National Identity and the Conflict at Oka*. New York: Routledge, 2004.
Keeshig-Tobias, Lenore. 'Stop Stealing Native Stories' [1990]. Ziff and Rao 71-73.
Kelly, Fred. 'Confession of a Born Again Pagan.' Castellano et al. 11-40.
Kelly, Jennifer. 'Coming out of the House: A Conversation with Lee Maracle.' *ARIEL* 25.1 (1994): 73-88.
Kew, Michael. 'Anthropologists and First Nations in British Columbia.' *BC Studies* 100 (1993-94): 78-105.
King, Thomas. 'Godzilla vs. Post-Colonial.' *World Literature Written in English* 30.2 (1990): 10-16.
–. *Green Grass, Running Water*. Toronto: HarperCollins, 1993.
–, Cheryl Calver, and Helen Hoy, eds. *The Native in Literature*. Toronto: ECW P, 1987.
Kirshenblatt-Gimblett, Barbara. 'Objects of Ethnography.' *Exhibiting Cultures: The Poetics and Politics of Museum Display*. Ed. Ivan Karp and Steven Lavine. Washington and London: Smithsonian Institution P, 1991. 386-443.
Kroeber, Karl, ed. *Native American Storytelling: A Reader of Myths and Legends*. Malden, MA: Blackwell, 2004.
Krupat, Arnold. '*Atanarjuat, the Fast Runner* and Its Audiences.' *Critical Inquiry* 33.3 (2007): 606-31.
–. 'Indian Autobiography: Origins, Type, Function.' Swann, *Smoothing the Ground* 261-82.
–. 'On the Translation of Native American Song and Story: A Theorized History.' Swann, *On the Translation* 3-32.
–. *Red Matters: Native American Studies*. Philadelphia: U Pennsylvania P, 2002.
–. *The Turn to the Native: Studies in Criticism and Culture*. Lincoln: U Nebraska P, 1996.
–. *The Voice in the Margin: Native American Literature and the Canon*. Berkeley: U California P, 1989.
Kulchyski, Peter. *Like the Sound of a Drum: Aboriginal Cultural Politics in Denendeh and Nunavut*. Winnipeg: U Manitoba P, 2005.
–, ed. *Unjust Relations: Aboriginal Rights in Canadian Courts*. Toronto: Oxford UP, 1994.
Kulchyski, Peter, Don McCaskill, and David Newhouse, eds. *In the Words of Elders: Aboriginal Cultures in Transition*. Toronto: U Toronto P, 1999.
Kunuk, Zacharias. 'I First Heard the Story of Atanarjuat from My Mother.' Angilirq et al. 13-15.
–. 'The Public Art of Inuit Storytelling.' 2002 Spry Memorial Lecture, Simon Fraser U, Burnaby, 25 November 2002. <http://www.com.umontreal.ca/spry/spry-kz-lec.html>. 5 September 2009.

–, dir. *From Inuk Point of View*. Igloolik: Igloolik Isuma Productions, 1985.
–, dir. *The Journals of Knud Rasmussen*. Inuktitut with English subtitles. Igloolik: Igloolik Isuma Productions, 2006.
–, dir. *Nipi (Voice)*. Inuktitut with English subtitles. Igloolik: Igloolik Isuma Productions, 1999.
–, dir. *Nunaqpa (Going Inland)*. Inuktitut with English subtitles. Igloolik: Igloolik Isuma Productions, 1991.
–, dir. *Nunavut (Our Land)*. Inuktitut with English subtitles. Igloolik: Igloolik Isuma Productions, 1994-95.
–, dir. *Qaggiq (Gathering Place)*. Inuktitut with English subtitles. Igloolik: Igloolik Isuma Productions, 1989.
–, dir. *Qulliq (Oil Lamp)* Dir. Zacharias Kunuk. Inuktitut with English subtitles. Igloolik: Igloolik Isuma Productions, 1993.
–, dir. *Saputi (Fish Traps)*. Inuktitut with English subtitles. Igloolik: Igloolik Isuma Productions, 1993.
–, dir., with Paul Apak Angilirq and Norman Cohn. *Atanarjuat, the Fast Runner*. Igloolik: Igloolik Isuma Productions, 2001.
Lang, Robert, Shelia Petzold, and Michael Fuller, dirs. *Almost Home: A Sayisi Dene Journey*. Title House, 2003.
Laub, Dori. 'Truth and Testimony: The Process and the Struggle.' *American Imago* 48 (1991): 75-91.
Leggatt, Judith. 'Raven's Plague: Pollution and Disease in Lee Maracle's *Ravensong*.' *Mosaic* 33/34 (2000): 163-78.
Lejeune, Philippe. 'Autobiography for Those Who Do Not Write.' *On Autobiography*. Ed. Paul John Eakin. Tr. Katherine Leary. Minneapolis: U Minnesota P, 1989. 185-219.
Lewis, Randolph. *Alanis Obomsawin: The Vision of a Native Filmmaker*. Lincoln: U Nebraska P, 2006.
Lloyd, Robert B. 'Expecting Satisfaction: Negotiating a Durable Peace in South Africa.' *Peace Versus Justice: Negotiating Forward- and Backward-Looking Outcomes*. Ed. William Zartman and Viktor Aleksandrovich Kremenyuk. Lanham, MD: Rowman and Littlefield, 2005. 221-42.
Loreto, Frank. Rev. of *Is the Crown at War with Us?* In *CM Magazine: Canadian Review of Materials*. Winnipeg: U Manitoba. 2 January 2004. <http://www.umanitoba.ca/outreach/cm/vol10/no9/isthecrownatwarwithus.html>. 28 July 2009.
Lutz, Hartmut, ed. *Contemporary Challenges: Conversations with Canadian Native Authors*. Saskatoon: Fifth House, 1991.
Manne, Robert. *The Culture of Forgetting: Helen Demidenko and the Holocaust*. Melbourne: Text, 1996.
Maracle, Lee. *Bent Box*. Penticton: Theytus, 2000.
–. *Bobbi Lee, Indian Rebel*. Toronto: Women's P, 1990.
–. *I am Woman: A Native Perspective on Sociology and Feminism*. 2nd ed. Vancouver: Press Gang, 1996.
–. 'Oratory: Coming to Theory.' Campbell et al. 85-93.
–. 'Moving Over.' *Trivia* 14 (1988): 9-12.
–. 'Ramparts Hanging in the Air.' Telling It Book Collective 161-75.
– *Ravensong*. Vancouver: Press Gang, 1993.
–. *Sojourner's Truth and Other Stories*. Vancouver: Press Gang, 1990.
–. *Sundogs*. Penticton, BC: Theytus, 1992.

Marken, Ron. Foreword. Campbell, *Stories* 4-5.

Marlatt, Daphne. 'Introduction: Meeting on Fractured Margins.' Telling It Book Collective 9-18.

Martin, Keavy. '"Are we also here for that?": *Inuit Qaujimajatuqangit* – Traditional Knowledge, or Critical Theory?' *Canadian Journal of Native Studies* 29 1.2 (2009): 183-202.

McCall, Sophie. '1997: The Supreme Court of Canada rules that the laws of evidence must be adapted to accommodate Aboriginal oral histories.' *Translation Effects: Literary Translation in Canada.* Ed. Kathy Mezei, Sherry Simon, and Luise Von Flotow. Ottawa: U Ottawa P (forthcoming).

McEachern, Allan. *Reasons for Judgment: Delgamuukw v. British Columbia. Western Weekly Reports* 3 (1991).

McKay, Stan. 'Expanding the Dialogue on Truth and Reconciliation – In a Good Way.' Castellano et al. 101-15.

McNeil, Kent. *Defining Aboriginal Title in the 90s: Has the Supreme Court Finally Got It Right?* Toronto: York U, Robarts Centre for Canadian Studies, 1998.

Metallic, Candace, and Patricia Monture-Angus. 'Domestic Laws versus Aboriginal Visions: An Analysis of the *Delgamuukw* Decision.' *Borderlands* 1.2 (2002): par. 1-64. <http://www.borderlands.net.au/vol1no2_2002/metallic_angus.html>. 26 February 2009.

Mildon, Drew. 'A Bad Connection: First Nations Oral Histories in the Canadian Courts.' Hulan and Eigenbrod 79-97.

Monet, Don, and Skanu'u (Ardythe Wilson). *Colonialism on Trial: Indigenous Rights and the Gitksan and Wet'suwet'en Sovereignty Case.* Gabriola, BC: Reflections, 1992.

Monture-Angus, Patricia. *Journeying Forward: Dreaming First Nations' Independence.* Halifax: Fernwood P, 1999.

Moses, Daniel David, and Terry Goldie, eds. *An Anthology of Canadian Native Literature in English.* 3rd ed. Toronto: Oxford UP, 2005.

Mosionier, Beatrice Culleton. *In Search of April Raintree.* Winnipeg: Pemmican, 1983.

Murray, David. *Forked Tongues: Speech, Writing and Representation in American Indian Texts.* London: Pinter, 1991.

Murray, Laura, and Keren Rice, eds. *Talking on the Page: Editing Aboriginal Oral Texts.* Toronto: U Toronto P, 1999.

Nahanni, Phoebe. 'The Mapping Project.' Watkins 21-27.

Nahanni, Phoebe, Charlie Snowshoe, Freddy Greenland, Wilson Pellissey, and Betty Menicoche. Presentation. *The Mackenzie Valley Pipeline Inquiry: Proceedings at the Inquiry* 147 (26 April 1976): 22,475-538.

Napoleon, Val. '*Delgamuukw*: A Legal Straitjacket for Oral Histories?' *Canadian Journal of Law and Society* 20.2 (2005): 123-55.

Ned, Annie. *Old People in Those Days, They Told Their Story All the Time.* Comp. Julie Cruikshank. Whitehorse: Yukon Native Languages Project, 1984.

Nicholas, Andrea Bear. 'The Assault on Aboriginal Oral Traditions: Past and Present.' Hulan and Eigenbrod 13-43.

NourbeSe Phillip, Marlene. 'The Disappearing Debate: Racism and Censorship.' *Language in Her Eye: Writing and Gender.* Ed. Libby Scheier et al. Toronto: Coach House, 1990. 209-19.

Obomsawin, Alanis, dir. *Is the Crown at War with Us?* Montreal: National Film Board, 2003.

–, dir. *Kanehsatake: 270 Years of Resistance*. Montreal: Studio B, Office national du film du Canada, 1993.
–, dir. *My Name is Kahentiiosta*. Montreal: Studio B, Office national du film du Canada, 1995.
–, dir. *Rocks at Whiskey Trench*. Montreal: Studio B, Office national du film du Canada, 2000.
–, dir. *Spudwrench*. Montreal: Studio B, Office national du film du Canada, 1997.
O'Brien, Susie. "'Please, Eunice, Don't Be Ignorant': The White Reader as Trickster in Lee Maracle's Fiction." *Canadian Literature* 144 (1995): 82-96.
Oman, Natalie Benva. 'The Gitxan-Wet'suwet'en Model.' *Sharing Horizons: A Paradigm for Political Accommodation in Intercultural Settings*. PhD diss. Montreal: McGill U, 1997: 105-57.
'Our Mission.' About Us. 2006. <http://www.isuma.ca/about_us/index.html>. 5 September 2009.
Owens, Louis. *Other Destinies: Understanding the American Indian Novel*. Norman, OK: U Oklahoma P, 1992.
Pelletier, Wilfred, and Ted Poole. *No Foreign Land: The Biography of a North American Indian*. Toronto: McClelland and Stewart, 1973.
Persky, Stan, ed. *Delgamuukw: The Supreme Court of Canada Decision on Aboriginal Title*. Vancouver: Greystone Books, 1998.
Petch, Virginia. 'The Relocation of the Sayisi Dene of Tadoule Lake.' 1995. In Canada, *For Seven Generations*, CD-ROM. Sections 1.0-9.0.
Petrone, Penny. *First People, First Voices*. Toronto: U Toronto P, 1983.
Pick, Zuzana. 'Storytelling and Resistance: The Documentary Practice of Alanis Obomsawin.' *Gendering the Nation: Canadian Women's Cinema*. Ed. Kay Armatage et al. Toronto: U Toronto P, 1999. 76-93.
Pinder, Leslie Hall. *The Carriers of No: After the Land Claims Trial*. Vancouver: Lazara, 1991.
Posluns, Michael W. 'Evading the Unspeakable: A Comment on *Looking Back, Looking Forward* [sic], Volume 1 of the Report of the RCAP.' *Canada Watch* 5.5 (1997): 86-88.
Rasmussen, Knud. *Across Arctic America: Narrative of the Fifth Thule Expedition*. New York and London: G.P. Putnam's Sons, 1927.
–. *Intellectual Culture of the Iglulik Eskimos: Report of the Fifth Thule Expedition 1921-24*. Vol. 7. 1 [1929]. Trans. William Worster. New York: AMS P, 1976.
'Reconcile.' *The Concise Oxford English Dictionary*. 9th ed. Ed. Della Thompson. First edited by H.W. Fowler and F.G. Fowler. Oxford: Oxford UP, 1995. 1148.
Rios, Theodore, and Kathleen Mullen Sands. *Telling a Good One: The Process of a Native American Collaborative Autobiography*. Lincoln and London: U Nebraska P, 2000.
Roberts, Helen, and Diamond Jenness. *Eskimo Songs: Songs of the Copper Eskimos*. Vol. 14, *Report of the Canadian Arctic Expedition, 1913-18*. Ottawa: F.A. Acland, 1925.
Robinson, Eden. *Monkey Beach*. Toronto: Alfred A. Knopf, 2000.
Robinson, Harry. *Living by Stories: A Journey of Landscape and Memory*. Comp., ed. Wendy Wickwire. Vancouver: Talon Books, 2005.
–. *Nature Power: In the Spirit of an Okanagan Storyteller*. Comp., ed. Wendy Wickwire. Vancouver: Douglas and McIntyre, 1992.
–. *Write It on Your Heart: The Epic World of an Okanagan Storyteller*. Comp., ed. Wendy Wickwire. Vancouver: Talon Books, 1989.
Rotha, Paul. *Robert J. Flaherty: A Biography*. Ed. Jay Ruby. Philadelphia: U of Pennsylvania P, 1983.

Rothenberg, Jerome, ed. *Shaking the Pumpkin: Traditional Poetry of the Indian North Americas* [1972]. New York: A. van der Marck, 1986.
Rothman, William. 'The Filmmaker as Hunter: Robert Flaherty's *Nanook of the North*.' *Documenting the Documentary*. Ed. Barry Keith Grant and Jeannette Sloniowski. Detroit: Wayne State UP, 1998. 23-39.
*Royal Proclamation of 1763*. <http://www.bloorstreet.com/200block/rp1763.htm#2>. 10 October 2008.
Ruffo, Armand, ed. *(Ad)dressing Our Words: Aboriginal Perspectives on Aboriginal Literatures*. Penticton, BC: Theytus, 2001.
Rymhs, Deena. 'Appropriating Guilt: Reconciliation in an Aboriginal Canadian Context.' *English Studies in Canada* 32.1 (2006): 105-23.
–. 'Auto/biographical Jurisdictions: Collaboration, Self-Representation, and the Law in *Stolen Life: The Journey of a Cree Woman*.' *Auto/biography in Canada: Critical Directions*. Ed. Julie Rak. Waterloo, ON: Wilfred Laurier UP, 2005. 89-108.
Said, S.F. 'Northern Exposure.' *Sight and Sound*. 12.2 (2002): 22-25.
Saladin d'Anglure, Bernard. 'An Ethnographic Commentary.' Angilirq et al. 197-227.
Samper, David A. '"Love, Peace, and Unity": Romantic Nationalism and the Role of Oral Literature in Kenya's Secondary Schools.' *Folklore Forum* 28.1 (1997): 29-47.
Sanders, Mark. 'Truth, Telling, Questioning: The Truth and Reconciliation Commission, Antjie Krog's *Country of My Skull*, and Literature after Apartheid.' *Modern Fiction Studies* 46.1 (2000): 13-41.
Sands, Kathleen Mullen. 'Collaboration or Colonialism: Text and Process in Native American Women's Autobiographies.' *MELUS* 22.4 (1997): 39-59.
–. 'Narrative Resistance: Native American Collaborative Autobiography.' *SAIL* 10.1 (1998): 1-18.
Sarris, Greg. *Keeping Slug Woman Alive*. Berkeley: U California P, 1993.
Schorcht, Blanca [Blanca Chester]. *Storied Voices in Native American Texts: Harry Robinson, Thomas King, James Welch and Leslie Marmon Silko*. New York: Routledge, 2003.
Scott, A.O. 'A Far-Off Inuit World, in a Dozen Shades of White.' Rev. of *Atanarjuat, the Fast Runner*, dir. Zacharias Kunuk. *New York Times Online* 30 March 2002. <http://www.nytimes.com/2002/03/30/movies/html>. 5 September 2009.
Sekyi-Otu, Ato. *Fanon's Dialectic of Experience*. Cambridge, MA: Harvard UP, 1996.
Sidney, Angela. *Haa Shagóon/Our Family History*. Comp. Julie Cruikshank. Whitehorse: Yukon Native Languages Project, 1983.
–. *Place Names of the Tagish Region, Southern Yukon*. Whitehorse: Yukon Native Languages Project, 1980.
–. *Tagish Tlaagú/Tagish Stories*. Rec. Julie Cruikshank. Whitehorse: Council for Yukon Indians, 1982.
–, Kitty Smith, and Rachel Dawson, *My Stories Are My Wealth*. Rec. Julie Cruikshank. Whitehorse: Council for Yukon Indians, 1977.
Siebert, Monika. '*Atanarjuat* and the Ideological Work of Contemporary Indigenous Filmmaking.' *Public Culture* 18.3 (2006): 531-50.
Silman, Janet, ed. *Enough Is Enough: Aboriginal Women Speak Out*. Toronto: Women's P, 1987.
Skea, Walter. 'The Canadian Newspaper Industry's Portrayal of the Oka Crisis.' *Native Studies Review* 9.1 (1993-94): 15-31.
Skinner, Constance Lindsay. *Songs of the Coast Dwellers*. New York: Coward-McCann, 1930.

Smith, A.J.M., ed. *The Book of Canadian Poetry: A Critical and Historical Anthology.* 3rd. ed. Toronto: WJ Gage, 1957.
Smith, Kitty. *Nindal Kwädindür/I'm Going to Tell You a Story.* Rec. Julie Cruikshank. Whitehorse: Council for Yukon Indians, 1982.
Smith, Linda Tuhiwai. *Decolonizing Methodologies: Research and Indigenous Peoples.* London: Zed Books, 1999.
Smith, Sidonie, and Julia Watson, eds. *De/Colonizing the Subject: The Politics of Gender in Women's Autobiography.* Minneapolis: U Minnesota P, 1992.
Soens, A.L., ed. *I, The Song: Classical Poetry of Native North America.* Salt Lake City: U Utah P, 1999.
Speare, Jean, ed. *The Days of Augusta.* Vancouver: J.J. Douglas, 1973.
Spivak, Gayatri Chakravorty. *A Critique of Postcolonial Reason: Toward a History of the Vanishing Present.* Cambridge, MA: Harvard UP, 1999.
–. 'Translator's Preface.' In Mahasweta Devi, *Imaginary Maps: Three Stories by Mahasweta Devi.* Tr. Gayatri Chakravorty Spivak. New York: Routledge, 1995. xxiii-xxx.
Stoll, David. *Rigoberta Menchú and the Story of All Poor Guatemalans.* Boulder, CO: Westview P, 1999.
'*Sui generis.*' *The Concise Oxford English Dictionary.* 9th ed. Ed. Della Thompson. First edited by H.W. Fowler and F.G. Fowler. Oxford: Oxford UP, 1995. 1393.
Suzack, Cheryl. 'Always Indigenize!' *English Studies in Canada* 30.2 (2004): 1-48.
–. 'Land Claims, Identity Claims: Mapping Indigenous Feminism in Literary Criticism and in Winona LaDuke's *Last Standing Woman*.' Acoose et al. 169-92.
–. 'Law Stories as Life Stories: Jeanette Lavell, Yvonne Bédard, and *Halfbreed*: Tracing the Autobiographical.* Ed. Marlene Kadar, Linda Warley, Jeanne Perreault, and Susanna Egan. Waterloo, ON: Wilfred Laurier UP, 2005. 117-41.
Swann, Brian. Introduction. *Coming to Light: Contemporary Translations of Native Literatures of North America.* Ed. Brian Swann. New York: Vintage, 1996. xiii-xlvi.
–, ed. *On the Translation of Native American Literatures.* Washington: Smithsonian Institution P, 1992.
–, ed. *Smoothing the Ground: Essays on Native American Oral Literatures.* Berkeley: U California P, 1983.
Swann, Brian, and Arnold Krupat, eds. *Voices from the Four Directions: Contemporary Translations of the Native Literature of North America.* Lincoln: U Nebraska P, 2004.
Swayze, Carolyn. *Hard Choices: A Life of Tom Berger.* Vancouver: Douglas and McIntyre, 1987.
Tedlock, Dennis. *The Spoken Word and the Work of Interpretation.* Philadelphia: U Pennsylvania P, 1983.
Telling It Book Collective. *Telling It: Women and Language Across Cultures.* Vancouver: Press Gang, 1990.
Tester, Frank James, and Peter Irniq. '*Inuit Qaujimajatuqangit*: Social History, Politics and the Practice of Resistance.' *Arctic* 61 [supplement 1] (2008): 48-61.
Tester, Frank James, and Peter Kulchyski. *Tammarniit (Mistakes): Inuit Relocation in the Eastern Arctic, 1939-63.* Vancouver: UBC P, 1994.
Thompson, E.P. 'Eighteenth-century English Society: Class Struggle Without Class.' *Social History* 3 (1978): 133-61.
Turner, Dale. 'Introduction.' '*This Is Not a Peace Pipe*': *Towards an Understanding of Aboriginal Sovereignty.* PhD diss. Ann Arbor, MI: UMI, 2005.

–. *This Is Not a Peace Pipe: Toward A Critical Indigenous Philosophy.* Toronto: U Toronto P, 2006.
Valaskakis, Gail Guthrie. *Indian Country: Essays on Contemporary Native Culture.* Waterloo, ON: Wilfred Laurier UP, 2004.
–. 'Parallel Voices: Indians and Others – Narratives of Cultural Struggle.' *Canadian Journal of Communication* 18.3 (1993): 283-96.
Vanderburgh, Rosamond. *I am Nokomis, Too: The Biography of Verna Patronella Johnston.* Toronto: General, 1977.
Venne, Sharon. 'Treaty-Making with the Crown.' Bird et al. 44-52.
–. 'Understanding Treaty 6: An Indigenous Perspective.' Asch 173-207.
Wachowich, Nancy, in collaboration with Apphia Agalakti Awa, Rhoda Kaukjak Katsak, and Sandra Pikujak Katsak. *Saqiyuq: Stories from the Lives of Three Inuit Women.* Montreal: McGill-Queen's UP, 1999.
Wakeham, Pauline. 'Discourses of Reconciliation, Aboriginal-State Relations, and the Production of Postcolonial Closure.' Abstract for the conference, TransCanada II: Literature, Institutions, Citizenship. U of Guelph (11-14 October 2007).
Warkentin, Germaine. 'In Search of "The Word of the Other": Aboriginal Sign Systems and the History of the Book in Canada.' *Book History* 2 (1999): 1-27.
Warley, Linda. 'Reviewing Past and Future: Postcolonial Canadian Autobiography and Lee Maracle's *Bobbi Lee, Indian Rebel*.' *ECW* 60 (1996): 59-77.
Warrior, Robert Allen. 'Native Critics in the World: Edward Said and Nationalism.' Weaver et al. 179-223.
–. *Tribal Secrets: Recovering American Indian Intellectual Traditions.* Minneapolis: U Minnesota P, 1995.
Watkins, Mel, ed. *Dene Nation – The Colony Within.* Toronto and Buffalo: U Toronto P, 1977.
Weaver, Jace. *That the People Might Live: Native American Literatures and Native American Community.* New York: Oxford UP, 1997.
Weaver, Jace, Craig S. Womack, and Robert Warrior. *American Indian Literary Nationalism.* Albuquerque: U New Mexico P, 2006.
Wentz, Cynthia. 'Jackpine Roots: Autobiography, Tradition, and Resistance in the Stories of Three Elders.' *American Indian Culture and Research Journal* 22. 1 (1998): 1-21.
Wenzel, George W. 'From TEK to IQ: *Inuit Qaujimajatuqangit* and Inuit Cultural Ecology.' *Arctic Anthropology* 41. 2 (2004): 238-50.
Wheeler, Jordan. 'Voice.' *Aboriginal Voices: Amerindian, Inuit and Sami Theater.* Baltimore: Johns Hopkins UP, 1992. 37-43.
Whitlock, Gillian. 'In the Second Person: Narrative Transactions in Stolen Generations Testimony.' *Biography* 24.1 (2001): 197-214.
Wickwire, Wendy. Interview. *BC BookWorld* (2005). <http://www.abcbookworld.com/view_author.php?id=2450>. 28 July 2009.
–. Introduction. Robinson, *Nature* 1-22.
–. Introduction. Robinson, *Living by Stories* 7-33.
–. Introduction. Robinson, *Write* 11-28.
Wiebe, Rudy. 'Where Is the Voice Coming From?' *Where Is the Voice Coming From?* Toronto: McClelland and Stewart, 1974. 135-43.
Wiebe, Rudy, and Yvonne Johnson. *Stolen Life: The Journey of a Cree Woman.* Toronto : A.A. Knopf, 1998.

Willmott, Glenn. 'Modernism and Aboriginal Modernity: The Appropriation of Products of West Coast Native Heritage as National Goods.' *Essays on Canadian Writing* 83 (2004): 75-139.

Winter, James. *Common Cents: Media Portrayal of the Gulf War and Other Events.* Montreal: Black Rose, 1992.

Womack, Craig. 'The Integrity of American Indian Claims (Or, How I Learned to Stop Worrying and Love My Hybridity).' Weaver et al. 91-177.

–. *Red on Red: Native American Literary Separatism.* Minneapolis: U Minnesota P, 1999.

–. 'A Single Decade: Book-Length Native Literary Criticism between 1986 and 1997.' Acoose et al. 3-104.

Wong, Hertha Dawn. *Sending My Heart Back across the Years: Tradition and Innovation in Native American Autobiography.* New York: Oxford UP, 1992.

Yaga'lahl (Dora Wilson). 'It Will Always Be the Truth.' Cassidy (ed) 199-205.

–. 'The Time of the Trial.' *BC Studies* 95 (1992): 3-11.

Ziff, Bruce, and Pratima V. Rao, eds. *Borrowed Power: Essays on Cultural Appropriation.* New Brunswick: Rutgers UP, 1997.

# Index

*Note:* 'IBC' stands for Inuit Broadcasting Corporation; 'RCAP,' for Royal Commission on Aboriginal Peoples

Aboriginal rights: and Canada, 10-11, 49-52, 216n8; and corporate rights, 108, 203, 226n6; and land claims, 57-58, 91, 106, 139, 140-48, 179, 210, 225n3; and liberalism in Canada, 11, 13, 43-51, 216n8; and self-government, 118; *sui generis*, 142, 226n5; and title, 140-45, 225n2. *See also* Aboriginal sovereignty; Aboriginal title; Canada; land; self-government

Aboriginal sovereignty, 11-16, 78, 107-8, 214n1, 216n8, 218n15, 229n2; *Delgamuukw*, 144, 147, intellectual sovereignty, 34-35, 218n15; literary sovereignty, 5-6, 11-12, 15-16, 33-35, 76-78, 96-99, 108, 207-13, 216n9, 218n15, 229n1; Mackenzie Valley Pipeline hearings, 43, 54; nationhood, 20, 38, 43-45, 58, 90-94, 114, 207-8, 214n1, 222n7; nation-to-nation relations, 33, 108, 114, 117-18, 120; Oka crisis, 83-84, 88-89, 91, 93-95, 99-101, 108; Royal Commission on Aboriginal Peoples, 114; self-determination, 33, 43-44, 46, 50-51, 84, 89, 93-94, 112, 120, 183, 206, 216n14. *See also* Aboriginal rights; Aboriginal title; Canada; land; self-government

Aboriginal title, 14-15, 55, 138, 168, 175, 179-80, 226n5; *Calder v. British Columbia*, 43, 220n6; *Delgamuukw*, 138, 140-54, 153-55, 160-61, 209-12, 226n6; 'exhaustion' of, 58, 81, 108, 144; 'extinguishment' of, 57-58, 108, 140-44, 161, 220n8; and jurisdiction, 56, 74-75, 139-41, 144-45, 147, 149-52, 179-80, 209-10, 226n6, 227n7; Oka crisis, 81, 86; Harry Robinson, 155, 160-61, 163-66; 'use and occupancy,' 55, 59, 67, 72, 152-53, 141-42, 220n6. *See also* Aboriginal rights; Aboriginal sovereignty; Canada; land; self-government

Acoose, Janice, 11, 206, 229n1

*adaawk*, 145-51, 160, 178-79, 210

Ahenakew, Edward, 221n3

Ahenakew, Freda, 37, 221n3

Alfred, Taiaiake, 33, 94, 222n7

*Almost Home: A Sayisi Dene Journey*, 134-35, 224n16, 225n21

Angilirq, Paul Apak, 182, 184, 189-99

Apak, Paul. *See* Angilirq, Paul Apak

*Atanarjuat, the Fast Runner*, 3, 15, 182-204, 228n9, 228n9; Jimmy Ettuk's adaptation, 192-94; success of, 196-97
*at.óow*, 26
Armstrong, Jeanette, 33, 206; Aboriginal literary nationalism, 229n1; 'land speaking,' 162; and Lee Maracle, 95
Austin, Mary, 19, 22
Australia, 111, 214n1; Human Rights and Equal Opportunity Commission (HREOC), 114, 223n6; reconciliation, 121
authorship, 2, 28-39, 171, 218n13, 227n13; 'bi-cultural composite authorship' (Krupat), 35; collaborative authorship, 2, 14, 36-39, 138-40, 168-71, 178-80, 205-13; and land jurisdiction, 139-41, 167, 178-80, 209-10; oral authorship, 37, 39, 170-71, 212, 221n3, 227n12

**B**akhtin, Mikhail, 9, 39-40; authorship, 39, 170-71; heteroglossia, 98, 215n7; *Speech Genres and Other Late Essays*, 70-71, 98, 170-71, 215n7, 222n9
Barnett, Don, 29, 104; and *Bobbi Lee, Indian Rebel*, 76-77, 95-98. See also Maracle, Lee
Bauman, Richard, 22
Bennett, John, 37-38
Berger, Sally, 188
Berger, Thomas, 74-75, 114, 117, 209, 220n5, 220n9; Berger Inquiry, 13, 43-59, 75, 209; Jean Chrétien, 56; *Ghosts of Futures Past: Tom Berger in the North*, 220n7; Mackenzie Valley Pipeline Inquiry, 3, 13, 44-62, 219n4; *Northern Frontier, Northern Homeland*, 44-74, 114, 117, 219n1; on Pierre Elliott Trudeau, 49. See also Mackenzie Valley Pipeline Inquiry
Beverley, John, 8-9, 95-98, 215n6. See also *testimonio*
Bilgen-Reinart, Üstün, 6, 110, 125; and Ila Bussidor, 14, 37-38, 110-11, 208-9, 221n3, 225n18, 225n19; collective life history, 122-23; role in collaboration, 110-11, 127-31; settler history, 130-34; witnessing, 127-31. See also Bussidor, Ila; *Night Spirits: The Story of the Relocation of the Sayisi Dene*
Bill C-31, 119, 224n10
Blackman, Margaret, 7-8
Blaeser, Kimberly, 33, 36; literary sovereignty, 206
Blondin, Ethel, 119-20
Blondin, George, 37, 221n3
*Bobbi Lee, Indian Rebel*, 76, 95-99, 104-5
*Book of Jessica*, 30
Borrows, John, 225n3
Boyce Davies, Carole, 30, 111
Brandon, William, 19-20, 24-25
Briggs, Charles L., 22
British sovereignty, 140, 143
Brody, Hugh, 3, 13, 36, 127, 219n1, 219n3, 220n7, 220n9; Dunne-za, 68-72; *Hunters and Bombers*, 61; land claims, 59-60, 73-74, 152; *Living Arctic*, 61-63, 114; Mackenzie Valley Pipeline Inquiry, 43-45; *Maps and Dreams*, 59, 67-74; *People's Land*, 63-67; voice and representation, 13, 59-75
Brumble, David: 'absent editor,' 6, 221n2
Burgos-Debray, Elizabeth, 29. See also *I, Rigoberta Menchú: An Indian Woman in Guatemala*
Bussidor, Ila, 110, 124-25; and Üstün Bilgen-Reinart, 14, 37-38, 110-11, 208-9, 221n3, 225n18, 225n19; collective life history, 122-23; and RCAP, 110-11, 124-26, 208-9; role in collaboration, 124-30, 133-35. See also Bilgen-Reinart, Üstün; *Night Spirits: The Story of the Relocation of the Sayisi Dene*
Byrne, Nympha, 37-38, 221n3

**C**airns, Alan, 34; on RCAP, 113-18; two-row wampum, 34, 218n16
*Calder v. British Columbia*, 43, 60, 143, 220n6
Campbell, Maria, 30-31, 37-38, 78, 221n3; *Book of Jessica*, 30-31; literary nationalism, 206, 229n1
Canada: assimilation, 11, 13, 19, 43-44, 66-67, 116-17, 123-24, 132-34, 216n1, 224n9; Berger Inquiry, 45-52; colonial policies, 10-11, 31-33, 49-50, 56-59, 66-67,

120-21; 'Indian policy,' 10, 13, 44, 121; and the law, 31-33, 140-45, 154-55, 161-62; liberalism, 11, 13, 43-51, 216n8; nation-to-nation relations, 33, 108, 114, 117-18, 120; relationship with Aboriginal peoples, 10, 33, 43-44, 90-93, 100-2, 109, 123-24. *See also* Aboriginal rights; Mackenzie Valley Pipeline Inquiry; Nunavut; Oka crisis; Royal Commission on Aboriginal Peoples
Canadian Broadcasting Corporation (CBC), 47, 125, 198
Caruth, Cathy, 129
Castellano, Marlene Brant, 121
censorship, 102-3
Chamberlin, J. Edward, 175-76
Chester, Blanca, 215n4. *See also* Schorcht, Blanca
Cheyfitz, Eric, 5
citizenship, 50-52
Clements, William, 5, 217n4; comparison between museum practices and Aboriginal literary anthologies, 22, 217n5, 217n6
Coates, Kenneth, 52
Cohn, Norman, 184, 191-202, 228n15, 229n19
collaboration: as ethics, 154-56, 162-68; as process, 32, 122-30, 191-92; as struggle, 76-78, 98; collaborative authorship, 2, 14, 36-39, 139, 168-71, 178-80, 205-13; critical approaches to, 1-18, 29, 36-40, 138-39, 168-69, 205, 209-13. *See also* authorship; Cruikshank, Julie; told-to narratives
Colombo, John Robert, 12, 23-25, 184; *Songs of the Indians*, 23-25
copyright, 30, 38, 170; oral copyright, 26-27, 180
Coyes, Greg, 115
Cronyn, George W., 12, 19, 22, 25, 184
Cruikshank, Julie, 12-13, 72, 221n13, 226n8, 227n12; collaboration, 12-13, 36-40, 138-40, 167-71; *Delgamuukw*, 145, 210; incorporation of Native voice, 28-29; 'layered tellings,' 71-72, 171, 221n13; *Life Lived Like a Story*, 36-37, 138, 167-78, 215n4, 218n18, 220n7; stories as wealth, 37, 168-78. *See also* Ned, Annie; Sidney, Angela; Smith, Kitty
Culhane, Dara, 140
Curtis, Natalie, 12, 19-25; *Indians' Book*, 20-21, 24, 217n4
Cuthand, Beth, 108, 211

**D**auenhauer, Nora Marks, 26, 37-38, 172, 221n3. *See also Haa Shuká/Our Ancestors: Tlingit Oral Narratives*
Dauenhauer, Richard, 26, 37-38, 172, 221n3. *See also Haa Shuká/Our Ancestors: Tlingit Oral Narratives*
decolonization, 2-3, 203, 74-75, 107-8, 120-22, 211-13; and Dene nation, 51-56; Gitksan-Wet'suwet'en legal approach, 139-40, 144-45, 210; land rights, 54-56, 89-94; and Mohawk nation, 89-94; Nunavut, 199-203, 211-12; voice, 44-45, 94-99, 102-4, 124-26; Linda Tuhiwai Smith, 218n14; literary, 2-3, 6, 76-78
Delgam Uukw, 145-47, 210
*Delgamuukw v. British Columbia*, 10, 15, 74, 209, 225n6; and collaborative authorship, 168-80, 212; oral traditions, 137-80; performance, 150-51; Harry Robinson, 155, 160-67; Supreme Court decision (1997), 137-39, 140-41, 144-45, 178-79, 225n1, 225n3, 227n15. *See also adaawk;* Gitksan-Wet'suwet'en land claims; *kungax;* McEachern, Allan
Dene Declaration, 43, 50, 53-54, 75
Dene nation, 50-59, 222n1; Dogrib First Nation, 46-48, 58, 220n8; Gwichin Dene First Nation, 46, 48, 58, 220n8; Sahtu Dene First Nation, 46, 53, 58, 220n7, 220n8
Department of Indian Affairs and Northern Development, 44, 81-83, 117, 124, 131-33; and Thomas Berger, 56, 64-65, 219n1; and Hugh Brody, 44-45, 219n3; Jean Chrétien, 56-57; and Alanis Obomsawin, 107; relocation of Sayisi Dene, 124, 131-33; residential schools, 107, 117, 224n9; Tom Siddon, 83-84. *See also* Canada
*During My Time: Florence Edenshaw Davidson*, 7, 224n13

Emberley, Julia V., 167-68
Erasmus, Georges, 51-52, 222n1, 223n5
ethnography, 2, 7-8, 12-15, 18-22, 27, 167-68, 181, 206; autoethnography, 182, 194, 197; Hugh Brody, 60-74; compared to *testimonio*, 94-98; counter-ethnography, 79-80, 182-97, 203-4; and film, 107, 181-97. *See also* narrative; told-to narratives
*e'thzil*, 122, 130-35
Evans, Michael Robert, 194, 198

Fagan, Kristina, 33, 206-7, 216n9
Fanon, Frantz, 63, 100, 220n11
Fee, Margery, 20
First Nations studies, 2, 4, 205, 216n9; appropriation of voice, 103; 'insider' and 'outsider' perspectives, 33
Flaherty, Robert, 195-96, 227n5, 228n7; filmic vision, 185, 195; influence on *Atanarjuat*, 183-88; relationship to Inuit, 187-88. *See also Nanook of the North*
Fouillard, Camille, 37-38, 221n3

*Gathering Voices: Finding Strength to Help Our Children*, 122, 224n14
Gingell, Susan, 4, 214n2, 215n3, 227n2
Gisday Wa, 145-47
Gitksan-Wet'suwet'en land claims, 15, 60, 140-41, 143-55, 168, 171, 174, 179, 209-12, 225n3, 226n6, 226n8; *adaawk* and *kungax*, 145-55, 179; legal approach, 139-40, 144-45, 210; title and jurisdiction, 139-41, 144-45, 147, 149-52, 179-80, 209-10, 226n6, 227n7. *See also Delgamuukw v. British Columbia*; McEachern, Allan
Godard, Barbara, 227n13
Grant, Peter, 150-51
Great Law of Peace, 84, 94, 222n7, 229n3. *See also* Alfred, Taiaiake; Turner, Dale; Valaskakis, Gail Guthrie
Griffiths, Linda, 30-31
*Guswentha* (Two Row Wampum), 207, 218n16

*Haa Shuká/Our Ancestors: Tlingit Oral Narratives*, 26, 37, 221n3

Hall, Anthony, 223n4
Hamilton, John David, 219n5
Hanna, Darwin, 226n9; and Mamie Henry, *Our Tellings*, 37-38, 221n3
Harper, Elijah, 94, 99-101, 222n6. *See also* Meech Lake, constitutional talks
Henderson, Ailsa, 200-1, 228n16
Henry, Mamie: *Our Tellings*, 37-38, 221n3
hooks, bell, 28
Huhndorf, Shari, 185, 190
Hungry Wolf, Beverly, 37, 221n3
Hymes, Dell, 5

*I, Rigoberta Menchú: An Indian Woman in Guatemala*, 29, 32, 217n11. *See also testimonio*
*I am Nokomis, Too: The Biography of Verna Patronella Johnston*, 7, 224n13
identity politics, 3-4, 44-45, 74-75, 77-78, 102, 106; 'parallel voices,' 18, 31-41, 77, 212, 218n16
Igloolik Isuma Productions, 15, 182-204, 211, 227n6, 228n9, 229n19; impact on Igloolik community, 183, 201-2; 'Inuit culture of production', 15, 197-99, 211; *Inuit Qaujimajatuqangit*, 203-4, 211; *Nipi*, 183, 202-3, 211; and Nunavut, 199-204; *Nunavut* series, 191; *Qulliq*, 184; and Telefilm, 191, 199, 202, 228n15. *See also Atanarjuat, the Fast Runner*; *Journals of Knud Rasmussen*; Kunuk, Zacharias
*Indian Act*, 11, 216n1, 224n10
Indian Brotherhood, 43, 52-57, 75
Indian Residential Schools' Truth and Reconciliation Commission, 111-13, 116, 223n8
*Indians' Book*, 20-24, 217n4
Innu nation, 26, 37, 122, 221n3, 224n14
Inuit Broadcasting Corporation (IBC), 184, 198, 211
*Inuit Qaujimajatuqangit*, 183, 191, 211, 229n17; and filmmaking, 197; and *Nipi*, 183; Nunavut, 200-4, 228n16
Inuit Tapirisat, 43, 199, 222n1
Iroquois Confederacy, 31, 84, 88, 93, 217n7, 222n7. *See also* Great Law of Peace; *Guswentha*; Turner, Dale; Valaskakis, Gail Guthrie

## Index

Jameson, Fredric, 227n13
Johnson, A.P., 26, 172
Johnson, Pauline, 25-27
Johnson, Yvonne, 31-33, 218n13. *See also* Wiebe, Rudy
*Journals of Knud Rasmussen*, 183, 190, 227n3, 228n9
Justice, Daniel Heath, 33, 206-7, 229n1, 229n2

'Kaax̱'achgóok,' 26, 171-73, 217n10, 227n14
Kahnawake, 78, 79, 83, 89-93, 102. *See also* Oka Crisis
Kalant, Amelia, 81, 83-84, 88
Kanehsatake, 3, 13, 77-109, 221n4, 221n5. *See also* Oka Crisis
*Kanehsatake: 270 Years of Resistance*, 79-93, 210
Keeshig-Tobias, Lenore, 27, 205
Kelly, Fred, 112, 118
Krupat, Arnold, 5, 215n5, 215n7, 228n10; authorship, 35-36; on Bakhtin, 215n7; intellectual sovereignty, 34-40; on Zacharias Kunuk, 185-86; orality, 215n4
Kulchyski, Peter, 10, 161, 219n2, 220n7, 220n8; exhaustion vs. extinguishment, 58, 140, 220n8; 'grammar' of land claims, 161-62; law and Aboriginal rights in Canada, 141-44, 210; self-government, 53-54, 58-59, 212; RCAP, 114
*kungax*, 145-49, 160, 178-79, 210. *See also adaawk*
Kunuk, Zacharias, 3, 181-202, 211; IBC, 198-99, 202, 211; Inuit oral traditions, 184; 'Inuit style' filmmaking, 188, 229n18; funding difficulties, 199; 'Public Art of Inuit Storytelling,' 181, 185, 196. *See also Atanarjuat, the Fast Runner;* Igloolik Isuma Productions; *Journals of Knud Rasmussen*

land, 77-102, 107-8, 138-80, 205-13, 216n3, 219n4, 220n7, 221n4, 221n5, 221n17, 221n19, 225n3, 226n6, 226n7, 227n15, 228n16; Thomas Berger, 49-51, 72-75; Hugh Brody, 59-60, 72-75, 219n3; *Calder v. British Columbia*, 43, 60, 143, 220n6; connection to story and property, 3-4, 26-27, 31, 37-40, 102-3, 137-40, 145-55, 160-68, 171-80, 210, 214n2, 217n10; *Delgamuukw*, 38-60, 138-55, 155, 161-62, 171; land claims, 2, 9-16, 37-39, 49-51, 53-59, 107-8, 140-55, 177, 209-10, 221n5, 225n3; 'land ownership,' 145-47, 149-55, 168-69, 171-78; Lee Maracle, 98-102; Allan McEachern, 151-53; and Mohawk nation, 77, 80-89, 91-94; a new ethics of, 138-39, 155, 160-67, 179; and *Night Spirits*, 123-25, 131-35; *Nipi*, 202-3; Alanis Obomsawin, 93-94, 107-8; and RCAP, 117-20; Harry Robinson, 160-67; sovereignty, 206-12; *St. Catherine's Milling and Lumber Co. v. The Queen*, 142-43; and travel, 54-56, 68-69, 146-54, 164, 168-75. *See also* Aboriginal rights; Aboriginal sovereignty; Aboriginal title; Canada; storytelling
Laub, Dori, 127-31
Lejeune, Philippe, 8-9, 30
Lewis, Randolph, 93
*Life Lived Like a Story*, 15, 36-40, 138-39, 154, 167-80, 212, 215n4, 218n18, 226n11
literary sovereignty, 5-6, 11-12, 15-16, 33-35, 76-78, 96-99, 108, 207-13, 216n9, 218n15, 229n1. *See also* Aboriginal sovereignty
*Living Arctic: Hunters of the Canadian North*, 61-63, 114

Mackenzie Valley Pipeline Inquiry, 3, 10, 13, 43-59, 61-63, 74-75, 114, 209; Hugh Brody, 59-63, 114; *The Inquiry Film: A Report on the Mackenzie Valley Pipeline Inquiry*, 48; and land claims, 49-51, 54-59, 219n4. *See also* Berger, Thomas
'Mapping Project,' 54-56, 68-69, 75, 209, 220n7. *See also* Nahanni, Phoebe
maps: conflicts over, 54-56, 68-70, 146-47, 175-76; 'dream maps,' 67-72; mapping projects, 54-56, 67-72, 75, 146, 174-76, 209, 220n7; relationship to storytelling, 71-72, 89, 137-79. *See also* Brody, Hugh; land; Nahanni, Phoebe; storytelling
*Maps and Dreams: Indians and the British Columbia Frontier*, 59-60, 67-74

Maracle, Lee, 12, 14, 33, 206; *Bobbi Lee, Indian Rebel,* 29, 76-78, 95-99; collaboration with Don Barnett, 29, 76-78, 95-99; doublevoicedness, 77-78, 94-106; feminist perspectives, 229n1; interview with Jennifer Kelly, 99; Oka crisis, 77-78, 98-102, 210; *Ravensong,* 98, 105; 'Rusty,' 104-5; *Sundogs,* 98-102

Martin, Keavy, 200-2

McEachern, Allan, 15, 174, 225n3; *adaawk* and *kungax,* 178-79; 'palpable errors,' 178-79; *Reasons for Judgment,* 74, 140, 144-55, 226n8; 'tin ear,' 150-52. *See also Delgamuukw v. British Columbia,* Gitksan-Wet'suwet'en land claims

Meech Lake, constitutional talks, 84, 94; accord, 100-1, 222n6

Mercier Bridge blockade, 86, 92-93; Lee Maracle, 101-2; *My Name Is Kahentiiosta,* 82-83; *Rocks at Whiskey Trench,* 92-93. *See also* Oka Crisis

Mohawk nation, 77, 80-94, 222n7. *See also* Kanehsatake; Oka crisis

Monture-Angus, Patricia, 120-22, 209, 217n12, 225n3

Mulroney, Brian, 81, 109

Murray, David, 5, 24, 215n5

Murray, Laura, 219n19

*My Name Is Kahentiiosta,* 79, 82-83, 89-91, 93

**N**ahanni, Phoebe, 54-56, 68, 75, 209, 220n7. *See also* 'Mapping Project'

*Nanook of the North,* 185-89, 194-96, 227n5, 227n5, 227n6, 228n7. *See also* Flaherty, Robert

narrative: (auto)biography, 2-3, 7-8, 29-35, 105, 215n5 ; collective life story, 6-7, 14, 110-11, 122-25, 130-31, 135, 208, 224n14; life narrative, 2, 6-14, 30, 76-77, 95-110, 122-26, 224n13, 226n11; narrative frames, 8, 13-14, 21, 26, 28-29, 30-31, 76-108, 121-22, 124-29, 172-78; oral narrative, 3-47, 104, 138-39, 154-79, 215n2, 215n4, 215n7, 221n3, 226n9. *See also* oral traditions; *testimonio;* told-to narratives

National Film Board (NFB), 106, 115, 199

nationalism: Aboriginal, 33-35, 53-54, 87-88, 90-92, 117-18, 205-13, 229n2; Canadian, 19-20, 83, 90-91, 114, 120; cultural, 3, 100, 183, 194-96, 197-204, 211; Inuit, 15, 43, 66-67, 197-204; Québécois, 10-11, 82-84, 88, 90-91; Romantic, 12, 18-26, 216n3; settler, 12, 19-20, 83, 90-91, 214n1. *See also* Aboriginal rights; Canada

*Nature Power: In the Spirit of an Okanagan Storyteller,* 155-57

Ned, Annie, 13, 37, 138, 167, 169-70, 174-75, 218n18, 220n7. *See also* Cruikshank, Julie; Sidney, Angela; Smith, Kitty

*Night Spirits: The Story of the Relocation of the Sayisi Dene,* 6, 14, 36-37, 221n3; mistranslation and nontranslation, 122-36; response to RCAP, 110-11, 122, 208-9, 225n20. *See also* Bilgen-Reinart, Üstün; Bussidor, Ila

*Northern Frontier, Northern Homeland: The Report of the Mackenzie Valley Pipeline Inquiry,* 44-54, 56, 61-63, 74-75, 114, 219n1

Northern Pipeline Agency, 59, 67-69, 72

NourbeSe Phillip, Marlene, 102-4

Nunavut: and *Atanarjuat,* 3, 10, 15, 182-83, 192, 197-204, 211; Government of Nunavut (GN), 200; *Inuit Qaujimajatuqangit,* 183, 197, 200-3, 211; *Nipi,* 202; *Nunavut (Our Land),* 191, 198, 228n6; Nunavut Tunngavik Inc (NTI), 200; self-government, 124, 135, 202-4, 211-12, 225n17, 225n19, 228n16, 229n19

**O**bomsawin, Alanis, 14, 106-8, 221n4; identity politics, 106-7; *Kanehsatake,* 79-93, 210; multiple tellings, 79-94, 107; *My Name Is Kahentiiosta,* 79, 82-83, 89-91, 93; *Rocks at Whiskey Trench,* 79, 83, 89, 92-93; sovereignty, 107-8; *Spudwrench,* 79, 85, 91-93; told-to narratives, 77-94

Oka crisis, 3, 10, 14, 33, 75, 76-108, 221n1, 221n4, 221n5, 223n4; artistic interpretations, 77-108; and journalism, 28-29; Lee Maracle, 95, 98-102, 107-8; Alanis Obomsawin, 77-94, 210-11; 'parallel voices,' 27-28, 31, 77; Quebec and

Canada, 83-84, 88, 90-91; Warrior Society, 88. *See also* Kanehsatake; Maracle, Lee; Obomsawin, Alanis
Okanagan nation, 100, 155-66, 226n9
Onasakenrat, Joseph, 80, 221n5
oral traditions: 217n5, 217n9, 225n3; and audience, 15, 37, 40, 67-68, 138-39, 155, 157-60, 168-78, 228n10; Igloolik Isuma, 182-84, 188-90, 193-96, 227n3, 227n4, 228n12, 228n13; and literary anthologies, 12, 18-26, 183-84, 216n2, 217n5, 227n4; and performance, 26-27, 38-41, 137-40, 145-47, 149-52, 188-90; relationship to writing, 4-6, 18-26, 30, 34, 122-31, 155-56, 161-63, 190-94, 206-7, 217n7; textualization of, 2-26, 28-32, 35-42, 45-48, 60-74, 76-78, 79-80, 94-98, 104-5, 114-17, 124-28, 147-48, 157-58, 214n2, 215n4, 215n5, 215n6, 217n5, 217n9. *See also adaawk;* authorship; Cruikshank, Julie; *kungax;* storytelling; told-to narratives; translation

*People to People, Nation to Nation: Highlights from the Report on the Royal Commission on Aboriginal Peoples,* 114-18
*People's Land,* 63-67, 221n12
Persky, Stan, 144
Petch, Virginia, 110, 122, 124-25, 208. *See also* Bilgen-Reinart, Üstün; Bussidor, Ila; *Night Spirits: The Story of the Relocation of the Sayisi Dene*
Pinder, Leslie, 148-51
'Post-Oka Kinda Woman,' 108, 211
potlatch, 26, 176
Powell, Judith, 52
property: cultural, 4, 26, 38-39, 102, 172, 179, 209; songs and stories, 26-27, 37-41, 54-78, 139, 145-94, 204, 209, 218n18, 226n9. *See also* Aboriginal title; land; storytelling; voice

Québécois sovereignty, 11, 83-84, 90-91, 222n6

reconciliation, 223n2, 223n4, 223n8; and collaboration, 168; Alanis Obomsawin, 93; and RCAP, 14, 109-36; and South Africa, 109, 112; and testimony, 109-16, 121-22, 128-29; and witnessing, 135-36
reported speech, 60, 70-75
residential schools, 161, 216n1, 223n8, 224n9; Isuma, 202, 211; Lenore Keeshig-Tobias, 27; Lee Maracle, 99; *Night Spirits,* 132-33; Alanis Obomsawin, 107; RCAP, 111-17
Rice, Keren, 219n19
Robinson, Harry, 15, 155-67, 174, 226n10; Aboriginal title, 163-68; biography, 155-56; creation story, 160-62; and *Delgamuukw,* 160-63; relationship with Wickwire, 156-60; storytelling practice, 139, 155-60, 167. *See also* Wickwire, Wendy
*Rocks at Whiskey Trench,* 79, 83, 89-93
Romantic nationalism. *See* nationalism
Rotinohshonni, 84, 94, 222n7, 229n3. *See also* Alfred, Taiaiake; Great Law of Peace
Rowley, Susan, 37-38
Royal Commission on Aboriginal Peoples (RCAP), 10, 14, 109-35, 213, 223n3, 223n4; *Looking Forward,* 116, 123, 126, 134-35, 223n4, 224n9, 225n17; *People to People,* 114-18; 'Residential Schools,' 116-17, 224n9; *Restructuring the Relationship,* 118-19; 'Women's Perspectives,' 119-20
*Royal Proclamation* (1763), 141-42, 225n4
'Rusty,' 36, 104-5
Rymhs, Deena, 32, 112, 218n13

Saladin d'Anglure, Bernard, 192, 194, 228n12
Sands, Kathleen, 215n4, 221n3
Sarris, Greg, 6, 13, 36, 40-41, 215n4, 219n19
Sayisi Dene First Nation, 14, 110-11, 122-36, 225n17, 225n19, 225n21
Schorcht, Blanca, 157-59. *See also* Chester, Blanca
self-government, 10, 118, 180, 206-9, 211-12, 218-21, 226n6, 225n18; and assimilation, 43-44, 56-59, 113, 183; Berger Inquiry, 13-14, 48-59, 75; Hugh Brody, 67; Nunavut, 197-98, 203-4; RCAP, 110-35; and the White Paper, 43; and women, 118-21. *See also* Aboriginal

rights; Aboriginal sovereignty; Aboriginal title; Canada; land
Sidney, Angela, 12, 37, 138, 167-76, 212, 217n10, 218n18, 220n7; 'Ḵaax̱'achgóok,' 171-73; *Shagóon*, 173-74; 'Wolf Story,' 175-77. *See also* Cruikshank, Julie; Smith, Kitty
Silman, Janet, 6
Smith, Kitty, 13, 37, 138, 167, 169-70, 174, 177, 218n18; 'Mountain Man,' 177-78. *See also* Cruikshank, Julie; Sidney, Angela
*Songs of the Indians (Volumes I and II)*, 23-25
Spivak, Gayatri Chakravorty, 224n15
Spudwrench, 79, 85-93
*St. Catherine's Milling and Lumber Co. v. The Queen*, 142-43
*Stolen Life: The Journey of a Cree Woman*, 31-32, 218n13. *See also* Johnson, Yvonne; Wiebe, Rudy
storytelling, 15, 26, 34-40, 138-39, 146, 154-85, 196, 204-12, 216n2, 220n7, 226n9, 226n11; and land, 3-4, 26-27, 31, 37-40, 102-3, 137-40, 145-55, 160-68, 171-80, 210, 214n2, 217n10; 'layered tellings,' 72, 171, 189, 221n13. *See also* authorship; oral traditions; told-to narratives
*Sundogs*, 98-102
Supreme Court of Canada: *Calder v. British Columbia*, 43; *Delgamuukw v. British Columbia*, 137-44, 178-79, 225n1, 225n3, 227n15
Suzack, Cheryl, 139, 229n1
Swann, Brian, 5, 215n4, 217n5
Swanton, John R., 8, 23

**T**edlock, Dennis, 5, 217n5
TELLING IT: Women and Language across Cultures, 102, 105-6
*testimonio*, 8, 29, 95-98, 215n6; and David Stoll, 217n11. *See also* Beverley, John
testimony, 64, 170; Berger Inquiry, 45-48, 54-56; Hugh Brody, 73; *Delgamuukw*, 139, 144-52, 160, 179; RCAP, 14, 109-16, 121-22; Alanis Obomsawin, 84; Sayisi Dene First Nation, 123-36. *See also* witnessing

told-to narratives: and Aboriginal writers and critics, 5-6, 78, 205-12, 215n4, 218n13, 218n17; Mikhail Bakhtin, 9, 39-40, 98, 215n7; collective life story, 6-7, 14, 110-11, 122-25, 130-31, 135, 208, 224n14; conflicts over, 27-28, 29-32, 37-39, 45, 76-78, 98, 218n13; critical approaches to, 3-12, 18-27, 28-29; definition, 2, 13, 40-41; Lee Maracle, 95-105; and public forums, 9-10, 12-16, 44, 114; and 'textual colonization,' 5-6, 18, 41-42, 78, 205-6. *See also* narrative; oral traditions; storytelling; translation
translation, 9-10, 15, 17-27, 90-91, 203, 212; Hugh Brody, 59-75; *Delgamuukw*, 137-40, 145-55, 161; failure of, 63-67, 73-75, 130-32, 149-51, 212-13; Zacharias Kunuk, 182, 189, 191, 197; *Night Spirits*, 122-33; nontranslation, 9-10, 72, 122-36, 221n14; RCAP, 110-11, 122; Brian Swann, 215n4. *See also* narrative; oral traditions; told-to narratives
Travis, Richard, 64-66. *See also* land: land claims
treaties, 10, 88, 99, 112, 118, 125, 160, 206-7; Treaty Three, 142-43; Treaty Five, 131; Treaty of Niagara, 141, 225n4; Two-Row Wampum, 31, 34
Trudeau, Pierre Elliott, 13, 43, 45-49
Truth and Reconciliation Commission (South Africa), 109, 111-12, 223n2
Turner, Dale, 216n8, 218n16, 223n5; RCAP, 114; sovereignty, 16, 207-8
two-row wampum belt, 34, 218n16; treaty, 31, 34

**V**alaskakis, Gail Guthrie: appropriation, 103; Oka crisis, 88; 'parallel voices,' 31-41; 'stereotypical inclusion,' 31, 50-51
Vanderburgh, Rosamond, 6-7
Venne, Sharon, 13, 36, 39
voice: and Aboriginal studies, 1-2; appropriation of voice, 3-4, 12-14, 20-27, 31-32, 38-39, 102-4, 182, 205-6, 218n13; and Berger Inquiry, 44-56; and Hugh Brody, 59-75; 'coming to voice,' 28-32, 43-56, 59, 74-75, 208, 215n6; Lee Maracle, 76-78, 94, 99, 103; and narrative frames, 8,

13-14, 21, 26, 28-29, 30-31, 76-108, 121-22, 124-29, 172-78; 'Native voice,' 12, 18, 28, 41, 62; and *Night Spirits*, 110, 125, 130-35; and *Nipi*, 202-5; Alanis Obomsawin, 79-93, 210; 'parallel voices,' 18, 31-41, 77, 212, 218n16; and representation, 3, 10, 13, 44-45, 59-75, 77-78, 102-6; and the Royal Commission on Aboriginal Peoples, 114-17; third-person voice, 73, 105, 113, 125, 135. *See also* identity politics; oral traditions; storytelling; told-to narratives

Wakeham, Pauline, 111
Warkentin, Germaine, 217n7
Warrior, Robert, 218n15, 229n1, 229n2; sovereignty, 34
Watkins, Mel, 52
Weaver, Jace, 206; orature, 5-6
Wenzel, George, 200-3
Wheeler, Jordan, 28-31, 101, 221n1
'Where Is the Voice Coming From?' 17, 41
White Paper, 11, 13, 43, 216n1; and Pierre Elliott Trudeau, 11
Whitlock, Gillian: 'second person,' 110, 114, 121

Wickwire, Wendy, 15, 155-67. *See also* Robinson, Harry
Wiebe, Rudy, 218n13; *Stolen Life: The Journey of a Cree Woman*, 31-32; 'Where Is the Voice Coming From?' 17-18, 41. *See also* Johnson, Yvonne
Willmott, Glenn, 20
Wilson, Dora, 153-54, 179
Winter, James, 82. *See also* Oka Crisis
witnessing, 210, 217n11, 224n15; *adaawk* and *kungax*, 146-47, 210; Berger Inquiry, 45; Cathy Caruth, 129; and *e'thzil*, 130-32; *Night Spirits*, 123-47; RCAP, 113; and reconciliation, 135-36. *See also* testimony
Wolfart, H.C., 37, 221n3
Womack, Craig: Indigenous sovereignty, 206; oral literatures, 5-6, 12, 34, 206; *Red on Red*, 33-34
*Write It on Your Heart: The Epic World of an Okanagan Storyteller*, 15, 138-39, 154-55, 168, 180

Yaga'lahl (Dora Wilson), 153-54, 179

Printed and bound in Canada by Friesens

Set in Sabon and Myriad by Artegraphica Design Co. Ltd.

Copy editor and proofreader: Jillian Shoichet